progress

future

promise

America
& the Spirit of Enterprise

century of progress, future of promise

James W. Robinson

CHERBO PUBLISHING GROUP, INC.
ENCINO, CALIFORNIA

From the Author

It was no easy task to get one's arms around a subject the size and scope of American business. Thankfully, I had a lot of help!

This book could not have been written without the creativity, expertise, and inspiration of colleagues at both Cherbo Publishing Group and the U.S. Chamber of Commerce.

Jack Cherbo, president of Cherbo Publishing Group, set the tone and themes for the book, put his company and resources on the line, and persevered through many hurdles to see it through. Margaret Martin lent her excellent editorial judgment to the effort and did a superb job smoothing and reshaping the prose.

At the Chamber, Julie deFalco helped research and draft major portions of the material covering various industry sectors. She is a fast, creative, and thorough writer. Jane Sanders also has my gratitude for her efforts and for involving me in this project.

I also gratefully acknowledge the work of William G. Van Meter and Charles R. Armentrout for their tireless work on an in-house U.S. Chamber of Commerce history on which much of chapter four of this book is based.

Finally, I thank my former boss and mentor Milt Mitler who, along with Jack Cherbo, conceived of the Cherbo-Chamber partnership that resulted in this volume. Many years ago, Milt helped me a great deal in the earliest stages of my career and now he has helped me again in creating this opportunity for me.

PRESIDENT Jack C. Cherbo

EXECUTIVE VICE PRESIDENT Elaine Hoffman

EDITORIAL DIRECTOR Christina M. Beausang

MANAGING FEATURE EDITOR Margaret L. Martin

SENIOR FEATURE EDITOR Tina G. Rubin

SENIOR PROFILES EDITOR J. Kelley Younger

ASSOCIATE EDITOR Sylvia Emrich-Toma

PROFILES WRITERS Camilla Denton, Beth Mattson-Teig,
    Felicia E. Molnar, Tina Rubin, Nancy Smith Seigle,
    Paul Sonnenburg, and Stan Ziemba

ART DIRECTOR/DESIGNER Peri A. Holguin

PHOTO EDITOR Catherine A. Vandenberg

SALES ADMINISTRATOR Joan K. Baker

ACQUISITIONS ADMINISTRATOR Bonnie J. Aharoni

PRODUCTION SERVICES MANAGER Ellen T. Kettenbeil

ADMINISTRATIVE COORDINATOR Jahnna Biddle

EASTERN REGIONAL MANAGER Marcia Weiss

EASTERN DEVELOPMENT DIRECTOR Glen Edwards

Cherbo Publishing Group, Inc., Encino, Calif. 91316

© 2001 by Cherbo Publishing Group, Inc.

All rights reserved. Published 2001

Printed in the United States of America

Visit CPG's Web site at www.cherbopub.com

Library of Congress Cataloging-in-Publication Data

Robinson, James W.

    America and the Spirit of Enterprise.

Library of Congress Control Number: 2001091930

    ISBN 1-882933-39-7

This book is dedicated to those brave individuals

whose lives were lost in the tragic events of September 11, 2001.

In their courage, in their day-to-day efforts to accomplish miracles large and small,

they were America personified.

Contents

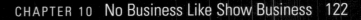

Consumer Cooperation is an expression of Economic Democracy

Photos: This page, below, © Underwood & Underwood/Corbis; opposite, © D. Boone/CORBIS

Corporations & Organizations Profiled

The following companies have made a valuable commitment to the quality of this publication. The U.S. Chamber of Commerce gratefully acknowledges their participation in *America & the Spirit of Enterprise: Century of Progress, Future of Promise.*

Fostering a
Future of Promise

As America entered the new millennium, thousands of words were spoken and written documenting virtually every aspect of the remarkable 20th century. Surely by now the story of what is rightly called the American Century has been fully told. Or has it?

One critical chapter has remained unwritten, undocumented, uncelebrated, and largely ignored. It is the story of free enterprise and the millions of men and women who seized its promise and brought about the most productive, prosperous period in human history. More than any other person, event, or institution, it is American business and its entrepreneurial leaders who are responsible for a century of unsurpassed economic and social progress.

Name almost any achievement in science, medicine, technology, or lifestyle, and you can trace its origins and success to the ideas, investments, risk-taking, and hard work of American business.

Cite virtually any positive development in American society and you will find that economic growth in the private sector, fueled by business, made it all possible.

Either directly through its own actions, or indirectly through the economic expansion it creates, American business:

- pays the bills for the nation's safety net for the poor and elderly;
- provides health care for more than 150 million citizens;
- supports the greatest network of educational and charitable organizations in the world;
- funds the cleaning of the natural environment and countless recreational opportunities;
- sustains the military defenses that preserve peace and freedom around the globe.

These and many other achievements are all the more remarkable when you consider that for much of the 20th century, two competing and completely opposite economic systems vied for the hearts and minds of people around the world.

One system placed its faith in the omnipotence of central economic planning and big government, backed by authoritarian rule deriving its ultimate power from the barrel of a gun.

The other system placed its faith in free people and free markets, governed only by simple rules of fair play.

The first system has been consigned to the ash heap of history, while America's spirit of enterprise has survived and thrived to become the economic model for the new millennium.

America & the Spirit of Enterprise: Century of Progress, Future of Promise tells the story of the free enterprise system that has enabled business and industry to grow and make America the envy of every country in the world. This book chronicles the entrepreneurial achievements, inventions, innovations, and growth of American business and profiles the industries and business leaders who made it all possible.

While it is a celebration of a brilliant past, *America & the Spirit of Enterprise* is very much a book about the future, daring the reader's imagination with the prospect of even greater business and economic achievements yet to come.

As we anticipate those future achievements, the greatest challenge facing our nation is that we understand that continued progress and prosperity are not automatic. They must be earned with hard work and bold decisions—and with government policies that foster, rather than smother, economic growth.

Therein lies the mission of the U.S. Chamber of Commerce: to fight for the open markets and the economic freedom our American entrepreneurs must have to continue making miracles for our entire society. If they are allowed to succeed, then the past century of remarkable accomplishment will stand as but a prologue to even greater achievements in the century we have just begun.

So join with the U.S. Chamber and me in celebrating the past and resolving to work hard and work together to make the future even brighter.

Thomas J. Donohue

President and CEO
U.S. Chamber of Commerce

part one
A Century of Growth & Progress

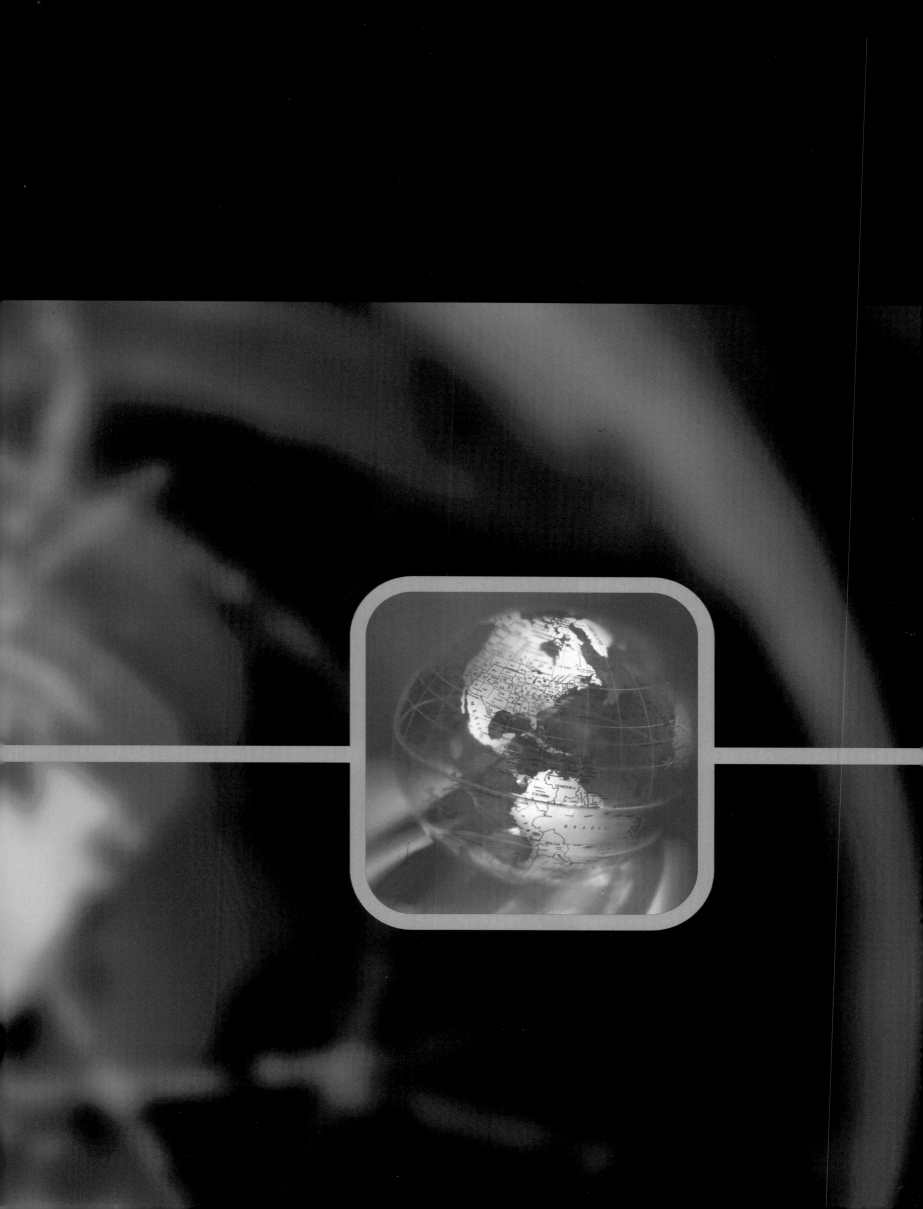

DATELINE: PROGRESS

KEY EVENTS & PEOPLE THAT SHAPED, & WERE SHAPED BY, AMERICAN BUSINESS

THE 20TH CENTURY WAS THE MOST PRODUCTIVE AND PROSPEROUS PERIOD IN HUMAN HISTORY. EVEN THROUGH TUMULTUOUS AND UNCERTAIN TIMES, AMERICAN BUSINESS TRIUMPHED, AS THE MEN AND WOMEN WHO PUT THEIR FAITH IN THE FREE ENTERPRISE SYSTEM ROSE TO MEET THE CHALLENGES OF A RAPIDLY CHANGING WORLD.

HENRY FORD

WILBUR AND ORVILLE WRIGHT AT KITTY HAWK

1900 America's population stands at 76,094,000; federal spending is less than $500 million.

1901 Theodore Roosevelt becomes president and sets out to "bust trusts." J. P. Morgan creates U.S. Steel, which will become the first billion-dollar corporation in history.

1902 150,000 miners strike in Philadelphia. British tobacco company Philip Morris is incorporated in the United States; by 2001, the company will rank number 11 on the Fortune 500 list of largest companies and will include the world's number two food company (Kraft) and the number two U.S. brewer (Miller).

1903 Henry Ford organizes Ford Motor Company. The Wright brothers make the first successful flight.

1904 The New York City subway opens. Construction begins on the Panama Canal.

1905 The first movie theater opens, in Pittsburgh. Albert Einstein proposes his theory of relativity.

1906 The San Francisco earthquake hits. Upton Sinclair writes his exposé of the meat-packing industry, *The Jungle*.

1907 The century's first stock crash triggers nationwide panic. Nineteen-year-old Jim Casey establishes the American Messenger Company in Seattle, which will grow into United Parcel Service, the number one package-delivery service in the world in 2001.

1908 Petroleum production begins in the Middle East. Ford develops the first Model T, which sells for $850. General Motors is organized; ninety-three years later, GM will reign as the world's number one automaker with $184.6 billion in annual revenues.

1909 Robert Peary and Matthew Henson reach the North Pole. The National Association

CONSTRUCTION OF THE EMPIRE STATE BUILDING

or the Advancement of Colored People (NAACP) is founded.

1910 America's population stands at 92,407,000. Federal spending totals $690 million.

1911 A fire in the Triangle Shirtwaist Company in New York kills 146 and sparks national outrage. The Supreme Court finds Standard Oil in violation of the Sherman Antitrust Act.

1912 The "unsinkable" *Titanic* sinks. William Randolph Hearst begins building his media empire.

1913 The 16th amendment is ratified, creating the income tax. The Federal Reserve System is created. Ford develops the first moving assembly line.

1914 World War I begins. The Panama Canal officially opens. The Clayton Antitrust Act is passed, further clamping down on monopolies.

1915 One million Ford autos have now rolled off the assembly lines.

1916 Jeannette Rankin of Montana is the first woman elected to Congress.

1917 The U.S. joins World War I. Vladimir Lenin and Leon Trotsky take control of Russia by a coup d'état.

1918 Daylight savings time first goes into effect. An influenza epidemic begins that will eventually kill 500,000 Americans and 21 million worldwide.

1919 The Treaty of Versailles ends World War I. Prohibition begins. Dial telephones are introduced. American Cornelius V. Starr opens a small insurance agency in Shanghai, China; the company eventually grows into American International Group (AIG), the United States' largest underwriter of commercial and industrial insurance.

1920 America's population stands at 106,461,000. Federal spending totals $6.36 billion. The 19th amendment gives women the right to vote.

1921 Vitamin D and E are discovered. The Roaring Twenties prosperity begins in earnest.

1922 Coal miner strikes cripple the industry. Insulin is developed to treat diabetes.

1923 ACNielsen is founded and behalf of advertisers. *Time* magazine makes its debut.

1924 Stalin seizes power in the Soviet Union. IBM is founded. In England, the first television image is transmitted.

1925 Al Capone rises to power in Chicago.

1926 RCA, General Electric, and Westinghouse form NBC. Auto antifreeze is introduced, making cars usable year-round.

1927 Charles Lindbergh makes the first nonstop solo flight across the Atlantic.

1928 General Electric introduces the television. Alexander Fleming discovers penicillin.

1929 The stock market crashes and the Great Depression begins.

1930 America's population stands at 123,076,741. Federal spending totals $3.32 billion. The Smoot-Hawley Tariff Act is passed and U.S. exports plummet.

1931 The Empire State Building is completed. There are 30,000 televisions in the United States. General Motors' Frigidaire makes refrigerators efficient for household use. Caterpillar Tractor Company, of Peoria, Illinois, offers the first diesel-powered tractor.

1932 24.1 percent of the American workforce is unemployed.

1933 Franklin Roosevelt takes office. Adolph Hitler becomes chancellor of Germany. Prohibition is repealed.

1934 The Securities Exchange Commission and the Federal Communications Commission are created. Cropland in the Midwest is ruined by dust-bowl conditions, spurring migration west.

1935 Social Security is created. Radar is pioneered.

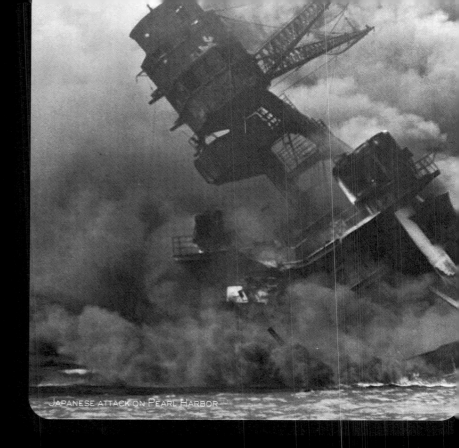
JAPANESE ATTACK ON PEARL HARBOR

1936 FDR is reelected by a landslide.

1937 The Golden Gate Bridge is completed. The *Hindenberg* explodes. Antihistamine is developed to treat allergies.

1938 The Fair Labor Standards Act establishes a minimum wage. The first xerographic copy and the ballpoint pen are created.

1939 World War II begins.

1940 America's population stands at 132,122,446. Federal spending totals $9.47 billion. The first monthly Social Security checks are distributed. FDR becomes the first and only president to be elected to a third term. Color television is introduced.

1941 The Japanese attack Pearl Harbor, bringing the United States into World War II. RCA introduces a powerful microscope that can magnify objects 100,000 times.

1942 The Manhattan Project is established to create the atom bomb.

1943 The withholding of tax from paychecks begins. Antibiotics and Pap smears are introduced.

1944 The D-Day invasion turns the tide in World War II. The World Bank and the International Monetary Fund are established. The GI Bill of Rights is passed. Harvard creates the first general-purpose digital computer.

1945 World War II ends with an atomic bomb attack on Japan. The first HMO, Kaiser-Permanente of Oakland, California, makes its health plan available to the public.

1946 The first United Nations General Assembly is convened. Winston Churchill warns the West about the Iron Curtain.

1947 The Marshall Plan to rebuild Europe begins. The Taft-Hartley Act is enacted over President Truman's veto, reining in some union practices. The transistor is first developed.

1948 The nation of Israel is declared. Edwin Land invents the Polaroid Land camera. Cable TV is invented.

1949 NATO and the People's Republic of China are formed. The 45 RPM record makes its debut. Otis introduces the first automatic elevator, in Dallas. The first Xerox machine is introduced.

TELEVISION IN THE 1950s

1950 America's population stands at 152,271,417. U.S. GDP is $294.6 billion. Federal spending totals $42.56 billion. The Korean War starts.

1951 The first nuclear power plant is built. The first business computer to handle both numeric and alphabetic data is introduced.

1952 *The Today Show* debuts. Jonas Salk develops the polio vaccine. The first open-heart surgery takes place.

1953 The Korean armistice is signed. The structure of DNA is discovered.

1954 The Supreme Court's *Brown v. Board of Education* decision outlaws segregated schools. Television outstrips radio in ad revenues for the first time.

1955 The AFL and CIO merge. Fiber optics are developed.

1956 Elvis Presley emerges as a big star and purveyor of the youth culture.

1957 Russia launches *Sputnik*, the first earth-orbiting satellite, triggering the space race. The pacemaker is invented.

1958 The United States launches its first satellite into orbit. The first transatlantic jet service begins. The integrated circuit is invented.

1959 Fidel Castro seizes power in Cuba. The St. Lawrence Seaway opens.

1960 America's population stands at 180,671,158. U.S. GDP is $526.6 billion. Federal spending totals $92.19 billion. Ninety percent of American homes have television, and 70 million citizens watch the Nixon-Kennedy debates on TV. The first communications satellite is launched. The first working laser is introduced.

1961 The Berlin Wall is erected. OPEC is established.

1962 The Cuban Missile Crisis brings the superpowers to the brink of nuclear war. The first transatlantic television transmission via satellite is accomplished. John Glenn becomes the first American to orbit the earth. Sam Walton opens the first Wal-Mart; by 2001 the company will be the world's largest retailer and rank number two on the Fortune 500 list.

1963 President John Kennedy is assassinated. The first artificial heart implantation takes place.

1964 The Beatles visit the United States. The Gulf of Tonkin Resolution triggers full-scale American involvement in Vietnam.

1965 ABC pays an unprecedented sum to broadcast NCAA football games.

1966 The Medicare program begins. The FDA declares the birth control pill safe for use.

1967 Racial violence breaks out in U.S. cities. The first successful human heart transplant takes place.

1968 Martin Luther King Jr. and Robert F. Kennedy are assassinated. The motion picture rating system is introduced. Oil is discovered in northern Alaska.

1969 President Richard Nixon begins withdrawing troops from Vietnam. Man walks on the moon for the first time. The Woodstock music festival draws more than half a million.

1970 America's population stands at 205,052,174. U.S. GDP is $1.03 trillion. Federal spending totals $195.6 billion. IBM introduces the floppy disk. The bar code is invented. The first Earth Day is observed, inaugurating a new era of environmental awareness and regulation.

1971 Intel introduces the microprocessor. The voting age is lowered to 18. Wage and price controls are imposed.

1972 Nixon visits China. HBO debuts and e-mail is introduced.

1973 U.S. involvement in the Vietnam War ends. OPEC raises prices and imposes an oil embargo.

RICHARD NIXON (RIGHT) AND ZHOU ENLAI IN CHINA

1974 Nixon resigns over the Watergate scandal. OPEC ends its embargo.

1975 South Vietnam falls to the communists. Bill Gates and Paul Allen form Microsoft, today the world's number one software company. The Altair 8800, the first personal computer, is introduced.

1976 America celebrates its bicentennial and elects Jimmy Carter president.

1977 The neutron bomb is developed. Megahits like *Star Wars* and the soundtrack from *Saturday Night Fever* signal a new era of mass marketing in entertainment. VCRs are developed.

1978 The U.S. Supreme Court upholds affirmative action, setting the stage for a new wave of workplace regulation and litigation. The Home Depot is founded in Atlanta, a company that in 2001 will rank as the nation's 23rd largest company and the largest home improvement retailer.

1979 The U.S. embassy in Tehran, Iran, is taken over by militants and Americans are held hostage. An era of deregulation of American industries begins with trucking and aviation. The Sony Walkman appears. An accident at the Three Mile Island nuclear power facility in Harrisburg, Pennsylvania, calls into question the future of this power source.

1980 America's population stands at 227,224,681. U.S. GDP is $2.78 trillion. Federal spending totals $591 billion. Ronald Reagan is elected president. The Supreme Court rules that genetically engineered organisms can be patented.

1981 Reagan's economic plan dramatically lowers taxes and cuts the growth of federal spending. The president fires striking air traffic controllers. MTV begins broadcasting. AIDS is first identified. Sandra Day O'Connor becomes the first woman nominated to the Supreme Court.

1982 A permanent artificial heart is implanted for the first time. The economy is beset by a deep recession.

1983 The first cellular telephone system begins operation, in Chicago, Illinois. Sally Ride becomes the first American woman astronaut to go into space.

1984 The AT&T monopoly is broken up. Apple introduces the Macintosh. A toxic gas leak at a Union Carbide plant in India kills 2,000.

1985 Mikhail Gorbachev takes over in the Soviet Union and begins a reform program. Enron, America's top buyer and seller of natural gas and power wholesaler, is formed through the merger of Houston Natural Gas and InterNorth Natural Gas.

1986 The Iran-Contra scandal grips Washington. Prozac is first used to treat depression.

1987 AZT becomes the first in a long line of anti-AIDS drugs.

1988 The United States and Canada conclude a free-trade deal. Compact disks outsell vinyl records for the first time.

1989 The *Exxon Valdez* ruptures and spills 11 million gallons of crude oil off the Alaskan coast. The first World Wide Web server and browser are developed.

1990 America's population stands at 249,438,712. U.S. GDP is $5.74 trillion.

GEORGE BUSH (LEFT) AND SADDAM HUSSEIN ON CNN DURING THE GULF WAR

Federal spending totals $1.25 trillion. The Americans with Disabilities Act is enacted.

1991 The Soviet Union is dissolved. Gopher, the first user-friendly Web interface, is created. Operation Desert Storm liberates Kuwait from invading Iraqi forces.

1992 A text-based Web browser is introduced. There are 900 million televisions around the world, 200 million in the United States. The FDA recognizes genetically engineered food as safe.

1993 The North American Free Trade Agreement (NAFTA) is approved. The dominant navigating system for the Web, MOSAIC, is developed.

1994 The first e-commerce sites are established.

1995 The first cloned sheep are created.

1996 A reform bill puts time limits and work requirements on welfare recipients. A major telecommunications deregulation bill is signed. 45 million are now using the Internet, 30 million of them are in North America.

1997 U.S. spacecraft *Pathfinder* lands on Mars. Boeing acquires rival and fellow aviation pioneer company McDonnell-Douglas, forming the 105th largest firm on the 2001 Fortune 500 list.

1998 President Clinton is impeached. The euro is approved.

1999 Hundreds of billions of dollars are spent by government and industry to reprogram computers to avert crashes over "Y2K." There are now 150 million Internet users, 50 percent residing in the United States. Oil giants Exxon and Mobil merge to form the number one company on the 2001 Fortune 500 list. ExxonMobil.

2000 America's population stands at 283,713,698. U.S. GDP is $10.11 trillion. Federal spending totals $1.79 trillion. The nation breaks a record for the longest period of sustained economic expansion in history. The human genetic code is mapped.

2001 George W. Bush takes office as president.

The Empire Builders

WILLIAM BOEING (1881–1956)
BOEING

Boeing began by building and flying seaplanes in the early days of flight. He then laid the foundation for a company that has outlasted all domestic competitors and still reigns supreme over global aviation.

WILLIAM BOEING (LEFT) AND A. T. HORNING

BUSINESS LEADERS

America's stellar economic performance in the 20th century took more than smart policies, desirable products, and good fortune. Unknown entrepreneurs and nationally renowned leaders with vision, inventiveness, and ceaseless energy grabbed hold of bold ideas and turned them into reality, propelling the nation to stratospheric levels of prosperity. There are those business giants who built corporate or financial empires. There are the visionaries whose fame is based on the development of an invention or an idea. Finally, there are those who may not have been in business but through their actions profoundly reshaped the business world.

WALT DISNEY (1901–1966)
THE WALT DISNEY COMPANY

Disney, an artist and filmmaker, was taking a train trip between New York and Los Angeles in the 1920s when the vision of a funny mouse popped into his head. From the creation of Mickey Mouse came an entertainment giant that today is valued at $20 billion and whose products are known around the world.

HENRY FORD (1863–1947)
FORD MOTOR COMPANY

Ford put the horseless carriage within reach of average families and thus created America's car culture. More than that, he revolutionized manufacturing with his assembly-line methods and was one of the first industry titans to understand the link between satisfied workers and productivity. (He reduced their time on the job to eight hours a day and paid them five dollars for that shift, an unheard of wage at the time.)

SAM WALTON

WILLIAM HENRY GATES III (1955–)
MICROSOFT

Just as Henry Ford's vision ushered in the automobile age, Gates's vision ushered in the Internet age. This Harvard dropout created the language and easy-to-use programs that turned the computer into one of the most powerful sets of tools ever placed in human hands. For his efforts, Gates became a billionaire in his twenties and today ranks as the world's richest person.

AMADEO PETER GIANNINI
(1870–1949)
BANK OF AMERICA

Giannini's innovations made consumer banking what it is today. Giannini devised the first system of bank branches, emphasizing convenience for customers. His Bank of America pioneered and popularized installment loans to individuals,

which today drive so much of the consumer economy.

WILLIAM HEWLETT (1913–2001)
& DAVID PACKARD (1912–1996)
HEWLETT PACKARD

Hewlett and Packard started their company in a garage with an investment of about $500. Beginning with sound-testing equipment and later moving into computers, Hewlett and Packard built a global powerhouse years before anyone had heard of Silicon Valley or the PC.

RAY KROC (1902–1984)
McDONALD'S

Kroc was already 52 when he saw the crowd of people pulling into the McDonald brothers' hamburger stand in San Bernardino, California. He surmised that the busy young families of the post–World War II years wanted restaurants that were fast and familiar, and whose products were consistent in quality and price. Thus the fast-food industry was born.

AKIO MORITA (1921–1999)
SONY

Penniless after the ravages of World War II, this Japanese industrialist almost single-handedly changed the image of Japanese-made products from cheap schlock to the highest quality. Morita and Sony also triggered a consumer electronics revolution by making affordable but reliable products available to the mass market, and with innovations like the Sony Walkman.

ALFRED P. SLOAN JR.
(1875–1966)
GENERAL MOTORS

If anyone could stand toe to toe with the legendary Henry Ford it was Sloan. He not only built the General Motors behemoth but also created a corporate management system that was emulated for decades.

SAM WALTON (1918–1992)
WAL-MART

Walton invented the modern retailing system with huge discount stores that became economic anchors in suburbs and rural areas. The seeds planted by this Arkansas businessman grew into what is today the second largest company in America.

HARRY (1881–1958) & JACK
WARNER (1892–1978)
WARNER BROS.

When the Warner brothers released *The Jazz Singer* in 1927, the first release with a sound track synchronized to the film images, they revolutionized the movie industry and ignited a golden age in Hollywood. Their efforts helped establish entertainment as a major 20th-century industry and America as its undisputed leader.

THOMAS WATSON JR.
(1914–1993)
IBM

This legendary businessman envisioned a great future in machines that tabulated data, and from that idea and other innovations, such as the electric typewriter, built IBM into a global giant and a much respected symbol of American economic power and excellence. Within the business world, Watson became equally known for motivating and training his sales force, imbuing them with a distinct corporate culture, and putting the concepts of service and quality on a par with the products themselves.

ROBERT WOODRUFF
(1889–1985)
THE COCA-COLA COMPANY

In 1923, Woodruff became president of a company his father and a group of investors had purchased several years earlier. He quickly began to pioneer many of the marketing strategies that are still effective today: He relied heavily on market research, linked his product to a distinctive lifestyle, and ensured consistency in the product worldwide. In the process, Woodruff made Coca-Cola one of the most recognizable brands in history.

The Visionaries

JEFF BEZOS (1964–)
AMAZON.COM

When Bezos founded Amazon.com in 1995, the popular use of the World Wide Web was in its infancy. In a few short years, this on-line retailer of books, music, movies, and other products set the pace of the exploding but turbulent e-commerce sector. The jury is still out on Amazon's long-term viability, but Bezos's legacy as one of the founding fathers of e-commerce is secure.

LEE IACOCCA (1924–)
FORD MOTOR COMPANY & CHRYSLER

At Ford, Iacocca oversaw the development and marketing of the Mustang. At Chrysler, he engineered that company's bold come-back in the 1980s. Beyond that, Iacocca

JEFF BEZOS

pioneered the concept of the businessman as just an average guy in the street, winning white-collar and blue-collar fans alike with his pithy comments about economic and trade issues.

HERB KELLEHER (1931–)
SOUTHWEST AIRLINES

This hard-charging chief of a small regional airline saw his business really take flight in the aftermath of airline deregulation in the early 1980s. Kelleher believed that air travel should not be confined to the upper strata of American society and he banked on the idea that average Americans would fill his no-frills "buses in the sky" in exchange for low fares. He was right, and today Southwest is America's fifth largest and most popular airline.

WILLIAM LEVITT (1907–1994)
RESIDENTIAL HOUSING

In the aftermath of World War II, Levitt did more than any other single person to create suburban America. His Levittown, New York, subdivision offered affordable detached homes in planned communities for the nation's growing middle class—and the concept rapidly spread across the country.

ROBERT N. NOYCE (1927–1990)
THE INTEGRATED CIRCUIT

In 1959, the man who would later found Intel developed an efficient method of connecting transistors and other electronic components into a single integrated circuit. Succeeding generations of these circuits would grow in speed and complexity but shrink in size. Today, Intel's most sophisticated microprocessor contains some 9.5 million transistors in a single chip. It is impossible to overstate the impact of these developments, spearheaded by Noyce and others, on today's technological revolution.

JACK WARNER (LEFT) AND HARRY WARNER

H. ROSS PEROT (1930–)
BUSINESS & POLITICS

Perot made his fortune by building Electronic Data Systems (EDS) but became a household name through his adventures in politics and international derring-do. In 1979, he staged a successful mission to free EDS employees held in Ayatollah Khomeini's Iran. In the 1992 presidential election, he garnered 19 million votes as an independent candidate and ranks to this day as one of the best known business people of all time.

WILLIAM SHOCKLEY (1910–1989)
THE TRANSISTOR

Shockley and his team of developers at Bell Labs orchestrated the first giant step into the age of technology by introducing the transistor in 1948. This device replaced the much larger and less reliable vacuum tube in electronic devices and spawned entire generations of new products and industries.

FREDERICK SMITH (1944–)
FEDERAL EXPRESS

When Smith was at Yale, he wrote a term paper arguing for an overnight delivery service that would meet the needs of a just-in-time economy and fill the service

TED TURNER

JACK WELCH (1935–)
GENERAL ELECTRIC

Welch not only revived a sluggish corporate giant, he pioneered many of today's modern management techniques and corporate strategies. He is frequently cited as the most respected CEO in America, and his pronouncements on business leadership are required reading for any student of enterprise.

ROBERT E. WOOD (1879–1969)
SEARS, ROEBUCK & CO.

Sears was a famous but faltering catalogue sales company when Wood jumped ship from rival Montgomery Ward and joined the company in 1924. He then transformed Sears into the largest retail chain in the nation, in part through innovations such as offering free and ample parking.

STEPHEN "STEVE" WOZNIAK
(1950–) & STEVE JOBS (1955–)
APPLE COMPUTER

Computers were supposed to be confined to offices. They were to be run by experts and would require huge amounts of space and energy to operate. Wozniak and Jobs were the first to reject those assumptions. Their vision, which they helped turn into reality through Apple, was to place

gaps left by the U.S. postal monopoly. While he earned only a C grade on the paper, Smith soon translated his ideas into Federal Express, which today delivers packages to more than 200 countries in 600 aircraft and 46,000 trucks.

TED TURNER (1938–)
CABLE NEWS NETWORK (CNN)

This media visionary popularized the concept of cable superstations that broadcast programming all over the nation. By creating CNN, Turner set out to challenge the news dominance of the three major networks and fill an increasing demand for 24-hour news. Today, CNN is considered by many to be the network of record, particularly in the international arena. On more than one occasion, world leaders engulfed in conflict have sent messages and signals to each other through the network's interviews.

THEODORE VAIL (1845–1920)
& WILLIAM G. MCGOWAN
(1927–1992)
AT&T AND COMPETITORS

In the early years of the 20th century, Vail built AT&T into a telecommunications

giant, introducing key service upgrades and extending service beyond the confinement of upper-class America. In the later decades of the century, McGowan would challenge AT&T's monopoly by starting MCI. The subsequent competition from the courtroom to the marketplace would leave consumers a little confused but clearly winners as the availability of cheap long-distance calling, cell phones, and pagers spread around the world.

JAY VAN ANDEL (1924–)
& RICH DEVOS (1926–)
AMWAY

By creating Amway, the direct-selling giant that markets consumer products and services in a network marketing system, these two Dutch Americans from a Grand Rapids, Michigan, suburb ignited a global entrepreneurial revolution. Some 30 million people worldwide have joined Amway and other companies like it, taking advantage of a low-cost business opportunity and building their own direct-selling organizations.

FRANKLIN D. ROOSEVELT

easy-to-use computers in the hands of average people. Their early efforts initiated the personal computer era.

Wilbur (1867–1912) & Orville (1871–1948) Wright
The airplane

They were better inventors than they were businessmen. And what an invention! By creating and successfully flying the first airplane, the Wright brothers altered man's sense of time, space, and reality forever.

The Reshapers

Theodore Roosevelt (1858–1919)

This turn-of-the-century president railed against business monopolies, emphasized conservation of natural resources, and set a pattern of presidential activism that through the century would have a tremendous impact on business and the economy.

Franklin D. Roosevelt (1882–1945)

Roosevelt brought the government into the economic arena as never before. Some believe FDR's New Deal and entitlement programs such as Social Security set the stage for a dangerous intrusion of government into the private economic affairs of citizens. Others see him as saving the free enterprise system from its own excesses and thus dissuading the public during the trauma of the Great Depression from turning to more radical solutions like socialism.

Douglas MacArthur (1880–1964) & George C. Marshall (1880–1959)

MacArthur and Marshall helped lead America to victory during wartime. In the aftermath of World War II, they were called upon to rebuild the economies of America's allies and enemies. MacArthur's role in postwar Japan and Marshall's leadership in rebuilding Europe would prepare the way for America's leading role in today's global economy.

Dwight D. Eisenhower (1890–1969)

As president, Ike's leadership in building the Interstate Highway System gave the U.S. economy its vast transportation network that today carries well over 90 percent of all the goods shipped around the nation.

George Meany (1894–1980)

This labor leader, along with cohorts like Walter Reuther, had a major impact on business, helping to establish basic workplace rules and benefits, many of which have now been codified into federal and state law.

Richard Nixon (1913–1994)

Nixon opened China, setting the stage for the development of a lucrative business relationship between the world's most populous country and the world's most successful economy. He also created the Environmental Protection Agency and the Occupational Safety and Health Administration (OSHA), tried wage and price controls, and broke the link between the dollar and gold.

Ronald Reagan (1911–)

In 1981, Reagan ushered in the "Reagan Revolution" that reaffirmed the role of free enterprise in American life through lower taxes, deregulation, and less government. Many historians and economists believe his actions, both economic and political, directed at the communist empire helped trigger the breakup of the Soviet Union, thus reshaping not only the U.S. military

but also the economic landscape of the entire world.

Harold Greene (1924–2000)

This federal judge presided over the breakup of AT&T in 1984, deregulating the telecommunications industry and creating the turbulent and competitive environment that would later foster the Internet age.

Alan Greenspan

Alan Greenspan (1926–)

From the late 1980s to the present day, this Federal Reserve Board chairman has been widely credited with crafting a monetary policy that fueled, but did not overheat, the longest and greatest period of economic expansion in this or any nation's history.

THE STORY OF THE CENTURY

THE ROLE OF AMERICAN BUSINESS IN THE NATION'S GOOD LIFE

Sir Winston Churchill said it as well as anyone ever has: 'Some regard private enterprise as if it were a predatory tiger to be shot. Others look upon it as a cow they can milk. Only a handful see it for what it really is: the strong horse that pulls the whole cart.'

During the past century, private enterprise pulled humanity's cart to the greatest heights of prosperity mankind has ever known. And much of the enterprise system's energy, inventiveness, and sheer resilience came from the United States.

The story of American business in the 20th century is a story of unsurpassed achievement that is fully understood only when one stands at the center of a complex intersection of biography, geography, longevity, demography, humanity, technology, philosophy, and most important, opportunity.

Biography: America's economic achievements were driven in good measure by hundreds of business visionaries and strong-willed corporate builders, as well as millions of courageous, risk-taking entrepreneurs.

Geography: Over the past 100 years, the nation continually expanded its economic borders, first to the Sunbelt and West Coast and then to the global marketplace.

Longevity: Business and the growth it fostered provided the foundation of wealth that enabled America to significantly upgrade its quality of life, public health, and medical advances, thus expanding U.S. life expectancy by an astounding 30 years in a single century.

Demography: The economic vitality of the nation was continually refreshed by the arrival of succeeding generations of hardworking immigrants, immigrants who also replenished the American workforce as domestic birthrates dropped.

Humanity: Over the course of the last century, business markedly improved its treatment of workers and the environment and became major contributors to society and the community.

Technology: Ceaseless advances spurred in large part by American business—from the Model T to the personal computer—not only increased personal comfort but unleashed stupendous increases in productivity, allowing citizens a lifestyle of abundance and leisure unimaginable just a century ago.

Philosophy: American business was a major player in determining a victorious outcome in the great 20th-century philosophical struggle between capitalism (and freedom) and communism (and totalitarianism).

Opportunity: Through the achievements it registered and the examples it set, American free enterprise in the last 100 years offered unsurpassed economic opportunities to millions

ABOVE: WILLIAM McKINLEY, SUPPORTED BY BUSINESSMEN, WORKERS, AND SOLDIERS, DOFFS HIS HAT TO AMERICA'S SPIRIT OF ENTERPRISE IN THIS CAMPAIGN POSTER CIRCA 1895–1900. • OPPOSITE: FOLLOWING A NATURALIZATION CEREMONY AT ELLIS ISLAND, THIS YOUNG AMERICAN PROUDLY DISPLAYS PROOF OF HIS NEW CITIZENSHIP.

at home and abroad. It is this empowering of individuals and the affirmation of the human spirit that stand as perhaps America's greatest achievement in the 20th century.

The following pages will illustrate in vivid detail each of these aspects of a most remarkable story, a story that was often overlooked as historians and analysts took stock of the 20th century in the year 2000 and one that prepares for and guides America into an even more exciting and challenging future.

WHAT A DIFFERENCE A CENTURY MAKES!

To understand the change, growth, and progress achieved by Americans during the 20th century, all one has to do is contrast

ABOVE: FIELDHANDS POSE ON A KANSAS FARM IN 1911. · BELOW: THE 20TH CENTURY SAW A RUSH OF WOMEN INTO THE WORKFORCE, AS THIS 1941 POSTER BY THE ILLINOIS STATE EMPLOYMENT OFFICE ILLUSTRATES. · OPPOSITE: TODAY, LIKE THIS HOSPITAL WORKER, 54 MILLION WOMEN WORK IN NONFARM JOBS.

what life must have been like in 1900 with what it is like today.

Various benchmarks help tell the story.

In 1900: America was home to 76 million people. Birthrates were high, but so were deaths. For every 1,000 people, there were approximately 30 births and 17.2 deaths. The five leading causes of death were pneumonia related to the flu, tuberculosis, diarrhea, heart disease, and stroke. Average life expectancy was just 48 years.

Today: America is home to 283 million people. The birthrate per thousand has dropped to 14.5 and the death rate to 8.6. The leading causes of death are heart disease, cancer, stroke, pulmonary diseases, and pneumonia. Life expectancy is 78 years.

In 1900: New York was the most populous state, with 7.2 million people. California was well down the list with 1.48 million. America's workforce totaled 29 million. Just under 19 percent of women participated in the workforce; 37.5 percent of working Americans worked on farms.

By 2000: California was the most populous state with nearly 34 million residents. New York slipped to third behind Texas, with just over 16 million. The labor force totaled 137.7 million. Nearly 60 percent of women worked. Ninety-eight million Americans worked in service industries. Just 1.6 percent worked on farms.

In 1900: Federal spending claimed just 3 percent of the gross domestic product (GDP). There was no federal income tax, but there were also no Social Security system, no Medicare program, and virtually no workplace or environmental rules. Few employers offered workers health services.

Today: Federal spending consumes 19 percent of a $10.11 trillion economy. The average American works into the month of May before he or she finishes paying off the year's taxes. Yet workers and their families are covered by a vast

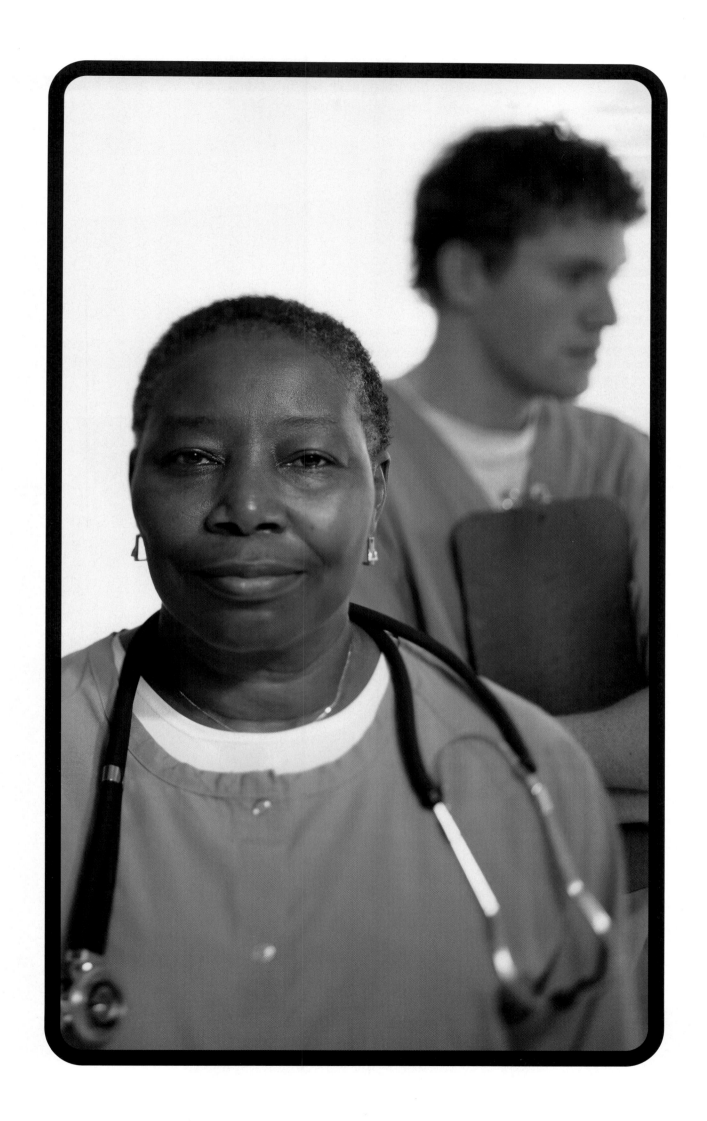

17

Above: The American dream comes true for a young couple in the 1950s. The average price of a home then was $22,000. · Opposite: The dream lives on 50 years later, as this couple watches their new home take shape. In 1999, the average price for a new house was $203,900.

array of safety-net programs designed to sustain life in the event of injury, illness, unemployment, and in old age. The voluntary system of employer-based health care coverage insures more than 170 million American workers and their families.

In 1900: Less than 13 percent of adults were high school graduates; 3 percent had college degrees; and 1,965 graduate degrees were awarded in the entire nation. Women earned just 20 percent of college degrees.

Today: Eighty-three percent of adults are high school graduates and 24 percent earn college degrees. More than 50 percent of these degrees are earned by women. Over 500,000 graduate degrees are awarded nationwide each year.

In 1900: Just 1 percent of Americans owned stock.

Today: Fifty-two percent own stock.

Stock ownership was but one manifestation of a century of economic and social progress, according to the American Enterprise Institute (AEI), based in Washington, D.C. The AEI scholars, along with economists such as Stanley Lebergott, have documented the tremendous changes for everyday Americans, pointing out that the typical work week has shrunk from six days to five, with daily hours on the job cut from ten to eight and lower. The other examples are many.

• Output per person increased eight times over the course of the century.

• U.S. investment in the global economy grew 140 times over.

• In 1919, only 152,000 Americans traveled overseas. In 1997, 22 million Americans went abroad.

• Accidental deaths in the home and workplace declined throughout the century.

• The average income of middle-income households rose from $15,745 in 1929 to $47,809 in 1998—after adjusting for inflation.

• The poverty rate declined from 22 percent in 1959 to 12 percent in 1999.

• Total miles traveled by all motor vehicles increased 25,000 times over from 1900 to 1997.

• American business revenues grew from $2 trillion in 1939 to $18 trillion in 1996.

• Stock exchange volume multiplied 3,000 times between 1900 and 1999.

• Sixty-five thousand new book titles were published in 1997, more than ten times the number of new titles published in 1900.

• The annual volume of mail per person increased from 147 pieces in 1900 to 1,103 pieces in 1998.

In addition, thanks to increased formal schooling, Americans are entering the workforce later than they did a century ago and leaving it sooner. And, whereas 87 percent of women reported doing four or more hours of housework a day in 1924, just 14 percent do today. Moreover, at the

involvement in economic affairs. As the 20th century began, America was just starting to flex its economic and military muscles. Theodore Roosevelt, a young president barely into his forties, challenged the monopolies that had come to dominate key industries, in his view busting trusts on behalf of consumers, workers, and small businesses. He established a new tradition of governmental activism that in 1913 would result in the Federal Reserve System and in 1914 a fully operating Panama Canal.

turn of the last century, making clothes and baking bread occupied major portions of the daily lives of American women. According to one estimate, in 1900 the typical housewife personally carried seven tons of coal, hauled 9,000 gallons of water, and baked half a ton of bread!

Together these and other developments have added up to a life of comparative leisure today as compared to 1900.

CONTRIBUTING TO AMERICA'S PROGRESS

What explains this century of progress in the abundance, quality, and longevity of American life?

Is it that the nation has been blessed by geography—a vast continent rich in natural resources and separated from prior centuries of turmoil by two vast oceans?

Is it that American society has been continually renewed and revitalized by succeeding waves of immigrants who brought their energies, talents, and dreams to these shores?

Is it because of a democratic political system and a form of government that protects the aspirations of individuals

from the plunder and tyranny of kings and dictators?

Has America been blessed with more than its share of brilliant scientists, inventors, doctors, and medical researchers whose developments and breakthroughs made the nation's citizens more productive, comfortable, and healthy?

And has the country been honored by millions of brave men and women who have repeatedly put their lives on the line defending America and its promise from enemies seeking to conquer or destroy it?

The answer to all of the above is a resounding "yes." Each of these blessings contributed strongly to creating the greatest and most prosperous nation on earth. But underlying it all has been a free enterprise system that while far from perfect has generated the growth, wealth, and opportunity to make all other advances possible.

Much of the last century was spent trying to find the right balance between unbridled free enterprise and government

Meanwhile, business visionaries like Henry Ford and William Boeing spent the pre–World War I years developing revolutionary new products such as the automobile and airplane as well as modern assembly-line techniques and principles of corporate management. Such advances helped place products that were once reserved for the super rich into the hands of the average American, setting the stage

Photos: Top, © Schenectady Museum; Hall of Electrical History Foundation/CORBIS; bottom, © Kevin Fleming/CORBIS

prosperity, with the nation's businesses making great strides in product development. Television became the country's dominant medium for entertainment and, later, for information. Seminal developments like the invention of the transistor sowed the seeds for the information age still to come. Rising incomes allowed Americans to attain greater education levels that in turn increased their productivity. The creation of suburbs with affordable housing further elevated the quality of life. In the meantime, the modern civil rights movement began to challenge the nation's conscience.

While the 1960s began as a decade of promise and further astounding economic progress, the country found

ABOVE: THIS GENERAL ELECTRIC TELEVISION WAS A FASCINATING NOVELTY IN 1939. · BELOW: PATRONS EXPLORE THE INTERNET AT THE @ CAFE IN NEW YORK'S EAST VILLAGE.

for the first great period of mass consumerism, the Roaring Twenties.

And roar they did. In the decade following World War I, giant companies like IBM were founded. Fledgling industries like the movies and radio came into their own. The momentum of rapid economic growth funded and fueled advances in health and the municipal environment. The country was sailing on a tide of prosperity such as it had never known. But the hopes and dreams of millions sank with the stock market crash of 1929.

Historians and economists still argue about whether it was Franklin Roosevelt's New Deal or America's entry into World War II that finally pulled the country out of the Great Depression. Whether or not the New Deal gets the credit, its policies sparked a debate that continues to this day. Following the depression, Americans

reached a consensus that a nation with such a rich and powerful economy should offer in an organized fashion at least a floor of basic income security for the poor, the elderly, and the workers. But how much government was enough? How much cradle-to-grave security could the government provide without eating away at fundamental economic principles of self-reliance and individual initiative that produced sufficient wealth to offer that security in the first place? Such issues had an enormous impact on business, for it was to business that America looked to generate the jobs and revenues needed to pay for those who were not able to produce and provide for themselves.

The post–World War II years unleashed an explosion of middle-class

itself divided on such issues as the Vietnam War and the War on Poverty. The nation also discovered that it had been a poor steward of the earth and was paying for it with a fouled environment. The first Earth Day, in 1970, signaled the beginning of a new environmental sensitivity but also an era of regulations.

The 1970s underscored the extent to which America's economy had become intertwined with and sometimes vulnerable to outside events. Increases in the price of oil by the Organization of the Petroleum Exporting Countries (OPEC) and an embargo in 1973 triggered the nation's first modern energy crisis.

The 1980s were the era of Ronald Reagan. His tax cuts, deregulation, and controls on the growth of federal spending unleashed business. Meanwhile, tough competition from overseas, especially from Japan, forced companies to restructure and change their management practices and corporate cultures.

Despite accumulating deficits and a stock market crash in 1987, the Reagan eighties produced a business sector that reengineered itself for fierce global competition and saw American companies further multiply choices for consumers, particularly in media, news, information, services, and high technology. MTV and CNN were born. VCRs and personal computers became commonplace, and American staples like automobiles were improved in order to recapture markets lost in the 1970s.

With the end of the Cold War, businesses had to refocus their efforts on new markets in a rapidly globalizing economy. During the 1990s, American companies moved quickly to expand their presence in world product, service, and financial markets and to form strategic alliances with foreign companies to maximize their reach around the globe.

The 1990s also saw the arrival of the Internet age. No single person, company, or country can lay claim to inventing it, but American business certainly led it. The Internet age burst upon humankind with breathtaking speed, shrinking the world, empowering average citizens everywhere with knowledge and capabilities, and significantly increasing the productivity of each worker.

Indeed, the last decade of the 20th century saw the longest period of economic growth in the nation's history. And while this age, like all others, will see its ups, downs, and uncertainties, one thing is certain: American free enterprise, and the visionaries, companies, and workers who power it, will continue to push the human condition across new frontiers, never flinching and never looking back.

GOOD NEIGHBOR TO THE WORLD
COMBATING SOCIAL & ENVIRONMENTAL PROBLEMS

FEW WOULD DISPUTE THE ARGUMENT THAT THE PRINCIPAL GOAL OF ANY BUSINESS IS AND MUST BE TO MAKE A PROFIT. FOR THE SMALL-BUSINESS OWNER, THAT PROFIT CONSTITUTES HIS OR HER LIVELIHOOD. FOR THE LARGE CORPORATION, THE PROFITS THAT AREN'T PLOWED BACK INTO BUSINESS EXPANSION ARE RETURNED TO INVESTORS IN THE FORM OF DIVIDENDS.

Increasingly, these investors include millions of Main Street Americans whose pensions depend on the growth of and income from stocks in the country's largest companies.

Free-market economists assert that making a profit should indeed be the only business of business, that the profit motive fuels growth, inventiveness, hard work, and product and lifestyle advances and helps explain the most successful and sustained broad-based prosperity ever known to mankind.

Yet over the course of the 20th century, it can be said that while the business community continued to focus on profit, it also developed a strong social conscience and commitment to the community, producing tremendous contributions that have enriched the lives of all Americans. As globalization proceeds apace, this commitment is now being extended to the international community as well.

The contrast with the past—in image if not in reality—is striking. At the end of the 19th century, images of robber baron monopolists living the high life off the labor of others in a gilded age were firmly fixed in the American mind. The modern labor movement was in its infancy. Laws protecting workers, even children, from exploitation were scarce. So, too, were unemployment and welfare programs that might protect them from the frequent boom-and-bust roller-coaster ride that characterized the economy of those times. As the industrial might of the nation grew, few gave any thought whatsoever to the environmental consequences.

Some would say that business not only had to be pushed to show concern for the plight of workers, the condition of the environment, or the social conditions of the community, it had to be shoved. But the more realistic assessment is that attitudes on these issues evolved in the business community as they did in society as a whole. Most businesspeople adopted a larger view of their role in society, believing that by enriching the entire community they were not only doing the right thing but helping improve the overall business environment and thus their company and its profit potential.

Call it enlightened self-interest. Ascribe it to the time-honored American values of being a good neighbor and giving something back to the community. Or more cynically chalk it up to the simple necessity of obeying new labor, environmental, and consumer laws or the mundane desire to gain publicity by doing good works. Whatever motive one wishes to credit, the

ABOVE: WATER IS TESTED AT A TREATMENT CENTER TO ASSURE THAT IT MEETS ENVIRONMENTAL PROTECTION AGENCY STANDARDS. · OPPOSITE: A VOLUNTEER PLANTS SEEDLINGS IN A CLEARED AREA OF FOREST.

business community's record of action in arenas extending far beyond the economic one is indisputable.

One critical point is clear when evaluating society's progress in the 20th century and the role of business in that progress: Without a strong economy and the broad-based prosperity produced by American business, little if any gains in working conditions, environmental quality, equality of opportunity, health care, or education and the arts would be possible. A strong, productive economy is what pays the bills for all these worthy goals and compelling missions.

INVESTING IN WORKERS

In the early stages of the industrial revolution, America's laborers and assembly-line workers were valued principally for their strong backs and nimble hands. With

waves of unskilled and poorly educated immigrants pouring in to man the nation's factories, mines, foundries, and oil fields, there was little interest or incentive on the part of the captains of industry to view labor as anything more than just another factor in the cost of doing business. And like all such factors, the goal was to secure it as cheaply as possible in order to maximize profit. With workers yet unorganized and few laws governing the workplace, the climate was ripe for unscrupulous operators to exploit their employees.

Yet in the late 19th century and the early years of the 20th century, conditions began to change as workers responded by organizing unions and waging strikes. These activities were often answered by violent crackdowns. Workplace fires and industrial accidents in sweatshops and mines opened

the nation's eyes to dangerous working conditions. Muckraking journalists exposed the plight and exploitation of child laborers. These events led to the first laws governing working hours and conditions.

More positive developments empowered workers as well. The economic growth and industrial development of America improved overall living conditions. A strong middle class and opportunities for upward mobility emerged. Advances in transportation, especially the invention and popularization of the automobile, would by the 1920s allow average citizens the flexibility to explore new opportunities rather than be tied down for life to one employer. Enlightened industrialists like Henry Ford began to recognize the importance of investing in human capital. By improving pay and conditions for assembly-line workers, Ford found he could more than make up for those higher costs in increased productivity and a higher quality of work. In other words, he and the rest of American business began to discover that treating workers well was a good investment.

All of these factors explain the remarkable strides made by American workers in the 20th century. Organized labor played a role, especially in the early decades. The unions' achievements include the enshrining of workers' rights and protections in the form of federal and state laws such as the National Labor Relations Act of 1935 and the Occupational Safety and Health Administration Act of 1971.

As America has become the knowledge and technology service center for the global economy, there is broad recognition in the business community that companies will prosper if and only if there is a genuine interest and investment in human talent and the well-being of the workforce. In fact, as the demographics of the nation have shifted and the supply of available workers has tightened, the best employees find themselves in increasingly high demand, with companies seeking to devise new strategies to attract and retain them.

By the end of the 20th century, workers were enjoying the best range of benefits from employers in American history. According to the U.S. Chamber of Commerce,

adults and 3.3 million children added to workplace health plans from 1994 through 1998. All told, companies on average spent over $4,100 per employee for health plan costs in 1998 and a total of $291 billion for group health insurance.

In addition, of the two out of three Medicare beneficiaries who had prescription drug coverage, 44 percent received it through their former workplace. Employer spending

Employers who offer retirement plans spend on average $3,244 per employee on retirement and savings programs. More than 90 percent of employers who offer a 401(k) plan match employee contributions to the plan. These plans are tremendously popular with employees: 87.4 percent of eligible employees participate in their 401(k) plan. The average employer contribution to 401(k) plans is 4.9 percent of payroll. Through

ABOVE: AN INSPECTOR STAMPS VATS OF POLYURETHANE RESIN DESTINED FOR SHIPMENT TO ATHENS, GREECE. AS THE 21ST CENTURY DAWNED, INTERNATIONAL TRADE'S IMPACT ON U.S. AND WORLD ECONOMICS GREW. IN MID 2001, THE UNITED STATES EXPORTED NEARLY $90 BILLION IN GOODS AND SERVICES WHILE IT IMPORTED NEARLY $120 BILLION'S WORTH. · OPPOSITE: THIS OFFICE IN MIAMI REFLECTS THE OPEN, FUNCTIONAL DESIGN AND INCREASED USE OF HIGH-TECH EQUIPMENT THAT DEFINED THE WORKSPACE AT THE END OF THE 20TH CENTURY.

employers spent $818 billion on employee benefits in 1998; 155 million Americans received their health insurance through employers (in 2001, that figure grew to more than 170 million), with 6.1 million

for prescription drugs accounted for 15 percent of total employer health plan costs in 1998, compared with 9 percent in 1993.

Companies also incur huge expense to help give workers a secure retirement.

retirement plans, 86 percent of employer-plan sponsors provide investment education to employees.

Paid leave is the most common benefit offered by employers. In companies with

25

more than 100 workers, 95 percent of full-time employees are eligible for paid vacation. In 1999, 74 percent of firms offered some type of alternative work arrangement, a sharp increase from 54 percent in 1990. Common types of work arrangements include flextime, compressed workweek, job-sharing, work at home/telecommuting, part-time employment, summer hours, and phased return from leave.

Workplaces are becoming safer as well. According to the Occupational Safety and Health Administration (OSHA), the number of workplace-related injuries and illnesses has fallen to the lowest level since record-keeping on the federal level began in the early 1970s.

American business is providing a level of safety in the workplace, security upon retirement and in case of illness, and flexibility on the job for parents juggling the responsibilities of family and work unsurpassed in our history and unmatched by any other economy.

PROTECTING THE DELICATE BALANCE

Cleaning the environment stands as one of the pivotal triumphs of the 20th century, and American business deserves a good measure of the credit. Critical environmental strides began early in the century, long before anyone ever conceived of Earth Day or the Environmental Protection Agency. Advances in municipal health, sanitation, and water supplies together represented one of the biggest factors in reducing the spread of disease and increasing life expectancy. Yet other environmental perils were ignored until the last three decades of the 20th century. But since the first Earth Day in 1970, a lot has changed for the better, due in no small measure to an investment of more than one trillion dollars by American business to clean the environment.

By almost every indicator, the air, water, and land are cleaner today than they were

ABOVE: MAJESTIC MOUNT RAINIER RISES 14,410 FEET NEAR ASHFORD, WASHINGTON. MOUNT RAINIER NATIONAL PARK WAS ESTABLISHED IN 1899. · BELOW: GENERAL MOTORS INTRODUCED THE EV1, THE WORLD'S FIRST MASS-PRODUCED ELECTRIC CAR, IN 1997.

30 years ago. In the last three decades, total emissions of the six principal air pollutants decreased by an overall 29 percent, even though the U.S. population increased 28 percent. Sulfur oxides are down 67 percent, nitrogen oxides by 38 percent. Smog has decreased 31 percent, while carbon monoxide levels have dropped by 66 percent. Airborne lead is down 97 percent, and particulates (tiny specks of material that can lodge in the lungs) have been reduced by 26 percent.

The water is also cleaner. The amount of fishable or swimmable waters has increased by almost 40 percent since 1975. Discharges of untreated organic wastes and toxic metals from industry have sharply declined, plunging by 98 percent from 1970s levels.

And, with less than 5 percent of this country's land covered by urban or suburban areas and roads, there are still many parts of the country where residents can go for recreation and scenic beauty as well as areas that can be responsibly developed. In fact, today states like Maine, Vermont, and New York have about 26 million more acres of forest than they had in 1900.

When it comes to the environment, American business on the whole has put up the cash, worked hard, and played by the rules. So, three decades after the first Earth Day, the nation has the cleanest environment in generations. Business will continue to make environmental improvements, with planned investments of $1.5 trillion in the first decade of the new century.

U.S. companies will apply money, research, and determination to develop technologies that make the economy more efficient, less wasteful, and more protective of the environment.

This commitment will build on achievements to date. Thanks to technologies developed by business, CD-ROMs can hold 200 phone books' worth of information, cutting down on paper usage. "Clean" fiber-optic cables are steadily replacing "dirty" copper wiring, not only streamlining communications but treading more lightly on the environment. Food biotechnology is increasing the productivity of American farms while helping to feed a hungry world. New strains of rice that include vitamins are combating disease in desperately poor countries.

The United States is producing more crops on less land than ever before. The transportation industry has developed cleaner and more efficient engines. In fact, a fleet of 20 fuel-efficient new cars produces less air pollution than one car built in 1960. And, streamlined logistics procedures, enabled by technology, ensure that each trip counts.

Whether it is fuel, forest products, steel, tires and rubber, or petrochemicals, American industries have developed methods and equipment to make their processes cleaner and more efficient. Technological advances have resulted in many benefits, from airplanes to the polio vaccine to the home computer. Technology has made the world cleaner, safer, and more comfortable. In the new century, American business will prove that technical innovation is now an effective agent for environmental progress.

The Spirit of Volunteerism

Since the frontier days when settlers pitched in to help raise barns or plow each other's fields, America has been known for a rich spirit of volunteerism. Business has participated in this spirit throughout U.S. history, and as the wealth and strength of the American private sector have grown, so, too, have its voluntary investments in schools, young people, health services, civil rights efforts, the arts, and community development projects.

In 1999, U.S. corporations and their foundations donated more than $11 billion, a 14.2 percent increase from the previous year. But these donations are only the tip of the iceberg. Private foundations, most of them funded by successful business leaders and families, in the course of the last century amassed enormous wealth for the purpose of supporting charitable works and institutions that better individuals and society.

According to the New York–based Foundation Center, a nonprofit clearinghouse

BELOW: A VOLUNTEER FROM HABITAT FOR HUMANITY INTERNATIONAL APPLIES PRIMER TO A NEW HOME. THE AMERICUS, GEORGIA–BASED, NONPROFIT ORGANIZATION, WHICH CONSTRUCTS HOUSING FOR NEEDY FAMILIES, WAS FOUNDED IN 1976 AND SINCE THEN HAS BUILT MORE THAN 100,000 HOMES AROUND THE WORLD, 30,000 IN THE UNITED STATES ALONE. · OPPOSITE: AMERICAN BUSINESS AND PHILANTHROPIC ORGANIZATIONS HAVE PROVIDED FUNDS TO BUILD SCHOOLS, LIKE THIS ONE IN KENYA, AND BRING OTHER FORMS OF AID TO THIRD WORLD COUNTRIES.

of information on foundations and charitable organizations, there are a total of 47,000 active independent, corporate, community, and grantsmaking foundations in the United States. By 1998, these entities had combined assets of $385 billion, more than a ten-fold increase since 1975. The foundations issue nearly $20 billion in grants, again, some ten times the amount given in 1975.

The names of the largest grantsmakers are familiar to many Americans and represent the giants of 20th-century American industry. Measured by assets, the top ten are the Bill and Melinda Gates Foundation; the David and Lucile Packard Foundation; the Ford Foundation; the Lilly Endowment; the J. Paul Getty Trust; the Robert Wood Johnson Foundation; Pew Charitable Trusts; the W. K. Kellogg Foundation; the John D. and Catherine T. MacArthur Foundation; and the Andrew F. Mellon Foundation.

These and many other organizations provide essential support to America's colleges and universities, museums and performing arts groups, hospitals and health organizations, civil rights groups, and youth and scholarship programs. In addition, countless corporations and small businesses donate their time and resources to community programs and organize workplace fund-raising drives that have become indispensable to organizations such as United Way and the American Red Cross.

As America has staked a bigger claim in the global economy, American business has extended its helping hand around the globe. Some of the critics of globalization claim that the U.S. presence in developing countries is an exploitative one. Yet invariably, American-owned factories and facilities in those countries offer the best pay, benefits, and working conditions available. Developments in technology, medicine, and

agriculture and environmental control have frequently been shared with poor countries, lifting living conditions in those societies. When tragedy strikes in the form of a flood or earthquake, American companies are among the first to aid in rescue and recovery.

To spread the word about these positive activities and show global corporations from all nations how to perform even greater community service and operate at a high ethical level, the U.S. Chamber of Commerce formed the Center for Corporate Citizenship in 1999. One group that the Center has recognized is the American Apparel Manufacturers Association for its program certifying factories that can demonstrate their clothing is manufactured under lawful, humane, and ethical conditions.

In addition, the Bank of America Foundation played a leadership role in organizing funds, food, medical supplies, and other relief for the tens of thousands of Hurricane Mitch victims throughout Central America. Cargill opened a model chicken-processing factory outside of Bangkok that is renowned for its clean conditions and safety record. The plant buys chickens from Thai farmers and pours a significant share of profits from the facility into scholarships for poor children in rural Thailand.

Conoco has initiated an environmentally friendly method of oil exploration and extraction in the central African countries of Angola, the Congo, and Gabon. The company built schools for the children of its workers and established hospitals and food banks to help the communities in which it operates. And closer to home, General Motors has established itself as the leading corporate giver to United Way, donating more than $38 million annually, while Discovery Communications, the parent company of the Discovery Channel, has worked to enhance the technology, literacy, and critical viewing skills of young people in the United States and abroad.

In these and countless other ways, American business has embraced the responsibilities of good corporate citizenship.

PITCHING IN TO DEFEND AMERICA

When one leafs through the pages of the *Saturday Evening Post* and other popular magazines of the wartime years of the early 1940s, it is striking how virtually every ad run by an American corporation puts product promotion on the back burner and instead implores readers to participate in the war effort. There are appeals to buy war bonds, conserve energy, and donate used products and scrap materials so they can be converted into weapons, ammunition, and matériel. There are warnings to

ABOVE: NAVY PILOTS PREPARE FOR A NIGHT RUN IN THEIR EA-6B *Prowler*. · BELOW: AIR NATIONAL GUARD MEMBERS AT NEW YORK'S WESTCHESTER COUNTY AIRPORT HEAD OFF FOR A TRAINING MISSION IN 1952.

keep quiet in the plant and on the street lest spies overhear conversations that could be helpful to the enemy.

The dissemination of such information is but one small example of how American business helped defend America during the great military challenges of the 20th century. Businesses converted their factories when necessary, rallied their workforces to the effort, invented technologies used to help the nation on the battlefield, and lent their logistical expertise to the gargantuan task of shipping men and supplies around the world.

And business has not been immune to the tragedy of war as tens of thousands of sons and daughters of business owners died on battlefields throughout the century.

As the 20th century drew to a close, America was at peace, but as the only remaining superpower it was necessarily primed for military missions around the globe that can occur at a moment's notice.

American business plays a leading role in this preparedness and sacrifice. For some three decades, most companies have supported the idea that dedicated Americans who serve in the National Guard or the reserves should not have to worry that their careers will suffer if they are called to active duty. Companies have embraced this patriotic principle, even as the disruptions and costs to do so have skyrocketed.

During the 1970s, the guard and reserve duty seldom entailed more than 39 days a year and most of that was during weekends. Thus, the impact on normal business operations was minimal. In the late 1980s, reservists spent less than one million days on active duty. In 1999, they spent nearly 13 million days on active duty—and the Pentagon says that in the next two decades, that number is bound to grow.

The reason this is happening is simple. In 1989, the Department of Defense had 2.2 million active duty military personnel and 1.2 million reserve personnel. After the collapse of the Soviet Union, Defense cut its active duty personnel by 34 percent and the reserve components of the services by 26 percent. Moreover, between 1989 and 1999, the Army was reduced from 28 divisions to 20; the Navy went from 567 ships to just over 300; and the Air Force dropped from 37 fighter wings to 20.

Business, in the form of the flexibility granted to National Guard reservists, has helped pick up the slack. Between 1975 and 1989, the military was deployed on 20 missions. By contrast, over the past 10 years the military has been deployed 48 times.

There is a small group of employers whose workers are in the highest demand by the military. In some cases, they are gone from the workplace more than 200 days each year.

It's a costly burden, but as it has done throughout the century, American business is today playing a leadership role in America's military readiness and its ability to defend its freedom, its economy, and its way of life.

From caring for employees and their families to cleaning the environment, from aiding the poor to defending the nation, American business has helped transform the nature of capitalism from dog-eat-dog to people helping people. Commercial success is still an overarching goal, but thousands of American companies operating around the globe demonstrate every day in many ways that making a profit and improving the community are not mutually exclusive. They go hand in hand.

INNOVATIVE ENTREPRENEURS
SMALL BUSINESS IN AMERICA

AS THE GLOBALIZATION OF THE AMERICAN ECONOMY PICKED UP STEAM AT THE END OF THE 20TH CENTURY, AND THROUGH AN INCREASING NUMBER OF MEGAMERGERS THE CONSOLIDATION OF INDUSTRIES CONTINUED UNABATED,

some wondered what was to become of the small-business person in the United States. In a high-speed, technologically sophisticated economy, would there be room for the individual entrepreneur?

In 2001, the answer is clear: Not only has the traditional role of small business in America been preserved, the small-business sector is thriving. Economic changes that some thought would imperil entrepreneurs have instead empowered them.

These changes include the reorganization of traditional industries and their purchasing and employment practices, resulting in an explosion of opportunities for consulting and subcontracting. In addition, the availability of relatively inexpensive information and communications technologies has enabled millions of Americans to start home-based enterprises with little more than a computer, phone, and fax and has allowed them to compete alongside the largest companies in the global marketplace.

Throughout the 20th century, there was a progressive decline in the percentage of Americans who worked for themselves as people moved from the farms and country towns to the cities. By the end of the 1970s, the overall decline in the self-employment economy was arrested as millions of Americans, reacting to frustrations in the breakneck corporate lifestyle and new opportunities in the service economy, began opening small businesses. Today, 12.9 million Americans are self-employed, which at 10 percent of the workforce equals the share of private sector workers who belong to labor unions. Millions more are proprietors and partners in small businesses that they own but which technically "employ" them. Many more maintain their traditional employment while engaging in some form of entrepreneurial activity on the side.

A PROFILE OF DYNAMISM

Research prepared by the U.S. government's Small Business Administration (SBA) paints a telling picture of this dynamic sector of American business. Small businesses (defined by the SBA as companies employing fewer than 500 workers) employ 53 percent of the private, nonfarm workforce and generate approximately 51 percent of the gross domestic product.

Based on the number of business-tax returns, there were 24.8 million businesses in America in 1998. This is a 73 percent increase over the number of businesses in 1982.

Above: This restaurateur joins the ranks of the growing number of women who own their own business. In 1999, 4.6 million American women were self-employed. · Opposite: Like this delicatessen owner, nearly 99 percent of all employers are small-business operators.

SMALL-BUSINESS ENTREPRENEURS, LIKE THESE YOUNG URBAN PLANNERS, ARE RESPONSIBLE FOR CREATING 75 PERCENT OF NEW JOBS.

Over 99 percent of these firms qualify as small businesses.

Furthermore, as the 21st century begins, entrepreneurship is clearly on the rise. About three-quarters of new business owners today start their enterprises while still employed in another job. Some 60 percent of new firms begin at home. All told, about 21 million Americans—17 percent of all nonfarm workers—are engaged in some form of entrepreneurial activity, on either a full-time or part-time basis.

Small-business ownership also opens the door to opportunity for millions of Americans, including many who have traditionally found doors closed to them.

Small firms provide most initial on-the-job training. They are more likely to employ younger and older workers as well as former welfare recipients. Women-owned businesses are booming. The number of women-owned businesses grew by 89 percent between 1987 and 1997. There are an estimated 8.5 million of these firms in the United States today.

The same holds true for minority-owned businesses. The number of companies owned by Hispanic Americans increased 232 percent, to an estimated 1.4 million, from 1987 to 1997. Asian Americans owned 1.1 million companies, a 180 percent increase over the same period. African American firms grew by 108 percent to 882,000.

Small business is clearly responsible for much of the inventiveness and new opportunities in American society. These firms accounted for more than 76 percent of all the new jobs created in the United States during the period 1990–1995. Some 55 percent of product and service innovations come from small firms. These companies obtain more patents per sales dollar than large firms.

And the future looks even brighter. According to the Bureau of Labor Statistics, small firms will contribute about 60 percent of all new jobs created in the nation between 1994 and 2005. The fastest growing small business–dominated sectors will be medical and dental laboratories, residential care, credit reporting, equipment leasing, child day care services, job training, architectural and engineering services, and restaurants.

Further propelling small-business owners will be the growth of global trade. Contrary to the impression that only the largest multinational corporations are involved in international commerce, small firms already account for some 47 percent of U.S. exports, based on the number of sales, and an overwhelming 96 percent of all firms that do export. Even so, less than 2 percent of American companies are engaged in international commerce, suggesting an avenue of tremendous opportunity for entrepreneurs in the new century.

SMALL ENTERPRISES: AMERICA'S DREAM-BUILDERS

But the facts and figures tell only part of the story. The presence of so many small-business success stories, there for everyone to see in virtually every community in the country, offers compelling proof that the American dream of personal advancement and family fulfillment is alive and well. Have an idea, work hard, play by the rules, and even those with the most limited means have a reasonably good shot at success. It is this dream that has attracted millions of immigrants to America's shores throughout the nation's history and does to this day.

To be sure, it's a road rich in opportunity but also peril. Proving that these

proprietors operate at great risk and long odds, statistics show that 85 percent close their doors in the first five years, although just one in seven closes due to financial failure. Standard businesses that start with less than $10,000 in the bank are especially vulnerable.

Yet small business in America perseveres and thrives. Entrepreneurs and companies most Americans have never heard of survive against tremendous odds. There are so many stories of such perseverance that the U.S. Chamber of Commerce and the MassMutual Financial Group have honored those who have demonstrated the greatest nerve and verve with the annual Blue Chip Enterprise Award.

Recently recognized was Utah businessman Mike Cameron whose small firm, Christopherson Business Travel, was threatened by reduced airline commissions and on-line bookings. When Cameron took over the firm in 1990, it had just $1 million in annual revenues. Faced with extinction, Cameron refused to scale back his operation—just the opposite. He gave employees early raises and bonuses and embraced on-line booking, even helping clients master the art. Rather than discard their travel agent, clients found new value in Cameron's services. By the year 2000, the company reached $100 million in sales.

The Small Business Administration also honors these courageous entrepreneurs. It recognized business owner David Cline of Costa Mesa, California, the owner of Balboa Instruments, as the National Small-Business Person of the Year in 2000. Since acquiring his firm in 1980, Cline has diversified and grown the small electronic and development firm and has constantly produced and patented new technologies.

Twenty percent of the company's pre-tax profit is used as a bonus allocation to employees.

Another SBA award recipient is Barbara Miller of Amarillo, Texas. Thirty-five years ago, she took an entry-level position with a paper company. Today she owns one. The Miller Paper Company, which offers more than 1,500 products, has grown so fast that employment has doubled since its founding in 1995.

The SBA also honored DelGrasso Foods of Tipton, Pennsylvania, which opened its doors as a "kitchen operation" based on an Italian immigrant's recipe for spaghetti sauce. Under the leadership of James and Joseph DelGrasso, the company has grown into a modern operation, manufacturing over 18 million jars of spaghetti and pizza sauce annually.

Nothing Succeeds Like Success

The story of 20th-century American business is full of examples of entrepreneurs—from Henry Ford to Bill Gates—who started like any other small-time business person, only to see their products and ideas transform the world.

The pace of the very small becoming the very big in business has accelerated in

it onto the magazine's list of the 400 Richest Americans, displacing an equal number of others. For the most part, they are founding their fortunes on clever and inventive ideas and technologies, bearing out a forecast made by writer and economist George Gilder at the beginning of the

"In the not-so-distant past, wealth was almost always based on possession of physical assets. Wealth was timber, oil, real estate, factories, or printing presses. Almost all of today's new fortunes are based not on hard assets but on ideas and organizing principles."

ABOVE: PRESIDENT BILL CLINTON GREETS BARBARA MILLER, PRESIDENT OF THE MILLER PAPER COMPANY, OF AMARILLO, TEXAS. OPPOSITE: PARTNERS IN A BAKERY, THESE BUSINESS OWNERS NOT ONLY MAKE A LOT OF DOUGH, THEY, ALONG WITH OTHER PIONEERING ENTREPRENEURS, PROVIDE THE IMPETUS FOR THE GROWTH OF THE AMERICAN ECONOMY AND INCREASED OPPORTUNITIES FOR MINORITIES. IN 1999, NEARLY 7 PERCENT OF AFRICAN AMERICANS, 5 PERCENT OF ASIANS, AND 7 PERCENT OF HISPANICS WERE SELF-EMPLOYED.

the age of technology. *Forbes* magazine observes that great fortunes are being created almost monthly in the United States today by young entrepreneurs who didn't have a dime 10 or 15 years ago. Since 1990, well over 200 new people have made

last decade that the 1990s would bring "a global economy dominated more and more by fortunes of thought rather than hoarding of things."

The Forbes staff discovered this when it analyzed the fortunes of the Forbes 400:

While not everyone will make the Forbes 400, America's entrepreneurs go about their business serving customers, employing neighbors, helping their communities, and building their dreams.

THE BATTLE FOR ECONOMIC FREEDOM

PRESERVING & ADVANCING FREE ENTERPRISE

VIRTUALLY EVERYONE WHO HAS EVER BUILT, OWNED, OR WORKED IN A BUSINESS LEARNS EARLY ON THAT SUCCESS DEPENDS ON MORE THAN INVENTING GOOD PRODUCTS, DEVISING DESIRABLE SERVICES, OR CREATING A UNIQUE MARKET NICHE.

Success depends in equal measure on the economic environment in which the business operates. And that environment is dominated by public policies crafted and implemented at all levels of government.

A GLOBAL STRUGGLE

The 20th century was witness to a political and philosophical battle of historic magnitude. At the century's outset, the doctrines of Marx and Engels ignited street protests, fueled the rise of the international labor movement, and captured the imagination of intellectual salons throughout Europe. Their ideology was based on the idea that the public—which really meant the government—should own the means of production and distribute wealth according to need rather than ability. It was an ideology that would give rise to centrally planned and run economies, communist dictatorships, and a costly and deadly Cold War with the West.

Most Americans had a different idea about the role of government in the economy, believing that economic freedom is the foundation of all other freedoms. Private enterprise, in which individuals were incentivized and rewarded for investment, risk, inventiveness, and hard work, and where wealth was owned by people and not the government, was not only the right system to have in a free society, it was by far the most productive.

By the close of the 20th century, one philosophy would prevail. The only surprise was the speed at which this great debate was eventually resolved. For a good part of the century, it was communism that was on the rise. Even in free societies such as the democracies of Western Europe, government amassed economic power at a staggering pace, creating the cradle-to-grave welfare state. No wonder that by the late 1950s, Soviet leaders were boldly predicting that Americans' grandchildren would be living under communism.

Instead it is Soviet children who are living in freedom. In the last two decades of the 20th century, the accumulated economic failures of socialism, the brutality and corruption of the Soviet Communist political system, the heroism of reformers like Lech Walesa and Mikhail Gorbachev, and the dogged determination of the West and leaders such as Ronald Reagan and Margaret Thatcher, resulted in the consignment of Soviet Communism to the ash heap of history.

Photo: © Bettmann/CORBIS

January — THE NATION'S BUSINESS — 1918

25 CENTS

ACHTUNG!
Sie verlassen jetzt
WEST-BERLIN

GOVERNMENT'S ROLE IN AMERICAN ENTERPRISE

The end of the Cold War was a triumph for America and especially its free enterprise economic system. But debate continued within the United States itself and does so to this day, a debate that in the end may never be fully resolved. What should the role of government be in America's free enterprise system? How much regulation is needed to make sure people compete fairly and honestly? How much of the wealth of those who succeed should be claimed to assist those who for whatever reason cannot? And good intentions aside, at what point is the accumulated weight of taxes, regulations, paperwork, and lawsuits so great that the engines of productivity simply stop turning, thereby depleting the very resources the proponents of bigger government seek for their social goals?

The relationship between government and business in 20th-century America has run the gamut from cozy cronyism to bitter antagonism to wary partnership. Few would deny that the role of government in the economic life of the nation increased substantially in the 20th century. This can be seen not only in specific policies directed at business and the American economy but also in the impact on the business environment of social programs such as education, welfare, Social Security, and Medicare. These and other programs have required massive infusions of capital drawn in the form of taxes levied on business and consumers.

Shortly before the 20th century began, the stage was set for a strong interventionist role by government in business with the passage of the Sherman Antitrust Act in 1890, designed to break up powerful monopolies in the rail, oil, and other industries.

Even more momentous events and policy decisions were to follow. In 1913, the federal income tax was introduced and the Federal Reserve System was established. The stock market crash of 1929 triggered the Great Depression. The ensuing "New Deal" changed the business-government relationship forever. The 1930s brought the Social Security System for retirees and the National Labor Relations Act, which along with other measures in previous years codified into law many demands of the labor union movement.

The 1941 Japanese attack on Pearl Harbor forced America's entry into World War II. On the home front, this meant rationing, price controls, the conversion of factories to wartime production, and the first large-scale introduction of women to jobs traditionally held by men. In the postwar years, the introduction of the G.I. Bill, along with a flood of pent-up postwar consumer demands, brought many young workers into the professional ranks, homeownership, and the middle class.

During the prosperous 1950s, what President Dwight Eisenhower would later call the "military industrial complex" emerged, with government pouring massive resources into the infrastructure and technologies needed to wage the Cold War. These investments boosted peaceful endeavors as well, bringing about advancements in aviation, energy production, communications, travel, and shipping.

America celebrated the first Earth Day, in 1970, signaling a new environmental consciousness. While addressing needed improvements in environmental practices, the movement also unleashed a wave of new restrictions on enterprise that continues to this day. In 1971, President Richard Nixon, a longtime foe of government intrusion in the economy, imposed wage and price controls to combat inflation. Reflecting changing attitudes and the political climate, his administration also created the Environmental Protection Agency (EPA) and the Occupational Safety and Health Administration (OSHA).

As the 1970s drew to a close, an era of deregulation began, first in oil, trucking, and aviation and later spreading to telecommunications. In 1981, President Ronald Reagan persuaded a Democratic Congress to enact historic tax relief on businesses and individuals, along with spending cuts. The policies triggered an economic boom tempered by the exponential growth of government debt as both Congress and the president failed to control expenditures.

A new era of globalization was ushered in with the 1993 approval of the North American Free Trade Agreement (NAFTA), facilitating trade between Canada, Mexico, and the United States. In 1999, the federal government initiated an antitrust action against Microsoft, signaling that regulators

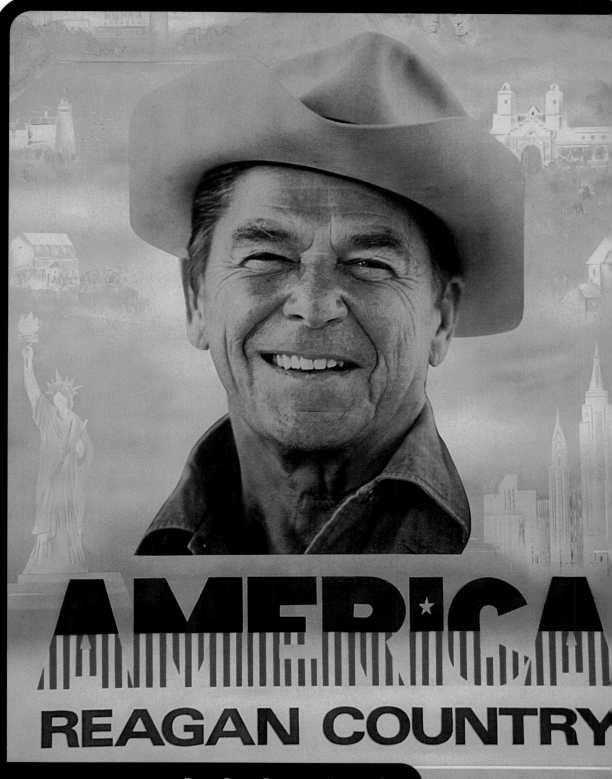

AMERICA

REAGAN COUNTRY

ABOVE: RONALD REAGAN EXUDES OPTIMISM IN THIS CAMPAIGN POSTER THAT HANGS IN THE RONALD REAGAN PRESIDENTIAL LIBRARY IN SIMI VALLEY, CALIFORNIA. HIS ECONOMIC POLICIES BROUGHT ABOUT A NEW ERA IN AMERICAN BUSINESS. • OPPOSITE: A SOBERING SYMBOL OF THE COLD WAR, BARBED WIRE IN FRONT OF THE BRANDENBURG GATE MARKS THE BOUNDARY BETWEEN EAST AND WEST BERLIN. THE BERLIN WALL WAS ERECTED IN AUGUST 1961 TO HALT THE MASSIVE DEFECTION OF EAST GERMANS (2.6 MILLION BETWEEN 1949 AND 1961) TO THE WEST.

would seek a major role in the development of a hitherto unregulated industry. In 2000, President Bill Clinton would cap his administration's open-trade policy with the passage of Permanent Normal Trade Relations

(PNTR) with China. The move would pave the way for the integration of the world's most populous nation into the global trading system, creating new export and investment opportunities for American business.

These and other governmental decisions—often reflecting the changing values of society—illustrate that in virtually all arenas of public policy, particularly at the federal level, there is potential impact on

43

The entrance to the U.S. Chamber of Commerce, at 1615 H Street, NW, in Washington, D.C., has greeted business and political leaders from the world over since 1925.

business and its ability to grow, compete, and create jobs. Thus, even those business people who believe that government's role in the free enterprise system should be strictly limited acknowledge the business community's compelling need to participate in the shaping of policy.

Indeed, by the year 2000, Uncle Sam's footprint loomed large on the landscape of American free enterprise. Today, the federal government's level of taxation, as a share of national income, rivals that of the World War II years, when the nation had to fund much of the global conflict. Federal regulations cost U.S. businesses an estimated $750 billion per year, while businesses, fearing that crippling liability will stunt the development of new products and life-saving drugs, incur $160 billion annually in legal fees.

Many believe that federal entitlements, especially Social Security and Medicare, are ill equipped to handle the changing demographics of American society. The impending retirement of 76 million baby boomers, along with lower birth rates, will in the first third of the new century reduce the ratio of workers to retirees to just two to one. These underfunded obligations are expected to impose an unprecedented financial burden on companies and younger workers.

At the same time, most business people support a reasonable level of regulation, a basic set of rules to ensure that competition is fair and conduct ethical. Furthermore, business looks to government to maintain a system of courts, keep the lanes of commerce open and free with a strong national defense, provide superior public schools to train the workforce of the future, and to build and maintain the essential infrastructure of the country such as highways and the air traffic control system.

CREATING A BUSINESS WATCHDOG IN WASHINGTON

How does business convince government to be less of a hindrance to growth and opportunity and to engage public resources where necessary to build the long-term economic strength of the nation? For most of the 20th century, it has looked to the U.S. Chamber of Commerce, the business community's advocate, watchdog, and leader in Washington, D.C., to handle this challenging and complex task.

It was a political leader, not a company executive, who first saw the need for a national chamber and rallied business to action. On March 1, 1912, President William Howard Taft sent a message to Congress calling for a conference in Washington of commercial and trade organizations. Just over a month later, on April 22, over 700 delegates from every state in the union gathered at the New Willard Hotel in Washington, D.C., for the purpose of forming a national commercial organization that would be called the Chamber of Commerce of the United States.

President Taft outlined his vision of its purpose in remarks to the delegates: "We want your assistance in carrying on the government in reference to those matters that affect the business and the business welfare of the country, and we do not wish to limit your discretion in that matter. We wish your advice should be as free and unrestricted as possible, but we need your assistance and ask for it."

With the group's first president, Chicago businessman Harry A. Wheeler, at the helm, the new organization moved quickly to attract a high-level board of directors and executive staff. In September 1912, the first issue of *Nation's Business* was released, a publication that would focus on business issues and concerns for the next 86 years. The group also prepared reports on national

BELOW: PRESIDENT WILLIAM HOWARD TAFT ADDRESSES A CROWD IN 1910. TWO YEARS LATER, HE WOULD CALL FOR THE CREATION OF THE CHAMBER OF COMMERCE OF THE UNITED STATES, AN ORGANIZATION THAT WOULD REPRESENT THE INTERESTS OF BUSINESS IN THIS COUNTRY. • OPPOSITE: THE ELEGANT INTERIOR OF THE U.S. CHAMBER OF COMMERCE HEADQUARTERS IS THE WORK OF THE BUILDING'S ARCHITECT CASS GILBERT, WHOSE ORIGINAL DESIGN INCLUDED AN OPEN-AIR COURTYARD. THE CORNERSTONE FOR THE BUILDING WAS LAID IN 1922.

issues, outlining the pros and cons of each for members of Congress.

It was in the aftermath of World War I that the U.S. Chamber made its first truly significant mark on national policy. Less than a month after the signing of the Armistice ending the war, the Chamber convened a Special Reconstruction Conference for December 3–6, 1918, to call for the removal of wartime restrictions on industry and to help companies make the adjustment from lucrative wartime contracts to peacetime pursuits.

The postwar period was also a time of great labor strife. Even though in ensuing years the Chamber would find itself at odds with the agenda of organized labor, the organization supported collective bargaining and the right of employees to join unions.

During the Roaring Twenties, the growth of the U.S. economy was reflected in substantial revenue and membership growth at the Chamber. Having outgrown its rented office space, the Chamber collected donations from all over the country to build a national headquarters on the northwest corner of Lafayette Square directly across the park from the White House on the site of the home of Daniel Webster. The building was designed by renowned New York architect Cass Gilbert, who would later design the building now housing the United States Supreme Court.

In May 1925, the headquarters of the U.S. Chamber of Commerce was formally dedicated. William Howard Taft, who had since become chief justice of the United States, was on hand for the dedication, saying, "With small beginnings . . . you have built a center of influence that has made, and will continue to make, for the great good of this country." The building, expanded and renovated over the years,

houses the Chamber to this day, serving as a meeting and rallying place for the business community.

LOYAL OPPOSITION TO BIG GOVERNMENT

The depression years of the 1930s brought new challenges to the Chamber. On the one hand, the organization led business efforts to work with the government to pull the country out of the depression. Yet members also became increasingly disturbed by the decade-long drift towards bigger government and an administration that often emphasized support for labor unions over industry.

This new adversarial position was by necessity put on hold during World War II, when the organization worked closely with

the Roosevelt administration to help meet wartime production needs. The Chamber also helped promote the sale of war bonds, disseminated information about the draft, and encouraged members to participate in exposing and guarding against acts of domestic espionage by America's enemies.

The postwar years of the late 1940s and 1950s presented a completely new landscape for American society and the business community. The Chamber changed and expanded its activities to reflect this new landscape. The organization began its first international programs, reflecting new opportunities in global trade. Regional offices were created around the country to organize grassroots support for business initiatives in

PERMANENT NORMAL TRADE
RELATIONS WITH CHINA

Congress. When it became clear that even the election of Republican Dwight Eisenhower to the presidency would not result in containing the excesses of the New Deal or curtailing the growth of government spending, the Chamber stepped up its aggressive lobbying against what it saw as a bloated federal government.

These activities prepared the organization for the 1960s when, confronted with President John F. Kennedy's New Frontier and President Lyndon Johnson's Great Society, the Chamber initiated its first political action programs to support pro-business candidates. It also initiated a massive economic education program that disseminated information about the free enterprise system. In 1974, this program was reformatted into Economics for Young Americans, which reached over 30 million high school students.

The 1970s were years of great upheaval for the U.S. economy and dramatic change at the U.S. Chamber. In 1975, Judge Lewis F. Powell, just before his elevation to the U.S. Supreme Court, prepared a lengthy memorandum calling on the Chamber and the business community to increase its activism in the face of mounting attacks on the enterprise system. These suggestions, combined with the ascension of a vigorous young leader to the presidency of the Chamber in the person of Richard L. Lesher, resulted in a burst of new activities and programs.

The National Chamber Litigation Center (NCLC) was formed to give the business community its own public-interest law firm. The NCLC routinely lodges or participates in lawsuits whose outcomes will have a broad impact on business. In 1999, for example, it was an NCLC legal action

that delayed the Environmental Protection Agency's implementation of new clean-air rules that the Chamber believed were based on unsound science.

The National Chamber Foundation, the business community's own "think tank," was created to encourage high-profile public dialogues on vital business issues. In January 2001, for example, a Foundation-sponsored aviation summit shed new light on the problems facing America's overburdened aviation system.

Grassroots, political, and communications activities were significantly expanded as well. A major investment was made in the Chamber's international programs as trade became an increasingly important part of the American economy. In 1983, the U.S. Chamber played a critical role in convincing Congress to pass President Ronald Reagan's economic program.

Revitalizing the 'Voice of Business'

While much of the 1980s and 1990s were prosperous, they were also years of seminal change for American business. Global competition triggered the need for major corporate restructuring. High technology created vast new markets while transforming the daily patterns of business and finance. The election of Bill Clinton as president brought with it strong support for the expansion of free trade, but also an increase in regulations and lawsuits against many businesses.

The membership of the Chamber had changed, too, and so had the political, regulatory, and legal climate facing the business community. It was this set of conditions that greeted the organization's new and current president and CEO, Tom Donohue, when he took the helm of the Chamber in September 1997.

Pledging to reinvigorate the venerable business institution and make it relevant for a new era of globalization, technology, and divided government, Donohue launched an aggressive revitalization campaign that has dramatically increased the Chamber's revenues, public profile, and lobbying activities. Programs that seemed to stray from the Chamber's core purpose—advocacy—were jettisoned in favor

The Chamber under Donohue has been credited with successfully stopping an $800 billion tax increase, passing legislation to prevent trial lawyers from taking unfair advantage of potential Y2K computer problems, and the enactment of permanent normal trade relations with China.

Perhaps most important, the Chamber has returned to prominence in the role envisioned for it by President Taft—as *the* voice of business in the halls of government here and

participate in Chamber activities—represents nearly three million companies. They are bound by a common agenda, vigorously pursued by Donohue and his team of lobbyists, issue experts, lawyers, and communicators.

It is an agenda that seeks to rein in the influence of trial lawyers, reduce taxes, weed out excessive regulations, reform entitlement programs, find and train enough workers, and expand U.S. trade and leadership in technology around the globe.

ABOVE: THOMAS J. DONOHUE (RIGHT), PRESIDENT AND CEO OF THE U.S. CHAMBER OF COMMERCE, GREETS SECRETARY OF STATE COLIN POWELL (LEFT) AND KING ABDULLAH II OF JORDAN. • OPPOSITE: PRESIDENT BILL CLINTON ADDRESSES THE PRESS FOLLOWING THE SIGNING OF THE PERMANENT NORMAL TRADE RELATIONS WITH CHINA BILL ON OCTOBER 10, 2000, AS SPEAKER OF THE HOUSE DENNIS HASTERT OF ILLINOIS LOOKS ON. THE BILL RECEIVED THE FULL SUPPORT OF THE U.S. CHAMBER OF COMMERCE.

of a tripling of the lobbying team, the creation of a new political program that greatly influenced the 2000 congressional elections, and a new aggressiveness on the legal reform front.

around the world, in the media, in the courts of law, and in the court of public opinion.

Today, the Chamber federation—the network of large and small businesses, state and local chambers, and industry associations that

And equally important, in the words of Donohue, the Chamber's goal is to insure "that business stops apologizing for being the one institution in America that really works."

FROM SEA TO SHINING SEA

AMERICA'S NEW BUSINESS LANDSCAPE

During the 20th century, America moved from farm to city to suburbs and from the rustbelt to the Sunbelt. The nation's consumers and employees lived longer and grew older, and women pushed toward parity in the professional ranks. Waves of immigrants continued to arrive, no longer through Ellis Island,

which today houses a museum, but more often through the international airports of Los Angeles and Miami and the border crossings of the Southwest. And the marketplace for American goods, services, ideas, and culture burst out of the insular borders of the United States to the global community.

American business helped shape—and was shaped by—all of these dramatic trends. It all added up to the century-long development of a profoundly different business landscape that carried the country into the new millennium.

THE SHIFTING AMERICAN POPULATION

Americans continued in the 20th century the pattern of urban migration that began in the 19th. There were some six million farms in 1900; a century later there were two million.

People moved from east to west and north to south. This shift can be seen in the ranking of the ten most populous U.S. cities in the year 2000 compared to the year 1900. A century ago, the top ten cities were, in order, New York, Chicago, Philadelphia, St. Louis, Boston, Baltimore, Cleveland, Buffalo, San Francisco, and Cincinnati.

By the end of the 20th century, the ten most populous U.S. cities were New York, Los Angeles, Chicago, Houston, Philadelphia, San Diego, Phoenix, San Antonio, Dallas, and Detroit.

Even more significant has been the growth of vast swaths of suburbia. These regions fail to show up on most top-ten lists because by their very nature they are amorphous conglomerates of people and businesses rather than more easily defined cities and towns. Many are known by monikers thought up by civic leaders or the media, such as the Southland (the Los Angeles basin and beyond), the Inland Empire (the urban areas of Riverside and San Bernardino Counties east of Los Angeles), Chicagoland, and the Boston–New York–Washington corridor. Still others are identified principally by county, for example, Westchester (New York), Cobb County (Georgia), and Orange County (Southern California).

Originally conceived of as pleasant middle-class escapes from the crowds and crime of urban centers (and mocked as bedroom communities without character or culture by many), the suburbs have become vibrant business centers in their own right. Companies have located

ABOVE: THIS NEWLY NATURALIZED CITIZEN REPRESENTS THE CHANGING FACE OF AMERICAN BUSINESS. IN THE 1990s, EACH YEAR APPROXIMATELY 460,000 IMMIGRANTS BECAME U.S. CITIZENS. · OPPOSITE: GRANT WOOD'S 1930 PAINTING AMERICAN GOTHIC SYMBOLIZES THE DIGNITY AND FORTITUDE OF THE AMERICAN FARMER AS HE CONFRONTS THE GREAT DEPRESSION AND AN UNCERTAIN FUTURE.

new facilities and even headquarters in these regions, and start-up firms occupy spacious suburban office parks. With this shift, however, have come problems and frustrations formerly associated more with the inner cities. Crime, overcrowding, traffic, and pollution in Southern California's Inland Empire, for example, are growing faster than in urban Los Angeles.

New Centers of Business, Commerce, and Culture

Along with the movement of people came the decentralization of American business power and commercial activity. The 20th century, particularly the last half, witnessed the rise of dozens of new business centers stretching across the Sunbelt and up the California coast to the Pacific Northwest. Business followed the flow of people and people followed the growth of business and job opportunities. Developments such as

air-conditioning, the interstate highway system, public universities, and the great water projects of the West also played an indispensable role in fueling America's new business "democracy."

The importance of traditional business centers such as New York, Chicago, Boston, and Philadelphia remains intact, particularly when one looks beyond the borders of those cities to the greater metropolitan areas for which they serve as communications, financial, and cultural anchors. The seven counties north, west, and south of the city of Chicago, for example, together comprise one of the most modern and thriving entrepreneurial regions in the country. Westchester County north of New York City, the Route 128 corridor near Boston, and the New Jersey suburbs of both the Big Apple and Philadelphia play host to both high-tech start-ups and behemoths such as IBM, PepsiCo, and AT&T.

By the end of the century, other regions had taken their place alongside the commercial centers of the Northeast and Midwest as vital cells of economic growth and opportunity.

One such region is Northern Virginia, home to an amazing concentration of high-tech companies stretching along I-66 and surrounding Dulles Airport. Companies such as America Online make their home here.

Charlotte, North Carolina, symbolizes the modernity and prosperity of what came to be known as the New South. Settled as far back as 1750, the city established its first claim to fame as the center of U.S. gold production in the early 19th century. Charlotte has since struck gold again. Bolstered by its outstanding university and research centers, educated workforce, cluster of high-tech companies, and headquarters of giants like Bank of America, the community today attracts highly skilled employees and entrepreneurial companies from all over the nation.

Atlanta, another region of growth, began in 1837 as a railroad town called Terminus. It gained sufficient economic strength in the ensuing years to become a major strategic target of General W. T. Sherman and his invading Union troops during the Civil War. Almost completely destroyed in the war, it was rebuilt quickly. Today, it is one of the nation's most important centers of finance, manufacturing, and transportation and headquarters to some of America's biggest companies, such as UPS and Home Depot.

The arrival of the railroad also spurred the growth of Miami. As the small, sleepy tropical town became more accessible, "snowbirds" from the North flocked to its warm climate. Tourism is still a staple of the entire south Florida economy, of which Miami serves as anchor. But Miami is much more. Fueled by a massive influx of industrious refugees from Cuba, as well as immigrants from both the northern states and Latin America, Miami has become a leading international trade center, with more than 170 multinational companies located there.

To the west, the "Texas Four" have taken their place as commercial centers. Houston, San Antonio, and Dallas, rank among America's ten largest cities; Austin is in the top 20.

in health sciences, technology, and shipping. In terms of tonnage, the Port of Houston is the busiest seaport in America.

San Antonio, the country's eighth most populous city, is home to the Alamo and played a leading role in the turbulent history intertwining the United States, Mexico, and Spain. With the arrival of the railroad after the Civil War, San Antonio became a top shipping center. It is still a major livestock center, as it has been for over a century. The military commands a strong presence in the community,

early spurts of growth courtesy of farming and ranching. The city first made its mark as the seat of government, but at the end of the 20th century, it had also become globally recognized as a center of research and development, fostering a pattern that has been duplicated in other capital cities from Sacramento to Washington, D.C. Like Austin, these cities have drawn upon the largesse of the government, the educated workforce government attracts, large consumer markets, and strong educational institutions to branch out into high technology.

ABOVE: THE 60-STORY FOUNTAIN PLACE SKYSCRAPER, WITH ITS POINTED ROOFTOP, IS ONE OF THE MORE DISTINCTIVE BUILDINGS THAT MAKE UP THE DALLAS SKYLINE. MORE THAN 40 PERCENT OF TEXAS'S HIGH-TECH JOBS ARE FOUND IN THE DALLAS–FORT WORTH AREA. • OPPOSITE: MORE THAN 500,000 PEOPLE LIVE IN CHARLOTTE, NORTH CAROLINA, THE NATION'S 26TH LARGEST CITY AND ITS SECOND LARGEST BANKING CENTER. OVER 300 FORTUNE 500 COMPANIES HAVE A PRESENCE IN THIS POWERHOUSE OF THE SOUTH.

Houston is America's fourth largest city. Named after Sam Houston and founded in 1837, it served as the first national capital of the Texas Republic. Today, it is not only the energy capital of the world but a leader

and tourists flock to the city to enjoy its unique culture.

Austin, the capital of Texas and America's 19th largest city, traces it roots to the arrival of the railroad and enjoyed its

Dallas was founded as a trading post and later became the nation's leading cotton market. Cattle, oil, and real estate development came next. All marked exciting and sometimes rocky chapters in the creation of

Commuters head home on the 110 freeway in downtown Los Angeles. More than 300,000 cars travel this stretch of road daily.

what residents call the "metroplex." With industries like insurance, aviation, and technology moving in in large numbers, Dallas's economy is highly diversified, buffering the city from the boom-and-bust cycles that characterized its history as a resource-based economy.

The Rocky Mountain hub of Denver also spent much of its history tied to the shifting fortunes of resource-based industries like mining, ranching, and energy. Like Dallas, it has diversified into a major center of finance, construction, marketing, and transportation. The region has attracted hundreds of thousands of refugees from

Sunbelt megalopolises such as Southern California, people seeking a cleaner environment and a more relaxed lifestyle.

Three major cities across the Southwest exemplify what became by the end of the 20th century the fastest growing region of America: Albuquerque, Phoenix, and Las Vegas.

Albuquerque is a leading center of health care, nuclear research, and technology manufacturing as well as a major focal point of the burgeoning economic and cultural power of the Latino community. Phoenix has grown so fast that most Americans are surprised to learn it is only the seventh largest city in the nation. It's a

center of aerospace and agriculture and a magnet for both retirees and young Hispanics seeking economic opportunity. Las Vegas is the worldwide center of gaming and America's fastest growing major city. Conventions flock to the city's renowned attractions, as do construction and retail services all hoping to take advantage of the area's stupendous growth.

The West Coast also experienced such growth throughout the second half of the 20th century. San Diego is the nation's sixth most populous city. Fueled by a large military presence, San Diego capitalized on that advantage (along with its perfect climate) to

BELOW: THE 675,000-SQUARE-FOOT PEPSI CENTER IN DENVER IS HOME TO THE COLORADO AVALANCHE HOCKEY TEAM AND BASKETBALL'S DENVER NUGGETS. · OPPOSITE: NAVAL BASE CORONADO, ON SOUTHERN CALIFORNIA'S SAN DIEGO BAY, IS MADE UP OF THE NAVAL AIR STATION NORTH ISLAND AND THE NAVAL AMPHIBIOUS BASE CORONADO. COMMISSIONED IN 1917, THE AIR STATION WAS OFFICIALLY RECOGNIZED BY THE HOUSE ARMED SERVICES COMMITTEE IN 1963 AS THE "BIRTHPLACE OF NAVAL AVIATION."

significantly diversify. It is a leading hub of aerospace, communications, tourism, and with the bustling Mexican border just a half-hour drive away, international trade.

The Los Angeles area is so big that it's hard to tell where it begins and where it ends. The city itself trails only New York in population, but the communities surrounding it, such as Orange County to the south, have become substantial business centers in their own right. As for Los Angeles, the city has seen it all. It's been an agricultural center, a major oil producer, defense contractor, manufacturing center, international trade hub, and the home of Hollywood and the entertainment industry. All of these industries remain important parts of the Southern California business landscape. The area is America's largest manufacturing center and through Hollywood the focal point of the development and dissemination of popular culture worldwide.

Farther up the coast is San Jose, the civic gateway to the Santa Clara Valley. Once known principally for its beautiful rolling countryside, wineries, and agricultural production, the Santa Clara Valley is now known worldwide as the Silicon Valley, the center of high technology that almost every city, state, and nation dreams of emulating. Despite challenges to its supremacy and the problems associated with rapid growth, the real Silicon Valley continues to lead. Today, it is home to nearly 6,400 high-tech firms, from small start-ups to giants like Hewlett-Packard, employing some 283,000 people.

The Pacific Northwest enjoyed tremendous growth in the last half of the 20th century. Seattle, first settled in the mid-1850s by five families from Illinois, is today the center of a 400-mile coastal

corridor from Eugene, Oregon, to Vancouver, British Columbia, that is inhabited by eight million people with an economic output of some $250 billion. Microsoft and Starbucks are just two of the global powerhouses of the Pacific Northwest economic kingdom.

THE GROWING RANKS OF IMMIGRANTS AND THE ELDERLY

The new business landscape of the 21st century must be defined in terms of people as well as places. As the new millennium begins, the U.S. population is more diverse and older than ever before.

Over the course of the last hundred years, immigrants began coming from a broader range of countries. The result was a change in the ethnic, cultural, and consumer makeup of the nation. From 1900 to 1910, 91 percent of immigrants came from Europe, with just 8 percent divided equally between North America (Mexico and Canada) and Asia. By the end of the 20th century, 38 percent were arriving from North America (mostly Mexico), 33 percent from Asia, 7 percent from South America, and 6 percent from Africa. Europeans now make up just under 14 percent of America's immigrants.

Demographically, the nation grew much older as well. In 1860, half the population was under the age of 20. By 1994, half was 34 or older. By 2020, half will be 39 or older. During the 20th century, the elderly population, those aged 65 and older, increased 11 times, compared to just a

United States, now fully engaged and obligated in the global arena, took the lead in not only rebuilding the economies of its enemies and allies, but in establishing the legal framework for international commerce, the General Agreement on Tariffs and Trade (GATT). The Bretton Woods (New Hampshire) Conference led to the creation of the World Bank, the International Monetary Fund, and the exchange rate system.

The new realities of the postwar world—combined with advances in

ABOVE: A NEW TRACT OF HOMES GOES UP IN LAS VEGAS, THE FASTEST GROWING METROPOLITAN AREA IN THE NATION FROM 1990 TO 2000. ITS POPULATION IS EXPECTED TO REACH TWO MILLION IN THE NEXT DECADE. · OPPOSITE: CITY LIGHTS ARE REFLECTED IN LAKE MICHIGAN ALONG CHICAGO'S NORTH AVENUE BEACH AS DAWN CASTS ITS DELICATE GLOW. LONG A CENTER FOR THE MANUFACTURING AND RETAIL INDUSTRIES, THE CHICAGO AREA IS ONE OF THE TOP RELOCATION DESTINATIONS FOR AMERICAN WORKERS.

threefold increase for those under 65. Since 1960, the ranks of elderly Americans have increased 100 percent, compared to 45 percent for the population as a whole. The number of people aged 85 and over has increased 274 percent.

America is now home to more than 35 million elderly, nearly 13 percent of the population. There are 12.4 million between the ages of 75 and 84 and 4.3 million who are 85 or older. By 2030, the number of people in these upper age brackets will explode to 70.1 million, 23.3 million, and 8.8 million respectively.

The 30-year increase in life expectancy during the century explains part of this major shift in age demographics. So do declining birth rates, which are due in part to the fact that over 50 percent of adult women now work in full- or close to full-time occupations outside of the home in search of both income and professional fulfillment.

THE GLOBALIZATION OF THE AMERICAN MARKET

International trade has always loomed large in American history. The nation was explored and founded by Europeans seeking to develop and export raw materials back to their homelands. During the first half of the 19th century, regional differences over tariffs exacerbated—and some historians say superceded—differences over slavery, leading to civil war. As U.S. industrial might and international clout grew in the post–Civil War years, America embarked on a mercantile policy of its own, seeking markets, minerals, raw materials—and colonies—beyond its borders.

When the stock market crashed in 1929, Congress responded with a step many believe transformed a serious recession into a Great Depression. It passed the Smoot-Hawley Tariff Act of 1930, which contained the highest tariffs and trade restrictions in U.S. history. Following World War II, the

travel and communications and the increasing prowess of U.S. industry, intellectual property, technology, and services—opened vast international opportunities for U.S. companies. At the same time, the nation invited global competitors to its markets and frequently learned painful but ultimately productive lessons from these competitors.

In the last 30 years of the 20th century, America's international trade exploded. In 2000, U.S. exports to the world totaled $1.068 trillion dollars, which is triple the level of 1990 and exceeds the total value of the entire U.S. economy of just 30 years ago.

American business has $1.13 trillion in investments abroad, including $581 billion invested in the European Union, $186 billion in Asia, and $111 billion in Canada. U.S. corporate presence in other countries has built a strong foundation for economic development. In the special Chinese region of Hong Kong, for example, 10 percent of the workforce is employed by U.S. firms. One such firm, Nike, employs 550,000 people in 54 countries including Vietnam, where the products it manufactures and ships to market account for 4 percent of that country's entire export portfolio.

U.S. companies are now looking beyond the nation's borders not only for markets and manufacturing but also for services and product development. Now that voice and data can be easily transmitted over the Internet and through high-speed fiber optics and satellite communications systems, why not? Computer programmers in India, customer service representatives in the Philippines, and credit card billing processors in Ireland now operate on behalf of U.S. companies and their customers.

The Changing Landscape of American Enterprise

Ninety-six percent of the world's population lives outside the United States. For American entrepreneurs and companies, this fundamental reality—along with profound changes in the domestic market and in demographics—has changed the business landscape forever.

That landscape once marginalized or excluded vital segments of the population. Today, companies fight like gladiators for market share among women, minorities, and immigrants.

That landscape was once confined to a handful of business, commercial, and population centers. Today, the vibrancy of American business stretches from sea to shining sea.

That landscape once reflected inward upon itself, marketing to and protecting the domestic market at all costs. Today, the entire world is America's marketplace, and as new commercial ventures in space multiply, perhaps tomorrow the heavens will be, too.

part two
Innovative Industries

60

LAND OF BOUNTY

AGRICULTURE & CONSUMER FOODS

FOR MOST OF HUMAN HISTORY, MANKIND HAS HAD TO DEVOTE INORDINATE AMOUNTS OF TIME, ENERGY, AND SACRIFICE SIMPLY TO MEET THE BASIC REQUIREMENTS OF SUSTENANCE. EVEN TODAY, WITH THE WORLD'S POPULATION HAVING JUST CROSSED THE SIX BILLION MARK, FEEDING THE PEOPLE IS A MAJOR PREOCCUPATION FOR MANY SOCIETIES AND A CRISIS FOR MORE THAN A FEW.

But not in the United States, not anymore, thanks to remarkable and multifaceted advances that took place in the 20th century.

The tremendous advances in agriculture, refrigeration, transportation, and storage have served Americans well. The strides in agricultural productivity and new technologies alone have been astonishing. In 1900, for example, the amount of labor needed to produce 100 bushels of corn was 200 hours, and only about 40 bushels per acre could be grown. By 2000, on average, 100 bushels could be produced on a single acre of land after two hours of labor. As a result of greater productivity and new technology, Americans today spend a smaller proportion of their incomes—about 11 percent—on food than most other industrialized countries.

AMERICAN AGRICULTURE: BREADBASKET OF THE WORLD

In 1880, there were about 22 million farmers in the United States. Today, there are fewer than five million, and less than 2 percent of Americans live on farms. Despite this dramatic decline in the number of farmers, not since animals and grain were first domesticated, around 8000 B.C., have there been productivity advances like those of the 20th century.

American farmers were the first to use the technological advances of the 1950s and 1960s such as high-yielding and high-protein plant hybrids, new chemical fertilizers, and new crop strategies and harvesting methods, which enabled them to dramatically increase production. These techniques inspired researchers who were seeking ways to help the third world feed itself, culminating in the 1960s Green Revolution, a dramatic advance in food production that enabled desperate countries to feed their people.

Farming also became more environmentally sound. In the 1990s, American farmers, again in the vanguard, began to use Integrated Pest Management (IPM) techniques that helped lessen the need for crop protectants. In addition, sophisticated hybridization and other advances in food biotechnology have not only increased production of foods but reduced harm to the environment. Instead of using chemical pesticides and fertilizers, farmers can plant crops that have been bioengineered to resist pests and grow in poor soil conditions.

Today, approximately $6 million worth of grains, oilseeds, cotton, meats, vegetables, and snack foods are exported to foreign markets daily. American farmers hold 19 percent of the

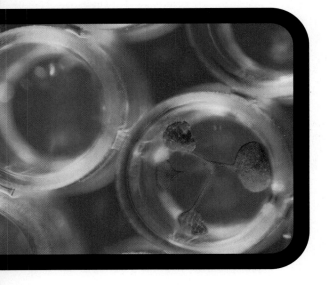

ABOVE: ON AVERAGE, ONE-THIRD OF THE WHEAT CONSUMED AROUND THE WORLD IS GROWN IN THE UNITED STATES; ONE-HALF OF THE WHEAT PRODUCED HERE IS SHIPPED OVERSEAS. · OPPOSITE: THESE MUSTARD SEEDLINGS HAVE BEEN GENETICALLY ENGINEERED TO BE HARDIER AND MORE RESISTANT TO PESTS.

database that will allow them to customize pesticide and fertilizer use for that site. Advances like this will enable American farmers, already the most productive in the world, to increase yields, improve the environment, and feed the world.

IN THE PANTRY, ON THE TABLE: THE COMPANIES BEHIND THE NAMES

Many Americans pour themselves a bowl of Kellogg's corn flakes for breakfast, grill some Kraft American cheese sandwiches for lunch, snack on a Coke or Pepsi and Fritos, and enjoy some Birds Eye vegetables and Gallo wine with dinner without giving any thought to the companies that provide the products. But behind every one of these names is a story of ingenuity and inventiveness and of the people whose ideas changed America's dining habits.

There were already about 40 breakfast cereal companies in Battle Creek, Michigan, when broom salesman William Kellogg

world market in cotton, 12 percent in wheat, 36 percent in corn, and nearly half the world market in soybeans.

Streamlined agricultural operations ensure a constant and bountiful supply of food. One of the leaders in this area is Archer Daniels Midland, which calls itself the "supermarket to the world." The Decatur, Illinois–based company is one of the world's largest processors of oilseeds, corn, and wheat, as well as soybeans, peanuts, and cocoa beans, and also offers worldwide transportation, storage, and sales services.

America's number one grain exporter is vertical integrator Cargill, the country's largest private corporation. Cargill began in 1865 when W. W. Cargill became the proprietor of a grain flat house in Conover, Iowa. Today, Cargill, headquartered in Minneapolis, Minnesota, incorporates diversified operations such as commodity trading, financial trading, futures brokering, and seed, feed, and fertilizer production. Through its Excel division, it is also responsible for processing about one-fifth of America's cattle.

The future of agriculture will be built on technology. At the start of the 21st century,

about 84 percent of American farmers use computers and 32 percent have Internet access; 73 percent of them communicate with each other by cellular telephone, a number that is likely to increase.

Farmers will also increasingly use satellite technology to pinpoint production. Using global positioning systems, they will be able to compare their exact position at any point in the field with a soil-conditions computer

FOOD FOR THOUGHT

TO CELEBRATE THE REPEAL OF PROHIBITION, ANHEUSER-BUSCH SENT A WAGON HAULED BY ITS FAMOUS CLYDESDALES TO THE WHITE HOUSE TO PRESENT PRESIDENT FRANKLIN ROOSEVELT WITH A HEFTY SUPPLY OF BEER. IN 2001, THE COMPANY LAUNCHED A NONALCOHOLIC ENERGY DRINK CALLED 180. · THE CENTER-PIVOT IRRIGATOR, INVENTED IN 1948 IN NEBRASKA, IS CONSIDERED BY MANY TO BE THE MOST SIGNIFICANT AGRICULTURAL DEVICE SINCE THE TRACTOR. · SWANSON FOODS, OF OMAHA, NEBRASKA, INTRODUCED THE TV DINNER IN 1954. IT CONSISTED OF TURKEY, DRESSING, GRAVY, PEAS, AND SWEET POTATOES. · THE FIRST MCDONALD'S FRANCHISE THAT RAY KROC OPENED WAS IN DES PLAINES, ILLINOIS, IN 1955. · IN THE 1990S, SALSA BEGAN TO OUTSELL KETCHUP, A SIGN OF THE GROWING POPULARITY OF ETHNIC FOODS. · THE HERSHEY COMPANY, OF HERSHEY, PENNSYLVANIA, PRODUCES ABOUT 33 MILLION CHOCOLATE KISSES EVERY DAY, USING THE MILK OF 50,000 COWS. · R.J. REYNOLDS TOBACCO COMPANY, OF WINSTON-SALEM, NORTH CAROLINA, IS TESTING ECLIPSE, A CIGARETTE THAT REDUCES SECONDHAND SMOKE BY HEATING, INSTEAD OF BURNING, TOBACCO.

joined his brother, the widely known physician Dr. John Harvey Kellogg, at the Adventist Battle Creek Sanatorium around 1900. Dr. Kellogg, the director of the sanatorium, had invented his share of healthful products, but it wasn't until the two brothers accidentally made corn flakes from boiled wheat that they scored a hit. The corn flakes became a favorite of the sanatorium's residents, and the factory produced 100,000 pounds of flakes in the first year. In 1906, Will broke with his brother, who was not interested in expanding the business, and started the Toasted Corn Flake Company, which eventually became the Kellogg Company. It pioneered many of the characteristics of cereal everyone is so familiar with today: sugar sweetening, free samples, and waxed paper inserts. Today, the Kellogg Company is tied with General Foods for the number one ready-to-eat breakfast cereal company and makes six of the top ten cereals in the world.

The grilled cheese sandwiches enjoyed by children and adults alike owe a great deal to a bright young Mennonite named

ABOVE: SUSPENDED 18 FEET OVER THE ENTRANCE TO THE WORLD OF COCA-COLA, THIS GLOBE FEATURES ONE OF THE MOST RECOGNIZED NAMES—AND LOGOS— IN THE WORLD. THE VISITOR'S CENTER, LOCATED IN ATLANTA, GEORGIA, FEATURES EXHIBITS THAT LOOK AT THE PAST, PRESENT, AND FUTURE OF THE FAMOUS SOFT DRINK. · OPPOSITE: A RAIL CAR STANDS AT THE READY TO RECEIVE GRAIN FROM SILOS AT ONE OF ARCHER DANIELS MIDLAND'S PROCESSING FACILITIES. THE COMPANY IS ONE OF THE LEADING GRAIN PROCESSORS IN THE WORLD.

James Lewis Kraft. In 1903, unemployed and with almost no money, Kraft resorted to the knowledge he had gained from working with a cheese company, rented a horse and wagon, and began selling cheese wholesale to grocers around Chicago. Soon he was doing so well that he invited his brothers to join the business and launched J. L. Kraft and Brothers in 1907. Over the years, Kraft experimented with ways to improve the quality of cheese, which dried up quickly or became moldy; indeed, at the beginning of

the century, people purchased less than a pound of cheese per year. In 1915, the company began processing cheese in tins, which it supplied to the U.S. government for the troops during World War I. A year later, James took out a patent on processed cheese. In 1921, Kraft introduced a five-pound loaf of pasteurized, blended cheese that had no rind and, therefore, no waste. Kraft had revolutionized the cheese industry. Total cheese production expanded from 418 million pounds in 1920 to six billion

pounds a year by the 1990s. Today, Kraft Foods, headquartered in Northfield, Illinois, and part of the Philip Morris Companies, is North America's largest food company.

The frozen-food industry was started almost single-handedly by naturalist Clarence Birdseye, who frequently traveled to the Arctic. In 1916, he even brought his wife and baby along while he traded fur, acted as a medical missionary, and hunted and fished to feed his family. Birdseye noted that the extra meat and fish that he hung

A NATURALIST AND FUR TRADER WHO TRAVELED TO SUCH FARAWAY LANDS AS THE ARCTIC AND LABRADOR, CLARENCE BIRDSEYE IS CREDITED WITH SINGLE-HANDEDLY CREATING THE FROZEN-FOOD INDUSTRY.

outside his cottage froze during the cold days and nights. When it was defrosted and fixed for dinner, the food retained its freshness.

Curious, he returned to his home in Massachusetts and began experimenting with freezing processes to find the secret to keeping foods fresh. As it turned out, the secret consisted in little more than ensuring that foods be frozen quickly. Birdseye patented the "Quick-Freezing Machine" which froze fresh foods at minus 50 degrees Fahrenheit and went into business for himself, but retailers were not interested in purchasing the specialized refrigeration equipment necessary to sell the frozen food. Birdseye persevered, however, and in 1924 formed the General Seafood Corporation, whose product line included a wide variety of frozen meats, fish, poultry, fruits, and vegetables.

In 1934, Birdseye contracted with the American Radiator Corporation to manufacture inexpensive, low-temperature retail-display cooling equipment. This equipment displayed only Birds Eye products and was leased to retailers for about eight dollars per month. In 1944, the company started using insulated railroad cars, which allowed distribution of his products nationwide. By the time Birdseye died in 1956, he held nearly 300 patents. Today, the Birds Eye brand is owned by Agrilink, of Rochester, New York, the country's largest frozen-vegetable processor.

Nearly 90 percent of frozen food companies belong to the American Frozen Food Institute, of McLean, Virginia, which, through nutrient analysis, microbiological research, and other services, ensures an ample supply of healthful frozen foods.

The beverage and snack food industries also grew up during the 20th century. John Pemberton invented the Coca-Cola syrup in 1886 from coca leaves and kola nuts (the coca was left out by the early 1900s). Today, Coca-Cola is not only the best-selling soft drink in the world, with about 45 percent share of the soft drink market, it is also the most recognized brand name after McDonald's.

Coke's top challenger, Pepsi, was invented in 1898 by Caleb Bradham of New Bern, North Carolina, and soon joined Coke as one of the world's favorite soft drinks. Today, however, nearly 60 percent of PepsiCo's sales come from its subsidiary Frito-Lay. In 1977, PepsiCo became involved in the restaurant business with its purchase of Pizza Hut, followed by the purchase of Taco Bell in 1978 and Kentucky Fried Chicken (now KFC) in 1986. These three companies were spun off as Tricon Global Restaurants in 1997. Tricon is right behind McDonald's in food sales. Today, PepsiCo, based in Purchase, New York, is the world leader in fruit drinks, which next to soft drinks have experienced steady growth along with bottled water. Indeed, before the fitness and health craze hit the United States in the 1970s, bottled water was an $80 million business; by 1989, it totaled $3 billion.

While soft drinks, fruit drinks, and bottled water hold a large share of the market, alcohol accounts for more than half of all beverage sales, with beer the most popular. The beer industry largely grew up with the great wave of German immigration in the 19th century. Famous names like Busch and Coors started out as regional brewers and soon went national.

Wine was a harder sell. Though Thomas Jefferson was the first of many Americans to attempt to inaugurate a true American wine industry, wine remained a luxury item and never caught on with the general public. The advent of Prohibition in 1919 didn't help either; only six vineyards were licensed to make wine, for sacramental and medicinal purposes. Meanwhile, the price of grapes soared as newly arrived European immigrants bought vines to make homemade wine. By the time of Repeal in 1933, the wine industry, such as it was, was in disarray.

That year, two California brothers named Ernest and Julio Gallo decided to popularize wine, a crazy idea at a time when only 33 million gallons were sold in the United States each year. Neither brother knew how to make wine, and the country was in the middle of the depression. The Gallo brothers moved ahead anyway, studying books on wine-making techniques, finding distributors, and managing the business. In their first year, they made $34,000 profit. In 1938, they began to put out their own brand of wine under the Gallo label. Unlike other Napa Valley vintners, Gallo focused not on creating a high-end premium product but on a wine that would appeal to the average American. The Gallos' instincts turned out to be correct. By the 1970s, Gallo's "popular" wines accounted for about one-third of all wines purchased in America, and the company decided to go into the premium wine business. Today, unlike many vintners, Gallo is vertically integrated, producing its wine in the vineyards and bottling and distributing it. The company is the largest wine-maker in the world, selling about a third of the 551 million gallons of wine purchased annually in the United States.

To Market, to Market: How America Shops

The profound changes that took place in the 19th century in Americans' eating habits would forever alter the food industry.

Back then, many families put up their own fruits and vegetables in the newly invented mason jars. Commercial canned foods began to appear on the eve of the Civil War and quickly became popular, allowing midwesterners to feast on shellfish and northerners to sample out-of-season fruits and vegetables. By 1900, sales had topped one billion dollars.

Two other common staples appeared during the 19th century: canned condensed milk and white flour. By 1900, almost a quarter of all bread loaves were store bought. (Commercially sold sliced bread, however, did not appear until 1930, when it was introduced as Wonderbread.) Meanwhile, changes were occurring on the

farms and ranches across the nation. Barbed wire was invented in 1867, a particularly important development for ranchers. The first silos were built in 1875, and in 1892, the gasoline tractor was invented.

Transportation advances also made an impact. The transcontinental railroad was completed in 1869, allowing agricultural products to be transported coast to coast. In 1876, Chicago meat magnate Gustavus Swift began shipping fresh, pre-dressed meat to the East Coast in a special refrigerator car. Twelve years later, the first refrigerated agricultural freight was shipped from California to New York.

The kitchen itself was becoming more civilized. Cast-iron stoves were reasonably good regulators of heat. Electric stoves were introduced to the public at the World's Columbian Exposition in Chicago in 1893 but were not really practical for home use for many years. Appliances like meat grinders, eggbeaters, apple corers, and iceboxes entered the American home.

In 1900, Americans in both urban and rural areas typically shopped at general stores for staples like tea, spices, and flour. City folk purchased their meat, greens, and bakery items from specialized shops; country folk produced most of their own.

BELOW: THE AMERICAN SHOPPER BENEFITS FROM THE ABUNDANCE OF PRODUCTS—AND CONSEQUENTLY, COMPETITIVE PRICES—AVAILABLE IN MARKETS ACROSS THE NATION. CONSUMERS MAKE APPROXIMATELY 2.3 TRIPS TO THE MARKET PER WEEK AND SPEND AN AVERAGE OF $23.04 PER TRANSACTION. · OPPOSITE, TOP: EMPLOYEES STAND BEHIND A SUMPTUOUS DISPLAY OF FISH. THE POPULARITY OF SEAFOOD IS ON THE RISE, WITH THE AVERAGE AMERICAN CONSUMING 14.9 POUNDS PER YEAR. · OPPOSITE, BOTTOM: GRAPES ARE READY FOR HARVESTING IN NORTHERN CALIFORNIA'S SONOMA VALLEY, OFTEN CALLED THE BIRTHPLACE OF THAT STATE'S WINE INDUSTRY.

Today's shoppers have a variety of choice and quantities their counterparts of 100 years ago could never have imagined. From local farmers' markets to upscale shops, grocery chains, bulk food stores, and now, even to the Internet, Americans have a variety of ways to purchase their food.

There are 126,000 grocery stores in the United States, with 1998 retail sales of almost $450 billion. The number one grocer in the United States, Kroger, of Cincinnati, Ohio, operates more than 2,300 stores around the country under such names as Kroger, Ralphs, and Smith's. Company founder Barney Kroger opened his first store in 1883 in Cincinnati, which quickly grew into a chain. In 1901, his was the first company to operate its own bakeries. Three years later, Kroger bought 14 Nagel meat markets and a packing house, adding meat to the grocery repertoire. In 1916, Kroger tried out the concept of self-service.

Meanwhile, in 1915, a young man named M. B. Skaggs of American Falls, Idaho, purchased a grocery store from his father. By 1926, he had expanded that small enterprise into 428 Skaggs stores

throughout ten states. Skaggs later merged with 322 Safeway (formerly Selig) stores. Today, there are 1,650 Safeway stores across the United States and Canada, with the company operating hundreds of additional regional stores, such as the Vons chain in Southern California.

Another grocery store giant, the Great Atlantic and Pacific Tea Company, or A&P for short, began as a single general store in Manhattan in 1859. By 1900, A&P had

almost 200 stores and was marketing its own brands of baking powder, canned peas, and tomatoes. Today, A&P is headquartered in Montvale, New Jersey, and operates more than 760 supermarkets under the A&P name and under regional names like Farmer Jack (in Michigan), Super Fresh (throughout the mid-Atlantic), and Sav-A-Center (in New Orleans), to name a few.

The first true supermarket was founded by a New Yorker named Michael Cullen. His King Kullen opened up to great fanfare on Long Island in 1930. Today, supermarkets (large, self-service grocery stores with full product lines and at least $2 million in annual sales) make up less than 25 percent of all grocery stores but sell 75 percent of all groceries in the country.

Another success story that grew from a single store into a diversified company is Houchens Industries, of Bowling Green, Kentucky. Started in 1917 with one country store, Houchens grew through the century and today consists of Houchens Markets, Save-A-Lot stores, and Jr. Food Stores. The company also has interests in

insurance, construction, warehousing, and recycling businesses.

Membership warehouse clubs such as Costco and Sam's Club are a growing segment of the industry. Ironically, what was common at the beginning of the century—grocers selling products in bulk—has come full circle as cost-conscious consumers flock to these warehouse clubs to purchase extra-large sizes of such staples as meats, olive oil, and cereal.

Supermarkets were built upon the notion that consumers would like to make a single stop to stock their kitchens. In the coming century, the process will become even more convenient as shoppers experiment with on-line grocery shopping.

BILLIONS SERVED: THE RESTAURANT BUSINESS

"You deserve a break today." "Have it your way." "Dominos does it." Advertising slogans for popular fast-food restaurants illustrate the greatest food trend of the 20th century: eating out. With families busier than ever, restaurants providing fast food, ethnic food, and, ironically, homestyle food have grown tremendously popular. In 1972, American consumers spent about a third of their food dollar dining out; in 1996, they spent 44 percent. During the 1990s, the restaurant industry grew every single year. Today, fast food accounts for about half of restaurant sales, bringing in $100 billion each year.

The fast-food trend began in the early 1900s. The 1904 St. Louis World's Fair introduced new snacks to Americans: the ice-cream cone (ice cream served in a waffle), iced tea, and the hamburger and hot dog.

From such humble beginnings sprang major industries. The sausage, for example, had always been a favorite of German and eastern European immigrants, but it took a Polish immigrant, Nathan Handwerker, to introduce it to a wider audience. Handwerker opened a frankfurter stand on Coney Island in 1916. To combat unfounded rumors that his hot dogs were substandard, Handwerker stationed college students wearing white professional jackets and stethoscopes around his stand. Soon, Nathan's became a fixture, and Governor Nelson Rockefeller declared that "no one can hope to be elected to public office in New York without having his picture taken eating a hot dog at Nathan's." In 2000, Nathan's Famous, based in Westbury, New York, had more than 400 locations throughout the world and sales of $47 million.

But the true fast-food star was the humble hamburger. After the burger's debut in St. Louis, J. Walter Anderson kicked off the first hamburger chain when he opened White Castle in 1921 in Wichita, Kansas. Headquartered today in Columbus, Ohio, the chain is still going strong with 350 restaurants. But the leader in the hamburger business—and the most famous of them all—is McDonald's.

The story is simple. Dick and Mac McDonald, two brothers living in San Bernardino, California, opened a small drive-in restaurant in 1940 and made a profit of $40,000 in their first year. That's because they knew what market they wanted to tap: young families, sometimes with two working parents, who wanted a fast, cheap, and good meal. What they didn't want was the other type of customer who often frequented this type of establishment: teenage boys, who sometimes became rowdy or even threatening.

The McDonalds figured that speeding up their operations would discourage loitering by the teenagers while increasing traffic from the young families. They were right. After streamlining hamburger production, trimming the menu down to a few essential items, and implementing the use of paper containers, McDonald's achieved the speedy service it sought and had almost more business than it could handle.

Meanwhile, a milkshake machine salesman named Ray Kroc noticed that while most drugstores that sold shakes were either dying out or buying fewer and fewer Multimixers, there was one shop that kept ordering more: McDonald's. Kroc decided to investigate. He visited just before lunchtime and was surprised to see that long lines had already formed. After watching for an entire afternoon, Kroc decided that he wanted to be in this business. He offered to be the brothers' franchising agent and eventually purchased the entire operation, name included. The institution he built, which not only resulted in a standard, popular, and reliable product but also provided the impetus for thousands of entrepreneurs to run their own franchises, is now the world's number one food chain. Headquartered in Oak Brook, Illinois, the company operates nearly 13,000 restaurants in the United States alone and an additional 15,000 abroad. In 2000, McDonald's had more than $14 billion in sales.

Will restaurants figure even more prominently in the 21st century? With serious labor shortages and higher minimum wage laws, it's not clear whether restaurants will be able to keep up with the demand. On the other hand, the food industry is becoming ever more productive and innovative. The industry that produces, processes, distributes, sells, and delivers the staff of life to consumers will always be there to help answer that daily question, "What's for dinner?"

Ray Kroc was so impressed with the customer traffic at the original McDonald's in San Bernardino, California, seen here in 1952, that he offered to franchise the operation. He opened his first franchise in Des Plaines, Illinois, and started the world's largest fast-food empire.

profiles
Agriculture &
Consumer Foods

THE COCA-COLA COMPANY

THE ATLANTA-BASED, $20.5 BILLION COCA-COLA COMPANY CONTINUES TO EXPAND, CREATING NEW REFRESHING AND WHOLESOME BEVERAGES TO ADD TO ITS IMPRESSIVE LIST OF 230 PRODUCTS, SOLD IN NEARLY 200 COUNTRIES.

In the annals of business there have been several brand names that have achieved icon status. None, however, have come close to the strength, recognition, and admiration achieved globally by Coca-Cola. For more than a century, Coca-Cola has been not only synonymous with soft drink beverages, but also the most successful product in the history of commerce. The familiar contour of its bottle, developed in 1915, and the flowing script of its trademark, designed in 1886, are the world's most widely recognized commercial symbols.

Through the years, the distinct, refreshing taste of Coca-Cola has provided simple moments of pleasure for an ever-expanding number of consumers. Today, Coca-Cola and the Company's other products are enjoyed more than a billion times every single day by individuals in nearly 200 countries.

In fact, just about everyone on the planet today has heard of Coca-Cola, and over 4 billion people have become consumers of Coke and the more than 230 other products of The Coca-Cola Company. But not everyone, perhaps, is familiar with the interesting history of the Atlanta, Georgia–based, $20.5 billion company and its impressive lineup of soft drinks, juices, sports drinks, water, and other beverages, with such well-known brand names as Sprite, diet Coke, Fanta, Minute Maid, Hi-C, POWERaDE, Nestea, Dasani, and Georgia Coffee.

Like most major corporations, The Coca-Cola Company, the world's largest beverage firm, sprang forth from modest beginnings. It all began in 1886 when an Atlanta pharmacist, John Stith Pemberton, produced the syrup for Coca-Cola and delivered it to a local pharmacy where, mixed with carbonated water, it was sold as a "delicious and refreshing" soda fountain drink.

Credit for the initial fame of Coca-Cola and the creation of The Coca-Cola Company belongs to an astute Atlanta pharmaceuticals businessman named Asa G. Candler, who purchased Pemberton's interest in the soft drink just prior to Pemberton's death in 1888. It was Candler who first marketed Coca-Cola in several major U.S. cities, in the late 1800s.

Another key figure in the Company's history was a Vicksburg, Mississippi, storekeeper, Joseph A. Biedenharn, who became the first to bottle the famous soft drink. So impressed was Biedenharn with the growing demand for Coca-Cola that in 1894 he installed bottling machinery in the back of his store and began selling cases of Coca-Cola up and down the Mississippi River.

Large-scale bottling of Coca-Cola began in 1899, when Chattanooga businessmen Benjamin F. Thomas and Joseph B. Whitehead built the first Coca-Cola bottling plant. Today, the vast network of mostly independently owned Coca-Cola bottling plants, located in some 200 countries around the globe, represents the largest, most widespread production and distribution system on earth.

The person chiefly responsible for achieving unrivaled heights of commercial success for Coca-Cola was Robert W. Woodruff, who became president of The Coca-Cola Company in 1923. During Woodruff's six decades at the helm of the firm, Coca-Cola established quality standards for every phase of its bottling operation and introduced such marketing innovations as the six-bottle carton; the standard metal cooler; and the automatic syrup dispenser for soda fountains. Most importantly, under Woodruff's leadership, the Company embarked on the road that carried it to every corner of the globe, making Coca-Cola a worldwide symbol of friendship and refreshment.

Today, under the leadership of Douglas N. Daft, chairman and chief executive officer, The Coca-Cola Company continues to expand its global reach and add innovative, refreshing, and wholesome ready-to-drink nonalcoholic beverages to its already impressive list of offerings. In addition, it continues to create model advertising campaigns that give consumers compelling reasons to choose Coca-Cola. And, as it has since its inception, the Company continues to be an involved, concerned, and committed citizen in the communities where it makes its products, helping people in times of crisis and taking steps to strengthen the communities.

When it comes to enterprise, progress, and a future of promise, The Coca-Cola Company itself, like the words in one of its memorable slogans for Coca-Cola, is "the real thing."

Life tastes good.

Opposite page: When this poster naming Coca-Cola as the "friendliest drink on earth" was made, in 1956, the drink was being served in more than 90 countries around the world. · Above: In 1905, when this advertisement appeared in magazines, Coca-Cola was most commonly purchased at soda fountains. · Left: The Company's current catchy slogan, "Life Tastes Good," reminds people that Coca-Cola products are often a part of life's special moments.

HOUCHENS INDUSTRIES, INC.

HOUCHENS INDUSTRIES, INC., HAS KEPT THE PREMISE OF ITS FIRST COUNTRY STORE—OPENED IN 1917—AND BUILT A MAJOR ENTERPRISE WITH DIVERSIFIED BUSINESSES IN 11 STATES.

Emergent technologies—from the latest NASA space flight to this week's dot-com—make headlines and the nightly news. But the foundation upon which such innovation is built remains America's core businesses—the companies large and small that, decade after decade, produce the goods and services on which every community's quality of life depends.

That reality underlies the business strategy pursued by the management team at Houchens Industries, Inc., of Bowling Green, Kentucky: Combine sound management practices and innovative systems to build a growth-oriented enterprise of diversified and complementary businesses. According to Jimmie Gipson, CEO and chairman of the board, "a key element of our success is the flexibility we have within our company, which allows us to quickly recognize and seize upon an opportunity when it presents itself."

The Houchens heritage began in 1917, when Ervin Houchens opened a 12-by-20–foot country store in Glasgow, Kentucky. It was steadily strengthened over the decades, primarily through the operation of conventional supermarkets in Kentucky and northern Tennessee. In 1988, the company's established supermarket and commercial property development and leasing operations were purchased by its employees. Through growth brought about by the positive attitude, productivity, and team spirit of its employees, the number of participants in its employee stock ownership plan ranks Houchens Industries, Inc., among the nation's top-ten companies that are 100 percent employee-owned.

During the 1990s, Houchens Industries management built on its core of conventional supermarkets to create a diversified parent company and compatible subsidiaries, acquired on the basis of superior management and solid performance records. As the 21st century began, Houchens employed more than

5,000 people in more than 340 retail facilities in 11 states, from Georgia to upstate New York.

At the core of the Houchens enterprise are the retail grocery operations of Houchens Industries. In 1991, Houchens Industries began focusing on limited-assortment grocery stores under the Save-A-Lot banner, expanding on the company's base of conventional supermarkets operating in Kentucky as Houchens Markets and IGA Food Stores. By the end of 2001, Houchens Industries will own and operate more than 200 Save-A-Lot Food Stores. Typically smaller than 15,000 square feet, the community-centered Save-A-Lot units offer shoppers an alternative to conventional supermarkets, with discount prices. The company's niche strategy includes locating its Save-A-Lot Food Stores in new buildings and small shopping centers, as well as in aging retail areas, often helping in the revitalization of older neighborhoods.

Since 1998, Houchens Industries has expanded its corporate family to include:

- Jr. Food Stores, Inc., a growing chain of convenience stores that owns and operates 42 units in Kentucky and Tennessee;

- Southern Recycling, Inc., a recycling company that exemplifies Houchens Industries' commitment to the environment. Southern Recycling operates an exclusive curbside recycling franchise in Bowling Green and processes recyclable materials for regional and national markets;

- Center of Insurance, Inc., a full-service insurance agency concentrating on the Kentucky region, representing major U.S. insurance companies and offering diverse lines of insurance coverage;

- Stewart and Richey Construction, Inc., which performs a full range of residential, commercial, and industrial contracting work, including the construction and renovation of homes, office buildings, shopping centers, and industrial facilities; and

- Houchens Warehousing, Inc., which owns and operates efficient and cost-effective warehousing facilities for Houchens grocery operations and the warehousing needs of other businesses.

Contributing to the community is one of the ways Houchens Industries fulfills its role as a good corporate citizen. The employees of the Houchens corporate family lend support to local communities through sponsorship and support of fund-raising events, charitable contributions, and volunteering for a variety of community services.

Devoted to four guiding principles—quality products and services, customer satisfaction, innovation and action, and open communication with customers and employees—Houchens Industries continues to offer a sound framework of dynamic commerce and quality service.

Opposite page: The first Houchens grocery store, just 12 by 20 feet in size, was opened in 1917. It is preserved at its original location, near Glasgow, Kentucky. · This page, top: Houchens Industries employees gather at Fountain Square Park, in Bowling Green, Kentucky. The company considers its employees to be its most valuable resource.

AMERICAN FROZEN FOOD

THE AMERICAN FROZEN FOOD INSTITUTE WORKS TO ENSURE THAT NOURISHING AND CONVENIENT FROZEN FOODS—WHICH PROVIDE SUPERIOR NUTRITION—ARE CONTINUALLY ABUNDANT, RELIABLE, VARIED, SATISFYING, AND ECONOMICAL.

The strongest proof of any technology's real significance may lie in its influence upon people's everyday lives. By such a test, during its 70 years of growing use and popularity, the technology of frozen foods has earned its place among modern America's most constructive innovations. When, one March morning in 1930, Clarence Birdseye optimistically combined an inventor's creativity with a salesman's confidence and arrayed his selection of neatly packaged, quick-frozen foods into a grocery store display case in Springfield, Massachusetts, he inaugurated an industry that would forever change the way the world eats.

HISTORY

From inception, the vital role of frozen food in the nation's economic and cultural life expanded swiftly—and for reasons that are compelling not only at mealtime, but also throughout the growing, harvesting, transporting, market-

ing, and storage of foods of nearly every kind. Major food producers promptly recognized the potential of the technology, and Birdseye's patents for package design and the double-plate freezer were soon acquired by the predecessor of General Foods Company. By the late 1940s, a grocery store without a frozen food case was becoming a rarity.

But if the industry's momentum was initially driven by the economy and convenience of frozen foods, a further reality would ultimately ensure their enthusiastic endorsement by health experts: frozen foods provide superior nutrition. Following years of scientific studies at the University of Illinois, in 1998 the U.S. Food and Drug Administration concluded that fruits and vegetables picked at peak freshness and immediately

frozen contain as many, and often more, nutrients than their "fresh" equivalents. Moreover, for foods of all kinds, modern freezing and packaging means unsurpassed food safety, reliable product consistency, and year-round availability everywhere.

American Frozen Food Institute

An Industry's Cooperative Center

Like other complex enterprises, the frozen foods industry benefits not only from competition, but from cooperative, coordinated action. Launched in 1942 by 19 frozen fruit and vegetable packers, the National Association of Frozen Food Packers became today's American Frozen Food Institute (AFFI), whose member firms compose some 90 percent of the industry. The professional staff of the institute, headquartered in McLean, Virginia, along with some 500 representatives of member companies who serve on 34 AFFI committees and task forces, accomplishes work ranging from nutrient analysis and international trade development to environmental protection, workplace safety, and microbiological research.

The 21st Century

Not surprisingly, the pace and diversity of developments in the frozen food universe largely reflect society's pattern of swift and profound change. Especially notable is the industry's success in meeting the needs of busy working families whose hectic schedules often leave little time for meal preparation. Today, complete meals, healthy and satisfying, can be served within minutes of arriving home. Paralleling refinements in freezing processes and packaging that ensure maximum nutrient retention and flavor stability have brought advances in prepared foods to earn the admiration of world class chefs, as well as hungry shoppers.

For the most adventurous diner as well as the busy parent, a stroll past the frozen food cases of a typical supermarket reveals a selection nothing less than

astonishing. From pizza rivaling that of the best restaurant and golden kernels of corn indistinguishable by farmers from fresh corn just shucked, through savory Thai specialities comparable to Bangkok's best, there is a cornucopia of nutritious foods from humble to elegant to tempt the palate and accommodate the budget.

The nation's frozen food industry continues not only to provide Americans with good nourishment, but also to ensure that all the values of abundant safe food can be enjoyed with unsurpassed convenience, variety, and economy.

OPPOSITE PAGE: FROZEN FOOD PRODUCTS, DUBBED "MIRACLE FOODS," WERE FIRST INTRODUCED BY CLARENCE BIRDSEYE AT A GROCERY STORE IN SPRINGFIELD, MASSACHUSETTS, IN 1930. · LEFT: TODAY'S SUPERMARKET FROZEN FOOD AISLE DISPLAYS A WIDE VARIETY OF MEAL SOLUTIONS, WITH HUNDREDS OF NEW PRODUCTS BEING INTRODUCED EACH YEAR.

BEYOND BOUNDARIES
AVIATION, DEFENSE, & SPACE EXPLORATION

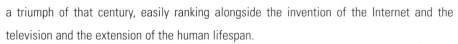

AS AMERICANS ROUTINELY BOARD FLIGHTS FOR DESTINATIONS ACROSS THE COUNTRY AND AROUND THE WORLD, IT'S EASY TO TAKE AVIATION'S 20TH-CENTURY ACHIEVEMENTS FOR GRANTED. THE CONQUEST OF SPACE AND DISTANCE WAS

a triumph of that century, easily ranking alongside the invention of the Internet and the television and the extension of the human lifespan.

Two significant events bracketed both the century and the development of flight. The first took place on December 17, 1903, when Orville Wright's plane flew 120 feet in 12 seconds over the beach at Kitty Hawk, North Carolina. The second occurred 96 years later, almost to the day, when on December 3, 1999, the National Aeronautics and Space Administration (NASA) launched a three-legged polar lander that was to dig for ice and study the atmosphere of Mars. Though ultimately this mission was unsuccessful, the dream remains of a manned mission to the red planet in the 21st century.

AVIATION TAKES OFF

Orville Wright once remarked that "flight was generally looked upon as an impossibility and scarcely anyone believed it until he actually saw it with his own eyes." Indeed, throughout most of human history, man has dreamed of traveling to the stars. In the 16th century, Leonardo da Vinci made sketches of a flying machine. But it was not until the 18th century that the first successful flight was recorded. In Paris on October 15, 1783, J. F. Pilâtre Rozier became the first human to fly, rising 80 feet above ground in a tethered hot-air balloon.

During the 19th century, many tried—and failed—to create a flying machine. It wasn't until the Wright brothers, Orville and Wilbur, applied themselves to the task that this age-old goal was finally achieved.

In the early days of flight, aviation was considered little more than entertainment—a hobby for rich enthusiasts, perhaps, and the source of great spectacle for the masses. In 1910, the first aviation meet was held in Los Angeles, but in the next three years, only five planes were sold to private individuals.

In 1911, Calbraith Perry Rodgers made early aviation history by flying from New York across the United States in the *Vin Fiz*, a single-engine, fixed-wing aircraft named for a grape-flavored drink. Rodgers crashed five times before reaching the Pacific 84 days after starting his journey.

ABOVE: HAVING ONCE TRAVELED INTO THE HEAVENS, THESE SPACECRAFT ARE FOREVER EARTHBOUND AT THE ROCKET GARDEN AT THE KENNEDY SPACE CENTER ON FLORIDA'S MERRITT ISLAND. · OPPOSITE: CHARLES LINDBERGH STANDS NEXT TO THE SPIRIT OF ST. LOUIS IN 1927, THE YEAR HE CROSSED THE ATLANTIC SOLO.

During aviation's barnstorming years in the 1920s, both men and women aviators were treated like the music, film, and sports celebrities of today, with adoring fans massing to watch their exciting exploits. When Donald Douglas, whose company would later become McDonnell-Douglas, established an airplane factory in Los Angeles, it was widely considered to be an entertainment undertaking rather than a manufacturing one.

There were a number of firsts recorded in those days. The most famous was Charles Lindbergh's nonstop solo flight across the Atlantic Ocean in the *Spirit of St. Louis* in 1927. It took 33 hours and 29 minutes. The Pacific was conquered in 1927 when Army Air Corps pilots Albert

Hegenberger and Lester Maitland flew from San Francisco to Hawaii, firmly linking the island to the mainland with this first flight. In 1932, Amelia Earhart became the first woman to cross the Atlantic solo.

Commercial air service did not begin in earnest for several years and was barely profitable, existing mainly on subsidies from carrying airmail. Though the first aerospace engineer graduated in 1911, it wasn't until the 1930s that aerospace became a discipline rather than a field dominated by intuition and trial and error.

Though certainly less romantic, this emphasis on science and professionalism sparked amazing advances. In 1933, the Boeing Company introduced the 247 aircraft, which made all planes to date obsolete. The 247 could fly 70 miles per hour faster than other planes and led to the establishment by United Airlines, then part of the Boeing holding company, of 10 daily round-trips between New York and Chicago. With only 10 seats, the 247 had its limits, but its introduction inspired then-competitor Douglas Aircraft to develop its 21-passenger

DC-3, introduced in 1935. The DC-3 flew across the country in record time: 17 hours, 30 minutes. With its focus on greater passenger comfort, improved navigational and flight control systems, and many technological advances, it was the first aircraft to make aviation profitable. Douglas produced more than 12,000 civil and military DC-3s over the years, many of which were used for decades afterward. In just five years, the DC-3 carried 80 percent of domestic scheduled airline service—and air travel rose 500 percent between 1936 and the start of World War II. In 1939, Boeing introduced the Stratoliner, the first civil airplane to feature a pressurized cabin.

While the airline companies were budding, private aviation was lagging due to high costs. The coming of World War II decimated the private aviation industry, as wartime requirements used all materials and pilots for the war effort. Hopes that returning pilots would be interested in continuing flying as a hobby were dashed in the postwar period as many veterans had had quite enough of flying and could not afford the expense.

Private aviation—or "general aviation"—survived, however, thanks to business travel. In 1937, Beech Aircraft introduced its Model 18, the first true executive aircraft. Its speed, range, and sophistication set the early standards for the burgeoning private-aircraft industry. In 1958, Grumman introduced the Gulfstream I, a twin turboprop plane whose greater speed and comfort made it the Rolls Royce of executive travel. In 1964, William Lear introduced the six-seat, 500-mile-per-hour Learjet, which quickly became a status symbol among top business leaders. Business aviation came into its own in the 1970s with the introduction of twin-engine business aircraft with better radios and instruments. Today, 35,000 American companies use 50,000 general aviation aircraft.

In 1939, the first successful helicopter, the VS300, was developed in the United States by the Russian designer Igor Sikorsky. Though helicopters were not the key to revitalizing private aviation, the jet age helicopters built in the coming decades would prove useful in everything from traffic reports, police and fire rescues and surveillance, and military support.

ABOVE: CHARLES "CHUCK" YEAGER, SEEN HERE IN 1962, HOLDS A MODEL OF THE BELL X-1, THE ROCKET IN WHICH HE BECAME THE FIRST PILOT TO BREAK THE SOUND BARRIER, IN 1947. · OPPOSITE, TOP: AMELIA EARHART WAS THE FIRST WOMAN TO FLY ACROSS THE ATLANTIC, IN 1932, AND THE FIRST PERSON TO FLY SOLO ACROSS THE PACIFIC, IN 1935, FROM HAWAII TO CALIFORNIA. IN 1937, DURING AN ATTEMPT TO CIRCUMNAVIGATE THE WORLD, HER PLANE DISAPPEARED. · OPPOSITE, BOTTOM: ROWS OF BOMBER NOSE CANOPIES SPARKLE UNDER THE FACTORY LIGHTS AT DOUGLAS AIRCRAFT'S LONG BEACH, CALIFORNIA, PLANT IN 1942.

In the post–World War II years, with the transition from piston engines to jet engines, planes could go faster than ever. In 1947, Chuck Yeager broke the sound barrier in a Bell X-1 named *Glamorous Glennis* for his wife. Its rocket engines were later used on manned rocket flights. The fastest flight ever was in 1967, when an X-15 flew to Mach 7, paving the way for space travel. However, supersonic travel never went very far due to the noise and the environmental impact and so was not pursued in the United States. Today, British Airways' and Air France's Concorde is the only commercial jet that flies faster than the speed of sound.

As commercial aviation came into its own, American companies in the 1940s and 1950s faced a great deal of competition

from each other, unlike their European counterparts. The result was constant improvements in safety, performance, and service, making American companies the best in the world. The greatest challenge at that time was to build a plane better than the DC-3, then the market leader. In 1954, Boeing introduced the 707, the first jet transport. It came as close as economically possible to supersonic transport, and even today few planes go faster. There followed many of today's familiar jet aircraft: the DC-8; the Boeing 727, with three jet engines; and the first wide-body, the Boeing 747. The introduction of faster and better planes that could fly at higher altitudes made cheaper flights possible, and by 1960 there were 52 million boardings annually and 30 million passenger miles traveled.

Air carriers were confronted with a major challenge in 1973 when an oil embargo by the Arab states drastically boosted the cost of jet fuel, slowing the growth of air travel and threatening the financial viability of airlines. At the same time, it spurred the development of more fuel-efficient engines.

The deregulation of the airline industry, spearheaded by President Jimmy Carter in 1978, brought with it a shock as great as the rise in fuel prices. Previously, the federal government essentially set airline routing and ticket prices, forcing airline companies to focus competition on the quality of passenger service, including such things as gourmet meals and novelty costumes for flight attendants.

Deregulation after years of stringent government control is difficult for any industry. In commercial aviation, many carriers merged, consolidated, or went out of business altogether. At first, destinations deemed unprofitable by airlines (especially in rural America) lost regular service. Many passengers complained of overcrowded planes and terminals and a general decline in service. Safety worries were expressed as well, although the overall safety record continued to improve. But as the industry adjusted, the benefits of deregulation became more apparent—chief among them, access to air travel by tens of millions of Americans who previously found it too expensive.

Spearheading this change was a man named Herb Kelleher, whose Southwest Airlines (initially a small regional carrier) took full advantage of the new climate of deregulation. The iconoclastic airline revolutionized U.S. air travel in the 1980s when it expanded across the country, providing bare-bones service at rock-bottom prices, and spawned a host of low-cost imitators. By 1998, there were 560 million domestic plane travelers—ten times as many as in 1960.

Southwest ranks among the top 10 U.S. airlines. Heading the list is United Airlines, followed by American, Delta, Northwest, and Continental Airlines, which serves the greatest number of international cities of all U.S. airlines.

As air travel enters its second century, the process of consolidation of major U.S. airlines continues. But so, too, does the appearance of new, no-frills, low-cost carriers that keep the competitive climate intact, while the growth of air cargo has opened a rich new business frontier for many carriers. With passenger complaints on the rise, the industry is leading efforts to persuade the federal government and local communities to modernize the air traffic control system and expand airport and runway construction. The early struggles focused simply on

A SLEEK, NEW 727 ROLLS OUT OF A HANGAR AT BOEING'S PLANT IN SEATTLE IN 1962. THE JET HAD A RANGE OF 3,110 MILES AND COULD HOLD 131 PASSENGERS AND REACH A TOP SPEED OF 632 MPH.

experts believed that naval superiority, rather than prowess in the air, would determine military dominance. Still, it was hard to overlook the performance of the World War I flying aces. The imperial Japanese government certainly didn't. On December 7, 1941, the United States Pacific Fleet was bombed at Pearl Harbor, Hawaii, by Japanese squadrons. The fact that the four aircraft carriers stationed there were away from the island at the time and survived brought little solace to American leaders. They still considered battleship strength more important, and this strength was decimated in the attack on Hawaii.

The United States was only slightly more prepared for World War II than it was for the first world war. In 1939, only

the task of keeping the aircraft aloft. Exceedingly safe and tremendously popular, commercial flight today is in some ways a victim of its own success. Demands for more flights, better service, and cheaper fares are creating new opportunities—and challenges—for America's airlines and aviation companies.

DEFENDING THE NATION FROM ON HIGH

Aviation in the 20th century not only revolutionized personal travel but warfare as well.

In 1914, at the start of World War I, neither of the opposing European factions saw aviation as anything more than a useful tool for air reconnaissance and surveillance. Nobody made plans for an organized mobilization of aircraft, and logistics and operations were not well understood.

But during the Great War, the offensive potential of aircraft was recognized. In 1917, Germany figured out how to drop

bombs on London; its wartime raids killed 162 people and injured 438.

World War I radically changed the aviation industry in America. When the United States entered the war in 1917, there was only a handful of obsolete aircraft and hardly any industry or industrial base. In a single year, this all turned around. By the end of the war, American companies were building 12,000 state-of-the-art aircraft per year.

In the interwar years, aviation's military advocates were few. After all, most military

2,200 military aircraft were produced. In 1942, the nation produced nearly 50,000 planes—twice as many as the Axis powers. The Battle of the Coral Sea that year was a turning point of the war. The Japanese and Allied powers fought a major naval engagement in the air; the surface ships never sighted each other.

It was clear by 1943 that air superiority was turning the tide for the Allies in both Europe and the Pacific. By 1944, the mobilized industry was putting out 100,000 planes

a year: Grumman F6F Hellcats, Northrup C-61 Black Widows (with radar equipment that let them fight at night), Douglas C-54s, and Lockheed P-38 Lightning (long-range fighters that shot down more Japanese aircraft than any other). By 1945, bombing in Europe was so successful in destroying German planes that it almost ceased because few such targets remained to be hit.

The development of the Boeing B-29 superfortress in 1944 was a major advance. It allowed for the first time the precision targeting of bombs. This led to the successful nuclear strikes on Hiroshima and Nagasaki

Francis Gary Powers, was denounced as a spy and imprisoned. The incident poisoned U.S.-Soviet relations and contributed to a buildup of tensions leading to the 1962 Cuban Missile Crisis. It was the introduction of Soviet nuclear missiles in communist Cuba, capable of reaching targets in the United States, and the Americans' insistence that they be removed that brought the two nations to the brink of nuclear war.

During the Vietnam War, the United States was again handicapped by the limitations of air warfare. The enemy's guerilla

ABOVE: IN 1962, JOHN GLENN POSES BEFORE THE FRIENDSHIP 7, IN WHICH HE BECAME THE FIRST MAN TO ORBIT THE EARTH. GLENN WOULD SET ANOTHER RECORD, THAT OF OLDEST PERSON TO GO INTO SPACE, 36 YEARS LATER WHEN HE TRAVELED ABOARD THE DISCOVERY. · OPPOSITE, TOP: A McDONNELL DOUGLAS F-15 EAGLE DISPLAYS BOTH GRACE AND POWER DURING AN AIR FORCE PRACTICE FLIGHT. · OPPOSITE, BOTTOM: PILOTS CHEER ABOARD THE U.S.S. LEXINGTON AIRCRAFT CARRIER IN 1943, AROUND THE TIME OF THE GILBERT ISLANDS OPERATION IN THE PACIFIC.

which brought the war in the Pacific to an end in August 1945.

In the ensuing Cold War years, aviation became a vital component to national defense. In 1947, the introduction of jet technology on Boeing's B-47 bomber made it the most important military aircraft at the time. The Soviets lagged somewhat behind America in aircraft development but managed to copy NATO designs enough to bolster their own air force. The Korean War showed some of the limitations of air power. Though the United Nations forces, led by the United States, had clear air superiority, the battle was fought to a stalemate on the ground.

In 1954, McDonnell introduced its F101 long-range interceptor and reconnaissance plane. This sophisticated device led to an unexpected twist in Cold War history. In May 1960, the United States was embarrassed when Soviet premier Nikita Khruschev announced that a U-2 spy plane had been downed over the U.S.S.R. Its pilot,

tactics made air strikes imprecise and inefficient. The controversial nature of the conflict led the White House and the Pentagon to restrict the choice of targets to military installations only. And with both competing camps in the Cold War armed to the teeth with nuclear weapons, dropping nuclear bombs was out of the question.

It was not until the 1991 Gulf War that air power became the last word in warfare. The air superiority of the Desert Storm Coalition enabled attacks that decimated Iraqi installations and forces with minimal losses on the United States' part.

Military aviation is but one component of a defense industry that has kept America strong and free. Over and over again, the companies that build the planes, ships, and motor vehicles, outfit and equip the soldiers, and invent the technologies that give those soldiers the edge in battle—these companies have been there whenever the country has called on them.

THE RACE TO THE STARS

The 20th century ended with U.S.-Soviet cooperation in the Mir space station (*mir* means "peace" in Russian). But the start of the space race was not nearly so sanguine. Defense was one of the motivating factors in the space race, and the development of U.S. space technology was interwoven with new defense technologies.

In 1926, scientist Robert Goddard launched the world's first liquid fuel rocket. Powered by gasoline and liquid oxygen, the rocket traveled a distance of 184 feet at 60 miles per hour. Early advances were motivated by war. In 1942, Germany changed the face of warfare forever by introducing the V-2 rocket, which could be launched from Germany at remote targets in London. Its principal inventor, the German scientist Wernher von Braun, was brought to America, as was valuable German rocketry research captured in the waning days of the war. Von Braun worked for the U.S. Army and NASA until his death in 1977. He is best known for his leadership and involvement in two projects: Von Braun created the Intercontinental Ballistic Missile System (ICBM), which Boeing turned into the Minuteman missile program, and led the invention of the Saturn V rocket, which sent man to the moon in 1969.

The dawn of the space age occurred when a 183-pound piece of metal about the size of a basketball spent 98 minutes orbiting the earth. The launch of *Sputnik I* by the Soviet Union on October 4, 1957, also launched the space race, the United States' attempt to catch up to the apparent Soviet technological superiority. Adding insult to injury, the U.S.S.R. launched *Sputnik II* just a month later, this time carrying a heavier payload that included a dog named Laika.

The United States was a quick study, kicking its nascent space program into high gear, so much so that on January 31, 1958, it successfully launched *Explorer I*, a satellite that carried a small scientific payload. Sputnik and subsequent firsts in manned space flight by the Soviets inspired the establishment of NASA and the United States' own early space achievements.

But the brass ring was landing an astronaut on the moon. In 1961, President John F. Kennedy envisioned this feat and called upon Congress, the space community, and the American people to achieve the goal before the end of the decade.

Thus the Apollo program was launched. William Allen, then-president of Boeing Company, was so enthusiastic about the program that he loaned 2,000 executives to NASA and provided overall systems integration for the entire project. On July 16, 1969, *Apollo 11*, manned by Neil Armstrong, Edwin "Buzz" Aldrin Jr., and Michael Collins, was launched toward the moon. Four days later, Armstrong became the first human to walk on the moon in what he called "one small step for man, one giant leap for mankind."

Though manned space missions got most of the headlines from the 1960s through 1980s, equally momentous developments were achieved on other space frontiers. In the decades following Apollo,

ABOVE: THE INTERNATIONAL SPACE STATION, A JOINT ENDEAVOR BY 16 NATIONS, IS BEING ASSEMBLED IN SPACE. ONCE COMPLETED, IT WILL HAVE 46,000 CUBIC FEET OF LIVING AND WORKING SPACE. · BELOW: A STRANGER IN A STRANGE LAND, NEIL ARMSTRONG STANDS NEXT TO HIS ONLY LINK TO EARTH, THE LUNAR LANDING MODULE OF APOLLO 11 IN 1969.

exploratory spacecraft were launched to Jupiter *(Pioneer 10* and *11)*, Saturn *(Pioneer 11)*, and Mars *(Viking 1* and *2)*, on the "grand tour" of the solar system *(Voyager 1* and *2*, which are still traveling), and to Venus *(Magellan)*. Developments in satellite launches and technologies would revolutionize defense (through their spying and tracking capabilities), weather forecasting, telecommunications, and mass media. The Hubble Space Telescope, built by Lockheed Martin and launched in 1990 on a 20-year mission, has provided scientists with millions of pieces of invaluable

data about the universe and spectacular photos, including shots of the births of stars, galactic black holes, and the surface of Pluto.

The last Apollo mission flew in 1972, and space missions became less frequent during the 1970s. That decade marked the development of the American cruise missile program and the modernization of the Soviet intercontinental ballistic missiles (ICBMs). The launch in 1981 of the *Columbia*, America's first reusable space shuttle, and President Ronald Reagan's 1983 announcement of the Strategic Defense Initiative (SDI) thrust space back into the limelight. The SDI, which envisioned earth-orbiting defensive weapons capable of knocking out missile attacks on the United States, proved to be a major factor in convincing an economically moribund Soviet Union that its days of competing militarily with the United States were numbered.

The end of the Soviet Union and the Cold War led to defense cutbacks in the 1990s, prompting defense and aviation companies to merge and to create new uses for modified military technology. The first year that commercial space expenditures exceeded defense space expenditures was 1998. And what Americans have reaped is tremendous. For example, airports use Raytheon's Terminal Doppler Weather Radar to detect wind shear before commercial flights take off, saving countless lives. Motorola's portable phones use satellite technology.

And today, anyone can add a special feature to his or her automobile: the Global Positioning System, which allows people to get directions whenever they want.

Space enthusiasts believe that the new century will bring the nation at least within reach of landing a man or woman on Mars. And where will that lead? Some, like Vinton Cerf, one of the inventors of the Internet and a senior executive at MCI-WorldCom, believe that Mars and Earth can be connected by the Internet. The first timid steps into space will likely be followed by bold strides, led by the increasing expansion of commercial activities in space—and by the imaginations of anyone who has ever dreamed about traveling to the stars.

profiles
Aviation, Defense, &
Space Exploration

LOCKHEED MARTIN

LOCKHEED MARTIN IS A LEADING SYSTEMS INTEGRATOR IN AEROSPACE, DEFENSE, AND TECHNOLOGY SERVICES SUPPORTING CUSTOMER REQUIREMENTS WORLDWIDE.

A company's strength is often measured by the relationships it develops with customers, employees, suppliers, and the communities it serves. As an advanced technology enterprise that conducts business all around this rapidly changing world, Lockheed Martin is committed to forging strong, dynamic partnerships.

Every day, in factories, offices, labs, and field sites worldwide, the 133,000 men and women of Lockheed Martin renew their commitment to making their company the world's best systems integrator in aerospace, defense, and technology services. With 17 lines of business, Lockheed Martin's major concentrations include systems integration, aeronautics, space systems, and technology services.

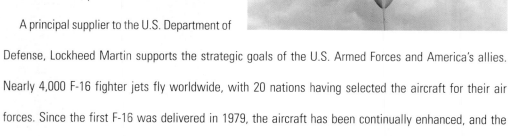

Headquartered in Bethesda, Maryland, the company has facilities in 44 states and the District of Columbia and is allied with more than 250 international partners in 30 countries.

A principal supplier to the U.S. Department of Defense, Lockheed Martin supports the strategic goals of the U.S. Armed Forces and America's allies. Nearly 4,000 F-16 fighter jets fly worldwide, with 20 nations having selected the aircraft for their air forces. Since the first F-16 was delivered in 1979, the aircraft has been continually enhanced, and the newest model—the Block 60—performs its multiple missions at remarkably low operating costs.

The company's next-generation combat aircraft, the F-22 Raptor, completed its flight test program in 1999. Combining stealth, integrated avionics, and "supercruise" (sustained supersonic flight without the use of afterburner) capabilities, the versatile Raptor is expected to ensure U.S. and allied air superiority well into the 21st century. Also in support of U.S. Air Force requirements for advanced tactical aircraft, Lockheed Martin is developing the Preferred Weapon System Concept as a contender in the 2001 Joint Strike Fighter competition.

For people in desperate need of aid in war or natural disaster, the silhouette of an approaching Hercules C-130 airlifter has long been a welcome sight. Lockheed Martin has built this workhorse for five decades. The most advanced Hercules, the C-130J, combines its proven airframe design with advanced cockpit and navigation technologies, and lightweight high-strength materials.

The company's LANTIRN 2000 (Low-Altitude Navigation and Targeting Infrared for Night) electronics system protects fixed-wing aircraft from attack and increases the pilot's situational awareness. Lockheed Martin's maintenance, modification, and logistics services help the Air Force affordably maintain its ready fleet.

Lockheed Martin produces the Aegis Combat System, a high-technology electronic shield for U.S. Navy and allied ships. Aegis can simultaneously engage threats from under the sea, on the surface, and in the air.

As a systems integrator, Lockheed Martin is a partner of choice for government and industry leaders in a range of projects that include air and vessel traffic management; advanced combat systems for aircraft and ships; and data-handling for vast information systems.

Lockheed Martin works with government agencies worldwide to build systems that manage large quantities of information. The corporation's systems integration for the U.S. government, beyond the Department of Defense, involves customers as diverse as the FBI, Postal Service, General Accounting Office, Social Security Administration, Internal Revenue Service, Immigration and Naturalization Service, Patent and Trademark Office, Environmental Protection Agency, Fannie Mae, Census Bureau, and Federal Aviation Administration (FAA).

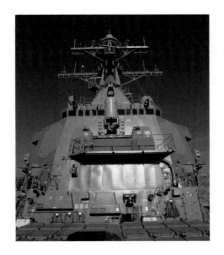

For the U.S. Census Bureau, Lockheed Martin systems are involved in processing the 120 million forms of Census 2000. Its Data Capture System (DCS) 2000 electronically reads some 1.5 billion pages of handwritten census returns and processes data for subsequent analysis. How fast? In 1890, U.S. Census data were compiled using a punch-card tabulating machine for the first time, and processing time dropped from nine years to seven years. Today, Lockheed Martin and its U.S. Census Bureau customer will deliver the Census 2000 data to the U.S. President's desk in just nine months.

OPPOSITE PAGE: THE F-22 RAPTOR IS LOCKHEED MARTIN'S NEXT-GENERATION COMBAT AIRCRAFT, COMBINING STEALTH, INTEGRATED AVIONICS, AND "SUPERCRUISE." · ABOVE: THE HERCULES C-130J AIRLIFTER COMBINES PROVEN DESIGN WITH ADVANCED COCKPIT AND NAVIGATION TECHNOLOGIES, AND LIGHTWEIGHT, HIGH-STRENGTH MATERIALS. · LEFT: THE AEGIS COMBAT SYSTEM IS A HIGH-TECHNOLOGY ELECTRONIC SHIELD FOR U.S. NAVY AND ALLIED SHIPS. AEGIS CAN SIMULTANEOUSLY ENGAGE THREATS FROM UNDER THE SEA, ON THE SURFACE, AND IN THE AIR.

Lockheed Martin works in partnership with the FAA and air traffic management customers worldwide to design and develop the most modern and efficient air traffic control operations, for safer and more efficient air traffic over busy skies.

PARTNERSHIP WITH NASA

Lockheed Martin has a long history of supporting America's space program and the NASA customer, as well as working with international space programs, such as the International Space Station. Space Shuttle operations is the job of United Space Alliance (USA), a joint venture established in 1996 between Lockheed Martin and The Boeing Company. Since the first shuttle flight in 1981, Lockheed Martin has supplied NASA with the external fuel tank for the Orbiter.

NASA's partnership with Lockheed Martin does not end with the shuttle program. Lockheed Martin Technology Services leads a team to consolidate mission and data services operations—the Consolidated Space Operations Contract (CSOC)—at five of NASA's major centers. With NASA, the Lockheed Martin team will move space operations to a commercially based structure and increase use by commercial customers. By reducing the cost of space operations, the team will save NASA funding that can be used for space and Earth science programs, as well as new research initiatives. Lockheed Martin's full partnership with NASA on the Hubble Space Telescope includes repair and service missions, along with planetary exploration.

For commercial, civil, and defense customers, Lockheed Martin provides launch vehicles including Athena for smaller payloads; Atlas and Proton for commercial payloads; and Titan for larger Department of Defense payloads. Launch services for Atlas and Proton are marketed through the International Launch Services (ILS) joint venture formed in 1995. The most advanced Atlas, the Atlas V, is being designed with the new Common Core Booster stage the company is developing. The goal: a more efficient, more powerful, lower-cost family of launchers that will be used to competitively support the commercial and U.S. government market for space launch services. The Common Core Booster will be powered by the

RIGHT: LOCKHEED MARTIN WORKS IN PARTNERSHIP WITH THE FEDERAL AVIATION ADMINISTRATION (FAA) AND AIR TRAFFIC MANAGEMENT CUSTOMERS WORLDWIDE TO DESIGN AND DEVELOP THE MOST MODERN AND EFFICIENT AIR TRAFFIC CONTROL OPERATIONS, FOR SAFER AND MORE EFFICIENT AIR TRAFFIC OVER BUSY SKIES. • OPPOSITE PAGE, TOP: THE ATLAS III LAUNCH IN SPRING 2000 IS AN EXAMPLE OF THE LAUNCH VEHICLES AND SERVICES PROVIDED BY LOCKHEED MARTIN FOR COMMERCIAL, CIVIL, AND DEFENSE CUSTOMERS. • OPPOSITE PAGE, BOTTOM: GLENN L. MARTIN, SHOWN HERE IN 1909, AND ALLAN AND MALCOLM LOUGHEAD, PHOTOGRAPHED IN 1913, WERE PIONEERS IN THE AEROSPACE RESEARCH AND INNOVATION THAT BECAME LOCKHEED MARTIN.

new Russian RD-180 engine. The RD-180 engine and a new Centaur upper stage were flight-proven on the Atlas III that was successfully launched on May 24, 2000.

Software Excellence

Lockheed Martin is a major developer of software and software-intensive systems. The company's foundation in advanced technology nourishes a corporate emphasis on innovation, a commitment backed by a $1 billion research budget. It also means the company can attract and retain skilled, imaginative scientists and engineers. In this regard, Lockheed Martin launched its Employer of Choice Initiative, an effort to continually assess and respond to the changing business environment.

Lockheed Martin also has a strong commitment to continual learning—about customers, technology, market dynamics, and emerging needs. The corporation offers employees the tools, information, and support to meet the next technical or business challenge. Programs include on-line and other self-study courses, leadership development, tuition reimbursement, and on-the-job training and mentoring.

Lockheed Martin keeps abreast of progressive trends in work plans that attract talented people—flexible hours, telecommuting, and other family-friendly practices. Its LifeWorks program offers consulting and referral services to help employees deal with the issues confronting working parents and caregivers responsible for older relatives. Its LMPeople Project, integrating payroll, benefits, and human resources practices, is designed to help retain talented employees by enabling them to manage their careers through a self-service database on the company's intranet.

Committed to excellence and customer focus in a world that accelerates relentlessly, Lockheed Martin has built its reputation on innovation in science, in technology, and in business. Lockheed Martin people take pride in a great company's heritage. That pride is matched by the company's sustained commitment to technological leadership and to the relationships that turn the once unimaginable into reality.

RESERVE OFFICERS ASSOCIATION

THE RESERVE OFFICERS ASSOCIATION OF THE UNITED STATES IS THE ONLY PROFESSIONAL MILITARY ASSOCIATION REPRESENTING ALL COMMISSIONED OFFICERS, ACTIVE AND RESERVE, FORMER AND RETIRED, OF THE SEVEN U.S. UNIFORMED SERVICES.

The Reserve Officers Association of the United States (ROA) has spent the last 80 years working to support and promote sound U.S. military policy and a secure nation.

Established in 1922 on the recommendation of World War I General of the Armies, John J. Pershing, ROA has worked tirelessly over the years to support, promote, and defend the rights of all its members, who are the front line of the nation's security.

ROA's body of members worldwide consists of nearly 78,000 officers of the U.S. Army, Navy, Air Force, Marine Corps, Coast Guard, Public Health Service, and National Oceanic and Atmospheric Administration. ROA is the only professional organization in the world of active, reserve, retired, and formerly federally commissioned officers and warrant officers from all branches of the nation's uniformed services.

Its Washington, D.C.–based professional staff works with Congress and Pentagon leaders, while its members work in their congressional districts across the nation. ROA has achieved a remarkable record of assuring that a fair share of the federal budget is earmarked for the nation's defense, even during periods when isolationist or disarmament tendencies in U.S. society threatened to degrade the nation's military strength.

The work of the ROA does not end with its members or the uniformed services. In line with its congressional charter, ROA educates the public on matters affecting global stability and national security. Through its Defense Education Forum (DEF), ROA provides unique leadership workshops for Fortune 500 firms. The DEF has established a reputation as a broker providing access to acknowledged authorities in the field of values-based leadership and strategic decision making.

OF THE UNITED STATES

ROA's efforts to obtain fair and equitable benefits for active and retired members of the uniformed services have been equally impressive. Among other things, the organization has been directly responsible for, or played a key role in securing from Congress, such gains as pay, medical, retirement, education, and survivor benefits for military Reserve members; as well as prohibitions against employment discrimination. In addition, ROA addresses concerns of all Americans on such issues as health care, taxes, and entitlements.

The organization offers its members networking opportunities, including semiannual conventions and regular local chapter and statewide meetings. Through its monthly members-only publication, *The Officer* magazine, and its weekly E-mail service, ROA provides updates on issues affecting national defense and the military Reserves and National Guard.

Although the Reserve Officers Association has worked closely with Congress from the time of its inception, its relationship to the nation's top legislative body was firmly established when, in 1950, Congress passed, and President Harry Truman signed into law, legislation granting ROA a congressional charter. The charter formally charges the organization with the mission of "supporting a military policy for the United States that will provide adequate national security and promote the development and execution thereof." Since 1968, ROA has conducted its business through national headquarters in the Minuteman Memorial Building in Washington, D.C. This building, dedicated to "the citizen-soldiers, -sailors, -Marines, -airmen, and -Coast Guardsmen who have given their lives in service to their country," is directly across the street from the U.S. Capitol.

ROA is represented by departments in each of the 50 states and the District of Columbia, as well as in Europe, Latin America, the Far East, and Puerto Rico. Worldwide, the organization has more than 500 chapters.

The strength of any organization is based upon the numbers of its members, so ROA is constantly seeking to add to its ranks, to increase its voice in Congress. For additional information about the organization, and for those eligible to obtain a membership application, visit the ROA Web site at www.roa.org.

OPPOSITE PAGE: AS PART OF HIS INITIATIVE TO COMBINE INTO ONE ORGANIZATION THE REGULAR ARMY, THE NATIONAL GUARD, AND THE PERMANENT RESERVES, GENERAL JOHN J. "BLACKJACK" PERSHING, WITH SEVERAL OTHER ARMY RESERVE OFFICERS, FOUNDED THE RESERVE OFFICERS ASSOCIATION (ROA) IN 1922. SINCE THEN, ROA HAS EXPANDED TO INCLUDE THE COMMISSIONED CORPS OF ALL SEVEN UNIFORMED SERVICES. · ABOVE: THE ROA HEADQUARTERS IS LOCATED IN THE MINUTEMAN MEMORIAL BUILDING, DIRECTLY ACROSS THE STREET FROM THE U.S. CAPITOL, ALLOWING ITS LOBBYISTS UNPARALLELED ACCESS TO THE NATION'S ELECTED REPRESENTATIVES. THE BUILDING, DEDICATED ON FEBRUARY 27, 1968, STANDS AS A MONUMENT ON CAPITOL HILL TO THE MEN AND WOMEN OF THE RESERVE COMPONENT. · LEFT: THE MINUTEMAN IS THE SYMBOL OF THE CITIZEN-SOLDIER, REPRESENTING ALL THE COMPONENTS OF THE RESERVE FORCES. IT IS THE IMAGE OF THE PATRIOT WHO LEAVES HIS OR HER FAMILY, HOME, AND JOB TO ANSWER THE CALL TO DEFEND THE COUNTRY IN TIME OF NEED. THE SYMBOL IS AS MEANINGFUL TODAY AS IT WAS 225 YEARS AGO.

WIRED TO THE FUTURE

COMPUTERS & INFORMATION TECHNOLOGY

THE 20TH CENTURY BEGAN WITH THE VIEW THAT THE RECENTLY INVENTED TELEPHONE WAS LITTLE MORE THAN AN EXTRAVAGANCE FOR THE WEALTHY. IT ENDED WITH THE CONVICTION THAT ELECTRONIC COMMUNICATION WOULD DEFINE AMERICA'S CULTURE AND CIVILIZATION IN SOMETHING CALLED 'THE INFORMATION AGE.'

IN TOUCH WITH THE WORLD

Alexander Graham Bell's invention of the telephone initially had its doubters and cynics. Mark Twain, for example, dismissed the new contraption with this legendary put-down: "If Bell had invented a muffler or gag, he would have done a real service." Others reacted with fear and superstition; they were afraid to talk to a disembodied voice and worried they would be electrocuted. Many saw the phone as a Gilded Age toy for the upper crust. Indeed, the cost of leasing a phone was prohibitively high for all but the wealthiest Americans.

The early notion that the telephone would remain an extravagance for a small segment of society was proved wrong as more and more Americans became accustomed to using it and recognized its value. In 1878, two years after Bell filed his patent, one was even installed at the White House, although it was only when Herbert Hoover took office, in 1929, that a telephone landed on the president's desk. By 1880, the first public pay telephone station had been established, and by 1892, phone lines linked New York and Chicago. There were 2.1 million telephones in the United States by 1902; that figure had shot up to 10 million at the start of World War I. The first transcontinental telephone call was placed by Bell and his former assistant, Thomas Watson, in 1915; to mark the occasion, Bell repeated their famous first telephone conversation of years before, saying, "Watson, come here, I want you." In 1927, the first overseas call was placed.

Over the years, many attempts were made to improve the quality of telephone calls. One such effort would lead to one of the greatest discoveries of modern times—and win its researchers a Nobel Prize. In the 1930s at Bell Laboratories in New Jersey, Karl Jansky was researching ways to reduce the noise produced from static on overseas telephone service. Jansky found that when he focused his radio antenna at the center of the Milky Way the noise increased. He published his findings in 1938, but the significance of his discovery would not be realized for nearly 30 years. In 1965, Bell Labs' Arno Penzias and Robert Wilson, who had been conducting radio astronomy experiments with an ultrasensitive antenna—and who experienced the same problems Jansky had with static—deducted that the static had nothing to do with the quality of the antenna. The sound came from background radiation, remnants of the explosion that began the universe. It was the most conclusive evidence to date of the Big Bang. Penzias and Wilson won the Nobel Prize in 1978 for putting the pieces together.

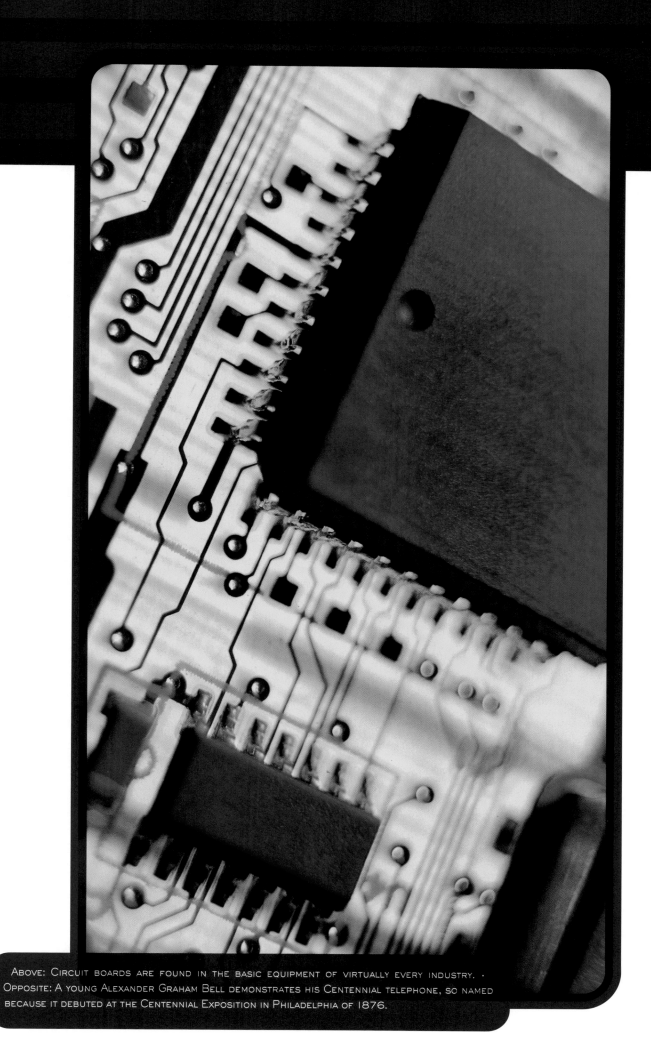

ABOVE: CIRCUIT BOARDS ARE FOUND IN THE BASIC EQUIPMENT OF VIRTUALLY EVERY INDUSTRY. ·
OPPOSITE: A YOUNG ALEXANDER GRAHAM BELL DEMONSTRATES HIS CENTENNIAL TELEPHONE, SO NAMED
BECAUSE IT DEBUTED AT THE CENTENNIAL EXPOSITION IN PHILADELPHIA OF 1876.

TELECOM ENTERS THE SPACE AGE

How did the clunky, plain, black rotary phone become the ubiquitous, pocket-sized, portable wireless phone of today? It started with the space race.

The launching of *Sputnik* in 1957 spurred the U.S. government and American companies to develop satellites and use them for communications systems. In 1965, the *Early Bird* satellite provided 10 times the capacity of submarine phone cables at one-tenth the cost. This price differential remained until the late 1970s, when AT&T created hair-thin, supertransparent, ultrastrong glass fibers. Fiber optics carry light impulses, as opposed to electric impulses, and can carry 65,000 times the information that copper wires can. Sprint completed the first nation-wide, 100 percent digital fiber-optic net-work in 1987. In 1989, the first transatlantic fiber optic–line phone call was made.

Today, satellites are used primarily for broadcasting, and fiber-optic and submarine cables carry telephone calls. Fiber optics are being increasingly used in local networks and will one day allow even the largest files to be transmitted quickly and easily.

Just as important as the creation of fiber optics and higher-capacity cables was the development of the portable phone system. The first cellular telephone system divided wireless communications into "cells," enabling telephones to be linked by microwave frequencies to base stations that connected the user to a conventional telephone network. The first system began operation in Japan in 1979; the first U.S. system began in Chicago in 1983. A decade ago, there were just 2.1 million cellular telephone subscribers. Today, there are 86 million American users and about 200 million worldwide.

Meanwhile, companies like Motorola are developing personal communications systems (PCS) that will provide global phone service via satellite. Not only does PCS revolutionize wireless capacity, it also allows e-mail, caller ID, paging, and a host of other services, as well as better sound and greater security from wireless eavesdroppers.

DAWN OF THE COMPUTER AGE

The incredible advances in telephony owe much to the invention of the computer. Throughout the 20th century, the developing technology for one industry was adapted to serve the needs of the other, and vice versa, and thus both industries fueled each others' growth.

Like the telephone, the computer had humble beginnings. In 1896, a German immigrant and Census Bureau statistician named Herman Hollerith started the Tabulating Machine Company in Washington, D.C., whose main product was a punch card tabulating machine that Hollerith had built for the 1890 census. In 1911, Hollerith's company merged with two others to become the Computing-Tabulating-Recording Co., which manufactured everything from commercial scales to industrial time recorders to meat and cheese slicers. A new general manager, Thomas Watson, came on board in 1914 and by 1924 had expanded the operations to other countries and renamed the company International Business Machines, or IBM.

Throughout the 1920s and 1930s, scientists and engineers considered how they could apply the new telephone technology to creating new computing machines. In 1927, an MIT scientist named Vannevar Bush created an analog computer that was able to solve simple equations. This was the basis of the Differential Analyzer, which Bush introduced three years later. A larger, more complex version than the analog computer, it weighed 100 tons, used 2,000 vacuum tubes, thousands of relays (an early form of digital switch), 150 motors, and 200 miles of wire. The Differential Analyzer was driven by electric motors but was internally mechanical, although later it was given electromechanical gears and used paper tapes to carry instructions.

Almost at the same time, the digital era was dawning. Claude Shannon published his watershed MIT master's thesis in 1938, which stated that Boolean algebra, invented in the 1850s by the mathematician George Boole, could be used to represent the functions of switches in electronic circuits. Electronics engineers could then use Boolean algebra to design digital electronic circuits.

of the first digital computer, the IBM automatic sequence-controlled calculator, or simply the Harvard Mark I, named for the university affiliated with the project. The Mark I, which was not finished until 1944, had 750,000 components. It was 50 feet long and eight feet tall and weighed five tons. The Mark I took less than a second to solve an addition problem but needed six seconds for multiplication and 12 for division, making it slower than any of today's cheap pocket calculators.

The Mark I and other primitive digital machines were merely prologue for the first

weighed 30 tons; contained 7,000 resistors, 10,000 capacitors, 6,000 switches, and 18,000 vacuum tubes; and needed 150 kilowatts of power—enough to power a small town. Having no internal source of memory, ENIAC had to be physically programmed with switches and dials. In order to correct this problem, ENIAC's fathers, John Mauchly and J. Presper Eckert Jr., soon began another project: the Electronic Discrete Variable Automatic Computer, or EDVAC, which contained stored programming. All future digital computers would be based upon EDVAC's central concept. The

BELOW: ARNOLD PENZIAS (LEFT) AND ROBERT WILSON STAND BEFORE THE ANTENNA THEY USED AT BELL LABS IN NEW JERSEY IN 1965 TO DETECT THE STATIC THAT LED TO THE CONFIRMATION OF THE BIG BANG THEORY. FOR THEIR DISCOVERY, THE TWO MEN SHARED THE NOBEL PRIZE FOR PHYSICS IN 1978. · OPPOSITE: ROBERT NOYCE, COINVENTOR OF THE INTEGRATED CIRCUIT AND FOUNDER OF INTEL, RECEIVES THE NATIONAL MEDAL OF TECHNOLOGY IN 1987 FROM PRESIDENT RONALD REAGAN AS VICE PRESIDENT GEORGE BUSH LOOKS ON.

If this were Shannon's only contribution to technology history it would be enough. However, a decade later he published another paper entitled "The Mathematical Theory of Communications," which showed how to make efficient, error-free transmission over noisy channels and made digital system development possible. Without this "information theory" the World Wide Web simply would not have been possible.

In 1940, many still believed in the possibilities of analog computing, but a scientist at Bell Labs changed that. George Robert Stibitz had built a digital machine in 1937 that evolved into a Complex Number Calculator two years later. This project, which he constructed with S. B. Williams, also of Bell Labs, was one of the first digital computers. It contained 450 telephone relays and 10 crossbar switches and could do simple arithmetic.

In 1939, Howard Aiken, an electrical engineer and physicist, began development

general-purpose electronic computer, the Electronic Numerical Integrator and Computer (ENIAC), developed at the University of Pennsylvania from 1943 through 1946. ENIAC was 10 feet tall; took up 1,000 square feet of floor space;

idea was refined and later published by the scientist Johann "John" von Neumann, who laid down the three main rules of computing: a stored program computer must contain memory; it must have a calculating unit; and it must include a control unit to help

interpret instruction. The first commercially available computer, the Universal Automatic Computer (UNIVAC I), was based on the EDVAC design. Built by Remington Rand, later a part of the Unisys Corporation, it was delivered to the U.S. Census Bureau in 1951.

The advances that occurred during the 1940s—due in no small part to World War II research—were stunning. At the same time, the marvelous machines that were developed and refined during this period were considered too large and impractical for all but institutional uses such as scientific calculations and data processing. Howard Aiken, of Mark I fame, predicted in 1947 that only six electronic digital computers would be required to satisfy the entire country's computing needs—understandably so since computers took up an enormous amount of space and were noisy and unwieldy. Who would want one?

Many companies, it turned out, because computers provided businesses with services they hadn't realized they could use. One of the earliest examples of the merging of telecommunications and information technology was AT&T's Direct Distance Dialing service, introduced in 1951. This uniform service interconnected millions of users and required thousands of switching centers. AT&T needed a new generation of switching systems that could think for themselves, remember a nationwide numbering system, and bill and process millions of transactions. By 1965, nine out of 10 Americans were using Direct Dialing, which made long-distance calls faster and less expensive. Thus ended two generations of operators intoning, "Number, please."

In 1952, IBM introduced its vacuum tube–based 701 model, which took the computer from government and research work to billing, payroll, and inventory control. But vacuum tubes added bulk and weight to computers—and they were slow. An alternative had to be found. It came in the form of the tiny point contact germanium transistor, created by Bell Lab researchers William Shockley, William Brattain, and John Bardeen in 1947. All three would share the Nobel Prize for physics in 1956.

By 1959, transistors, which were now being made of silicon, had replaced vacuum tubes. That year, IBM introduced the transistor-equipped IBM 7090, which could perform 229,000 calculations per second. That was so impressive that the U.S. Air Force used the 7090 for the Ballistic Missile Early Warning System. By 1964, American Airlines had implemented this new technology into its SABRE reservations system using two 7090 mainframes to link sales desks in 65 cities. And the transistor allowed AT&T to implement inexpensively the touch-tone dialing system, which had first been installed in 1941 but was too costly to become widespread.

As computers became more commercially viable, companies began to improve and refine these enormous machines. In 1957, IBM developed the first computer disk storage system, which could retrieve data in less than a second; in 1970, the company one-upped itself by introducing the first floppy disk. And in 1964, Big Blue introduced System 360, which allowed the use of interchangeable software and peripherals. This meant that instead of buying new

AT THE UNIVERSITY OF PENNSYLVANIA, J. PRESPER ECKERT JR. DEMONSTRATES THE ENIAC, THE FIRST GENERAL-PURPOSE ELECTRONIC COMPUTER. THE 1,500-SQUARE-FOOT DEVICE COULD PERFORM ADDITION PROBLEMS AT THE THEN-ASTOUNDING RATE OF 5,000 PER SECOND. TODAY'S COMPUTERS CAN PERFORM 100 MILLION SUCH PROBLEMS PER SECOND.

computers, users could upgrade by simply installing new hardware.

And the computer itself enabled businesses to clock dramatic performance gains. The 1960s were an era of "time sharing" of computers, which hooked up several users to mainframes, allowing them to feel like it was "their" computer. Later, the teleprinters that were hooked up to the computer were supplanted by keyboards and individual video displays, but it wasn't until 1982, with the founding of Sun Microsystems, that the first true workstation was introduced.

The PC Revolution

In 1975, an IBM mainframe that could perform 10 million instructions in a second cost $10 million. Two decades later, a computer video game capable of performing 500 trillion instructions per second was available for $50. Computer gamers—and everybody else—can thank the integrated circuit for this incredible advance in speed, size, and efficiency—not to mention affordability.

The pressures of World War II and the tensions of the 1950s space race spurred research into making computers faster and smaller. Semiconductor materials seemed a good bet: they had potential as amplifiers and switches and were therefore a good replacement for vacuum tubes. In 1958, Jack Kilby at Texas Instruments (TI) put entire multiple circuits on a single piece of semiconductor—including transistors, resistors, capacitors, and diodes—and created the greatest invention since the transistor: the integrated circuit. In 1961, Robert Noyce of Fairchild Semiconductor and TI introduced the first commercial planar integrated circuits that could perform simple logic. This was the beginning of the mass production of integrated circuits. Soon, improvements were added, like the epitaxy fabrication process that could grow silicon films on a silicon wafer, and transistors worked faster than ever before. By the end of the 1960s, companies could cram several thousand transistors on a single integrated circuit.

Despite all these improvements, computers were still out of the reach of the average American. After all, there were only about 30,000 computers in the world, and most of them were room-size mainframes that were programmed with punch cards. But there was one device that enabled individuals to do mathematical problems quickly and was small enough to fit on a desk: the

calculator. Its popularity would lead to an even greater discovery, one that would begin a new era in computer technology.

Interested in developing a line of calculators, the Japanese firm Busicom met with a brand-new American company, Intel, founded by former employees of Fairchild Semiconductor Robert Noyce, Gordon Moore, and Andy Grove. Busicom wanted Intel to develop 12 integrated circuits for the calculator. In 1971, Ted Hoff, one of Intel's engineers, decided to make one chip function as 12—and the microprocessor was born. Busicom—and even Intel—did not see any immediate use for this chip, but

ABOVE: PAUL ALLEN (LEFT) AND BILL GATES, SEEN HERE IN 1984, FOUNDED MICRO-SOFT (THE HYPHEN WAS LATER DROPPED) IN ALBUQUERQUE, NEW MEXICO, IN 1975 TO SELL THE BASIC COMPUTER LANGUAGE PROGRAM THEY HAD WRITTEN FOR THE ALTAIR MICROPROCESSOR. IN 1979, GATES MOVED THE COMPANY TO HIS HOME TOWN OF SEATTLE. · OPPOSITE: JOHN BARDEEN, WILLIAM SHOCKLEY, AND WALTER BRAITTAIN (LEFT TO RIGHT) INVENTED THE TRANSISTOR IN 1947. FOR THEIR EFFORTS, THEY WERE AWARDED THE NOBEL PRIZE FOR PHYSICS IN 1956.

having bought the rights to it from Busicom, Intel went ahead and released the 4004 chip anyway. It had as much computing power as ENIAC but was only 1/8 inch wide and 1/6 inch long and contained 2,300 transistors. The microprocessor made programmable intelligence cheap enough so that chips could be put into almost anything. The 4004 and its successor chip, the 8008, enabled the construction of affordable and general-purpose computers.

In 1974, Ed Roberts, head of an Albuquerque-based calculator company called MITS, used another of Intel's chips, the 8080, along with a build-it-yourself computer kit he had seen advertised in *Popular Mechanics* magazine to create the Altair 8800, the world's first personal computer. Supposedly named for a planet on the television show *Star Trek*, the Altair contained 256 bytes of random access memory and had to be programmed with a switch panel.

When the Altair 8800 appeared in the January 1, 1975, issue of *Popular Electronics*, it sparked the imaginations of a Honeywell employee named Paul Allen and his friend, Bill Gates. In one month, they created BASIC, the first computer language program written for a computer program, and quickly licensed it to MITS. Allen was hired as software director; Gates was still at Harvard. Thanks to BASIC, MITS sold 2,000 Altairs that year. Later that same year, Gates and Allen formed a company called Micro-Soft, the first created for the sole purpose of producing computer software.

Meanwhile, in 1976, while everyone was celebrating the bicentennial of the American Revolution, another revolution was brewing. Steve Wozniak and Steve Jobs, who had been fired from MITS, started a computer company, Apple, on April Fools' Day. Within a year it would offer the

first affordable and user-friendly personal computer (PC), the Apple II. For $1,300, a buyer would get 16 kilobytes of ROM, four kilobytes of RAM, a keyboard, and a display.

The Apple II kicked off a PC frenzy with new machines being introduced at lower prices with more extras, like the Commodore PET and the Tandy/Radio Shack TRS-80, both introduced in 1977. In 1981, IBM launched its first personal computer, which contained a microprocessor chip from Intel and a new disk operating system, MS-DOS, created by Microsoft. A year later, Sun Microsystems introduced the workstation. The industry was here to stay, with more amazing developments yet to come.

THE INTERNET PUTS THE WORLD ON-LINE

As computer technology developed, so, too, did advances in telecommunications, setting the stage for the Internet age.

During the 1950s and 1960s, as more and more satellites orbited the earth, scientists at the Department of Defense considered the grim question of how to ensure communications during a nuclear attack. In 1969, the U.S. Defense Advanced Research Projects Agency (DARPA) created the ARPANET, a decentralized, wide-area computer network that ensured that even if one part of the system were destroyed by a nuclear strike, messages would still be able to get through. It worked by splitting information into little packets, which then were assembled at the other end. During the 1970s, Vinton Cerf, a mathematician and scientist, and Robert Kahn, an engineer, created a way for ARPANET to interconnect with other independent networks, and the Internet was born.

Over the years, with varying degrees of government and private involvement, the Internet spread. Companies like IBM used the new technology in the mid-1980s to create intranets, which allowed companies to create private and secure networks for their employees. In 1985, Quantum Computer Services launched the first on-line service, Q-Link, on Commodore business machines. Soon, the company created joint ventures with computer companies like Tandy and Apple. By 1993, Commodore, which changed its name to America Online (AOL) in 1991, had half a million members. By the end of 1999, AOL had 20 million members and a movie named for its distinctive mail notification *(You've Got Mail)* and was powerful enough to make an offer to buy the megaconglomerate Time-Warner to provide it with enough content to satisfy all its customers.

AOL was a key reason for the spread of the Internet, but there were others. In 1989, a British scientist, Tim Berners-Lee, created Hypertext Markup Language, or HTML, and coined the term "World Wide Web." HTML let coders embed links to other pages and was necessary to create the easy-use interfaces that nonprogrammers depend upon today. With the introduction of the first browser, Mosaic, in 1993, the stage was set for widespread commercial use of the Internet.

Today, there are more than 242 million people on-line worldwide. Though e-commerce is not a serious threat to brick-and-mortar stores, 68 million Internet users purchased something on-line in 2000, spending $25.8 billion in the United States alone. Yet perhaps the biggest beneficiaries of the Internet are businesses, which, as of 1993, had done $43 billion worth of business over the Internet.

Meanwhile, innovative companies like Dell and Gateway continue to power the on-line revolution. Along with traditional mainstays like IBM, Apple, Toshiba, Compaq, and Sony, they are putting low-cost, high-quality, and user-friendly desktops, laptops, and video games in the hands of hundreds of millions of wired consumers around the globe.

In the coming decades, the integration of the Internet into people's daily lives will continue. "Smart" houses will monitor their own temperature and even figure out electronically what is in the refrigerator for dinner. General Motors is introducing Internet accessibility on automobiles so that among other things people don't have to ask for directions. And the venerable telephone may soon go on-line as well.

Around the world, these marvelous new communications technologies bring challenges and opportunities. While half of the people who live outside of the United States have never even used a telephone, technology has advanced to such a point that many of the areas they live in can leapfrog the installation of miles of telephone wires and go directly to wireless communications.

American companies—especially technology companies—have created an unstoppable juggernaut. They have fueled the longest economic expansion in this country's history, boosted productivity to unimaginable levels, and changed the way the world shops, socializes, and gets information. And it's due in large part to the ingenuity and hard work of America's businesses and free enterprise system.

ABOVE: MAC ENTHUSIASTS SELF-REGISTER VIA IMAC COMPUTERS AT THE SEMIANNUAL MACWORLD EXPO AT THE JACOB JAVITS CONVENTION CENTER IN NEW YORK IN JULY 1999. · OPPOSITE: APPLE COMPUTERS FOUNDERS STEVE JOBS (LEFT) AND STEVE WOZNIAK FLANK THEN-CEO JOHN SCULLEY AT A CONFERENCE IN SAN FRANCISCO IN 1984 TO INTRODUCE THE APPLE IIc.

profiles
Computers &
Information Technology

ONTARIO CORPORATION
A FAMILY OF TECHNOLOGY COMPANIES

AS A FAMILY OF TECHNOLOGY COMPANIES, ONTARIO CORPORATION IS COMPOSED OF ONTARIO SYSTEMS, SHERRY LABORATORIES, AND THE CDS GROUP, AS PROFILED IN THE FOLLOWING PAGES.

Ontario Corporation, headquartered in Muncie, Indiana, is a diversified corporation operating in three distinct industries, providing innovative computer-based products and services, contract manufacturing services, and proven independent third-party laboratory testing.

As an employee stock ownership company for more than 30 years, Ontario Corporation believes the ultimate credit for its success can be attributed to its employees, rich in talent and determination and dedicated to the delivery of superior products and services to their growing customer base. Led by co-founder and chairman, Van P. Smith, and vice chairman, president, and CEO, Kelly N. Stanley, Ontario Corporation is unique in being the first of only two companies to produce two U.S. Chamber of Commerce chairmen. Stanley completed his term in June 2001; Smith served as chairman in 1984.

ONTARIO CORPORATION'S VICE CHAIRMAN, PRESIDENT, AND CEO, KELLY N. STANLEY, LED THE WORLD'S LARGEST BUSINESS FEDERATION, THE U.S. CHAMBER OF COMMERCE, AS ITS CHAIRMAN FOR THE 2000–2001 TERM.

Serving more than 4,000 customers from 19 locations throughout the United States and the United Kingdom, Ontario Corporation supports clients in the semiconductor, telecommunications, computer, consumer electronics, medical, biomedical, aerospace, automotive, petrochemical, pressure vessel and heat exchanger, environmental, and food product industries. Ontario Corporation will pursue strategic growth opportunities and promote technology advances for the benefit of its employees, shareholders, and customers, as it looks to the future with enthusiasm and anticipation.

For additional information, call Ontario Corporation at 765-747-9001; or visit the company's Web site at www.ontario.com.

ONTARIOCorporation
A Family of Technology Companies

ONTARIO SYSTEMS
AN ONTARIO CORPORATION COMPANY

Ontario Systems is a technology company committed to providing innovative, computer-based products and services to niche receivables management markets. Virtually any business that sells its goods or services on credit could benefit from tools developed by Ontario Systems to help manage their accounts receivable.

As a technology leader in the receivables management industry, thousands of businesses (including hospitals, banks, collection agencies, credit card processors, student loan originators, utility companies, leasing, and teleservices companies) use Ontario Systems' products and services to manage their accounts. The company helps them maintain relationships with their customers, train and manage their employees, and increase profits using the latest technology.

Founded in 1978 by Wilbur R. Davis and Ronald K. Fauquher, the company was incorporated in 1980 and became a subsidiary of Ontario Corporation in 1985.

Ontario Systems has created a family of products to help its customers manage accounts receivable more effectively. For credit grantors (first party) or collection agencies (third party), Ontario Systems provides a seamlessly integrated suite of products that prioritize and track accounts receivable.

ONTARIOSystems

An Ontario Corporation Company

This integrated approach gives Ontario Systems' customers control over both their database and telephony tool set, enables them to streamline operations, and ultimately increases productivity, performance, and profits.

As a market-leading provider of receivables management products, Ontario Systems is recognized throughout its industry for its leadership in technology and customer service.

For additional information, call Ontario Systems at 765-751-7000; or visit the company's Web site at www.ontariosystems.com.

OPPOSITE PAGE, TOP: ONTARIO CORPORATION HEADQUARTERS IS LOCATED IN MUNCIE, INDIANA. • OPPOSITE PAGE, LEFT: KELLY N. STANLEY, ONTARIO CORPORATION'S VICE CHAIRMAN, PRESIDENT, AND CEO, SERVED AS CHAIRMAN OF THE BOARD OF THE U.S. CHAMBER OF COMMERCE FOR ITS 2000–2001 TERM. • ABOVE: ONTARIO SYSTEMS DEVELOPS RECEIVABLES MANAGEMENT SOFTWARE AND SYSTEMS AT ITS MUNCIE, INDIANA, TECHNOLOGY CAMPUS. • LEFT: AMONG THE SERVICES THAT ONTARIO SYSTEMS MAKES AVAILABLE FOR ITS CLIENTS IS HANDS-ON IN-HOUSE TRAINING.

SHERRY LABORATORIES

AN ONTARIO CORPORATION COMPANY

Throughout the United States and in 24 foreign countries, leading manufacturers and agencies trust the proven credibility of Sherry Laboratories as the leader in third-party independent laboratory testing.

Founded in 1947 and acquired by Ontario Corporation in 1969, Sherry Laboratories is a recognized leader in aerospace certification testing.

Testing facilities are strategically placed nationwide to serve a total cross section of industrial and government compliance testing requirements. Sherry Laboratories' eight facilities conduct more than 700,000 tests annually and staff 200 scientists, engineers, and technicians.

Few laboratories around the world carry the wide range of professional and governmental accreditations that Sherry has earned, including those awarded by the American Association of Laboratory Accreditation, ISO/IEC Guide 25, the American Petroleum Institute, and certifications by virtually all jet engine manufacturers.

The total range of Sherry Laboratories' capabilities and accreditations provides customers with a single source for independent metallurgical, nonmetallic, polymer, environmental, microbiological, bioassay, and petroleum-related testing services.

Customer satisfaction and market demand continue to propel Sherry Laboratories toward its goal to become the world's premier full-service, high integrity laboratory.

For additional information, call Sherry Laboratories at 765-747-9000; or visit the company's Web site at www.sherrylabs.com.

SHERRYLaboratories

An Ontario Corporation Company

Testing Today—Protecting Tomorrow

CDS GROUP
AN ONTARIO CORPORATION COMPANY

The CDS Group is a contract manufacturing company serving high-tech equipment industries, including the semiconductor equipment, commercial aviation, medical equipment, and telecommunications markets.

The CDS Group manufactures and tests complex, integrated electromechanical assemblies, modules, and systems. A large variety of subassembly components and structures are manufactured and assembled within the CDS Group network of manufacturing facilities, whose diversified network has been acknowledged as a world-class supplier of components and assemblies within those industries served.

With eight locations throughout the United States and the United Kingdom, the CDS Group is owned by Ontario Corporation and represents approximately 500,000 square feet of manufacturing capacity.

CDSGroup
An Ontario Corporation Company

As a recognized world-class supplier of components and assemblies for the semiconductor equipment industry, the CDS Group will continue to expand its relationships with other high-tech, capital equipment companies.

For additional information, call CDS Group at 650-595-5946; or visit the company's Web site at www.ontario.com/cdsg.html.

CORE COMPETENCIES

- Turnkey System Manufacturing
- Engineering and Design Services
- Large Envelope Machining
- Supply Chain Management
- Precision Welded Frames
- Sheet Metal Fabrication
- Cables and Harnesses
- Vacuum Chambers

COMMITMENT TO EXCELLENCE

PHILANTHROPY & EDUCATION

AMERICA'S ECONOMIC SUCCESS, SPEARHEADED BY BUSINESS, HAS NOT ONLY PRODUCED A WIDELY SHARED PROSPERITY, IT HAS FOSTERED A STRONG COMMITMENT TO CHARITABLE GIVING AND A PASSION FOR EMPOWERING FUTURE GENERATIONS THROUGH UNSURPASSED EDUCATIONAL OPPORTUNITIES. THIS DEVOTION TO PHILANTHROPY AND EDUCATION

has given rise to two sectors of activity that due to their size, innovation, and influence earn them a rightful place alongside America's other great industries.

MAGNANIMOUS UNDERTAKINGS: PHILANTHROPY IN AMERICA

American business's incredible ability to create new jobs and opportunities is widely recognized and acknowledged to be the direct result of the free-market system. Across the land, from self-employed consultants working in home offices to the bustling corporate centers of the world's biggest conglomerates, private companies employ more than 150 million Americans.

But jobs alone, as important as they are, do not fully depict business's impact on the community. Organizations at every level of society, from Little League baseball to the Metropolitan Opera, receive donations from companies large and small. American companies contribute more than $11 billion annually, and corporate foundations billions more, in charitable and educational pursuits. This is not a recent development. Indeed, today's wealthy high-tech entrepreneurs of the information age carry on a tradition established by some of the giants of the Industrial Revolution.

POWERFUL FORCES FOR GOOD: INDIVIDUAL AND CORPORATE FOUNDATIONS

John Davison Rockefeller. Andrew Carnegie. Henry Ford. These industrialists were called greedy and power hungry by some. Yet others revered them for their philanthropy and generosity. Many of America's most renowned educational, charitable, and medical institutions began with seed money from these individuals.

In 1863 at the age of 24, Rockefeller, a commission agent, entered the nascent oil business. Twenty years later, Rockefeller was the oil king. His Standard Oil Trust controlled 85 percent of all U.S. oil production and distribution and pioneered the development of the type of large-scale industrial organization that characterized much of 20th-century business.

Rockefeller's business acumen was matched by a strong sense of philanthropy. From his personal fortune and his own Rockefeller Foundation, he gave $500 million to causes large and small. He founded the University of Chicago in 1892, and in 1902 his foundation funded

ABOVE: A STUDENT USES AN INTERACTIVE PROGRAM TO SUPPLEMENT CLASSROOM INSTRUCTION. STUDIES BY THE U.S. DEPARTMENT OF EDUCATION SHOW THAT COMPUTER USE INCREASES LONG-TERM MEMORY AND SELF-ESTEEM. · OPPOSITE: LITTLE LEAGUE SLUGGERS EXHIBIT THE CAMARADERIE THAT COMES FROM PLAYING ON A TEAM. FOUNDED IN 1939, THE VOLUNTEER ORGANIZATION HAD NEARLY THREE MILLION PLAYERS IN 1999.

employees. Among Ford's numerous philanthropies was the Ford Foundation, which today ranks as the third largest in America, with an endowment of $12 billion.

The tradition of giving begun by America's early industrialists has developed into a powerful force for good. According to the Foundation Center, a group that monitors the nation's philanthropic sector, there are at least 49 foundations with assets of $1 billion or more. These foundations donate billions of dollars each year to education, social services, medical research, the arts, and other causes.

Leading the pack is the Bill and Melinda Gates Foundation, with an endowment of $15.5 billion. The Gates Foundation provides computers and technological training to public libraries in the United States and Canada, offers $1 billion worth of scholar-

ABOVE: PHILANTHROPIST AND INDUSTRIALIST ANDREW CARNEGIE, SEEN HERE IN 1906 AT HIS HOME IN NEW YORK, DONATED $333 MILLION TO A WIDE VARIETY OF CAUSES, INCLUDING $55 MILLION TO LIBRARIES ALONE. · OPPOSITE: CELEBRATING THE 57TH ANNIVERSARY OF THE UNITED NEGRO COLLEGE FUND IN 2001 ARE (LEFT TO RIGHT) MELINDA AND BILL GATES, EUNICE JOHNSON, AND WILLIAM GRAY III, THE ORGANIZATION'S PRESIDENT AND CEO.

a campaign to eradicate hookworm in the South, where the parasite had affected many citizens. He also established the Rockefeller Institute for Medical Research in New York City.

Rockefeller's progeny continued this philanthropic tradition, with John Davison Rockefeller Jr.'s funding of the restoration of Colonial Williamsburg, Virginia, and the donation of the site for the United Nations headquarters in New York City. J. D. Rockefeller III helped create New York's Lincoln Center for the Performing Arts and the United Negro College Fund.

A contemporary of Rockefeller senior, Andrew Carnegie began to build an empire of his own, the Carnegie Steel Company, in 1873. By the turn of the century, the company was producing about a quarter of the steel in the United States and had

interests in iron mines, ore, ships, and railroads. Carnegie retired in 1901 and spent the rest of his life establishing philanthropic organizations such as the Carnegie Endowment for International Peace and the Carnegie Corporation, educational institutions including the school now known as Carnegie-Mellon University, and more than 2,800 libraries.

Using Rockefeller oil and Carnegie steel, Henry Ford pioneered the American automobile industry. He also initiated the concept of paying workers five dollars for an eight-hour day, which doubled wages and reduced the work day by 90 minutes, and established a profit-sharing plan that eventually distributed $30 million annually among his

ships for academically talented but financially strapped minority students, and gives $750 million to the Global Fund for Children's Vaccines, among its many other good works.

Today, foundations sponsored by individual industrialists and large companies are commonplace. There are 28 corporate foundations with assets of $100 million or greater, contributing to a vast array of worthy projects.

In the early 1970s, for example, Control Data Corporation, a computer hardware manufacturer, created and launched Plato, a $900 million computer-based education system, as a direct result of its efforts to train a poor urban population in

Minneapolis. While government and businesses viewed the results positively, Control Data's founder, William Norris, was ahead of his time in trying to place computers in classrooms. Though Control Data is no longer around, Plato still is, albeit in a different form. Today, TRO Learning and Sylvan Learning Centers operate a joint venture using the program's basic skills courseware.

In 1941, the Westinghouse Electric Corporation began what is now the nation's oldest and most prestigious scholarship competition, the Westinghouse Science Talent Search. Open only to high school seniors, the Talent Search has provided hundreds of thousands of dollars every year in scholarships to 40 finalists. Five past winners of the search went on to become Nobel laureates. In 1998, Intel Corporation assumed sponsorship of the competition.

The World Food Prize was established in 1987 by Nobel laureate Norman Borlaug, widely credited with the Green Revolution in agricultural production in the 1960s. The prize is given every year to recognize outstanding individual achievement in improving the quality, quantity, or availability of food in the world. With the energy and resources of John Ruan, the trucking magnate, the World Food Prize has become one of the top international awards, recognizing advances in curbing hunger in poor countries everywhere.

In 1995, Exxon Corporation kicked off a $5 million campaign to help save its mascot, the tiger, from extinction. When the company merged in 1999 with Mobil Corporation, the new corporation, ExxonMobil, continued this effort along with Mobil's 30-year support of television's *Masterpiece Theater* and the Pegasus Prize for Literature. Through its corporation and its charitable foundation, the company also supported health and community efforts, and in 1998, contributed nearly $25 million to schools and educational programs.

Dow Chemical established several educational initiatives to strengthen science and mathematics training including the National Science Resources Center, created in 1985 and jointly operated by the Smithsonian Institution and the National Academy of Sciences; the Keystone Summer Initiatives Workshop, a school in the Rocky Mountains that teaches scientific principles to young people; and MATH-COUNTS, a national math coaching and competition program.

With the fall of the Soviet Union in 1991, the IBM Corporation was able to work with the Hermitage Museum in St. Petersburg,

Russia, to develop a digital library of high-resolution masterpieces. The end result of this project was to enable anyone in the world with Internet access to view the many treasures of this venerable museum.

Other gifts were designed to spark the imagination and foster the development of historic breakthroughs and new technologies. In the 1920s, for example, hotel owner Raymond Orteig offered $25,000 to the first person to cross the Atlantic from New York to Paris nonstop. It stimulated at least nine different attempts, culminating in the famous flight of Charles Lindbergh. In 1996, the X-Prize was established in St. Louis, Missouri, by a group of business leaders, astronauts, and other individuals interested in fostering the creation of reusable launch vehicles to carry passengers into space Since then, 20 teams have registered for the competition. The first team to create a successful reusable launch vehicle will receive the $10 million prize.

Besides donating on their own, many of America's largest corporations participate in a unique charity called AmeriCares, founded by industrialist Bob Macauley. Macauley made a name for himself in 1975 aiding Vietnamese orphans who were victims of a plane crash. In 1982, Pope John Paul II asked him if he could raise $50,000 worth of medicines and medical supplies for Poland. Macauley raised $3.2 million and AmeriCares was born. Today, it is one of the largest humanitarian relief agencies in the world. Approximately 1,000 corporations supply AmeriCares with medical equipment, drugs, nutritional supplements, and construction and other materials, some of which are surplus useable goods that would either go to waste or be destroyed. On its board of advisors are the heads of some of the nation's leading corporations.

Many corporations and businesses also contribute to society through membership in community associations. The Rotary Club is one of the most well-known of these associations. Established in 1905 by Chicago lawyer Paul Harris and three of his friends as a way to encourage humanitarian service, the Rotary Club promotes fellowship and charity by its business members. Today, the 1.2 million Rotarians around the world are involved in 29,000 clubs in 161 countries. Among its many activities, the Rotary Foundation fosters efforts to eradicate the polio virus around the world and provides study-abroad funds for high school students.

Corporations also serve their communities by providing training programs for their workers. According to the Bureau of Labor Statistics, 84.4 percent of employees at companies with more than 50 employees received formal training at some point during their employment; nearly 96 percent received informal training.

Sometimes, this formal training is in the form of a corporate university. For example, since 1961 more than 65,000 managers in McDonald's restaurants have graduated from the company's Hamburger University, the management-training center in Oak Brook, Illinois. McDonald's also runs

10 international training centers overseas including centers in England, Japan, and Germany. Motorola provides training and consulting to its employees, suppliers, and customers at Motorola University, which operates learning facilities at seven locations around the world.

BUSINESS STEPS UP TO THE PLATE: ENTREPRENEURSHIP AND TRAINING

With profound workforce shortages and the need for well-educated, technologically proficient workers, America's business community is taking steps to ensure that the nation has a viable workforce.

Its most ambitious effort yet, the Welfare-to-Work Partnership is a nonpartisan, national, and independent effort begun in 1996 by the UAL Corporation, Burger King, Monsanto, Sprint, and United Parcel Service. The Partnership is dedicated to moving people on public assistance to jobs in the private

sector by providing information, technical assistance, and support to businesses of all sizes, sectors, and industries.

Another example of local activism is the Work-Scholarship Connection established by Wegmans, a family-owned food retailer, in partnership with the Rochester (New York) City School District. The program supports 14- and 15-year-old high school students in need of special motivation and provides them with part-time jobs. Wegmans also offers a college scholarship as an incentive for students to complete the program. The first students to participate in the program graduated in 1990. Of the 13 graduates, 12 went on to college on the Wegmans scholarship.

The National Foundation for Teaching Entrepreneurship, or NFTE (pronounced "nifty"), was the brainchild of Steve Mariotti, a New York City businessman-turned-high-school-teacher who wanted to teach students academic and life skills

through a hands-on entrepreneurship and business ownership curriculum. Along with math, reading, and writing, NFTE teaches the basics of starting and operating a small business. By 1999, 28,000 students had participated in the NFTE program, more than half of whom were African American teenagers.

The desire for a good public image no doubt plays a part in motivating businesses to such philanthropic pursuits. Yet the legacy of giving—not just money but time and expertise—is so strong and vast that genuineness of the commitment cannot be questioned. During the 20th century and continuing to the present day, American business has succeeded in putting a human face on free enterprise.

ABOVE: STANFORD UNIVERSITY, IN PALO ALTO, CALIFORNIA, WELCOMES 1,600 FRESHMEN EACH YEAR. · OPPOSITE: FLOOD VICTIMS TAKE SHELTER AT A LOCAL AMERICAN RED CROSS. FOUNDED BY CLARA BARTON IN 1864, THE ORGANIZATION BOASTS 1.2 MILLION VOLUNTEERS.

THE KEY TO THE FUTURE: INVESTING IN EDUCATION

Americans approach few if any endeavors with the fervor and commitment they bring to education. In a democratic society devoid of caste and royalty and dedicated to equality of treatment, education is seen as the single most critical factor in breathing life into America's founding principles. Access to a good education, from kindergarten through graduate school, brings the nation's promise of equal opportunity to fruition.

From this fundamental American belief has risen the vast educational sector. Business has been front and center in its development, lending financial support as well as managerial and marketing know-how. More than idealism has motivated companies. It is the nation's educational institutions that equip students with the skills and work habits they need to be productive. In the knowledge economy of the information age, schools play a more critical role than ever before in determining the success of the economy and thus the nation. This helps explain why an astounding 55.8 percent of the population between the ages of 3 to 34 years—more than 55 million Americans—is enrolled full- or part-time in an educational institution.

In a sophisticated and technologically advanced society, access to and attendance at colleges, universities, and other institutions offering technical training are of vital importance. By the end of the 20th century, there were 4,070 such institutions certified to offer degrees at the associate level or higher. They not only boast an enrollment of at least 14.5 million students but also employ 2.75 million staff. Of particular importance to the business community are the more than 100,000 master's degrees in business awarded annually, supplying companies with the sophisticated managerial talent needed in the global economy.

Moreover, educational opportunities are now reaching a broader segment of society, including groups traditionally left behind. In 1960, for example, just 7.7 percent of American adults had completed four or more years of college. By 2000, that percentage had risen to nearly 25 percent. Women now outpace men in terms of college enrollment and in the number of degrees awarded at the associate, bachelor's, and master's levels. Whereas women earned just 3.9 percent of MBAs in 1970, that figure skyrocketed to 39 percent by 1996, and today women are at or near parity with men.

119

A Reputation for Excellence: The History of Higher Education

With its abundant educational opportunities, the United States attracts students from around the world seeking degrees from some of the world's best and most prestigious colleges and universities. The foundations of this reputation for excellence are older than the nation itself.

When the United States was still a collection of colonies, higher education was mainly intended to train theologians. Such was the original purpose of Harvard University, the nation's oldest institute of higher learning. Founded in 1636 in Cambridge, Massachusetts, it was named for John Harvard, an English clergyman who bequeathed the fledgling institution his library and half of his estate. Today, the university enrolls nearly 20,000 students and is reputed for its medical and business schools.

ABOVE: HARVARD'S APPLETON CHAPEL SHINES ON A WINTER'S DAY. · OPPOSITE: COLLEGE GRADS CELEBRATE THEIR ACHIEVEMENT. IN 1998, NEARLY TWO MILLION BACHELOR'S DEGREES WERE AWARDED.

The second oldest institute of higher learning in the United States was chartered by King William III and Queen Mary II in Williamsburg in 1693 and became a state-supported school in 1906. The honor society Phi Beta Kappa was founded on the campus in 1776. Today, there are 7,500 students enrolled at the College of William and Mary, named the best small public university in the nation by *U.S. News and World Report* in 2001.

Puritanism and the classics were the values upon which Yale University's original curriculum was based. Founded as the Collegiate School in 1701 in Killingworth, the university moved to its present location on 290 acres in New Haven, Connecticut, in 1716 and was renamed Yale College two years later. Today, Yale consists of a college,

graduate school, and 10 professional schools educating more than 11,000 students.

Established "for the Education of Youth in the Learned Languages and in the Liberal Arts and Sciences," as its charter states, the College of New Jersey opened in Elizabeth in 1746. A decade later, the campus was moved to the town of Princeton, and the school's name was changed to that of the town. Princeton University actually served as the capital of the United States for the several months that General Washington was encamped there in 1777 during the Revolutionary War. Today, Princeton has an enrollment of 4,600 undergraduates and 1,760 graduates.

The nation's first secular institution of higher education was the University of

Pennsylvania, founded in 1749 by Benjamin Franklin. More than 100 years later, in 1881, Joseph Wharton created the nation's first business school by endowing the Wharton School of Finance and Commerce at the University of Pennsylvania with $100,000.

Meanwhile, state governments became involved in education. The first state university, the University of North Carolina, was founded in 1795. In 1862, Congress passed the Merrill Act, which gave states federal land on which to establish colleges with programs offering agriculture, engineering, and military training. The Hatch Act, passed in 1887, expanded the mandate of land-grant schools to include research. Some of today's most venerable institutions of higher education, ranging from Texas A&M to Cornell University, are land-grant colleges.

As Americans moved west in the early 1800s to tame the vast continent, the creation of additional outstanding universities remained a priority. In 1842, Father Edward Sorin established the University of Notre Dame in South Bend, Indiana, as a Catholic university. While keeping faith with that mission, the university has also pioneered such secular pursuits as the study of the aerodynamics of flight and breakthroughs in the development of lasers, semiconductors, and synthetic rubber.

At the other end of the continent, Leland Stanford, the California businessman and public servant who was a driving force behind the completion of the transcontinental railroad, donated the land and a sizable grant to create a nondenominational, independent university admitting both men and women. Stanford University, in Palo Alto, California, founded in 1891 in memory of

Leland's late son, would become one of the world's most respected educational and research institutions.

By the turn of the last century, universities began to play an expanding role as centers of research as well as in training the growing ranks of the country's "white collar" professionals. Most colleges and universities had become secularized; many had already begun admitting women and African Americans years before. About 17 million Americans had some education, but only 4 percent had a college degree and even fewer had formal business training.

All that changed within half a century. First, the G.I. Bill of Rights, passed in the wake of World War II, provided federal money for veterans to attain higher education. The baby boom that followed meant more children would enter the educational system.

Today, nearly 25 percent of Americans have a college degree. About half of graduates receive degrees in a vocation; about a quarter receive degrees in business. A bachelor's degree is becoming increasingly important. According to the American Council on Education, people holding a bachelor's degree earn on average 86 percent more than those with only a high school diploma; 20 years ago that difference was 55 percent.

As a college degree becomes ever more important—and as the competition for tuition dollars becomes more intense—educational institutions are turning to the Internet to expand access and enrollment. Colleges and universities across the nation are going on-line; there are an estimated 90,000 courses delivered by distance learning. The University of Phoenix, for example, offers 800 on-line undergraduate and graduate courses with 35 degrees, including an MBA. Jones International University, founded in 1995, goes a step further: it is exclusively an on-line campus. Not only does it offer 80 courses and 26 certificate programs, it also provides custom courses for companies like AT&T Broadband Services and the Ball Corporation. Those courses are designed in part by faculty of the Wharton School and the London School of Economics. As more and more companies invest in and encourage extra training, the ability of people to learn what they want when they want will continue to grow, a benefit to both the employees and their employers.

With Americans having fewer children and reluctant to delay retirement despite longer life spans, the available pool of workers can barely keep pace with economic growth. This makes the training and productivity of the existing workforce more critical than ever. With their success tied to the quality of education, it is likely companies will become ever more involved with the students of tomorrow, whether it be through equipment donations, scholarship funds, hands-on training, or the advocacy of school reforms. Today, the nation spends about $557 billion on schools with an additional $93 billion spent on products and services that support the educational program.

By investing in their communities through generous philanthropy and in the future of the country through education, this nation's businessmen and -women have established that the true ethic of American free enterprise is not dog-eat-dog but people helping people.

chapter 11

NO BUSINESS LIKE SHOW BUSINESS

THE ENTERTAINMENT INDUSTRY

OVER THE PAST 100 YEARS, THE AMERICAN ENTERTAINMENT INDUSTRY HAS BECOME A POWERFUL FORCE IN THE GLOBAL ECONOMY, INFLUENCING CULTURES AND LIFESTYLES IN VIRTUALLY ALL NATIONS ON EARTH WHILE CREATING HUNDREDS OF THOUSANDS OF JOBS AND MULTIBILLION-DOLLAR BUSINESS EMPIRES HERE AT HOME.

YOU OUGHTA BE IN PICTURES

It's hard to conceive of now, but at the turn of the century, Hollywood was a humble little town of 5,000—mostly strict midwestern settlers who forbade saloons and theaters. How it became the epitome of glamour, intrigue, and talent is a story that begins with Thomas Edison.

In 1889, building on the early work of the French physician E. J. Marey, Edison invented the Kinetoscope, in his words, "an instrument which does for the eye what the phonograph does for the ear." The Kinetoscope was used to create short film clips, giving the illusion of movement by stringing together a series of slides.

The Kinetoscope was very popular but had one drawback: it could be viewed by only one person at a time. There was more money to be made in projecting films to large audiences, but Edison's company had not developed a projector, relying instead on the popularity of the Kinetoscope. So in 1895, Edison purchased the rights to the Phantoscope, a projector that had recently been introduced to the public by its inventor, Thomas Armat. Edison renamed the machine the Vitascope and unveiled it to a capacity audience in a vaudeville house in New York City in 1896. These "moving slides" were considered quite a novelty and attracted a great deal of attention. The first movie theater, called a nickelodeon, was built in Pittsburgh in 1905. Patrons paid five cents to see half an hour of various film bits set to live piano accompaniment. By 1907, there were 3,000 nickelodeons in business, and by 1909, nickelodeons had become relatively upscale, charging 25 cents for a show that often included vaudeville acts. Thus was the film industry born.

In its early days, film had a somewhat shady reputation. Many actors disdained the ten-minute "flickers" that mainly attracted poorly educated immigrants who found it good entertainment at an affordable price. Few, if any, theater and vaudeville producers saw any future in films. There were others, however, often newcomers to show business, who saw an opportunity there and grabbed it.

These men were newcomers not only to the field of entertainment but to America itself. Ironically, these immigrants had the clearest vision of what the American public would most want to see. In 1907, for example, the Russian Jewish immigrant Louis B. Mayer bought a nickelodeon in Boston, renamed it the Orpheum, and for Christmas that year produced *The Life of Jesus Christ in 27 Beautiful Scenes*. It was a hit with the public. Mayer went on to join

ABOVE: THE FORECOURT OF LEGENDARY MANN'S CHINESE THEATER IN HOLLYWOOD FEATURES THE FOOT- AND HANDPRINTS OF MOVIE STARS IN CEMENT. · OPPOSITE: IN 1999, MORE THAN 900 MILLION CDS WERE SHIPPED TO THE AMERICAN MARKET.

a production-distribution firm, Metro Pictures, and immediately bought the New England distribution rights to the first full-length picture ever made, D. W. Griffith's *The Birth of a Nation*, which came out the same year, 1915. In short order, Mayer stole actress Anita Stewart from Vitagraph Studios in Brooklyn, produced an early hit film called *Virtuous Wives*, and decamped to Hollywood. That once small, sedate town had, by 1920, vaulted to the top as the worldwide capital of moviemaking, producing four out of every five films and making the movie industry America's fifth largest, grossing $700 million every year.

Another immigrant, Hungarian Adolph Zukor, teamed up with Marcus Loew in 1904 to create Loews Theatres, a chain of penny arcades. In 1909, Loew started the enterprise that is today Loews Cineplex Entertainment, the country's second largest theater chain, with almost 3,000 screens in more than 400 theaters.

Loew also bought Metro Pictures in 1920, which Louis B. Mayer had abandoned. In 1924, Metro Pictures merged with Goldwyn Pictures Corporation, the brainchild of Samuel Goldwyn, and Loew hired Mayer to run the studio, now called Metro-Goldwyn-Mayer. MGM's first film was the original *Ben Hur* (1925). Today, MGM is a $672 million company and houses the largest film library in the world, with 4,000 film titles.

Meanwhile, Adolph Zukor was as busy as his occasional partner and friend, Loew. By 1918, Zukor had more than 200 major silent-film actors under contract. He joined with Jesse Lasky (another newcomer to America) to take over a distributor, Paramount Pictures, and a production company, Famous Players, to form Famous Players–Lasky. Famous Players was famous indeed, counting John Barrymore, Douglas Fairbanks, and Lillie Langtry among its founders. Its prestige made it an important link between the legitimate theater and film. By 1920, Famous Players–Lasky, which took on the Paramount Pictures name, had 300 theaters and dominated the industry.

By the 1920s, three studios led the film industry: MGM, Paramount, and 20th Century

CURTAIN UP! LIGHT THE LIGHTS!

RICHARD RODGERS AND OSCAR HAMMERSTEIN II INVENTED THE ART FORM KNOWN AS THE MUSI-CAL WITH THE DEBUT IN 1943 OF *OKLAHOMA!* AND WENT ON TO FORM THE MOST SUCCESSFUL PARTNERSHIP IN MUSICAL THEATER HISTORY. · SINCE ITS FOUNDING IN 1958, THE ALVIN AILEY AMERICAN DANCE THEATER HAS PERFORMED IN FRONT OF 19 MILLION PEOPLE IN 68 COUN-TRIES. · ESTABLISHED IN 1967 IN WATERBURY, CONNECTICUT, THE NATIONAL THEATRE OF THE DEAF IS THE NATION'S OLDEST TOURING THEATER COMPANY IN CONTINUOUS PRODUCTION. · AMERICA'S MOST SUCCESSFUL PLAYWRIGHT, NEIL SIMON HAS WRITTEN 28 PLAYS, INCLUDING *THE ODD COUPLE*, *PLAZA SUITE*, AND *CHAPTER TWO*, AND HAS HAD MORE PLAYS ADAPTED TO FILM THAN ANY OTHER WRITER. IN 1991, HE WON THE PULITZER PRIZE FOR *LOST IN YONKERS*. · IN 2001, MEL BROOKS'S *THE PRODUCERS* GARNERED A RECORD 12 TONY AWARDS.

Fox, with other studios like Columbia and Universal (which in 1962 merged with the Music Corporation of America to become the giant it is today) in supporting roles. The largest studios were producing a major feature every week, distributing it through their own channels. These films were all silents, which were especially adaptable to foreign audiences; all that was needed was a translation of the text on the title cards. They were typically accompanied by live orchestras and sound effects.

While the larger studios were churning out their silents, a small studio called Warner Bros. was waiting for its turn in the spotlight. It came in 1927 when Warner Bros. produced the first "talkie," *The Jazz Singer*, starring Al Jolson, whose improvised line "You ain't heard nothin' yet!" aptly characterized this brand-new development. Despite initial studio hostility to the idea of sound, the public loved it. Attendance at the movies doubled. By 1928, 300 theaters were equipped for sound, and by 1930, everybody was talking. By the end of that decade, timeless classics such as *Gone With the Wind* and *The Wizard of Oz* (both released in 1939) were being produced with regularity. Iconic figures would emerge over the middle years of the century—including Clark Gable, John Wayne, Cary Grant, Katharine Hepburn, James Dean, Marlon Brando, and Marilyn

frame of film. This painstaking process was replaced in 1932 with the invention of the three-color Technicolor cinematography system. The new process produced film with not only better color but which scratched less than hand-tinted film. Technicolor, along with sound, revolutionized the medium and profoundly affected the life and career of a young cartoonist named Walt Disney.

Of a Mouse and Men

With talkie fever sweeping the nation, Disney, a cartoonist with several silent cartoon series under his belt, and his partner Ub Iwerks decided to try the new sound technology in the 1928 cartoon *Steamboat*

best-known and most popular international figure of his day." That decade, Mickey went from being a crude, sketchy figure to the friendly face everyone knows today and was joined by other popular Disney creations Minnie Mouse, Donald Duck, and Goofy.

Sound was not the only new development that Disney took advantage of. He was the first to introduce the new Technicolor technology, in his 1932 short film, *Flowers and Trees*.

Disney also pioneered the full-length animated film with *Snow White* (1937) and used new advances in film technology to make classic films like *Pinocchio* and *Fantasia*, both released in 1940. Later, he delved into live-action films beginning with

ABOVE: WALT DISNEY, SEEN HERE IN HIS STUDIO CIRCA 1940, REVOLUTIONIZED THE ENTERTAINMENT INDUSTRY THROUGH HIS ANIMATED FILMS, TELEVISION PROGRAMS, AND THEME PARKS. DISNEY HOLDS THE RECORD FOR THE MOST ACADEMY AWARDS—32—WON BY A SINGLE PERSON. • OPPOSITE: FRED NIBLO DIRECTS THE FAMOUS CHARIOT RACE SCENE FROM THE ORIGINAL 1925 *BEN HUR*. THE SILENT CLASSIC WAS MADE AT MGM STUDIOS AND STARRED FRANCIS X. BUSHMAN AND RAMON NOVARRO.

Monroe—who would make indelible marks on American culture, style, and values.

The next major development—color—soon followed. Early experiments in this genre involved hand-tinting each individual

Willie, which marked the debut of a friendly little mouse named Mickey. It was an enormous hit, making Mickey Mouse a true American icon. In 1935, the *New York Times Magazine* noted that "Mickey Mouse is the

Treasure Island (1949). Disney himself adapted well to television, using it to screen talented actors and producers. And, with TV shows like the *Mickey Mouse Club*, which debuted in 1955, it became just another part

Frank Sinatra performs for a throng of adoring fans at the second annual Records for Our Fighting Men event in Central Park in July 1943.

of his growing entertainment empire. Today, the $1 billion Walt Disney Company owns three film studios, the ABC television network, and several cable channels.

Surviving Television

Not every studio was as successful as Disney's. The immediate post–World War II years turned out to be the sunset of the golden days of Hollywood. The heyday of Humphrey Bogart and Ingrid Bergman, Katharine Hepburn and Spencer Tracy, John Wayne and Bette Davis was over. Audience attendance peaked in 1946 with 90 million people per week as the widespread introduction of television took its toll on Hollywood. In some towns with only a handful of theaters, attendance dropped by as much as 40 percent due to that little black-and-white set. By the 1950s, the studio system was collapsing, the old-guard moguls were retiring, and rising costs and taxes were forcing many studios to Europe.

Help would later arrive in the form of another boxlike invention that would become almost as ubiquitous in American homes as the television itself: the VCR. Videocassette recording technology was initially created to save money in television production costs, but it also became the key to reviving the film industry.

The story of the VCR begins in the 1950s. At that time, the race was on to develop a substitute for the Kinescope, film-based recording equipment for television broadcasters that was relatively simple to use, if not of the highest quality. Film was becoming an outrageous expense, for so much of it was needed to tape all the television shows.

Charles Ginsburg led the research team at Ampex Corporation in developing the first practical videotape recorder (VTR). Ampex sold the first VTR for $50,000 in 1956; it only

recorded in black and white. RCA came out with equipment designed for color in 1959.

In 1977, RCA introduced the first four-hour home videocassette recorder. A year later, with the sales of the first programmable VCR and color home cameras, some 50 movie titles were available on videocassette. Soon, video rental stores were as common in the neighborhoods of America as gas stations. Today, the widespread availability of movies by cable and satellite has bit into the market of companies like Blockbuster, the number one video rental chain, although the increasingly popular DVD digital video format, which provides filmlike crispness and CD-like sound quality, may revitalize the movie rental industry.

Despite the influence of television and the availability of films on tape, going to the movies remains one of America's favorite pastimes. The movie industry survived by adapting to changes in society, as can be seen in the experimental films of the 1960s and 1970s, the megahits of the 1980s and 1990s, and the current popularity of the independents. And it will continue to find ways to draw audiences to the magic of the silver screen.

And the Beat Goes On

No matter what the form of entertainment, whether a TV show, a movie, a Broadway play—even a shopping outing—there is always music. Radio stations across the country play everything from pop to classical, from world music to the distinctively American jazz and bluegrass. People rush to buy the latest CDs by their favorite stars. At the dawn of the 21st century, music is hardly in the background of the entertainment industry; it's the headliner.

The recording industry traces its roots back to 1877, when Thomas Edison created the phonograph, which could record sound and play it back. As a telegraph operator at the Western Union office in Indianapolis, he discovered that he could hook together two old Morse code telegraph registers that would then capture incoming dots and dashes for later playback. Edison could sleep during his shift and catch up on work later.

Conceived as a laborsaving device for business, the machine consisted of a cylinder with tin foil wrapped around it. A stylus imprinted sound on the foil, a needle converted the indentations into sound, and a mouthpiece amplified it. It would take later

entrepreneurs to turn the cylinder phonograph into the more practical disk.

While Edison was experimenting with the phonograph, German immigrant Emile Berliner was working on an invention of his own: the electrical microphone. A decade later, he invented the gramophone, which played a wax disk. Berliner's inventions formed the basis for a recording industry, and in 1893 in Washington, D.C., he founded the United States Gramophone Company.

After a series of legal problems, Berliner's company was dissolved but was reborn in Camden, New Jersey, in 1901 as the Victor Talking Machine Company, featuring Nipper the dog on its phonographs and records. That year, two vaudevillians named Bert Williams and George Walker made a Victor record and

became the first African Americans to record on disk. In 1903, the first recordings of opera stars were released. And by the start of World War I, tenor Enrico Caruso had sold one million copies of a single, the first performer ever to do so.

In 1915, the Victor Talking Machine Company introduced the popular Victrola phonograph, and by 1919 Americans were spending more on phonographs and recordings than on music instruments, books, periodicals, and sporting goods combined. By the mid-1920s, most homes had a phonograph and millions of 78 RPM records were sold. In addition to Victor (which merged with RCA in

1929), other big labels, like Columbia, arose and created specialty labels for different kinds of music.

The music industry continued to expand through the 1930s, aided by advances in microphones, amplifiers, and phonographs, including stereo technology. After World War II, the music industry experienced significant changes. Many independent record labels consolidated with the bigger companies, and independent producers contracted with those major labels. The 78 RPM record was replaced by seven- and 12-inch longplaying (LP) records that were mainly used for classical, jazz, and soundtracks—that is,

BELOW: THOMAS EDISON POSES WITH HIS PHONOGRAPH, WHICH HE PATENTED IN 1878, JUST ONE OF HIS 1,093 PATENTS. · OPPOSITE: MAX V. MATHEWS PLAYS MUSIC ON A SYNTHESIZER. IN 1960, AS AN ELECTRICAL ENGINEER AT BELL LABS, MATHEWS INVENTED THE FIRST SYNTHETIC MUSIC LANGUAGE, CALLED MUSIC V.

until 1956 with the release of Frank Sinatra's *Songs for Swingin' Lovers* on LP, kicking off a trend in popular music that came to fruition with artists like Bob Dylan in the 1960s. Meanwhile, companies like Motorola were making transistor radios inexpensive enough for teenagers to purchase. By the end of the 1950s, portable record players were selling at a rate of 10 million every year. These devices introduced a new audience to musicians like Fats Domino, who popularized rhythm 'n' blues and helped turn it into rock 'n' roll. And of course, there was Elvis Presley, of whom it was said "was simply the most famous face in the world" between 1956 and 1959.

Rock 'n' roll created a new marketplace for producers and great opportunities for young men like Berry Gordy, who in 1959 created the Motown Record Corporation. By the end of the 1960s, it was the largest African American–owned corporation in the United

States. In the 1970s and 1980s, the industry would make room for labels such as trumpeter Herb Alpert's A&M Records, which headlined the Carpenters, and David Geffen's Geffen Records, which got its big break with the release in 1980 of John Lennon's comeback album, *Double Fantasy*, just months before the former Beatle was murdered.

The next big step was the transition from vinyl and tapes to digital compact disks (CDs). The CD was invented by James T. Russell in the late 1960s. A researcher at Battelle Memorial Institute's laboratory in Richland, Washington, Russell was a music lover who was confident that he could find a way to make the sound quality better on his vinyl phonograph records—and make them last longer. One Saturday afternoon, Russell had an inspiration: Use digital data recording, a technology he improved and refined throughout the 1970s. He eventually attracted the interest of the music industry. CDs didn't really catch on, however, until 1985 with the release of the Dire Straits album *Brothers in Arms*, but today they have virtually replaced all other formats of recorded music. CDs have also been merged with computers; CD-ROM games have revitalized the computer game industry, which began with the simple video game Pong in 1971.

By the end of the century, the music business, like the film business, was marked by a proliferation of independent producers and recording labels as well as do-it-yourself technology. Even so, the position of market leaders such as Sony, Universal, and Warner seemed secure.

At the beginning of the 21st century, the biggest challenge that the music industry faces is the MP3 format, which allows individuals to download music for free over the Internet. While a boon to undiscovered talent, the Internet's impact on the established industry is open to question.

THE ENTERTAINMENT ECONOMY

American music, films, and other forms of entertainment are a lightning rod, a magnet, and a mirror of U.S. culture and society. Some countries have expressed concern about "Americanization," but at the same time individuals everywhere have welcomed it, using it to define their goals and values as members of a burgeoning worldwide middle class.

The entertainment industry is a great tribute to the ingenuity and hard work of thousands of visionaries, inventors, and performers. Although most of its sectors are less than a century old, they have created icons and ideals that have become interwoven in the fabric of life. Movies, television shows, and songs create pictures in the mind, and for many eager artists, they are the stuff dreams are made of.

THE PLAY'S THE THING

PROFESSIONAL SPORTS PROVIDE ALL THE THRILLS, ACTION, AND EXCITEMENT OF AN INDIANA JONES MOVIE, CREATING LEGENDS AS BIG AS FILM STARS. · BABE RUTH IS THE ONLY PLAYER IN BASEBALL HISTORY TO HIT THREE HOME RUNS EACH IN TWO WORLD SERIES GAMES, IN 1926 AND 1928. REGGIE JACKSON HIT THREE HOMERS IN CONSECUTIVE AT-BATS IN THE FINAL GAME OF THE 1977 WORLD SERIES, EARNING HIM THE NICKNAME MR. OCTOBER. · JOHNNY UNITAS, IN HIS 17 YEARS WITH FOOTBALL'S BALTIMORE COLTS, THREW 47 TOUCHDOWN PASSES IN CONSECUTIVE GAMES, A RECORD THAT STILL STANDS. · BILLIE JEAN KING WON FOUR U.S. OPEN TENNIS TITLES AND SIX WIMBLEDON CROWNS AND WAS THE FIRST WOMAN ATHLETE TO EARN $100,000 IN A YEAR. · IN 1997, GOLF'S TIGER WOODS BECAME THE YOUNGEST PERSON TO WIN THE MASTERS. · LAFFIT PINCAY JR. HAS WON MORE THOROUGHBRED RACES—9,100 PLUS—THAN ANY OTHER JOCKEY.

MONEY MATTERS
FINANCIAL & INSURANCE SERVICES

A CENTURY AGO, ONLY A HANDFUL OF PRIVILEGED AMERICANS INVESTED IN THE STOCK MARKET. BY THE YEAR 2000, 52 PERCENT OF AMERICANS HELD STOCKS, AND EVEN MORE INVESTED IN MARKETS THROUGH 401(K) PLANS AND COMPANY OR UNION PENSION FUNDS. THIS INCREDIBLE GROWTH WAS DUE, IN LARGE PART TO THE INNOVATIONS OF THE

financial services sector. Encompassing everything from investments to insurance, America's financial services have helped millions of people achieve income and retirement security.

DOLLARS AND SENSE: BANKS AND THE SPREAD OF CONSUMER CREDIT

At the turn of the 20th century, the most powerful banker in America was the formidable J. P. Morgan, a financier who made his name creating enormous companies like General Electric in the waning days of the 19th century. At one point, Morgan was more powerful financially than the U.S. government. He single-handedly staved off the banking panic of 1907 with coolheaded orders given to Treasury Secretary George Cortelyou, Mayor George McClellan of New York City, and the major bankers on Wall Street. Indeed, the development of the Federal Reserve System in 1913 to regulate the money supply was a direct response to concerns about what would happen to the economy if J. P. Morgan died and was no longer there to quell another bank panic.

Even in his greatest triumph, however, Morgan would find that the times were changing and that banks, national currency, and credit were about to be democratized, opening up areas previously reserved for a fortunate few.

Back then, people were more likely to hide their meager savings under their mattresses than to put the money in a bank. This was in large part due to the fact that most banks wouldn't take small deposits. That bothered Amadeo Peter Giannini, the son of an Italian immigrant. A successful San Francisco business leader, Giannini became a director of the Columbus Savings and Loan Company in North Beach. Soon, he realized that the bank was missing a great opportunity: There were tradesmen, workers, and housewives in the local Italian American community who could form the customer base for a profitable business.

Giannini left Columbus and opened the Bank of Italy in 1904. It took in $8,780 from 28 depositors on its first day and grew quickly thereafter. Much of Giannini's success was due to his sales practices, which were rather unorthodox for the times. He would canvas the neighborhood to explain the benefits of interest-bearing savings accounts. He kept a desk at the center of the bank's main floor to meet customers and entertain their children and required that the bank staff carefully explain passbooks and deposit slips to the

ABOVE: THE DAILY AUCTION GETS UNDER WAY ON THE TRADING FLOOR OF THE NYSE. · OPPOSITE: J. P. MORGAN
ESTABLISHED ONE OF THE WORLD'S MOST POWERFUL BANKING HOUSES OF THE LATE 19TH CENTURY.

customers, many of whom could not read or write English. These practices paid off: within a year, the bank's assets were over $1 million.

During the San Francisco earthquake of 1906, Giannini's quick thinking saved his customers' assets. He and his staff piled the bank's cash and valuables in produce carts provided by Giannini's stepfather's produce company. Five days later, Giannini was back at work making loans. Bigger banks took a month to resume operations. The Bank of Italy went on to become Bank of America Corporation, the country's first coast-to-coast bank.

CREDIT WHERE CREDIT IS DUE

While Giannini was rescuing countless small assets from the deadly earthquake, another story in the finance industry was being written. One spring day in 1906, a railroad clerk came to the law offices of Arthur J. Morris, scion of an old Virginia family, wanting to borrow money to help his sick wife. Morris couldn't believe that nobody would give the man a loan. Even though he had no assets, the man clearly appeared to be a worthy credit risk. Morris secretly arranged to back a bank loan for him—and gave birth to the consumer credit industry.

After commissioning a survey of the American credit situation, Morris was surprised to learn that 80 percent of Americans had no access to bank credit and were borrowing from loan sharks at high interest

MONETARY GAINS

MAGGIE LENA WALKER BECAME THE FIRST AFRICAN AMERICAN WOMAN BANK PRESIDENT WHEN SHE FOUNDED THE SAINT LUKE PENNY SAVINGS BANK IN RICHMOND, VIRGINIA, IN 1903. · THE FIRST COIN TO BEAR THE LIKENESS OF A PRESIDENT (LINCOLN) WAS ISSUED IN 1908; IT WAS ALSO THE FIRST TO INCLUDE THE PHRASE "IN GOD WE TRUST." · THE FIRST ATM MACHINE WAS INSTALLED AT THE CHEMICAL BANK IN NEW YORK IN 1969. A YEAR LATER, A SURETY NATIONAL BANK BRANCH IN LOS ANGELES BECAME THE FIRST TO DISPENSE WITH HUMAN TELLERS ALTOGETHER. · ORIGINALLY LISTED IN 1824 AS THE NEW YORK GAS LIGHT COMPANY, CONSOLIDATED EDISON COMPANY OF NEW YORK HAS BEEN LISTED LONGER THAN ANY OTHER COMPANY ON THE NEW YORK STOCK EXCHANGE. · THE YEAR 2000 SAW BOTH THE BIGGEST ONE-DAY RISE (499.19 POINTS) AND FALL (617.78 POINTS) IN DOW JONES HISTORY.

rates. Morris thought that by lending money at reasonable rates to honest, hardworking people and letting them pay it back in sensible installments he could do good and do well at the same time. In 1910, he opened the Fidelity Savings and Trust in Norfolk, Virginia. The company provided savings accounts and personal loans.

Within just a few years, "Morris Plan" banking took off. Morris Plan banks were established as far west as Denver, and soon became a nationwide network. Other financiers joined in, understanding that the credit industry provided a useful service to worthy people and also helped stimulate the economy. (Nearly half of the first loans Morris issued in 1910 were for automobile purchases). In 1928, City Bank of New York (today's Citibank) became the first commercial bank to offer unsecured personal loans, charging 6 percent interest. And Giannini's Bank of America became the leader in consumer credit.

Today, there are only a handful of Morris Plan banks left, scattered across the country. They faded out not because they were no longer needed. On the contrary, Morris's banks had institutionalized the consumer credit industry to the point where consumers didn't even need to go to a bank anymore; they could just use a credit card.

be used in different locations and which had to be paid back within a short period of time. Within a year, the response was so enthusiastic that many banks began issuing local charge cards. Revolving credit cards were introduced and popularized in the years following World War II.

In 1958, Bank of America began issuing its own red, white, and blue credit card. In 1970, the bank formed an association with banks outside of California that was called National BankAmericard, which became Visa U.S.A. in 1976. In 1974,

Meanwhile, some banks that hadn't signed on with Bank of America formed a competitor to Visa that is today called MasterCard International and has its headquarters in Purchase, New York. In 1978, Visa and MasterCard worked out a deal in which banks could honor and issue both cards.

Visa surpassed MasterCard as the largest in the world in the 1980s, largely as a result of the efforts of Dee Ward Hock, who was the first CEO of Visa. A mountain boy from Utah, Hock developed the idea to create a decentralized system for the

ABOVE: TELLERS USE A SOPHISTICATED SOFTWARE PROGRAM AT THEIR BANK'S COMPUTER CENTER TO HELP THEM MANAGE CLIENTS' TELEPHONE INQUIRIES AND REQUESTS AS THEY ARISE. · OPPOSITE: A. P. GIANNINI, FOUNDER OF THE BANK OF ITALY (TODAY'S BANK OF AMERICA), CHECKS A LOAN DOCUMENT AT HIS SAN FRANCISCO DESK CIRCA 1923. ALWAYS AN INNOVATOR, GIANNINI CREATED THE WORLD'S FIRST MULTIBRANCH BANKING SYSTEM AND ESTABLISHED THE WEST AS A FINANCIAL CENTER SEPARATE FROM EASTERN INTERESTS.

Another credit service, deferred payment, went into effect in 1914 when Western Union began offering it to its best customers. In 1950, Diner's Club issued the first tangible card, a charge card that could

Bank of America formed a similar company for banks outside the United States, which was eventually named Visa International and today is based in Foster City, California.

company. After all, the participating banks were competitors in other areas. Why shouldn't they, after complying with basic standards, also compete with each other in offering Visa cards? Today, with 800 million

133

Indianapolis's central business district includes (left to right) American United Life Insurance Co.'s One American Square Tower, the Bank One Tower, and the 101 Ohio Street Tower.

cards in circulation, Visa provides the largest consumer payment system in the world. Visa also issues debit cards and "smart" cards.

A Secure Future

As the 21st century begins, several major factors are redefining the landscape of an industry that plays such a leading role in fueling and financing America's business development, foreign trade, and economic growth. According to the *U.S. Business Reporter*, a Web-based industry analysis service, banks have recently been focusing on the development of noninterest income , such as mergers, to boost overall profits. Facing increased competition from other financial service organizations as well as deregulation on the state, federal, and global levels, major banks have been engineering megamergers not only with each other but with other financial service companies.

In April 1998, for example, Citicorp and Traveler's Group agreed to a merger that created a $70 billion company, New York–based Citigroup, the nation's largest bank. A year later, Bank of America and Nation's Bank combined to form Bank of America Corporation, of Charlotte, North Carolina, now at number three. The second largest bank in the nation is J. P. Morgan Chase & Co. (formerly Chase Manhattan), of New York, while number four is Wells Fargo, of San Francisco. Other large and influential players on the scene include Bank One Corporation, of Chicago; Fleet Boston Financial Group; First Union Corporation, based in Charlotte, North Carolina; and Minneapolis-based U.S. Bancorp. They are buttressed by thousands of regional and community banks that bring their own innovations and dedication to service to the banking sector. For example, First Security Corporation, whose headquarters are in Salt Lake City, Utah, and which recently merged with Wells Fargo, is one of the leading banks in the West, with $4 billion in assets.

Despite concerns about poor customer service and lack of competitiveness voiced by some consumer groups, for individual consumers and business customers these developments mean having a package of financial services at their fingertips and convenient access to cash and other transactions anywhere in the world on a 24-hour, seven-days-a-week basis. The growing availability of on-line banking, including the ability to pay bills and transfer funds between accounts, adds to this focus on convenience and service.

Bulls, Bears, and Bullion: The Stock Market

Enterprising individuals in ancient Greece had to raise capital. The Romans created the idea of joint-stock organizations, which raised capital by selling shares. Medieval Japan had a rice-futures market. And the New York Stock Exchange was established under a buttonwood tree on Wall Street in 1790. Today, the NYSE handles more than 70 percent of all transactions' market value.

The first corporation in America to issue stock was the Baltimore & Ohio Railroad in 1829. Soon, many companies followed suit, finding it a more effective way of raising large amounts of capital than the old-fashioned method of borrowing from family or creating a partnership. One problem with this new method, however, was that potential investors had no idea whether the company was accurately reporting information or whether it was even collecting it in the first place. In 1852, Henry Varnum Poor, head of the American Railroad Journal, published an exposé of the Erie Railroad, a story that launched his reputation as an advocate for investors. Although his initial attempts to gather information about companies were rebuffed, investors trusted Poor and clamored for more information. Companies that were eager to be on Poor's good side furnished him with lots of statistics. In 1860, the first Poor's manual was issued. By the time Poor died, in 1905, his many publications had made him a well-respected institution. In 1941, Poor's company merged with Standard Statistics, which was founded in 1914, to create Standard & Poor's Publishing Company. Today, S&P is owned by the New York–based McGraw Hill Companies, one of the world's leading publishers. The S&P 500 market index of top companies is a respected indicator of the health of the economy.

Now that investors had a reliable source for information—indeed, now that businesses had an interest in providing that information—they needed ways to invest. Florida-born financial whiz Charlie Merrill thought he could do something about that. After relocating to New York City, he formed Charles E. Merrill & Co., an underwriting firm, in 1914. Sixteen months later, he teamed up with a soda fountain–equipment salesman named Edmund Lynch and formed Merrill Lynch & Co.

Through shrewd investments, the firm soon attracted some of the largest companies in the nation as clients, and because of Merrill's business acumen, its investors were prepared for the stock market crash in 1929 that ruined so many others. In 1940, Merrill Lynch became the first Wall Street company to issue an annual report. As the stock business turned toward the small investor, Merrill Lynch began an unprecedented advertising campaign in 1948 entitled "What Everyone Ought to

Know About this Stock and Bond Business." Aimed at the general public, this powerful newspaper ad succeeded in making Lynch a trusted household name. After a series of mergers at the end of the century, Merrill Lynch became the top brokerage firm in the country, fulfilling its founder's original vision of "bringing Main Street to Wall Street."

Today, other powerful players vie for the portfolios of America's individual and institutional investors. In 1997, the merger of the brokerage and financial services company Dean Witter, Discover with Morgan Stanley Group made New York–based Morgan Stanley a global powerhouse. The firm offers securities sales and trading, mergers and acquisitions financing and counsel, and a broad range of investment services and strategic advice.

New Ways of Investing

As the 1980s dawned, the stock market saw the stirrings of a revolution. In 1980, 4.6 million households—about 6 percent of the total—owned mutual funds either on their own or in part through their employers. (Mutual funds put shareholder money in a portion of a wide range of stocks.) In 1999, that figure mushroomed to a whopping 48.4 million households—nearly half of households in the country—a figure that included those who own mutual funds only through their employers. All told, at the turn of the 21st century, about 83 million people had invested in mutual funds and were taking advantage of the professional management, diversification, and potential for high returns that come with them.

Two of the largest mutual funds today are Boston-based Fidelity Management & Research Corporation (FMR), founded in 1946, and the Vanguard Group, of Malvern, Pennsylvania, founded in 1974. Both companies cater to smaller investors. Fidelity's

Fidelity Brokerage Services was the first mutual-fund company to offer discount brokerage services. Vanguard is known for its index funds (funds that mimic the top stocks in the stock market) and for its low costs.

As with nearly all aspects of business, the Internet is causing major changes in access to the stock market. Charles Schwab, an upstart San Francisco discount brokerage founded in 1975, has become the number one on-line trader. It was one of Schwab's customers, a physicist named Bill Porter, who invented on-line trading technology in 1982, in the early days of personal computers and the Internet. He realized that one day everyone would be on-line. In 1992, he founded E*Trade Securities, which began offering its services through America Online and CompuServe. In 1995, www.etrade.com set up shop on the Web. Today, E*Trade, of Menlo Park, California, is the third largest on-line broker, right behind New York–based TD Waterhouse (at number two) and Charles Schwab.

While the Internet will continue to provide valuable information for the individual investor, Americans will still rely on their stockbrokers for the expert advice and financial services that only they can provide.

The Business of Managing Risk: The Insurance Industry

The vast American insurance industry, which covers everything from health to property and casualty to life insurance, can trace its roots far back in time. References to insurance appear in the Code of Hammurabi. Medieval guilds provided some measure of insurance for members.

Insurance in this country goes back to colonial times. The British put into practice loss insurance as companies ensured merchant ships traveling to and from the colonies. But it was a colonist who can be credited with starting the insurance business here. Benjamin Franklin, ambassador to France, inventor of bifocals, founder of the University of Pennsylvania, among many other accomplishments, put into action hundreds of the ideas that bubbled over in his imagination. One of those concepts was fire insurance, which he created in 1752. Under Franklin's plan, property owners would purchase a plaque from the fire brigade and mount it on their houses. In the event of an emergency, the fire brigade would know that the occupants had purchased fire insurance—fire extinguishing services, really—and therefore put out the fire. Independence Hall, which was originally insured for $130, still displays its plaque.

The brigade system eventually broke down because of disorganization, yet there remained a need for the service. Thus, to stabilize the nascent industry, Franklin's company and others like it banded together to form the Fire Association of Philadelphia in 1817, the corporate ancestor of the Reliance Insurance Group, now a part of Reliance Group Holdings. This $3 billion company insures commercial property and provides worker's compensation insurance, among many other activities—a long way from the fire brigades of old.

Another Philadelphia-born company, the Insurance Company of North America was founded in 1792 in Independence Hall by a group of merchants and other important citizens. They offered marine and fire insurance for ships, cargoes, warehouses, and homes. Nearly 200 years later, in 1982, the INA Corporation, as it later became, merged with a life insurance company called Connecticut General Corporation, founded in 1865. The result was CIGNA, an $18 billion company that provides a variety of health insurance, property-casualty, and even retirement plans.

In 1875, New Jersey insurance agent John Fairfield Dryden opened the doors of the Prudential Friendly Society, offering life insurance for the working man. Life insurance companies had enjoyed a modest boom in the previous decades, but it was affordable only to the wealthiest people. Dryden, the son of factory workers, targeted his insurance to working-class people, who often found themselves wiped out from funeral expenses when the family breadwinner died. His unusual methods of business included visiting factories during lunch hours and staying open late to allow any curious workers to come in after the day was done. In Dryden's first year, 279 policies were sold,

some with premiums as low as three cents per week. By the end of the second year, 5,000 policies had been sold. Primarily a life insurance company, by the early 1950s the Prudential Insurance Company of America, as it was then known, was offering major medical insurance and individual health insurance. Today, Prudential, of Newark, is the country's number one life insurer.

Aetna also started out as a life insurer. Founded in 1853 in Hartford, Connecticut, Aetna entered the health insurance market in 1899. As the business grew, so did Aetna's reputation. Indeed, in 1963, Aetna insured the lives of America's first seven astronauts. In 1996, Aetna sold its property-casualty business to focus on health care and merged with U.S. Healthcare. Today, Aetna and its subsidiaries comprise one of the nation's largest health benefits groups.

Another giant of the industry, the State Farm Group began in 1922 as an automobile insurance company in Bloomington, Illinois. Founder George Mercherle sold policies to local Farm Bureau members and made policyholders owners of the company. His approach proved so popular that the

company quickly expanded beyond Illinois's borders. Today, State Farm is the nation's leading insurer of automobiles and homes.

CUNA Mutual Group of Madison, Wisconsin, is another example of a successful mutual company (a company owned by policyholders). CUNA was founded in 1935 by members of the early credit union movement and today, with assets of more than $8.5 billion, insures virtually 95 percent of this nation's credit unions.

With its vast array of products, AEGON Americas is representative of the wave of companies offering a multitude of financial services. A subsidiary of Aegon N.V., whose roots go back to 1844 Holland, AEGON Americas operates, among other companies, Baltimore-based AEGON USA and Transamerica, of San Francisco. AEGON offers life insurance, reinsurance, pension, investment, supplemental health insurance, and a wealth of other services.

The insurance industry is likely in store for some dramatic changes. Mutual companies like Prudential are considering extending their ownership to outside investors, a move that would help raise capital to continue growing. Another promising development is the keen interest of many baby boomers in purchasing long-term care insurance. From 1987 to 1996, sales of this insurance increased by 22 percent annually to five million policies.

Insurance companies are in an extremely risky business. The 1906 San Francisco earthquake nearly decimated the industry. Almost a century later, in 1992, Hurricane Andrew hit the East Coast. Since customers experience their greatest interaction with insurers during times of loss and emotional duress, maintaining a positive public image is always difficult. Yet the insurance industry has persevered and will continue to provide Americans with a cushion of security during life's hardships.

RISKY BUSINESS

TRAVELERS INSURANCE COMPANY OF HARTFORD, CONNECTICUT, WAS THE FIRST TO ISSUE AUTOMOBILE INSURANCE, IN 1898. THE POLICY WAS FOR $5,000 TO $10,000 IN LIABILITY; THE PREMIUM WAS $11.25. · THE FIRST NO-FAULT AUTOMOBILE INSURANCE LAW WENT INTO EFFECT IN MASSACHUSETTS IN 1970. · CALIFORNIA HAS THE HIGHEST HOMEOWNERS INSURANCE PREMIUMS IN THE NATION, WITH AN AVERAGE OF $595. WHEN IT COMES TO AUTOMOBILE INSURANCE, NEW JERSEY HEADS THE LIST WITH AN AVERAGE EXPENDITURE OF $1,138. · THE GROSS DOMESTIC PRODUCT IN 1999 OF ALL U.S. INSURANCE CARRIERS WAS $165 BILLION. · IN 2000, OF THE 20 MOST COSTLY INSURANCE LOSSES AROUND THE WORLD, HALF OCCURRED IN THE UNITED STATES AND WERE ALL DUE TO HAIL, STORM, AND/OR FLOODS. TOTAL U.S. INSURED LOSSES AMOUNTED TO $2.8 BILLION. · THE UNITED STATES LEADS THE WORLD IN THE TOTAL VALUE OF OVERALL INSURANCE PREMIUMS, WITH 34 PERCENT OF THE SHARE.

REFLECTING THE VITALITY OF THE DENVER BUSINESS DISTRICT ARE (LEFT TO RIGHT) UMB BANK, COLORADO-BASED 1ST BANK, AND MILE HIGH CENTER, WHICH CONNECTS TO THE WELLS FARGO CENTER BY SKYWALK.

profiles
Financial &
Insurance Services

STATE FARM GROUP

THE STATE FARM GROUP PROVIDES CAR, HOME, LIFE, AND HEALTH INSURANCE—PLUS BANKING AND MUTUAL FUND SERVICES—WITH A COMMITMENT TO GOOD NEIGHBOR SERVICE AND FINANCIAL STRENGTH.

At the core of the advertisements for the State Farm Group companies is a phrase familiar to just about everyone: "Like a good neighbor, State Farm is there."® For the Bloomington, Illinois–based firm—one of the largest property and casualty insurance companies in the nation, with over 71 million policies in force—that phrase is not just a slogan, but a way of life that comes just as naturally as breathing the clean air that blows across the Prairie State where State Farm was founded almost 80 years ago.

Since 1922, when the company was started by George J. Mecherle, a retired farmer turned insurance salesman, State Farm has experienced phenomenal growth. Today it is one of the largest financial institutions in the world. What began as a small mutual automobile insurance firm among Mecherle's friends in the local Farm Bureau in Bloomington grew to become a company that today insures one of every five automobiles in the United States, making State

Farm the nation's largest insurer of automobiles. In addition, State Farm is the leading insurer of homes in the United States. It has a life insurance business, begun in 1929, that ranks fifth among all life insurance groups doing business in the United States. It even founded a federal savings bank in 1998, State Farm Bank®, which provides a variety of financial products, available through State Farm's vast network of insurance agents and via the Internet. And it now markets 10 State Farm–branded mutual funds to the public.

The State Farm network of agents has grown to more than 16,000 people, and its workforce now includes more than 78,000 people, with more than 37,000 persons who deal with claims. The company that was started in a single, one-room office in Bloomington now maintains nearly 1,000 claim offices across the United States and Canada, as well as 13 zone operations that underwrite insurance policies, process claims, and oversee the company's business in their respective areas.

Despite its impressive growth, State Farm remains true to the principles on which Mecherle founded the company three-quarters of a century ago. While working for a small insurance firm, Mecherle came up with what was then a novel idea of how an automobile insurance company should operate—six-month policies, lower rates for drivers with less risk of loss, and honest and fair treatment of customers. So refreshing and appealing was his concept that within three years of establishing State Farm, people outside of Central Illinois were clamoring to become part of Mecherle's mutual automobile insurance company. The company quickly expanded to other states, including Indiana, South Dakota, and Missouri, and has continued to add new friends and neighbors in cities, towns, and rural areas in all 50 states, the District of Columbia, and three Canadian provinces.

When he established his firm, Mecherle made it clear that the company would be unlike any insurance firm that preceded it: "It will not be the policy of our company to build its membership by other than straightforward business methods, conducted honorably and fairly so that no one connected will ever be forced to make an apology." He told his original policyholders, "Your company will have every benefit, the same as though you were conducting your own company with the added benefit of a larger company." That philosophy continues to be the driving force behind State Farm's mission—to help people manage the risks of everyday life, recover from the unexpected, and realize their dreams.

Today, State Farm provides millions of families with assistance in managing the risks of everyday life. The company offers customers the confidence of association with a financially strong, enduring firm, one that has long inspired trust that it will keep its promises if the unexpected occurs.

Because State Farm is a mutual insurance company, free from any demands of Wall Street or stockholders, its profits are targeted to benefit its policyholders, through lower rates or initiatives to support their companies' growth.

According to company chairman and CEO, Edward B. Rust Jr., "Although State Farm today is a very large company with all the technology that such an enterprise entails, our policyholders always have a State Farm agent nearby—a person the policyholder knows and a good neighbor who can be trusted and turned to when help is needed."

OPPOSITE PAGE: RETIRED FARMER GEORGE J. MECHERLE FORMED STATE FARM MUTUAL IN 1922 TO TREAT AUTO INSURANCE CUSTOMERS "HONESTLY AND FAIRLY." • ABOVE: EDWARD B. RUST JR., CHAIRMAN AND CEO, LEADS THE ENTERPRISE AS IT ADDS FINANCIAL SERVICES TO ITS TRADITIONAL INSURANCE OFFERINGS. • LEFT: TITLE SPONSOR OF THE LPGA RAIL CLASSIC SINCE 1993, STATE FARM IS A LEADING SUPPORTER OF WOMEN'S EVENTS AND INTERESTS, INCLUDING THE WOMEN'S MUSEUM OF DALLAS.

RIGHT: WHEN A DISASTER SUCH AS A HURRICANE STRIKES, STATE FARM MOBILIZES ITS FORCES TO HELP ITS CUSTOMERS RECOVER AS QUICKLY AS POSSIBLE. • BELOW RIGHT: THE LATE EDWARD B. RUST SR. WAS U.S. CHAMBER OF COMMERCE PRESIDENT DURING 1973 AND 1974, AFTER SERVING ON THE CHAMBER BOARD SINCE 1966. AT HIS DEATH IN 1985, RUST WAS STATE FARM PRESIDENT AND BOARD CHAIRMAN. • OPPOSITE PAGE, TOP: SERVING COMMUNITIES MEANS REACHING OUT WITH RESOURCES AND VOLUNTEERS FOR CLASSROOM PROGRAMS, COMMUNITY REDEVELOPMENT, AND GRANTS. • OPPOSITE PAGE, BOTTOM: THE STATE FARM LOGO, LONG ASSOCIATED WITH THE NATION'S LARGEST INSURER OF CARS AND HOMES, SYMBOLIZES THE MISSION OF THE COMPANY'S AGENTS AND EMPLOYEES: "WE ARE PEOPLE WHO MAKE IT OUR BUSINESS TO BE LIKE A GOOD NEIGHBOR."

The companies that make up the State Farm Group today include the parent firm, State Farm Mutual Automobile Insurance Company—the original firm founded by Mecherle—which now markets both automobile insurance and health insurance; State Farm Indemnity Company, which handles automobile insurance business in New Jersey; State Farm Life Insurance Company; State Farm Life and Accident Assurance Company, which meets special requirements for life insurance in New York and Wisconsin; and State Farm Fire and Casualty Company, providing insurance for homeowners and boat owners and many commercial lines.

State Farm County Mutual Insurance Company of Texas insures standard-risk motorists in that state; State Farm General Insurance Company is a property insurance affiliate; and State Farm Florida Insurance Company insures homes, rental units, and condominiums in Florida. State Farm Bank is a nontraditional financial institution established to complement the insurance focus of State Farm. It provides banking services nationwide, including a range of deposit and loan products.

State Farm has been an innovative company ever since George Mecherle founded it. In 1960, it became the first automobile insurance company to establish drive-up claim service centers to reduce the time a customer spent dealing with a claim. A few years

later, it also was among the first to inaugurate a public awareness campaign focusing on highway safety. In 1971, State Farm was among the first to establish a special disaster service to handle claims on-site wherever and whenever natural disasters occur.

Because being a good neighbor means coming to the aid of those in need, State Farm and its employees have, since the company's founding, taken the extra step to give back to the communities they serve. The company's employees give hours of volunteer service, monetary assistance, and in-kind contributions when help is needed most.

State Farm plays a direct role in serving the communities where its policyholders live. Through its Good Neighbor Teacher Award™, it recognizes outstanding primary and secondary school teachers; through its foundation, it makes grants to higher education, human

services, community, and disease-preventing organizations; and among its employees and agents, it raises more than $3 million annually for the United Way. State Farm supports charitable causes such as the Special Olympics and the American Red Cross, and in conjunction with neighborhood-based groups, it helps provide housing for financially disadvantaged families and assists in the revitalization of deteriorating neighborhoods.

With the beginning of the new century, State Farm has embarked on a series of initiatives designed to ensure that its next 75 years in business will be as successful as its first 75. Rust says the organization must "be aware of the changes occurring in our business environment, and especially the new competitive business forces around us; and be certain our activities today are leading in the necessary direction so that we remain the number one insurance choice of State Farm customers."

But no matter how many changes are made, one thing at State Farm remains a constant: Like a good neighbor, State Farm is there for its policyholders. Neither George Mecherle nor his successors at State Farm would have it any other way.

CUNA MUTUAL GROUP

CUNA MUTUAL GROUP PROVIDES FINANCIAL SERVICES, INCLUDING INSURANCE, INVESTMENT, AND TECHNOLOGY SOLUTIONS, TO CREDIT UNIONS AND THEIR MEMBERS AROUND THE GLOBE.

CUNA Mutual Group, formed nearly 70 years ago with just $25,000, is now a Fortune 1000 financial services company and the leading provider of financial services to credit unions and their members all over the world.

CUNA Mutual offers more than 300 insurance, investment, and technological solutions through strategic relationships and multiple service channels. No other company in the world offers so many credit union–specific products. Headquartered in Madison, Wisconsin, CUNA Mutual also has offices in Waverly, Iowa, and Rancho Cucamonga, California. In addition, it maintains six regional offices across the country and has an affiliate, The CUMIS Group, in Burlington, Ontario, Canada.

"We exist for three main reasons: To help credit unions strengthen their relationships with members, to help credit unions strengthen their relationships with employees, and to help protect credit unions," says James L. Bryan, chairman of the board of CUNA Mutual and president and CEO of Texans Credit Union, in suburban Dallas. "In each area, we offer high-value solutions and maximum convenience. In short, we are capable of and committed to helping credit unions thrive. And ultimately, we help credit unions offer their members better deals in financial services."

According to Michael B. Kitchen, president and chief executive officer, CUNA Mutual partners with credit unions, working side by side with them as they compete for new members and work to retain existing ones. Because it is a mutual company, CUNA Mutual belongs to its credit union policyowners.

"Our philosophy of service matches that of the credit unions we serve," Kitchen says. "Together, credit unions and CUNA Mutual match sophisticated financial service products and services with members' needs and wants. Our strategy is simple and sustainable: Do whatever it takes to help establish and facilitate a lifetime relationship between credit unions and their members."

The confidence that credit unions have in CUNA Mutual is reflected in the fact that today it protects, with one or more coverages, more than 95 percent of the 10,500 credit unions in the United States and serves credit unions in more than 30 other countries. In addition, CUNA Mutual protects individual members directly, providing insurance, annuities, mutual funds, and other investment products to approximately 8 million credit union members.

Equally important is the confidence placed in CUNA Mutual by independent evaluators of financial services firms. Fitch rates the company AA (Very High), and A.M. Best has given CUNA Mutual affiliates CUNA Mutual Insurance Society, CUMIS Insurance Society, Inc., and CUNA Mutual Life Insurance Company its A (Excellent) rating. In 2000, *Inc.* magazine cited another CUNA Mutual affiliate, CMG Mortgage Insurance Company, as the 98th fastest growing privately held company in America. And in 2001, two of the mutual funds managed by CUNA Mutual's investment affiliate, MEMBERS Capital Advisors, were ranked "Best in Class" by *Mutual Funds* magazine.

The history of CUNA Mutual is as rich as that of the credit union movement itself. In fact, the pioneers of the credit union movement were the ones who, in 1935, established the CUNA Mutual Insurance Society, now the parent organization of all the companies that together form the CUNA Mutual Group. Chief among those pioneers was Edward A. Filene, a wealthy Boston merchant who ran the well-known department store that carries his family name and who was instrumental in establishing the U.S. Chamber of Commerce.

It was Filene who started and financed the campaign to establish credit unions throughout the nation in the early 1900s as a means for curing poverty through the principle of self help. And it was Filene who, with the legal assistance of Massachusetts attorney Roy F. Bergengren, engineered the passage of the Federal Credit Union Act of 1934, which gave legitimacy to the credit union movement. Later, a need emerged for affordable, easily available credit life insurance, to cover credit union loans not fully repaid when a member died. To fill this need, Filene helped establish CUNA Mutual

OPPOSITE PAGE: THE FIRST MEETING OF THE BOARD OF DIRECTORS OF THE CREDIT UNION NATIONAL ASSOCIATION (CUNA) WAS HELD IN KANSAS CITY, MISSOURI, IN JANUARY 1935. · ABOVE: THE CUNA MUTUAL GROUP HOME OFFICE IS IN MADISON, WISCONSIN. · LEFT: EDWARD A. FILENE, OF BOSTON, MASSACHUSETTS, KNOWN AS THE FATHER OF THE U.S. CREDIT UNION MOVEMENT, SPENT MORE THAN $1 MILLION OF HIS OWN MONEY TO START CREDIT UNIONS. HE WAS THE FIRST ELECTED CHAIRMAN OF THE CREDIT UNION NATIONAL ASSOCIATION (CUNA) AND CUNA MUTUAL INSURANCE SOCIETY.

RIGHT: CUNA MUTUAL GROUP PRESIDENT AND CEO, MICHAEL B. KITCHEN, AT LEFT, WAS INDUCTED INTO THE CREDIT UNION EXECUTIVES SOCIETY'S HALL OF FAME FOR HIS CONTRIBUTIONS TO THE CREDIT UNION MOVEMENT. AT RIGHT IS PAST SOCIETY CHAIRMAN AND DIRECTOR EDWIN R. BIGBY JR. · OPPOSITE PAGE, TOP: CUNA MUTUAL'S INVESTMENT UNIT, MEMBERS CAPITAL ADVISORS, IS RECOGNIZED BY INDEPENDENT EVALUATORS FOR TOP PERFORMANCE IN MANAGING PENSIONS AND VARIABLE INVESTMENTS. LEADERSHIP TEAM MEMBERS, FROM LEFT, ARE MARY HOFFMANN, FINANCE AND OPERATIONS OFFICER; MICHAEL DAUBS, PRESIDENT; JEFF PANTAGES, SENIOR VICE PRESIDENT; TOM MERFELD, SENIOR VICE PRESIDENT; DAN LARSON, VICE PRESIDENT; AND LARRY HALVERSON, SENIOR VICE PRESIDENT. · OPPOSITE PAGE, BOTTOM: CUNA MUTUAL GROUP'S BUSINESS-TO-BUSINESS BRAND IS "CUNA MUTUAL," AND THE BRAND PROMISE IS "THE POWER TO HELP CREDIT UNIONS COMPETE." THE COMPANY'S BUSINESS-TO-MEMBER COBRANDING STRATEGY IS CENTERED AROUND MEMBERS FINANCIAL SERVICES, WHOSE OFFERINGS ARE FUEL FOR CREDIT UNIONS' ENGINES.

with a $25,000 low-interest capitalization loan from his own pocket. He also helped guide the fledgling mutual insurance company, serving as its first president until his death in 1937. His cohort, Bergengren, was the company's first full-time managing director.

In 1937, just two years after its founding, CUNA Mutual became the leading provider of credit life insurance in the United States. And as time went on, it offered additional financial services, beginning with ordinary life insurance and renewable term life insurance. Over the years, the company has continued to pioneer additional financial service vehicles, initiating products a step ahead of banks and nontraditional financial services providers. Some of the numerous CUNA Mutual Group enterprises are:

- CUNA Mutual Life Insurance Company, CUNA Mutual Group's permanent affiliate, which provides life and long-term care insurance and annuities;

- CUNA Mutual Insurance Society, which provides accident, health, life insurance, and executive benefits;

- CUMIS Insurance Society, Inc., a property and casualty insurance subsidiary, which underwrites the Credit Union Fidelity Bond and provides loss prevention information to more than 95 percent of all U.S. credit unions;

- CUNA Brokerage Services, Inc., a registered broker dealer, which provides investments and mutual funds;

- MEMBERS Capital Advisors, which functions as the company's registered investment adviser;

- CUNA Mutual Mortgage Corporation, which provides mortgage loan origination, purchasing, and servicing;

- CMG Mortgage Insurance Company, which provides private mortgage insurance;

- CUNA Mutual Insurance Agency, Inc., which helps distribute insurance and annuity products to meet the special needs of CUNA Mutual customers; and

• Stewart Associates, which provides mechanical breakdown insurance.

The assets of CUNA Mutual now exceed $8.5 billion—a far cry from the $25,000 with which it was started—and its annual revenues currently exceed $3 billion.

As CUNA Mutual's product offerings expanded, so did its workforce, growing from just one employee in 1935, its managing director, to today's 5,000 employees, half of whom are based in Madison, Wisconsin. CUNA Mutual employees are not only dedicated to serving credit unions and their members; they are also committed to practicing the credit union philosophy of People Helping People, volunteering their time and money to help nonprofit organizations in the communities where the company's operations are based. The company itself makes grants to such organizations to ensure continued community health and welfare. In 1967, CUNA Mutual established the CUNA Mutual Group Foundation, to formalize its investment of corporate resources in maintaining healthy communities.

In this new millennium, CUNA Mutual is steadfastly committed to keeping credit unions at the forefront of financial services providers. It continually refines its traditional products and services and adds new ones. For instance, it has embraced new electronic delivery channels to give credit unions and their members the most efficiency and convenience.

"Among other things, we have developed new strategies for business-to-business and business-to-member relationships," says Kitchen. "We have created electronic access for our product lines: Credit Union Protection, Credit Union Employee Benefits, Lending, Investments, and Education. These lines now encompass new opportunities in customer relationships, using the Internet as a key channel for communications." But the Internet is simply an additional, convenient way of accessing CUNA Mutual products and services, he points out. As it has from the beginning, the company will always provide members with personal control of their finances through face-to-face and/or telephone contact with company representatives.

"Our commitment to serve credit unions and their members will never waver," Kitchen says. "Electronic communication is part of our successful evolution into a high-performance organization designed to help them create financial security and thrive, through the 21st century and beyond."

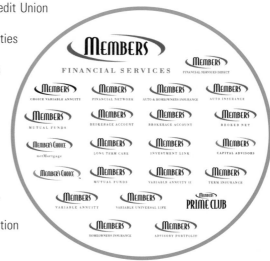

SPIRIT OF

AEGON AMERICAS

The operations of AEGON Americas include AEGON USA and Transamerica companies in the United States and Canada and AEGON's partnership with Banamex in Mexico.

Offering life and health insurance, pension and investment, reinsurance, and other related financial products and services, the AEGON Americas companies employ over 15,000 people. Its parent company is Netherlands-based AEGON N.V., one of the largest financial services groups worldwide. In addition to the Americas and the Netherlands, AEGON has major country units in Hungary, Spain, and the United Kingdom, as well as businesses in many other countries.

"Respect people, make money, and have fun" is the uncomplicated mission statement for AEGON.

"We have always kept things very simple," says Donald J. Shepard, member of the AEGON N.V. executive board and chairman, president, and chief executive officer of AEGON USA. "We have concentrated on our core businesses—life insurance, pensions, supplemental health, and asset accumulation products—all of which are growth businesses supported by promising demographics . . . and we have maintained an organizational structure that works well for us.

"Decentralized management has been key. It encourages a high degree of independence and autonomy, which gives our people the energy and ability to get things done. It also lets the people who run the business do the planning and handle the long-term thinking."

Afore Banamex AEGON
AUSA
Bankers United
Creditor Resources
Diversified Investment Advisors
IDEX
Life Investors
Monumental
AEGON Americas
Peoples Benefit
Seguros Banamex AEGON
Transamerica Canada
Transamerica Finance Corporation
Transamerica Life
Transamerica Occidental
Transamerica Reinsurance
Western Reserve

This entrepreneurial spirit—along with consistent emphasis on the cost controls and strict return rates that enable AEGON to remain a profitable low-cost provider—is central to its strategy for continuing growth. AEGON markets its products to companies and middle- and upper-income individuals. The opportunities for growth within these sectors continue to accelerate as the nation enjoys a healthy economy and the baby boom generation moves into its peak earning and retirement-planning years.

150

The main product areas of the AEGON Americas companies include traditional, universal, variable universal, and term life insurances, supplemental health insurance, guaranteed investment contracts, reinsurance, bank- and corporate-owned life insurance, mutual funds, and annuities. AEGON also creates special products and services for particular market segments in line with today's changes in consumer behavior, finance, and technology. AEGON distributes its products through independent and employee agents, brokers, partnerships, financial institutions, affinity groups, direct response marketing, and work site representation.

AEGON's consistency in delivering superior financial results is helped by its vision for positive change in the ever-evolving world of business technology and communications. "AEGON continues to increase its competitive edge by providing technological initiatives designed to make doing business with our companies easier," says Shepard. "E-business will lead to dramatic changes in the ways we interact with our customers and distributors and deliver service to them. Numerous initiatives are under way throughout our businesses to provide our customers, distributors, and employees with Internet access to information on the performance of products, accounts, and funds. There will also be access to policy transactions and financial planning tools."

AEGON believes businesses should contribute to the communities in which they operate. It places emphasis on community health and well-being and education. The company participates locally and nationally in many charitable organizations, such as the United Way, and gives individual grants to cultural, civic, educational, and health organizations. The AEGON Scholars program is designed to encourage the exchange of ideas and information between research scientists at Johns Hopkins University in Baltimore, Maryland, and Vrije Universiteit in Amsterdam,

the Netherlands. AEGON is also proud of its record for establishing energy conservation and recycling programs at its various divisions.

"Fulfilling our obligation to be a good corporate citizen is a source of great pride," says Shepard. "We are also proud of our employees' active participation in the betterment of their communities. We believe that the investment of not only financial resources, but also time, energy, and community leadership by businesses rewards all parties."

ABOVE: Shown here, from left, are Brenda K. Clancy, senior vice president, information and finance, treasurer; Douglas C. Kolsrud, executive vice president, asset allocation and risk management; Donald J. Shepard, chairman, president, and chief executive officer; Bart Herbert Jr., executive vice president and chief marketing officer; Patrick S. Baird, executive vice president and chief operating officer; and Tom A. Schlossberg, president, Diversified Investment Advisors. · Left: AEGON's success is based on the strong relationships its agents and distributors develop with their customers. Knowing their respective marketplaces and what products and services their customers want provides a great competitive advantage. Shown here is Transamerica agent Lynne Rosenberg-Kidd, in the center, with clients.

FANNIE MAE

FANNIE MAE IS A PRIVATE CORPORATION THAT HELPS AMERICANS ACHIEVE THE DREAM OF HOMEOWNERSHIP BY PROVIDING FINANCING FOR SINGLE-FAMILY AND MULTIFAMILY HOUSING THROUGHOUT THE UNITED STATES.

Fannie Mae is a perfect example of the American "century of progress." The company was created during the New Deal as a federal agency to fund home loans nationwide. In 1968, Fannie Mae was chartered by Congress as a private company to harness private capital, using private sector management and efficiency to achieve the public mission of expanding homeownership in America. The results? Nothing short of spectacular.

Today, Fannie Mae is the Fortune 500's largest nonbank financial services company, with a book of business of over $1 trillion. A shareholder-owned company traded on the New York Stock Exchange (FNM), Fannie Mae has helped more than 38 million families achieve the American Dream of homeownership.

Fannie Mae is headquartered in Washington, D.C., with five regional offices and over 50 local Fannie Mae Partnership Offices across the United States. The company raises capital from Wall Street and global investors to purchase or guarantee home loans originated by mortgage lenders. In the process, Fannie Mae provides a steady, nationwide flow of mortgage funds in all communities, at all times, under all economic conditions.

To help mortgage lenders serve more consumers and provide better service, Fannie Mae also develops and offers a range of technology products and services to make the mortgage process simpler, faster, and more cost-efficient.

For example, Fannie Mae was an early pioneer in making low down payment mortgages a national standard and now offers lenders the ability to make 30-year, fixed-rate, conventional loans with as little as three percent down. Fannie Mae's market-leading Desktop Originator® and Desktop Underwriter® technology, available to mortgage lenders on the Internet via www.efanniemae.com, enables lenders of all sizes and business models—from large national banks with mortgage subsidiaries to small community thrifts—to originate and process a range of innovative mortgage products from any desktop personal computer.

And, as one of the world's largest E-business companies, Fannie Mae harnesses the power of the Internet to help mortgage lenders offer consumers the best possible low-cost mortgage experience.

Beyond simply financing mortgages, Fannie Mae focuses on expanding homeownership particularly among underserved families. In 1994, Fannie Mae pledged to provide $1 trillion in funds to 10 million low- and moderate-income families, minorities, and immigrants and to achieve this target by the end of 2000. After meeting the goal early, Fannie Mae launched a redoubled new pledge to provide $2 trillion to 18 million underserved families before 2010.

Within this commitment, Fannie Mae has launched a series of multibillion-dollar investment plans in communities across the country with a range of local housing partners, including local chamber of commerce members such as banks, home builders, real estate professionals, and commercial developers. Notably, Fannie Mae invests capital and offers other financing strategies to make affordable homes and multifamily rental housing available to renew distressed neighborhoods.

Lest anybody question whether a private company with a public mission can have a profitable business, consider this: Fannie Mae has delivered 14 years of record earnings—over 50 consecutive quarters—a performance few Fortune 500 financial services companies can match.

Thus, instead of government subsidizing low-cost mortgages using taxpayer funds, Fannie Mae lowers mortgage costs using private capital and market forces, delivering the public benefits of homeownership without a penny of public money. Adam Smith and Alexis de Tocqueville might be very proud of how Fannie Mae continues to harness the restless American spirit of enterprise and ingenuity to deliver the American Dream of homeownership.

OPPOSITE PAGE: FANNIE MAE HAS HELPED MORE THAN 38 MILLION FAMILIES ACHIEVE THE AMERICAN DREAM OF HOME-OWNERSHIP BY PROVIDING A STEADY FLOW OF MORTGAGE FUNDS NATIONWIDE. · ABOVE: WITH ITS HOME OFFICE IN WASHINGTON, D.C., FANNIE MAE HAS FIVE REGIONAL OFFICES AND OVER 50 LOCAL FANNIE MAE PARTNERSHIP OFFICES IN CITIES ACROSS THE UNITED STATES. · LEFT: FRANKLIN D. RAINES IS CHAIRMAN AND CHIEF EXECUTIVE OFFICER OF FANNIE MAE. FANNIE MAE PROVIDES ADVANCED TECHNOLOGY VIA THE INTERNET TO ASSIST LENDERS IN EFFICIENTLY ORIGINATING AND PROCESSING A RANGE OF MORTGAGES. ALL PHOTOS © FANNIE MAE

With a successful and enduring heritage, First Security Corporation is now engaged in furthering its brand of service, 'Giving 110 percent,' as a partner in the 'Next Stage' with Wells Fargo.

First Security Corporation was organized in 1928 with resources of $28 million. The "multibank holding company"—an innovation of Marriner S. Eccles, who served as the corporation's first president—made it possible to operate 25 independent banks under a central corporate entity, thus benefiting from economies of scale.

First Security weathered the 1929 Crash and the ensuing Great Depression without losing a penny of its depositors' money. In fact, it helped to avert a banking crisis in the Intermountain West by acquiring a number of failing competitor banks. One of those acquisitions—the Deseret National Bank, founded in 1871 by Brigham Young—tied First Security to Utah's pioneer history.

In 1934, President Roosevelt appointed Marriner chairman of the Federal Reserve Board, a post Marriner held until 1951. Leadership of First Security fell to its vice president and general manager, E. G. Bennett, who was just back from a six-month assignment in Washington, D.C., where he had supervised the examination of 8,000 banks for the newly formed FDIC. Poor health prompted Bennett's early retirement in 1945, and George Eccles, secretary/treasurer of First Security and Marriner's younger brother, who had gradually taken on more responsibilities during Bennett's illness, became president of the corporation.

By 1970, the First Security executive management team consisted of George Eccles, president and CEO, Marriner Eccles, chairman, and their nephew, Spencer F. Eccles, executive vice president. In 1975, George became chairman and CEO, Marriner took the title of honorary chairman, and Spencer was elected president and COO.

With the deaths of Marriner, in 1977, and George, in 1982, Spencer Eccles was named president, chairman, and CEO of First Security. The corporation had become the leading banking organization in the Utah–Idaho–southwestern Wyoming area, with assets totaling $4 billion.

Under Spencer's leadership, First Security expanded into Oregon, Nevada, New Mexico, and California, and by 1999, its assets had grown to $23 billion. Spencer, now age 65, faced complex choices relative to First Security's future. He needed to double the size of the organization to be able to effectively compete in national and international markets, and he needed to find a successor. One solution would be a "merger of equals" with Zions Bancorp, the only other independent banking company of size between the Mississippi River and California. Zions Bancorp, formerly owned by the Mormon Church, was also headquartered in Salt Lake City and was led by a bright young CEO. The merger would retain the First Security name and Spencer would serve as chairman and co-CEO until his 68th birthday, in 2002. The merger, announced in June 1999, promised to be ideal, but proved to be doomed.

In the wake of the failed merger with Zions, Spencer formed an alliance with Wells Fargo, a $225 billion bank holding company with roots in Utah and a history dating back to 1852. These two companies successfully merged under the Wells Fargo name on October 25, 2000.

First Security Corporation and the Eccles family have been major players in the development of the Intermountain West. They have provided for accumulation of wealth by financing businesses, farms, real estate, and consumer

loans; by generating thousands of jobs; by financially supporting communities; and by securing the holdings of depositors and shareholders.

Though the First Security name is retired, the heritage is permanent. First Security's motto/logo has been "Giving 110 percent" and it is now engaged in furthering its brand of service as a partner in the "Next Stage" with Wells Fargo.

OPPOSITE PAGE: FIRST SECURITY WEATHERED THE GREAT DEPRESSION OF 1929 WITHOUT LOSING A PENNY OF ITS DEPOSITORS' MONEY. IN OCTOBER 1929, A LARGE SIGN ON THE BANK'S BOISE, IDAHO, BRANCH EXTENDS TO ITS PATRONS THE IDEAL INVITATION OF THE DAY: "IF YOU WANT YOUR MONEY COME AND GET IT." · ABOVE: MARRINER ECCLES'S NEPHEW SPENCER F. ECCLES, CHAIRMAN AND CEO OF FIRST SECURITY CORPORATION, STANDS IN FRONT OF THE COMPANY'S SALT LAKE CITY, UTAH, CORPORATE HEADQUARTERS BUILDING IN APRIL 2001. · LEFT: A PHOTOGRAPH TAKEN TOWARD THE END OF THE GREAT DEPRESSION SHOWS (SECOND FROM THE RIGHT, SEATED) FIRST SECURITY BANKING PIONEER MARRINER S. ECCLES, WITH HIS BROTHERS (FROM LEFT) SPENCER, WILLARD, AND GEORGE.

HEALING IN A NEW CENTURY

HEALTH CARE, PHARMACEUTICALS, & MEDICAL TECHNOLOGY

LIFE EXPECTANCY IN THE UNITED STATES INCREASED BY AN ASTOUNDING 30 YEARS IN THE 20TH CENTURY. IN THE PAST 100 YEARS, MORE PROGRESS WAS MADE IN SAVING AND EXTENDING HUMAN LIFE THAN IN THE PREVIOUS 5,000 YEARS. ADVANCES IN HEALTH CARE, FUELED BY MEDICAL TECHNOLOGIES, MODERN TREATMENT FACILITIES,

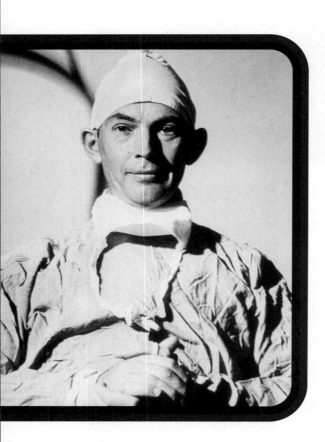

and miracle drug therapies—all powered by economic growth—deserve a great share of the credit.

Health care in all its aspects encompasses one-seventh of the American economy. More than 11 million people work in the health services industry, including five million who work in the nearly 7,000 hospitals across the country and nearly a million people who work in the growing area of home health care. All told, the vital drug, medical device, and hospital industries not only extend lives and ease pain but have a huge economic impact. The drug industry employs more than 212,000 people, the medical instruments industry more than 274,000. The drug industry alone spent more than $20 billion on research and development during the year 2000.

SAFE SURGERY, PURE DRUGS

The foundations for some of the medical miracles of the 20th century were laid by 19th-century scientists, doctors, and businessmen. French chemist Louis Pasteur hypothesized that miniscule organisms called "germs" were responsible for making people sick. In 1865, Dr. Joseph Lister, a British surgeon, applied Pasteur's thinking to surgery and used carbolic acid to sterilize instruments, wounds, and dressings.

An American advocate of Lister's techniques, Robert Wood Johnson joined the medical products company founded by his two brothers, Johnson & Johnson, which began operations in 1886 in New Brunswick, New Jersey. Within a year, the company was manufacturing antiseptic surgical dressings. In 1888, it released its first catalog, 32 pages long, with 14 pages devoted to medicated plasters that were used to keep applied medicines close to the skin.

Later, Robert published a booklet entitled *Modern Methods of Antiseptic Wound Treatment.* Intended to educate the public about germs and heat sterilization for surgery, the booklet also described related Johnson & Johnson products like bandages and sutures. The company distributed four million copies worldwide.

Johnson & Johnson products were soon ubiquitous. The first "First Aid Kits" were distributed to railroad workers in the 1890s, and during the Spanish-American War, Johnson & Johnson products were used to treat injured soldiers. In 1921, Johnson & Johnson introduced Band-Aid adhesive bandages, which became so widely used that the product name became

Above: A pharmaceutical technician processes one of the nation's 1,000 medicines under development. · Opposite: South African surgeon Dr. Christiaan Barnard, who studied at the University of Minnesota, in 1967 became the world's first doctor to perform a heart transplant.

the generic name for all such bandages. Today, Johnson & Johnson is a family of 190 companies in 175 countries, providing a wide range of consumer and professional products and medical drugs.

The 19th-century pharmaceutical industry was in its infancy rather unsavory. Slick patent-medicine salesmen peddled their wares to ignorant consumers. While many patent medicines had an herbal base, others were often simply alcohol- or cocaine-based. Navy surgeon Dr. Edward Robinson Squibb, disgusted with the erratic—and occasionally dangerous—quality of the drugs he was issued to treat soldiers, began his own company in New York City in 1856. Among other products, he produced chloroform, a recently invented anesthetic. With the advent of the

Civil War, demand for chloroform increased so rapidly that his company could hardly keep up with production.

Meanwhile, Squibb embarked on a campaign to ensure the purity and quality of drugs in America and to stop charlatans. Squibb started a medical journal called *An Ephemeris*, in which he discussed new medicines and procedures and exposed quacks. Squibb petitioned the federal government to pass legislation requiring pure food and drugs, which eventually led to the Pure Food and Drug Act of 1906. In 1989, Squibb's company merged with Bristol-Myers, another venerable pharmaceutical firm developed in the 19th century. Today, 70 percent of Bristol-Myers Squibb's business is devoted to developing pharmaceuticals like Taxol, the landmark anticancer drug, which in 1992 was approved to treat ovarian cancer.

Even with drugs that were pure, many were often useless because the human body could not dissolve them. In 1885, a Michigan doctor named William Erastus Upjohn patented a new "friable" pill that could be crushed by a thumb—an image he later used extensively in advertising his new invention. He formed the Upjohn Pill and Granule Company in Kalamazoo, and by 1900, his company was selling

MILESTONES IN MEDICINE

Drs. Varaztad Kazanjian of Boston and Vilray Blair of St. Louis pioneered modern plastic surgery, repairing the disfigured faces of World War I soldiers. · The first blood bank in the nation was opened at the Cook County Hospital in Chicago in 1937. · A leader in the study of birth defects, Dr. Virginia Apgar, of Westfield, New Jersey, developed a system in 1952 of five criteria for determining if a newborn needs resuscitation. Today, the Apgar Score is a common procedure. · The first successful surgery to separate Siamese twins was performed in 1953 on two-month-old girls at the Ochsner Foundation Hospital in New Orleans. · The technique for DNA cloning was invented by Herbert Boyer of the University of California, San Francisco, and Stanley Cohen of Stanford University in 1973. · Artificial skin was developed at Massachusetts General Hospital in 1981 by Ioannis Yannas and John Burke.

2,000 items. In 1908, he created a laxative called Phenolax in the then-unusual tablet form. In just six years, the company was selling 100 million Phenolax tablets annually. Upjohn's company continued to develop new products, but the doctor wanted to take the company in a different direction, toward a world-class, research-based pharmaceutical firm.

Over the years, his vision was realized and expanded upon. In 1995, the Upjohn Company merged with the European firm Pharmacia, and in 2000, the firm of Pharmacia and Upjohn merged with the Monsanto Corporation to become one of the world's fastest growing pharmaceutical companies, the Pharmacia Corporation, whose American headquarters are in Peapack, New Jersey. The company invests more than $2 billion each year in research and development of pharmaceuticals.

Another major pioneer and player in the development of life-saving drugs was Eli Lilly. Eli Lilly and Company was founded in Indianapolis in 1876 by Civil War veteran Colonel Lilly, a chemist who was frustrated by the poor quality of the medicines available. Lilly pioneered the use of solid research and science to make and improve medical drugs, and insisted that only doctors be allowed to dispense drugs. True to its founder, today the $10 billion

A Century of Achievement

Over the course of the 20th century, these and other companies and their researchers developed therapies that have conquered diseases and afflictions that have plagued mankind since the dawn of time.

At the turn of the century, diseases that for most people today are mere annoyances were literally life threatening. The influenza epidemic of 1918–1919 started out of the blue and in a short time had killed 21 million people, one percent of the world's population. It was the third worst epidemic in

named Jonas Salk teamed up with a microbiologist named Thomas Francis Jr., who was working on an influenza vaccine. They developed one in time to treat the U.S. military during World War II. When Salk became head of the Virus Research Lab at the University of Pittsburgh, he began to examine a different virus, the polio virus, which attacked nerve cells and the central nervous system and could cause paralysis and even death. Polio outbreaks, which had steadily increased since the turn of the century, affected tens of thousands of people

ABOVE: THANKS TO PHARMACIA CORPORATION'S $2 BILLION-A-YEAR INVESTMENT IN RESEARCH AND DEVELOPMENT, THIS SENIOR RESEARCH MICROBIOLOGIST AND OTHERS LIKE HER AT THE GLOBAL COMPANY CAN DEVELOP MEDICINES TO TREAT CANCER, ARTHRITIS/INFLAMMATION, INFECTIOUS DISEASES, AND DISORDERS OF THE CENTRAL NERVOUS SYSTEM. · OPPOSITE: ALONG WITH DILIGENCE, A CLEAN ROOM IS A PREREQUISITE FOR PACKAGING MEDICAL SUPPLIES AT THIS AMERICAN FIRM, ONE OF MANY THAT EXCEL IN PACKAGE DESIGN AND COST EFFECTIVENESS.

Eli Lilly and Company is best known for the world's biggest selling antidepressant, Prozac, and for anticancer treatments like Gemzar, insulin, and the osteoporosis medicine Evista.

recorded history. It disappeared as suddenly as it came, but not before leaving a billion people affected in its wake.

The fight against influenza led to other breakthrough discoveries. In 1938, a doctor

every year. Salk developed an experimental vaccine in 1952 that he eventually tested on volunteers including himself, his wife, and his children. They all produced antibodies to the virus. Within two years, schoolchildren

DR. JONAS SALK WORKS IN THE UNIVERSITY OF PITTSBURGH MEDICAL SCHOOL'S VIRUS RESEARCH LABORATORY IN 1955, THE YEAR HIS CREATION OF THE FIRST SUCCESSFUL POLIO VACCINE WAS ANNOUNCED.

across the country were inoculated. In 1962, scientist Albert Sabin, working at the University of Cincinnati College of Medicine, developed an oral version of the vaccine, which became the standard. Today, while there is still no cure for polio, cases in the United States are extremely rare.

Another major advance was the discovery of antibiotics in 1928 by Alexander Fleming, a Scottish scientist, who was the first to identify *Penicillium notatum*. However, he was not able to grow significant amounts of the mold, and it was turned over to a team of chemists who soon lost interest in pursuing its development.

In 1935, two British chemists named Howard Florey and Ernst Chain revived interest in penicillin and enlisted an American agricultural research center, which was successful in growing the mold. By 1943, at the height of World War II, only 400 million units of penicillin had been made, but the U.S. government recruited 21 pharmaceutical companies to help, and by the end of the war, 650 billion units of penicillin were being made every month. In 1945, Fleming, Florey, and Chain shared a Nobel Prize for their great lifesaving contribution.

Besides making tremendous strides in this country, pharmaceutical companies and their teams of scientists and researchers are also leading the way when it comes to helping people in other countries. Merck and Company, based in Whitehouse Station, New Jersey, is donating vaccines for measles, mumps, and rubella for use in Honduras to help eradicate measles and rubella in the western hemisphere. Philadelphia-based Wyeth-Ayerst Laboratories has donated more than 1.5 million doses of oral polio vaccine (worth $10 million) to national immunization programs in Guatemala, Romania, and Bulgaria.

SmithKline Beecham, also of Philadelphia, supplies free drugs to treat elephantiasis in about one-fifth of the world's population. And Bristol-Myers Squibb is spending $100 million in five southern African countries to fund Acquired Immune Deficiency Syndrome (AIDS) research trials, train physicians, and help private organizations with AIDS prevention and treatment programs.

The Drug Development Process

Almost half of the 152 major medicines released in the last two decades were developed by American drug companies. Before their release, these drugs went through a development process which is longer and more complex than ever before. Average drug development time steadily increased from just over eight years in the 1960s to 11.6 years in the 1970s, 14.2 in the 1980s, and 15.3 in the early 1990s. On average, a developer will evaluate about 5,000 compounds and select 250 for laboratory testing. Of those, only five will make it to clinical testing on human volunteers. And only one will pass clinical trials and gain approval by the Food and Drug Administration (FDA).

The process is expensive as well. Developing one drug costs an average of $500 million. Since the 1970s, research spending on pharmaceuticals has almost doubled every five years. In 1997, companies spent more than $20 billion on finding and developing new medicines.

Despite the expense and lengthy delays, the pharmaceutical industry has tackled some of the most intractable diseases. America's pharmaceutical companies currently have more than 1,000 new medicines in development, including 96 new drugs for heart disease and stroke, 316 anticancer medicines,

17 new treatments for Alzheimer's disease, and 29 medicines for arthritis.

Working side by side with these drugs are generics and over-the-counter medicines. Generics are produced by companies like Miami-based IVAX; Schein Pharmaceutical, of Florham Park, New Jersey; and Mylan Laboratories, headquartered in Pittsburgh. Generic medicines typically cost 50 percent to 90 percent less than name brands. Over-the-counter drugs are produced by developers like Bristol-Myers Squibb, New York–based Pfizer, and Schering-Plough, of Madison, New Jersey, and address everything from minor aches and pains to coughs, sunburn, and a myriad of life's other little problems.

Instruments of Good Health

Robert Wood Johnson's first gauzes and antiseptics were the beginning of what is today a $16 billion industry encompassing nearly 130,000 medical products, from eyeglasses and hospital gowns to wheelchairs. The related $120 billion medical device industry produces vital equipment, like pacemakers and shunts, and is responsible for many other developments, such as devices that permit diabetics to test their blood-sugar level with a minimum of pain.

One leader in the medical device field is Medtronic, which manufactures pacemakers, spinal implant devices, and implantable drug delivery systems, among its many products. Founded by Earl Bakken and Palmer Hermundslie in Minneapolis in 1949 as a medical equipment repair and sales company, Medtronic soon began manufacturing custom-made equipment for midwestern customers. One of those customers was Dr. C. Walton Lillehei, an open-heart surgeon at the University of Minnesota's medical school. In 1957, Lillehei decided to make a better pacemaker. At the time, the only pacemakers available were bulky and unreliable, had to be plugged into a wall outlet, and occasionally shocked the patient. Lillehei's device was better but still needed to be plugged in. He tapped Medtronic to build a battery pack for the device. Soon, the battery-powered pacemaker became a major advance for patients. Eventually, the electronic components of the device were also improved, and by 1960, Medtronic had become a major manufacturer of biomedical devices including newly developed implantable pacemakers. Over the years, Medtronic made many new technological developments and is today a $4 billion company.

The incredible progress made in organ transplants—a procedure that was unthinkable half a century ago—and the drugs that prevent organ transplants from being rejected have ironically caused a new problem, one the medical devices industry hopes to solve.

Every year, 30,000 Americans qualify for a heart transplant; only 2,000 will get one. An artificial heart would help those 28,000 Americans who can't get a transplant. Danvers, Massachusetts–based Abiomed has created an artificial, battery-powered heart called AbioCor. It weighs just two pounds—a pound more than a real heart—and has a seamless surface that discourages the creation of blood clots and decreases the need for many strong blood thinners. The AbioCor was first implanted in a patient at the University of Louisville and Jewish Hospital in 2001.

THE HEALTH CARE SYSTEM

The great advances in medical treatments and procedures have been accompanied by changes in the way health care is administered. For much of the 20th century, most Americans had indemnity insurance. They could go to any doctor, hospital, or provider, and the insurer and patient would each pay

BELOW: RESEARCHERS USE A MODEL TO STUDY THE STRUCTURE AND FUNCTION OF A MOLECULE IN RELATION TO THEIR WORK DEVELOPING GENE THERAPIES THAT CAN REMEDY DISEASE AND IMPROVE THE QUALITY OF LIFE. · OPPOSITE: A RESEARCHER EXAMINES A FILM OF DNA, ON THE LOOKOUT FOR EVEN THE TINIEST ERRORS THAT CAN CAUSE DISEASE. AS PROGRESS IN MAPPING THE HUMAN GENOME HAS UNFOLDED OVER THE LAST DECADE, THE FEDERAL GOVERNMENT HAS TRANSFERRED TECHNOLOGY TO THE PRIVATE SECTOR TO DEVELOP NEW MEDICAL APPLICATIONS.

part of the bill. When *Marcus Welby, MD* premiered on television in 1969, only 10 percent of Americans lacked some form of private or public health insurance. Of those who did have insurance, almost 100 percent had fee-for-service plans in which the doctor's judgment ruled. Yet public dissatisfaction with health care was rampant.

The 1970s saw the rise of the health maintenance organizations, or HMOs, led by Dr. Paul Ellwood, the "father of the HMO" and the founder of United Healthcare. Although the idea behind the HMO—that is, a plan in which members prepaid for comprehensive health care—had been around since Henry J. Kaiser and Dr. Sidney R. Garfield offered such a plan to the public in 1945 through Kaiser-Permanente in Oakland, California, it was Ellwood who coined the term and helped contribute to the HMOs' growth. Today, 67 million Americans belong to HMOs, including Kaiser Foundation Health Plan, Aetna–U.S. Healthcare, and Humana.

Health care insurance also brings up the related question of long-term care. One of the greatest challenges of the 21st century is figuring out how to take care of people at the end of their lives and maintain their dignity and comfort. In an aging society, this issue has become increasingly important. There is no single model for this type of care. It could encompass the $87 billion nursing home industry or the $34 billion home health care industry. By the year 2005, about nine million Americans will need long-term care. With the number of elderly increasing, it is no surprise that more than 100 companies offer long-term care insurance. For example, First Penn–Pacific Life Insurance Company, of Schaumburg, Illinois, offers plans to protect retirees' assets against the rising cost of living and of long-term care and provides

financial planning, term insurance, and emergency-fund planning products.

GETTING BETTER ALL THE TIME

With the many health care options available to them, consumers are seeking more information about health and medicine. According to the Washington, D.C.–based American Association of Health Plans, a trade association that seeks to keep the public informed about issues involving managed health care, consumers will increasingly use the Internet to interact with their doctors and make informed decisions about their health care.

It is estimated that 17 million Americans use the Internet to find disease-related information; more than one-third are seeking cancer information. The National Cancer Institute helps individuals find information about clinical trials of experimental drugs. Some drug companies have also helped fund a site that provides information on soon-to-be released drugs and helps

individuals find clinical trials in their area. The University of Pennsylvania operates a database of medical articles.

In addition to the Internet, patients also turn to their pharmacists for information. According to the National Association of Chain Drug Stores, an Alexandria, Virginia–based organization that represents retailers and consumers, pharmacists are increasingly working with doctors to offer advice on patient care.

The fields of medicine and health care have advanced to levels unimagined even by the most forward-thinking individuals a century ago. Yet ahead are even more exciting developments. Life spans are longer and people are healthier than ever. Diseases of the developing world are increasingly being brought under control. And in the next 100 years, the world will witness amazing advances in gene research and therapies— all led by the vision and funding of America's companies.

SPECIAL REPORT: BIOTECHNOLOGY

COAXING MIRACLES FROM MOLECULES

The future of the pharmaceutical industry increasingly lies in biotechnology, in which companies use sophisticated techniques to coax miracles out of mere molecules. Of the industry as a whole, which ranges from agriculture to criminal forensics, medical biotechnology accounts for nearly a quarter of the U.S. industry's sales.

The biotechnology industry was born in 1953 when James D. Watson and Francis Crick outlined DNA's double-helix structure. More recent events have shaped today's biotechnology industry. In 1980, the U.S. Supreme Court ruled that life forms can be patented, and in 1988, patent protection was extended to genetically engineered mice, moving the ball forward on the search for gene therapies. In 1989, researchers in the United States and Great Britain embarked on an ambitious effort to map the 30,000 genes on 23 chromosomes and sequence their three billion DNA base pairs. On June 26, 2000, the Anglo-U.S. Human Genome Project (whose U.S. base is the National Institutes of Health in Washington, D.C.) and Celera Genomics Corporation, of Rockville, Maryland, announced jointly that they had deciphered the human genetic code. (Both entities had worked independently on the project.) This breakthrough may well provide the key to understanding the basis of genetic diseases like muscular dystrophy and Alzheimer's.

A global biotechnology company that has made invaluable contributions in the fields of oncology, nephrology, and rheumatology is Amgen, based in Thousand Oaks, California. The company's products treat such diseases as chronic renal failure and fight infection associated with certain types of chemotherapy. Amgen's research program is developing small-molecule drugs and protein therapeutics that may eventually serve in the treatment of such debilitating diseases as osteoporosis, Parkinson's, and cancer.

Other leading biotechnology firms include Chiron, of Emeryville, California, which manufactures Proleukin for the treatment of metastic renal cell carcinoma or metastic melanoma, and San Francisco–based Genentech, maker of the metastic breast cancer medicine Herceptin. The companies are partially owned by Novartis and Hoffman–La Roche respectively. Another top biotechnology firm, Centocor, of Malvern, Pennsylvania, produces the well-known heart drug ReoPro. America's biotech companies will continue their quest for cures to diseases like diabetes, leukemia, and AIDS.

The biotechnology industry is as risky as it is promising; only one drug in 10,000 makes it to market. Nevertheless, the industry continues to make tremendous strides in bringing better health—and longer and better lives—to all.

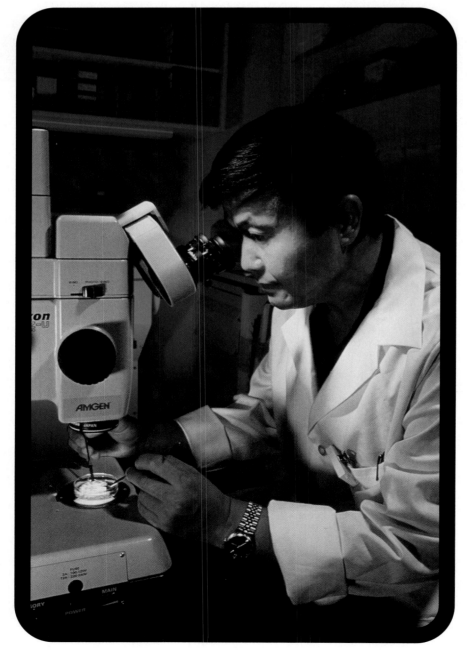

ABOVE: EPOGEN, DEVELOPED BY AMGEN FOR THE TREATMENT OF ANEMIA ASSOCIATED WITH CHRONIC RENAL FAILURE, UNDERGOES PROCESSING IN ROLLER BOTTLES. THE MEDICINE IS ONE OF THE BEST-SELLING PHARMACEUTICALS IN THE WORLD. · OPPOSITE: A SCIENTIST AT AMGEN OBSERVES THE MICROSCOPIC STRUCTURE OF THE BRAIN.

profiles
Biotechnology &
Pharmaceuticals

AMGEN

A GLOBAL BIOTECHNOLOGY COMPANY, AMGEN DEVELOPS HUMAN THERAPEUTICS, USING SCIENCE AND INNOVATION TO DRAMATICALLY IMPROVE PEOPLE'S LIVES.

Launched just over two decades ago, Amgen today is the world's largest independent biotechnology company—a Fortune 500 firm with 2000 revenues of more than $3.6 billion and net income of more than $1.1 billion. Its business success story provides inspiration for countless entrepreneurs. In its earliest years, Amgen (then Applied Molecular Genetics), pioneered the development of novel and innovative products based on advances in recombinant DNA and molecular biology. The company invested its hard-earned capital in manufacturing recombinant dyes, detergents, and animal growth hormones; it employed just a few people and operated from small, shared corporate offices.

Today, Amgen researches potential therapeutic products for nephrology, cancer, rheumatoid arthritis, and metabolic and neurodegenerative diseases, employing some 7,500 people worldwide. Its corporate head-quarters are on a 120-acre campus in Thousand Oaks, a location chosen for its proximity to the major research centers of Southern California's leading educational institutes. The company also maintains research facilities in Boulder, Colorado; Cambridge, Massachusetts; and Cambridge, England; manufacturing facilities in Longmont and Boulder, Colorado, and Juncos, Puerto Rico; distribution centers in Louisville, Kentucky, and Breda, the Netherlands; and other operations in Australia, Canada, Europe, and Asia.

The Amgen workforce is dedicated to achieving the company's aspiration to be the world's best human therapeutics company, living the Amgen values and using science and innovation to dramatically improve people's lives. As part of an industry that has been described as the incubator of most of the progress that will be made in human health care in the coming decades, the company attracts some of the brightest scientists and researchers from leading universities around the globe. These men and women are engaged in strenuous competition with the nation's largest pharmaceutical and biotechnology companies to create new therapeutics.

Biotechnology uses high-tech procedures to extend the reach of science to unleash the body's own powerful therapeutic responses. Biotechnology-based therapeutics act with a direct physiological role at the molecular and cellular levels. Ever since Francis Crick and James Watson started unraveling the secrets of DNA in 1953—for which they, with Maurice Wilkins, became Nobel laureates in medicine in 1962—genetic researchers have devoted careers to determining how to put the ensuing breakthroughs to work for mankind.

Under the leadership of its first chairman and CEO, George B. Rathmann, Ph.D., Amgen's success began with its first product, a breakthrough drug named EPOGEN® (Epoetin alfa). EPOGEN has improved the health and quality of life for dialysis patients by helping their bodies produce needed red blood cells. Until the landmark product EPOGEN was available, kidney dialysis patients who experienced anemia often received blood transfusions to help restore their supply of red blood cells. EPOGEN is now the seventh largest–selling drug therapy in the United States.

Amgen's second product, NEUPOGEN® (Filgrastim), which stimulates the production of white blood cells, also has broad acceptance. It is widely administered to chemotherapy patients to fight infection.

For its extraordinary achievements in the commercial application of technology, Amgen became the first biotechnology company to receive the National Medal of Technology, earning this presidential award in 1994.

And Amgen has a pipeline of promising new therapeutics. Among these is Aranesp™ (darbepoetin alfa), which is designed to represent a new standard of care in treating anemia in patients with chronic kidney disease. The company invests heavily in research and development (R&D expenses were equal to 26 percent of sales in 2000), and it forms academic and corporate collaborations to further accelerate its progress.

Amgen also invests in the community, contributing more than $5.5 million annually through the Amgen Foundation and a wide range of other corporate contributions, as well as providing hands-on volunteer assistance via the Amgen Staff Community Involvement Program.

Under the leadership of current chairman and CEO, Kevin W. Sharer, Amgen pursues its enduring goals of launching a stream of products that will dramatically improve people's lives, creating an environment where the best people choose to work, and delivering superior shareholder returns compared to its industry peer group.

OPPOSITE PAGE: SHOWN HERE IS THE MOLECULAR STRUCTURE OF ARANESP™, A NEW ANEMIA TREATMENT FOR CHRONIC KIDNEY DISEASE. ARANESP IS IN AMGEN'S PIPELINE. · THIS PAGE: AMGEN HEADQUARTERS INCLUDES MORE THAN 3.8 MILLION SQUARE FEET AND 40 BUILDINGS, ON 120 ACRES IN THOUSAND OAKS, IN VENTURA COUNTY, CALIFORNIA. BUILDING 10 (ABOVE), ONE OF AMGEN'S ORIGINAL BUILDINGS, HOUSES THE COMPUTER INFORMATION SYSTEMS (CIS), INFORMATION MANAGEMENT, AND QUALITY ASSURANCE STAFFS. BUILDING 14 (LEFT) IS THE SITE OF AMGEN'S MOLECULAR AND CELLULAR BIOLOGICAL RESEARCH.

profiles
Health Care Associations

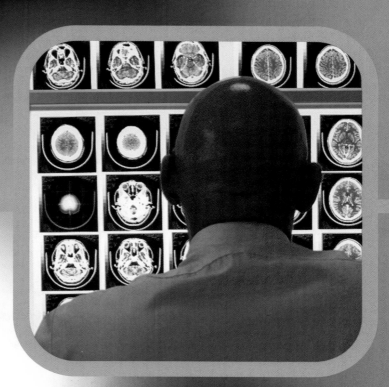

AMERICAN ASSOCIATION OF

THE AMERICAN ASSOCIATION OF HEALTH PLANS PERFORMS AN ADVOCACY ROLE ON BEHALF OF ITS MEMBERS—MORE THAN 1,000 MANAGED HEALTH CARE ORGANIZATIONS LOCATED NATIONWIDE.

Over the last decade, managed health care has moved to the forefront of the health industry, facing many challenges on various fronts. The American Association of Health Plans (AAHP), the largest managed health care trade association, has played a lead role in helping this diverse, growing industry participate in the national health care debate, while leading the effort to address the challenges and seize the opportunities of health care in the 21st century. In the process, AAHP's efforts have helped revolutionize the way issues are advocated in Washington and across the nation.

AAHP's membership is as extensive as it is diverse, consisting of more than 1,000 managed health care organizations throughout the United States, from large companies, serving millions of enrollees, to community-based plans, serving just a few thousand people. These organizations differ not only in size, but also in the nature of care they provide. AAHP's membership includes nonprofit and for-profit health maintenance organizations, preferred provider organizations, point-of-service organizations, and others. The AAHP membership is a dynamic, forward-looking force, providing high quality health care and keeping it affordable.

The managed care industry has faced many challenges—from proposals for anticonsumer legislation that would compromise health plan organizations' ability to provide consumers with quality, affordable health care, to demands by a rapidly expanding industry that health plan organizations adapt. AAHP, led by its president and CEO, Karen Ignagni, stands at the helm as the managed care industry sails into uncharted waters and new opportunities.

"Our mission is to help create a political environment that allows health plan organizations to provide the best and most affordable health care to consumers," explains Ignagni, who joined AAHP in 1993, just as the trend toward managed care began to grow. Some politicians used this opportunity to try to advance proposals that would expose health plan organizations and employers to lawsuits

HEALTH PLANS

that were seen by some as frivolous. Ignagni's wide-ranging experience in Washington has helped protect health plans and others from frivolous lawsuits.

ISSUE ADVOCACY IN THE 21ST CENTURY

Ignagni laid the groundwork for facing such challenges by transforming AAHP into a new style of association: one that is nimble, proactive, and tailored to seize the emerging opportunities of the 21st century. Political campaign veterans were hired, along with high-technology specialists who brought ideas for leveraging the possibilities of the Internet. AAHP also built a state-of-the-art database of information on 32 million health care consumers, which enables the association's member organizations to quickly enlist an army of grassroots activists to send Washington policymakers a message on any important issue. Further capitalizing on new technology, AAHP now makes regular Internet broadcasts, reaching more consumers and policymakers than ever before.

All these efforts led toward the demise of dated lobbying strategies and the beginning of a new brand of outreach that resembles more an agile political campaign than a traditional lobbyists' battle. "Most people think of trade associations as groups that buttonhole legislators and make back room deals," says Ignagni. "This is not the way it is now. Today, it is necessary to aggressively drive the debate. We send out our message using all the vehicles of a political campaign, with polling, grassroots organizing, and all the earned media attention we can gain."

As AAHP put these strategies to work and successes accrued for its membership, even its opponents took notice, crediting Ignagni with revitalizing AAHP and strengthening its influence.

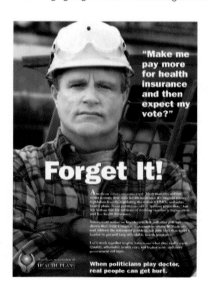

One illustration of the way AAHP has influenced lobbying is the strategy it used to mute health maintenance organization (HMO) reform as a significant issue in the 2000 presidential primaries. In early 1999, the potential candidates had begun focusing on the politically critical states of Iowa and New Hampshire, testing the issues and the rhetoric for their campaigns in the 2000 primaries. At the time, efforts in Washington to expose HMOs to lawsuits were in full swing, and HMO reform was perceived to be a popular theme with voters. The potential existed that patient protection would gain momentum as a major campaign issue, just as universal health insurance had in 1992.

Who's **delivering** more **healthy** full-term **babies?**

America's Health Plans are.

American Association of
HEALTH PLANS

Working to Make Health Care Better.

AAHP executed a strategy that proved successful in convincing candidates that managed care liability was a losing issue on the campaign trail. AAHP polled voters in Iowa and New Hampshire and, after finding relatively little active interest for HMO reform in either state, AAHP shared this information with the candidates and their staffs, as well as with local reporters and officials. HMO reform never emerged as a significant issue in either primary. Indeed, in the general election, the issues of prescription drug coverage and of reducing the ranks of the uninsured received far more debate than that of HMO reform.

The success of AAHP's strategy captured the attention of Washington lobbyists, and the *National Journal* devoted a feature to the association's "new tack." National Public Radio predicted that the effort would usher in a new approach to lobbying. AAHP's work heralded a new style of issue advocacy for trade groups of all kinds.

AAHP also worked to debunk another weapon of managed care foes: the infamous "HMO horror story." Such stories were basic to the efforts of special interest groups campaigning for HMO reform. These groups solicited people's most dramatically negative experiences with HMOs and passed them on to the media, where they became tools for reporters presenting the complex issues of managed care. Press coverage of the issue tended to be quite one-sided.

AAHP proactively researched the facts of the most widely circulated negative anecdotes and discovered that these stories were often based solely on the patients' own words, with little independent evidence to back them up. Health plan organizations, bound by privacy guidelines prohibiting them from discussing medical records, were unable to confirm or deny these accounts. AAHP prepared a report documenting the lack of confirmation for these stories, and challenged the press to approach its coverage with greater objectivity. The AAHP report led to a

Who's **helping** America's **kids** breathe a little easier?

We are.

Working to Make Health Care Better.

HEALTH PLANS CONTINUED

spate of news articles that questioned the appropriateness of the press when using such anecdotes to cover the HMO debate. The *Washington Post* said that journalists and politicians rarely hear the other side in the HMO debate. The *New York Times* observed that complex tragedies usually have two sides and that it is rare for both sides to be adequately covered.

PUTTING PATIENTS FIRST

Along with its political work, AAHP devotes time to helping members take steps to improve their record in providing quality, affordable health care. AAHP members adopted an industrywide Code of Conduct in 1997 as a means to hold themselves and their fellow organizations accountable to offer quality health care. The Code of Conduct was implemented with the goal of improving communication with patients and physicians and following through on their concerns.

"Managed health care is an evolving industry, and we will never cease our efforts to keep health care affordable while continuing to improve quality and to address consumer concerns and needs within the health care system," says Ignagni. One such step, adopted by the AAHP board of directors in summer 2000, is a set of principles that seeks to help health plan organizations simplify their administrative procedures for both patients and doctors. Another important industry-led initiative has been the Coalition for Affordable Quality Healthcare (CAQH), a coalition of 26 health plans and insurers and their trade associations working to streamline administrative procedures and improve the health care experience for more than 100 million Americans and their doctors.

AAHP also is focused on leveraging the opportunities being created by the Internet for health care consumers. According to Ignagni, a new era is imminent in which Internet technology will empower consumers to take control of their health care decisions and choices. Consumers have the ability to easily find and use the latest medical information and will soon be able to interact with their physician and receive medical advice via their personal computer.

These opportunities also bring new challenges; among them, how to maintain high standards of quality and affordability amid a period of such rapid change. In June 2000, AAHP began addressing this question, ratifying a set of principles intended to guide health plan organizations as they combine the power of 21st century technology with the high standards they spent years developing.

"We will continue to look to the future for new ways to make health care better for consumers," Ignagni says. "And we will never lose sight of the high standards to which the managed care community has always been committed."

MADE IN THE U.S.A.

MANUFACTURING & CONSUMER PRODUCTS

'WE WORK IN A SERVICE ECONOMY.' 'WE LIVE IN THE INFORMATION AGE.' 'THE INTERNET ERA IS UPON US.' 'WHAT WE DO WITH OUR BRAINS IS MORE IMPORTANT THAN WHAT WE DO WITH OUR HANDS.'

These statements reflect some of Americans' common assumptions of the times. Each one of them is true; none can be seriously challenged. Yet when all is said and done, America's prosperity, economic strength, and quality of life still depend largely on an industry born in the 19th century: manufacturing.

The manufacturing industry that arose in America as a result of the Industrial Revolution soon became a bedrock part of the economy. By the 1940s, manufacturing made up one-fifth of the American economy. Today, with the many advances and changes in the industry, manufacturing still occupies this spot. But, because gross domestic product only accounts for final sales, not for intermediate activity, economic figures actually understate the contribution that manufacturing makes. Indeed, a full three-fifths of the $3 trillion in total manufacturing sales can be attributed to intermediate activity, which includes the production of everything from primary metals to car engines.

Manufacturers also perform the nation's largest share of research and development, a whopping 57 percent. R&D by the transportation equipment, electronics, and chemical industries alone comprises 38 percent of the total. Even in the information age, where intangibles like knowledge are of utmost importance, manufacturing's role is as vital as ever.

TOOLS OF THE TRADE

The foundation of the manufacturing industry is the machine tools sector, which makes the machines that make everything else. In 1997, the production machinery, tools, and general components industry shipped $82 billion worth of goods, a figure growing 2 percent per year.

Machine tool companies started forming midway through the 19th century and by the early 1900s led the world market for industrial machinery. One of the early success stories began in Fond du Lac, Wisconsin, where the sawmills and gristmills that sprang up created demand for shops that could supply and repair machines. John Bonnell opened a small machine shop in 1859 in the middle of town and began selling sawmill equipment, farm plows, and steam engines. In 1902, the company, now called Giddings & Lewis, began designing and manufacturing machine tools such as engine lathes and horizontal boring machines. Later, it even manufactured shell lathes for use in World War I. Over the century, Giddings & Lewis continually added to and refined its product line. In 1997, the company became a subsidiary of Germany's

ABOVE: A WOMAN WEAVES COTTON BY MACHINE IN AN EARLY 1900S MILL. • OPPOSITE: HIGH-SPEED EQUIPMENT PRINTS FABRIC FOR FLOOR COVERINGS, A QUARTER OF THE U.S. TEXTILE MARKET TODAY.

Thyssen Krupp AG. Today, Giddings & Lewis is the number one maker of industrial automation products and machine tools in North America.

Another manufacturing giant got its start in the industrial age. Ingersoll-Rand is the result of the 1905 merger of Ingersoll-Sergeant Drill Company—itself a merger of the Ingersoll Rock Drill Company, established in 1871 by Simon Ingersoll, and the Sergeant Drill Company, founded in 1885 by Henry Sergeant—and Rand & Waring Drill and Compressor Company, founded by Albert Rand in 1872. Today Ingersoll-Rand, whose headquarters are in Woodcliff Lake, New Jersey, is one of the world's top manufacturers of construction and industrial machinery. The incredibly diversified company makes everything from tractors to golf carts to Schlage combination locks.

The top production equipment manufacturer in the United States is Peoria,

Illinois–based Caterpillar, which started modestly in the 1890s. Benjamin Holt and Daniel Best were two entrepreneurs experimenting with building steam tractors, each within his own company. Both worked on developing track-type tractors and gasoline-powered tractor engines. Holt's "caterpillar" track-type tractor was used by the Allies to fight in World War I. The Holt and Best companies merged in 1925 and formed the Caterpillar Tractor Company. Innovation followed innovation: diesel engines, motor graders, blade graders—even a special M4 tank engine that was used during World War II. Today, Caterpillar is the world's number one maker of earth moving machinery.

Another example of a manufacturer whose products serve a wide variety of uses is the Gorman-Rupp Company of Mansfield, Ohio. Their pumps are used in everything from clearing flood waters to delivering

clean water supplies to cities to removing water from construction sites.

The automotive parts industry owes its success to America's love affair with the car. By the end of the 20th century, the industry comprised 15,000 different companies making everything from wheel assemblies to car alarms. Employing 750,000 Americans, the automotive parts industry accounts for more than $23 billion in direct retail sales and more than $90 billion when sales to car manufacturers are included.

Dramatic Advances

Manufacturing changed dynamically over the course of the 20th century as exciting new techniques were developed. One of the earliest and perhaps one of the most important advances was the ability to control the temperature of buildings and homes. Air-conditioning, a purely 20th-century invention, fundamentally changed the way people live and work and the way products like pharmaceuticals and microchips are manufactured. Indeed, air-conditioning has been credited with creating the modern South and giving rise to important Sunbelt business centers such as Atlanta and Dallas. Many also attribute massive cultural changes to air-conditioning. For example, former news broadcaster David Brinkley credited the invention of air-conditioning, which enabled Congress to stay in Washington over the sweltering summers, with the growth of the federal government in the 1930s and 1940s.

The "father of air-conditioning," Willis Carrier was a mechanical engineer who lived in New York at the turn of the century. A thoughtful, imaginative, and determined scientist, Carrier was asked in 1902 by the Sackett-Wilhelms Lithographing and Publishing Company to figure out a way to chill the air inside the factory. The heat and humidity were changing the papers' dimensions and misaligning the colored inks, thus inhibiting the publisher's ability to print color images. After long hours of poring over Weather Bureau tables and scientific texts, Carrier invented a machine that would draw air over coils holding a cold chemical, thereby cooling the air. Later that same year, while pacing late at night on a foggy train platform in Pittsburgh, Carrier envisioned

all fundamental calculations in the air-conditioning industry.

In 1915, Carrier and some friends formed the Carrier Engineering Company and developed other products such as the centrifugal refrigeration machine, a key invention that enabled homes, schools, hospitals, stores, airports, and office buildings to be air-conditioned. "Comfort cooling" was first installed at the J. L. Hudson Department Store in Detroit in 1924. Later that year,

Great Depression and World War II prevented the further development of residential air-conditioning systems, but during the postwar boom, cooling units sprouted in houses across the country.

Today, the Carrier Corporation, of Farmington, Connecticut, is a subsidiary of United Technologies and the world's largest manufacturer of heating, ventilation, air-conditioning, and refrigeration (HVAC) equipment. Carrier's company, which

ABOVE: DR. WILLIS CARRIER, THE "FATHER" OF AIR-CONDITIONING, HOLDS A THERMOMETER INSIDE AN IGLOO DISPLAY AT THE 1939 WORLD'S FAIR IN ST. LOUIS TO DEMONSTRATE THE STEADY 68-DEGREE TEMPERATURE INSIDE. CARRIER'S 20TH-CENTURY INVENTION DRAMATICALLY IMPACTED THE AMERICAN WAY OF LIFE AND IS EVEN CREDITED WITH GIVING RISE TO THE MODERN SOUTH. • OPPOSITE: A ROAD PAVING COMPACTOR BY INGERSOLL-RAND, ONE OF THE WORLD'S TOP MANUFACTURERS OF INDUSTRIAL AND CONSTRUCTION MACHINERY, IS READY TO ROLL.

yet another machine that would "wash" the air in a foggy mist. He patented his invention, Apparatus for Treating Air, in 1906. His 1911 paper formally explaining his ideas would become the intellectual basis of

Will Horowitz Jr., a movie theater owner in Texas, asked Carrier to air condition some of his properties. By 1930, 300 theaters across the country had air-conditioning, and going to the movies would never be the same. The

started with $32,000, is now worth more than a cool $5 billion.

While air-conditioning proved to be one of the most important inventions of the early 20th century, the last 50 years saw its share

A MODEL DEMONSTRATES THE NEW COMBINATION WASHER-DRYER IN THE RCA WHIRLPOOL "MRS. AMERICA" GAS KITCHEN OF THE 1950S. TODAY, HOME APPLIANCES ARE PART OF A $34 BILLION A YEAR INDUSTRY.

of rapid advances that led to great improvements in manufacturing techniques. Waterjet technology was one such innovation. In the early 1970s, Michael Pao, a former scientist at Boeing, was looking for a way to use a superhigh-pressure jet of water to cut through metal. Flow, the company Pao started in his basement, patented the first abrasive waterjet system that could cut heavy materials up to a foot thick. Today, Flow International, of Kent, Washington, leads the world in the development of waterjet technology. The technology is used in many industries, from aerospace to automotive to ship building. Flow has even developed an entirely new way of preserving food through its ultrahigh-pressure water technology that can sterilize food without heat.

MAKING LIFE EASIER: APPLIANCES, ELECTRONICS, AND FURNISHINGS

It's hard to imagine that just a century ago, the iceman would come around to homes and inquire whether the family would need ice for the day. Today, more than 95 percent of U.S. households have refrigerators, and the iceman comes no more. Refrigerators—along with ranges, washing machines, dishwashers, microwaves, and myriad other devices that didn't exist a century ago—have contributed not only to an improved quality of life but to the economy. The home appliance and consumer electronics industry totals more than $34 billion a year; its growth follows that of the new housing industry and of the improving economies overseas.

The electric refrigerator was the invention of Alfred Mellowes of Fort Wayne, Indiana, and was first produced by the Guardian Frigerator Company in 1916. The company was purchased three years later by General Motors and eventually operated under the name Frigidaire. Today Frigidaire is a subsidiary of the joint company comprised of Cleveland-based White Consolidated Industries and AB Electrolux, of Stockholm, Sweden.

One of the most popular of all time-saving appliances, the dishwasher, traces its roots to a wooden, hand-powered device patented by Joel Houghton in 1850; but the device never worked well. In 1886, an Illinois society lady named Josephine Garis Cochrane came up with her own version of the machine and, four years later, a company to market it. Her creation, a series of wire compartments inside a copper boiler, was displayed at the 1893 World's Fair in Chicago. Only hotels and restaurants, however, were interested in purchasing the new dishwashing machine, and in the 1920s, the Garis-Cochran Dish-Washing Machine Company was sold. It went through various owners until 1940 when it became KitchenAid, which is today a subsidiary of Whirlpool, headquartered in Benton Harbor, Michigan.

The invention of the microwave oven came about by accident. In 1945, Percy Spencer, an engineer at the radio-tube maker Raytheon Corporation, of Cambridge, Massachusetts, was standing in front of a magnetron tube when he noticed that the candy bar in his pocket was melting. He grabbed some corn kernels and placed them in front of the tube, and they began to pop. Two years later, Raytheon introduced the Radarange, the first microwave oven. Intended for the commercial market, it sold for nearly $3,000. The first microwave for use in the home was produced by Tappan in the early 1950s and cost nearly $1,300. Today, the Radarange is manufactured by Amana Appliances of Amana, Iowa. Tappan, headquartered in Dublin, Ohio, is a division of Frigidaire.

The largest producer of major home appliances in the United States today—and the second largest in the world—is the Whirlpool Corporation. The number two manufacturer is General Electric Appliances, of Louisville, Kentucky, followed by Maytag, headquartered in Newton, Iowa.

Just as Americans depend on their appliances to make their lives easier, no American household, it seems, could survive without a vast array of electronic

MAKING IT BIG

In 1904, Carl Fisher of Indianapolis, Indiana, founded the Prest-O-Lite Company to manufacture acetylene gas lamps which made night driving possible. In 1909, Fisher was one of four men who raised $250,000 to start the Indianapolis Motor Speedway Company, builder of the legendary racecourse. · Using vulcanization, a process discovered by Charles Goodyear of melding rubber to cloth, the U.S. Rubber Company began producing rubber-soled shoes in the late 1800s. The firm adopted the name Keds for the shoes in 1916. U.S. Rubber went on to become Uniroyal and Keds are now made by Stride Rite. · Edwin Land's 1932 invention of the Polaroid sheet led to its use in everything from camera filters to sunglasses to military equipment. In 1947, Land would again revolutionize the industry with his invention of instant photography.

gadgets. In 1999, Americans purchased $80 billion worth of consumer electronics, ranging from color TVs and VCRs to camcorders and telephone answering machines. Despite the fact that imports account for 55 percent of annual purchases, domestic production is alive and well, encompassing 725 factories in 35 states. The industry directly employs 179,000 Americans and contributes to another 3.8 million jobs in the retail sector.

All told, there are 1.6 billion consumer electronic products in use in American households. These products bear the names of popular American brands such as Motorola (Schaumberg, Illinois), Emerson (St. Louis, Missouri), RCA (Indianapolis, Indiana), Zenith (Glen View, Illinois), and General Electric (Fairfield, Connecticut), while companies with headquarters outside the United States, such as Tokyo-based Sony, Casio, and Hitachi and Amsterdam-based Philips, maintain a strong North American presence through manufacturing, distribution, and service operations, or a combination of all three.

Furnishings for the home and office would become another major component of American consumerism in the 20th century. The office furniture market alone would exceed $12 billion by century's end. Ten U.S. furniture companies boasted revenues of $1 billion or more, topped by market leaders Steelcase ($4 billion), of Grand Rapids, Michigan; St. Louis–based Furniture Brands International ($2 billion); LifeStyle Furnishings International ($2 billion), of High Point, North Carolina; and Herman Miller ($1.8 billion), with headquarters in Zeeland, Michigan.

NEW MATERIALS: CHEMICALS AND PLASTICS

A famous scene in the 1967 movie *The Graduate* featured Dustin Hoffman's sneer at the "one word" of career advice given to him by his parents' friend: "Plastics."

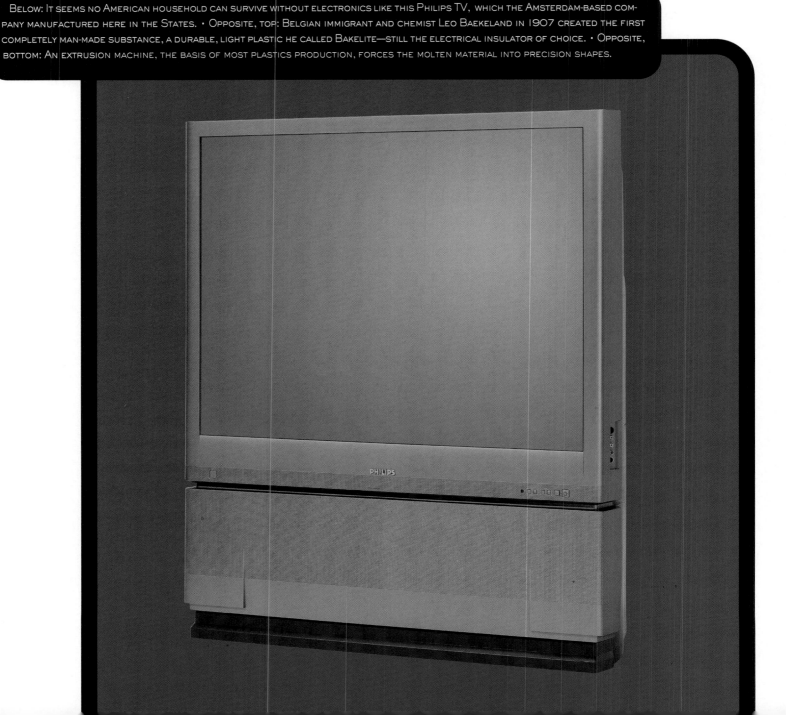

BELOW: IT SEEMS NO AMERICAN HOUSEHOLD CAN SURVIVE WITHOUT ELECTRONICS LIKE THIS PHILIPS TV, WHICH THE AMSTERDAM-BASED COMPANY MANUFACTURED HERE IN THE STATES. • OPPOSITE, TOP: BELGIAN IMMIGRANT AND CHEMIST LEO BAEKELAND IN 1907 CREATED THE FIRST COMPLETELY MAN-MADE SUBSTANCE, A DURABLE, LIGHT PLASTIC HE CALLED BAKELITE—STILL THE ELECTRICAL INSULATOR OF CHOICE. • OPPOSITE, BOTTOM: AN EXTRUSION MACHINE, THE BASIS OF MOST PLASTICS PRODUCTION, FORCES THE MOLTEN MATERIAL INTO PRECISION SHAPES.

Maybe he should have listened. In 1996, plastics shipments totaled $274 billion, and the industry accounted for 1.3 million jobs. The $437 billion U.S. chemical industry as a whole is the largest export industry in the country, holding 10 percent of the export market. It invests $26 billion in research and development annually.

The chemical industry produces more than 70,000 products, products that are found literally everywhere. Each automobile, for example, contains on average about $2,000 worth of chemical processing and products, ranging from polyurethane seat cushions to brake fluids and rustproofing. Other products simply would not exist without chemicals. Microprocessors, for instance, were created from advances in silicon chemistry and high-performance polymers.

One of the earliest and most important discoveries in the industry occurred in 1868. Chemist John Wesley Hyatt was searching for a material that would be a good substitute for ivory in billiard balls. The demand for ivory was threatening the elephant population. The substance Hyatt first tried, collodion, produced balls that adopted the proper shape but exploded when they hit each other. Undaunted, Hyatt tinkered with the formula and added camphor. The result was the first thermoplastic, a substance molded under heat and pressure that retains its shape. The material, Celluloid, was later used in the first flexible photographic films.

In 1907, while searching for a replacement for shellac, a naturally occurring product used to insulate wire, chemist Leo Baekeland created the first completely man-made substance. The liquid resin he produced, called Bakelite, would adopt the same shape as the vessel in which it was contained and never lose its shape. Another valuable property of Bakelite was its strength; it could fortify softwoods and make them more durable. Bakelite was particularly valuable during World War II for it made possible the production of new and lighter weapons. And because it is electrically resistant, chemically stable, and heat resistant, does not break, and does not dissolve when exposed to the elements, Bakelite is still the electrical insulator of choice, its original purpose fulfilled many times over.

Today, the U.S. chemical industry is led by E. I. DuPont de Nemours and Company, founded in Wilmington, Delaware, in 1802 by a French immigrant. Originally a producer of "black powder" used for gun and blasting powder, DuPont was entirely reorganized a century later when it established the Eastern Laboratory in New Jersey, one of the first industrial research labs in the United States. Soon the company constructed the Experimental Station that eventually investigated the manufacture of synthetic fibers.

DuPont's groundbreaking research into polymers led to the development of several vital new products, including neoprene synthetic rubber, invented in 1933.

But DuPont's greatest product, at least in the minds of many women, was yet to come. In the 1920s, Wallace Hume Carothers, the head of the DuPont lab, was working on a new tough plastic called Fiber 66. Later called nylon, the fiber replaced animal hair in toothbrushes and silk in stockings. In fact, May 15, 1940, the day nylon stockings first

became widely available, was known as "N-day." American women purchased five million pairs. Later, the versatile nylon was used during the war for parachutes and to reinforce tires. The popular nylon stockings were soon discontinued as part of the war effort. When production resumed, women lined up around the block to buy the fantastic sheer stockings. Over the years, DuPont introduced new materials like Lycra and Kevlar and chemicals like Suva, a chlorofluorocarbon substitute.

DuPont's close competitor, the Dow Chemical Company, is also one of the world's top makers of agents that process chemicals, treat contaminated water, and refine petroleum and is active in the markets for other materials used in the automotive and packaging industries. One of Dow's greatest innovations was accidental. One day in 1933, Ralph Wiley, a college student, was cleaning glassware in the Dow labs and found that one vial would not get clean. The indestructible material that was in that vial was transformed into

a dark green film, polyvinylidene chloride, more felicitously known as Saran. The U.S. military sprayed it on fighter planes to protect them against sea spray. Later, Dow refined Saran and sold it to consumers as Saran Wrap.

From long-playing records to nonstick Teflon to spandex, plastics—and the chemical industry as a whole—have profoundly improved the lives of Americans. Since 1976, plastics have been the most widely used material in the United States, from housing materials to car parts, from computers and peripherals to artificial joints and medical devices. Plastic packaging has been a major boon to Americans, keeping foods fresh and free of contamination. Each pound of packaging reduces up to 1.7 pounds of food waste. Plastic containers require less packaging overall and are often recyclable. New kinds of plastics are biodegradable. In short, it seems as if the old industry slogan still holds true: We can have "better living through chemistry."

Woven into the Economy: Textiles

Rayon, Dacron, Gore-Tex, Thinsulate—today's high-tech fabrics have progressed a long way from the expensive novelty of nylon hose. Today, plastics and synthetic fabrics are used in about 60 percent of all apparel fabrics and 80 percent of all home textiles.

The textile industry has had many success stories resulting from companies experimenting with synthetic fabrics. One such company, Burlington Industries, was founded in Burlington, North Carolina, in 1923 as Burlington Mills by J. Spencer Love, a World War I veteran. The plant's first employees wove typical cotton fabrics for products ranging from flags to dresses, curtains to diapers. A year after opening the business, Love decided to start making fabrics from the newly invented rayon. The fabrics were an instant hit. By the end of 1936, Burlington had 22 plants. By 1960, Burlington was the parent of 17 other companies and produced everything from ribbon to carpeting in its 100 plants. Today, Burlington has 18,000 employees and is a $1.6 billion company.

One of Burlington's biggest competitors is the Spartanburg, South Carolina–based Milliken & Company, one of the world's largest textile companies. Its roots stretch back to 1865, when it was a small woolen-fabrics firm. Today, the mostly family-owned enterprise has 65 facilities and makes more than 48,000 textile and chemical products such as fabrics for uniforms (including spacesuits) as well as for rugs, carpets, tennis balls, sails, and printer ribbons.

Quaker Fabric Corporation, of Fall River, Massachusetts, is one of the world leaders in upholstery fabrics. Established in 1945, the company is renowned for its jacquard fabrics and specialty yarns. Quaker sells

Above: Levi's, a staple of life since 1853, await shipment at the Levi Strauss factory in San Francisco. • Opposite: College women in 1944 try on DuPont's "greatest hit," nylon stockings.

No bird soars too high,
If he soars with his own wings.
—William Blake

INSPIRED BY A WALL-SIZED MICHAEL JORDAN POSTER, A CUSTOMER JUMPS FOR THE NET AT NIKE TOWN'S BASKETBALL COURT IN CHICAGO. JORDAN'S ENDORSEMENT HELPED NIKE BECOME PART OF POP CULTURE.

approximately 40 million yards of material, the majority of which are custom made, to furniture manufacturers around the world.

DRESSED FOR SUCCESS: THE APPAREL INDUSTRY

Despite the many changes in fabrics—and fashions—over the century, one item of clothing remained constant: the trusty pair of blue jeans. In fact, jeans are arguably the only apparel item that has remained much the way it was 100 years ago.

The top manufacturer of jeans in the United States is Greensboro, North Carolina–based VF Corporation, which holds more than 25 percent of the U.S. market with brands such as Lee and Wrangler. VF also produces lingerie, swimwear and sportswear, backpacks, industrial clothes, and infant and children's clothes. This $5.5 billion company—the largest publicly traded apparel company in the world—is a combination of a few smaller companies.

The VF Corporation began in Pennsylvania as the Reading Glove and Mitten Manufacturing Company in 1899 and changed its name to Vanity Fair Silk Mills in 1919. Meanwhile, in 1912, the H. D. Lee Mercantile Company began marketing overalls, jackets, and dungarees to workers in Kansas City, Kansas. Lee also introduced the Lee Union-All, which became the official uniform for doughboys in World War I. Vanity Fair Silk Mills bought the H. D. Lee Company in 1969 and changed its name to VF Corporation. In 1986, VF bought Wrangler Westernwear, which was founded in 1947 to make jeans with input from working cowboys. Today, 98 percent of working cowboys and rodeo performers wear Wranglers.

VF may be the largest jeans maker, but the world's top maker of brand-name clothing is its close competitor, Levi Strauss

& Co. In 1853, Levi Strauss, a German immigrant, settled in San Francisco and established a successful dry goods store. One of his most popular items was denim pants. One day about 20 years later, a tailor named Jacob Davis approached Strauss with a business proposition. Davis, who had been a regular customer for years, had invented a special rivet that reinforced the denim pants. The rivets were becoming very popular, and Davis wanted to patent them, but he couldn't put together the $68 to file the papers. Would Strauss help? He did, the patent was filed in 1873, and the business partnership that ensued—named for Levi Strauss—still benefits jeans wearers worldwide.

BEST FOOT FORWARD: THE SHOEMAKERS

While the basic jeans style remained fairly constant over a century, shoes evolved into an incredible assortment of styles, from casual to dress to athletic, each one with its own infinite array of designs.

Total footwear retail sales in the United States hit 1.1 billion pairs in 1998. A large chunk of that amount went to Nike, the world's number one athletic shoe company. Nike controls nearly half of the U.S. athletic shoe market and is the parent company of Cole Haan dress and casual shoes.

The Nike story began in California. While a business student at Stanford in 1962, former college track athlete Phil Knight wrote a paper setting forth his plan to overcome German dominance of the U.S. athletic shoe industry by importing high-tech shoes from Japan. He tapped his former college coach from the University of Oregon, Bill Bowerman, who crafted shoes for the U of O track team, to set up a new company, Blue Ribbon Sports. BRS imported

shoes from Japan, and by 1968, the company was having shoes made according to Bowerman's designs. In 1972, BRS started a new brand, Nike, named for the ancient Greek goddess of victory, and renamed the company Nike. A year later, American record-holding track star Steve Prefontaine wore Nike shoes, the company's first endorsement by a major athlete.

The endorsements continued throughout the 1970s, 1980s, and 1990s, from the likes of tennis star John McEnroe to basketball great Michael Jordan (after whom the Air Jordan line was named) to top golfer Tiger Woods. Nike's footwear grew more technologically advanced, and with a popular advertising campaign ("Just Do It"), the $8 billion Nike also became part of pop culture.

A POSITIVE OUTLOOK

The future of the textile industry is unclear. Half the apparel sold in this country is imported, and the trend is likely to continue. As the U.S. workforce becomes more highly skilled and technologically advanced, companies requiring less-skilled labor, particularly those in the textile industry, are sending work to China, Brazil, or Indonesia. In addition, with new free-trade agreements in Congress, this trend may well accelerate. On the other hand, those very same agreements could be a boon to America's manufacturers, opening markets closed to U.S. companies abroad. With lower trade barriers all around, almost all American companies are likely to benefit. Today, about two-thirds of imported goods are intermediate products that are finished in American factories. The quality of manufactured products in this country has substantially increased, and the American manufacturing industry enters the next century on a highly positive note.

profiles
Manufacturing &
Consumer Products

R.J. REYNOLDS TOBACCO

R.J. REYNOLDS TOBACCO COMPANY'S RICH HERITAGE OF INNOVATION IN THE LABORATORY AND THE MARKETPLACE CONTINUES TO SERVE THE FIRM IN SUCCESSFULLY MEETING THE CIGARETTE BRAND PREFERENCES OF ADULT SMOKERS.

R.J. Reynolds Tobacco Company, the second-largest cigarette manufacturer in the United States, began the 21st century fresh on the heels of two enviable achievements: the company celebrated its 125th anniversary and it was recognized as one of *Fortune* magazine's "100 Best Companies to Work For."

The fact that Reynolds Tobacco has succeeded for this length of time and to this degree is a tribute to the company's rich heritage of innovation in the laboratory and in the marketplace. It is also a testament to the company's ethical approach to manufacturing and marketing a legal but controversial product that is enjoyed by more than 46 million American adults.

R.J. Reynolds Tobacco Company's success in responsibly addressing the challenges of the tobacco industry and in serving its customers, shareholders, employees, and community provides a useful glimpse into contemporary American management.

Reynolds Tobacco commands about 24 percent of the U.S. cigarette market, with four of its products (Winston, Camel, Salem, and Doral) ranking among the nation's 10 best-selling cigarette brands. The company is a subsidiary of R.J. Reynolds Tobacco Holdings, Inc., a Fortune 500 firm that became a free-standing, publicly traded company in 1999. Reynolds Tobacco is headquartered in Winston-Salem, North Carolina, in the historic 1929 Reynolds Building, whose architects later designed the Empire State Building. The company operates a million-square-foot Whitaker Park facility in Winston-Salem and a two-million-square-foot plant in the nearby town of Tobaccoville.

The company was begun in 1875 when 25-year-old Richard Joshua (R.J.) Reynolds launched a chewing tobacco operation in Winston, North Carolina, then a production center for flue-cured tobacco leaf. Reynolds, a hands-on manager who knew his employees by name and personally oversaw operations, also spearheaded local road building, helped establish a savings bank, and served as a city commissioner.

COMPANY

Anticipating the popularity of smoking tobaccos, he introduced pipe tobaccos supported by memorable advertising campaigns.

In 1913, R.J. Reynolds introduced Camel cigarettes, which became the first nationally popular cigarette brand. The firm's packaging innovations became U.S. industry standards—the 20-cigarette pack, introduced in 1913; the one-piece, 10-pack carton, in 1915; the clear, moistureproof outer wrap to preserve freshness, in 1931. The nation's leading cigarette manufacturer from 1958 to 1983, Reynolds Tobacco has occupied a leadership position in the industry throughout its history.

The major issues concerning cigarette marketing and underage smoking were comprehensively addressed through a Master Settlement Agreement (MSA) signed in 1998 by the major U.S. tobacco companies, 46 states, and several U.S. territories. Its provisions were similar to those previously reached in settlements with the other four states. Reynolds Tobacco has demonstrated its ability to meet the rigorous provisions of the agreement while sustaining excellent financial results and improving its long record of corporate responsibility in critical areas.

Emphasizing ethical responsibilities, the company's management uses three guidelines in operating Reynolds Tobacco: to meet the preferences of adult smokers with distinctive, high-quality products and to develop technologies with the potential to reduce health risks associated with smoking; to deliver an attractive, long-term return to shareholders; and to provide an open work environment where employees can fully express their creativity and competitiveness. In addition to responsible corporate operation, Reynolds Tobacco and its 8,100 employees are committed to serving their greater community by supporting education, culture, and human services. Increasing educational opportunities has been a focus of the company's corporate giving since the founder's first documented community gift in 1891—$500 to help establish

the school now known as Winston-Salem State University. Reynolds Tobacco has given tens of millions of dollars for education, economic development, the arts, and social programs in its home state of North Carolina.

Reynolds Tobacco team members are proud of their company's responsible approach to marketing a controversial product. They have ensured that their firm remains a sound financial investment, paying competitive dividends while providing leadership in developing solutions to issues involving cigarettes. Each employee remains determined to meet business challenges and continually seeks new ways to serve adult smokers and the community.

OPPOSITE PAGE: THE CORPORATE CULTURE OF R.J. REYNOLDS TOBACCO COMPANY (RJRT) HAS EARNED THE COMPANY RECOGNITION AS ONE OF *FORTUNE* MAGAZINE'S "100 BEST COMPANIES TO WORK FOR." • ABOVE: THE REYNOLDS TOBACCO TOBACCOVILLE MANUFACTURING CENTER IS AMONG THE LARGEST AND MOST AUTOMATED CIGARETTE MANUFACTURING FACILITIES IN THE WORLD. • LEFT: REYNOLDS TOBACCO AND ITS EMPLOYEES SHARE A LONG HISTORY OF GIVING TO THE COMMUNITY. RJRT'S EMPLOYEES ARE THE LARGEST CORPORATE GROUP OF VOLUNTEERS WHO PARTICIPATE IN THE UNITED WAY OF FORSYTH COUNTY'S ANNUAL "DAYS OF CARING." DURING THIS THREE-DAY EVENT IN 2000, NEARLY 1,000 RJRT EMPLOYEES DONATED APPROXIMATELY 3,750 HOURS TO COMPLETE LANDSCAPING, CARPENTRY, CLEANING, AND OTHER PROJECTS AT MANY OF THE AREA'S 37 UNITED WAY AGENCIES.

EMERSON

AT EMERSON, TECHNOLOGY AND ENGINEERING COME TOGETHER TO CREATE SOLUTIONS FOR CUSTOMERS, DRIVEN WITHOUT COMPROMISE FOR A WORLD IN ACTION.

It was nearing the end of the 19th century, a time when most Americans were skeptical of a new energy source called "electricity." This new source of power was seen by some to be dangerous and unreliable, but it was soon to be harnessed into a history of success for Emerson, today a global technology leader heralded by *IndustryWeek* as one of the world's "100 Best Managed Companies."

Emerson's road to success started with two Scottish-born brothers, Charles and Alexander Meston. The pair were inventors who created new uses for the electric motor. They saw the patenting of a

reliable electric motor as a promising business opportunity and persuaded John Wesley Emerson, a former Union army colonel, judge, and lawyer, to be the principal investor in their business. From its 1890 beginnings, the company grew and expanded its product line. In 1892, Emerson sold the first electric fan in America—a product that would strengthen the Emerson name. Emerson continued its product expansion, attaching electric motors to new products such as sewing machines, player pianos, dental drills, and power tools.

New leadership for Emerson in 1954 brought big changes. The company began a continuing process of expansion. As a result, Emerson's operations grew from 4,000 employees in two plants in 1954, to 31,000 employees in 82 facilities in 1973. Product lines flourished as well, going from five basic lines to hundreds, and, in the process, by 1973 Emerson became a diversified corporation with nearly $1 billion in sales.

Under Emerson chairman Charles F. Knight, who took over as CEO from 1973 until October 2000, Emerson became a global leader in each of the businesses in which it competes. The company's broad

range of products and systems serve industrial, commercial, and consumer markets. Sales in 2000 were $15.5 billion, representing Emerson's 43rd consecutive year of increased earnings and 44th consecutive year of increased earnings per share.

Today, Emerson operates on every continent, in almost every country, with more than 120,000 employees working in 380 facilities. Emerson provides customers with innovative technologies and solutions in five business segments: electronics and telecommunications; process automation; industrial automation; heating, ventilating, and air-conditioning; and appliance and tools.

Emerson has continued its commitment to growth with new product programs, acquisitions, joint ventures, and international expansion, including into Asia-Pacific markets. Some 35 percent of Emerson's revenues are derived from new products that have been developed within the last five years. By pursuing a strategic, targeted pattern of acquisitions and divestitures—some 200 since 1973—Emerson keeps its businesses focused on fast-growing markets.

Today, Emerson has repositioned itself to be able to power the digital economy and participate in the rapid expansion of the global communications infrastructure. Emerson provides complete systems and services for reliable backup power systems for such applications as computer and telecommunications networks. The company is also developing E-commerce platforms that will enable its divisions to integrate their systems with partners worldwide.

To drive additional growth, Emerson is developing technology platforms such as PlantWeb process automation architecture; and Copeland Scroll compressor systems for the HVAC and other industries, and is creating service and solution capabilities that strengthen its leadership in serving customers around the world.

As Emerson looks ahead to the coming years, it will continue implementing the strategic growth initiatives that have led to high profitability and worldwide recognition for Emerson's technology and engineering leadership.

OPPOSITE PAGE: IN ITS CLIMATE TECHNOLOGY BUSINESS, EMERSON'S COPELAND HAS DEVELOPED SCROLL COMPRESSOR TECHNOLOGY THAT HAS REVOLUTIONIZED AIR-CONDITIONING APPLICATIONS WORLDWIDE. IN FISCAL 2000, EMERSON OPENED ITS NINTH COPELAND SCROLL COMPRESSOR PLANT, THIS ONE IN SUZHOU, CHINA, TO MEET THE GROWING DEMAND FOR THIS TECHNOLOGY IN ASIAN MARKETS. · ABOVE: EMERSON'S PLANTWEB PROCESS AUTOMATION TECHNOLOGY, WHICH COMBINES THE LEADING-EDGE DELTA V CONTROL SYSTEM WITH INTELLIGENT FIELD DEVICES AND INNOVATIVE SOFTWARE, ENABLES CUSTOMERS TO REALIZE NEW LEVELS OF EFFICIENCY IN THEIR OPERATIONS. AN ARCO/PETROECUADOR JOINT VENTURE HARNESSED THIS TECHNOLOGY TO INCREASE DAILY TRANSPORT OF OIL THROUGH A 498-KILOMETER PIPELINE BY OVER 11 PERCENT. · LEFT: TO BETTER FOCUS ON ITS CORE TELECOMMUNICATIONS BUSINESS, TELEFÓNICA DEL PERU RELIES ON EMERSON NETWORK POWER TO MANAGE ITS ENTIRE POWER INFRASTRUCTURE TO SUPPORT THIS REGION. EMERSON MAINTAINS OVER 2,000 INDIVIDUAL SITES, WITH SERVICES RANGING FROM UTILITY POWER PROCUREMENT TO NEW EQUIPMENT DEPLOYMENT TO ONGOING MAINTENANCE AND REPAIR.

SPIRIT OF DOW

IN FULFILLING ITS MISSION, 'IMPROVING THE ESSENTIALS OF LIFE,' DOW TRANSLATES SCIENTIFIC DISCOVERY INTO COMMERCIALLY SUCCESSFUL CHEMICALS, PLASTICS, AND AGRICULTURAL PRODUCTS AND SERVICES.

Since 1897, Dow has been propelled by ingenuity and innovation. As a global science and technology leader, Dow is committed to finding new and imaginative ways to constantly improve the things that are essential to human progress—food, water, shelter, transportation, workplaces, health, and medicine.

Based in Midland, Michigan, with more than 50,000 employees serving customers in more than 170 countries, Dow taps into its employees' rich diversity of thought and style to develop solutions that best meet the needs of a rapidly changing world.

A great diversity of Dow products—from SiLK™ semiconductor resin to STYROFOAM™ brand insulation—have reached the marketplace, placing the $30 billion corporation among the top 100 Fortune 500 firms. With an unending commitment to research and development, Dow brings to the world a passion for using technology to help lead society forward.

'LIVING. IMPROVED DAILY.'

Dow advanced packaging results in a safer food supply. The company's foam insulation systems create homes with greater energy efficiency. Stronger, brighter, and more uniform papers and coatings enabled by Dow products provide better readability and longer shelf life for printed matter, from newspapers to laser prints to photographs. Dow materials even make contact lenses more pliable, diapers softer and more absorbent, and pills easier to swallow. Through these and hundreds of other product applications, Dow is fulfilling its promise of "Living. Improved Daily." Around the globe, Dow strives to reach millions of people every day with products and services they need to thrive. Whether it is purifying drinking water in Africa, developing new crop-protection solutions for South America, or enabling today's computer systems to run

194

with unprecedented efficiency, Dow is committed to helping to make the world a better place.

Dow also is an active force in the economies and communities it directly serves, and beyond. From Malaysia to Brazil to Switzerland to Africa, Dow takes social responsibility seriously, working hard to uphold the three pillars of sustainable development—economic excellence, environmental integrity, and social responsibility—to meet the needs of today without compromising the needs of the future. Dow tracks its progress toward sustainable development and reports on it publicly in its annual report.

GRABBING HOLD OF THE FUTURE

To maintain its competitive advantage, Dow has taken a leadership role in its industry in integrating electronic business technology into its strategic framework. In 2000, the company expanded its private Internet site MyAccount@Dow, which enables Dow customers to place orders, track inventory, and access technical support.

Information technology also has enabled Dow employees to work with increased efficiency as one united global team, with standardized workstations that were first installed in 1996 and continually undergo regular worldwide upgrades. And, to remain at the forefront of communications tools and technology, the company is now piloting an innovation named "DowNET," which is a common, global integrated network for voice, data, and video communications.

In 104 years, Dow has come a long way from its humble beginnings as a bromine producer, now offering more than 2,500 products and services to customers in a wide variety of industries. Its 2001 merger with Union Carbide has catapulted Dow into position as the world's largest producer of chemicals, plastics, and agricultural products, creating an even greater opportunity to use science and technology to improve the basics of life for all the world's people.

OPPOSITE PAGE: DOW SPONSORS FREQUENT OPEN HOUSES AND EDUCATIONAL OUTREACH PROGRAMS. · ABOVE: DOW'S PRESENCE IN 170 COUNTRIES, COMBINED WITH A TRULY GLOBAL BUSINESS STRUCTURE, HELPS THE COMPANY "THINK GLOBALLY AND ACT LOCALLY" IN ALL REGIONS OF THE WORLD. · LEFT: DOW REMAINS COMMITTED TO THE ENVIRONMENTAL HEALTH AND SAFETY "VISION OF ZERO"— NO HARM TO THE ENVIRONMENT, TO DOW EMPLOYEES, OR TO THE COMMUNITIES IN WHICH THE COMPANY OPERATES.

QUAKER FABRIC CORPORATION

QUAKER FABRIC CORPORATION—AN 'OLD ECONOMY' COMPANY WITH A 'NEW ECONOMY' BENT—HAS INVESTED IN ALL PHASES OF ITS BUSINESS TOWARD BECOMING THE SUPPLIER OF CHOICE TO THE FURNITURE INDUSTRY WORLDWIDE.

In 1989, Larry Liebenow took the helm at Quaker Fabric Corporation, then an $85 million upholstery fabric manufacturer with 1,000 employees, an unexciting product line, and old buildings with even older equipment in them. Twelve years later, Quaker is a highly profitable, publicly traded company with 2,500 employees, the best product line in the industry, and millions of dollars worth of new high-speed, high-tech manufacturing equipment. To top it off, fiscal year 2000 revenues of $303 million set a new company record, with strong bottom-line results as well.

This dramatic turnaround at Quaker reflects the net effect of 12 years of focused investments under the leadership of president and CEO Liebenow. The investments, including investments in new product development, market positioning, marketing and distribution systems, technology, production equipment, state-of-the-art systems, and workforce development, have been made to position Quaker as the supplier of choice to the furniture industry worldwide. Quaker also is an employer of choice in Fall River, Massachusetts, where the company's seven manufacturing facilities are located, and an investment opportunity of choice for those investors interested in an "old economy" company with a decidedly "new economy" bent.

INVESTMENTS IN PRODUCTS

In 1989, driven by the vision of making Quaker the supplier of choice to the furniture industry worldwide—and convinced that it would take a combination of great products, great service, and great people to do that—Liebenow set out to help Quaker capture the top spot in the industry from the standpoint of fabric design and style. The first step in this process involved moving the company away from its historical focus on products for the promotional side of the market and toward the development of new collections of fabrics intended to meet the needs of middle- to higher-end furniture manufacturers.

To support this change in Quaker's product direction, the company turned its design area into an industry powerhouse. The result has been the introduction of line after line of enormously successful, and uniquely different, upholstery fabrics for both the domestic and international upholstery fabric markets. More than 500 new fabric designs are unveiled each season, with more than 1,000 new fabric designs released annually.

INVESTMENTS IN THE INTERNATIONAL MARKET

Armed with great products, Quaker's next move was to use these products not only to gain domestic market share, but also to expand distribution to other major markets around the world. The company has built a strong $40 million-per-year export business, and Liebenow, a vocal advocate for free trade, is convinced that "Quaker's success outside the United States demonstrates that we can design, produce, and sell our products in any market that is open to us."

INVESTMENTS IN MANUFACTURING

One walk through Quaker's manufacturing areas is generally enough to convince even a casual observer of the scope and complexity of the company's ISO-9001–certified production operations. With production equipment occupying more than two million square feet of manufacturing space, Quaker is able to handle the volume requirements of even the world's largest furniture manufacturers.

In response to growing demand for the new products developed by Quaker's design staff, the company has invested more than $90 million since 1996 in high-speed, high-tech manufacturing equipment. This ranges from new yarn manufacturing equipment for Quaker's specialty yarns, including its patented Ankyra™ chenille yarns, to new high-speed looms

with electronic Jacquard heads for weaving fabrics. The company also has added technologically sophisticated finishing and post-finishing equipment to support the competitive edge Quaker maintains with respect to the texture and feel of its fabrics.

With each new equipment purchase, Quaker's ability to seamlessly integrate new technology and processes into its

OPPOSITE PAGE: LARRY LIEBENOW IS PRESIDENT AND CEO OF QUAKER FABRIC. · ABOVE: UNDER LIEBENOW'S LEADERSHIP, QUAKER HAS INVESTED MILLIONS OF DOLLARS IN THE DEVELOPMENT OF NEW PRODUCTS TO SERVE THE FURNITURE INDUSTRY WORLDWIDE. · LEFT: QUAKER HAS PURCHASED HIGH-SPEED TEXTILE MANUFACTURING EQUIPMENT TO INCREASE CAPACITY, IMPROVE MANUFACTURING EFFICIENCIES, AND SUPPORT THE COMPANY'S MARKETING, QUALITY, AND DELIVERY OBJECTIVES. PHOTOS, © CONSTANCE BROWN

QUAKER FABRIC CORPORATION

1998

operations has grown accordingly. This is important, because the ability to quickly respond to
changes in market conditions, customer needs,
and technology is a core value and a major
competitive strength at Quaker. According to
Liebenow, "Mass customization is the name of
the game being played at the consumer level
today—and any company that isn't ready to play runs the risk of being sidelined. Quaker is ready to play."

INVESTMENTS IN SUPPLY CHAIN MANAGEMENT

Consumers today, whether shopping on-line or in a neighborhood furniture store, demand *what* they
want, *when* they want it, Liebenow believes. They want to buy it at a price that reflects fair value, and
they want it to perform as advertised. "The long-term winners in our industry will be those who do the
best job of consistently meeting and moving beyond those expectations," he says. "We are determined
to be among them. And we believe that our focus on supply chain management will allow Quaker to
continue to deliver on the commitment it has made to offer great products and great service to every
furniture manufacturer and fabric distributor we deal with."

In 1998, Quaker hired an experienced supply chain management professional to serve as a catalyst
for the kinds of changes the company felt it needed to make in its warehousing and shipping, purchasing, customer service, forecasting, and scheduling practices.

As Liebenow puts it, "Our initial efforts were focused on working to reduce our logistics expenses and
trying to better understand our own suppliers' information needs so that we could do a better job of
'helping them help us.'" Quaker then began redesigning its internal processes and improving its systems in
general to achieve operational excellence. To support that goal, significant investments were made in
Quaker's information technology (IT) systems and IT staff, including about $5 million for the Enterprise
Resources Planning system, which the company installed in 1998, and another $1.5 million–plus for the new

finite-scheduling system Quaker brought on-line in late 2000. Together, these investments were intended to serve as the backbone of Quaker's efforts to establish closer ties with its customers.

Summing up the effects these investments have had on his business, Liebenow states, "So far, Quaker's focus on supply chain management has had a positive effect on the company's performance in a number of areas, including a dramatic reduction in our delivery lead times, from 12 weeks in late 1998 to just four to six weeks today. These improvements have made our customers much happier, leading to increased revenues. More effective asset-use practices have allowed us to reduce both inventory levels and waste. And, of course, the more effective our use of these techniques, the greater the benefits we have derived, including decreased time to market for our new products, greater returns on our asset base, and reduced inventory carrying costs."

INVESTMENTS IN PEOPLE

Hire the best. Invest in the best. Keep the best. These three principles reflect the belief at Quaker that the 2,500 individuals working at the company are Quaker's most valuable corporate asset—and most important competitive advantage. All candidates for employment at Quaker are evaluated not only on the basis of their expertise and work experience, but also on their ability to understand that something special is happening at Quaker—something that brings out the best in those people who are genuinely interested in making a difference at a company that not only permits but also encourages that.

Training at Quaker begins on the first day of employment for every new employee. The company's recently revamped new-hire orientation program covers everything from which products are made at Quaker and how they are made, to fringe benefits, company policies, and safety procedures. Quaker is committed to making sure that all new staff members feel welcome and comfortable in their new environment. Thereafter, job-specific training begins for new members of the company's production staff, new company managers are enrolled in the next scheduled series of management training classes, and additional technical and professional training opportunities are made available to all company employees. In addition, Quaker places a premium on skill building, and hardly a day

goes by without a full schedule of classes taking place in the company's Learning Center, where books, videotapes, and other training materials also are made available to all company employees.

Liebenow is quick to acknowledge the contributions the company's workforce has made to Quaker's success. "Great people make the difference—at every company, in every industry, every time. We have great people at Quaker. They have a strong work ethic. They really care about the company. And they understand and embrace those core values that make Quaker the special place that it is."

THE GORMAN-RUPP COMPANY

KNOWN FOR PRODUCT INNOVATION, RELIABILITY, AND PERFORMANCE, THE GORMAN-RUPP COMPANY IS A WORLD LEADER IN MANUFACTURING PUMPS OF SUPERIOR DESIGN AND ENGINEERING FOR JUST ABOUT EVERY INDUSTRY AND NEED.

In 1933, while America was in the midst of the Great Depression, two entrepreneurs, J.C. Gorman and H.E. Rupp, pooled $1,500—along with their considerable talents and fortitude—and started a pump business in a barn on the outskirts of Mansfield, Ohio. From those modest beginnings, Gorman-Rupp has evolved into one of the leading pump companies in the world.

Throughout the years, Gorman-Rupp's continued growth has focused on superior pump design and engineering. As a result, the company has become known for market innovations and improvements that continue to set standards in the pump industry.

Whether operating at the remote fisheries of Dutch Harbor or at oil rigs in the Gulf of Mexico, delivering clean water supplies to major cities, protecting families when rivers rise, or putting out fires in Kuwait after the war, Gorman-Rupp pumps are on the job around the world—moving fluids that are essential to people's daily lives.

With facilities in the United States, Canada, and Ireland, Gorman-Rupp manufactures a wide variety of pumps: heavy-duty self-priming centrifugals, standard centrifugals, submersible pumps, positive displacement pumps, diaphragm pumps, and a full line of packaged stations for municipalities. Knowing that matching the right pump to the job is critical, Gorman-Rupp works with customers around the world to make sure they are getting the products they need.

The markets Gorman-Rupp serves are as diversified as its product lines. Gorman-Rupp is a leader in the municipal clean water supply and sewage-handling pump markets, manufacturing an extensive line of above- and below-ground sewage pumping systems, as well as booster stations with motors, controls, and piping. On the clean water side, the company's Patterson Pump division manufactures large-volume

split-case centrifugal, axial flow, and vertical turbine pumps to supply water to cities throughout the world.

In the industrial market, pumps are needed to move fluids in steel and paper mills, wineries, canneries, automotive and appliance facilities, and hundreds of other manufacturing applications. Gorman-Rupp pumps have proven to be more reliable and easier to service than other pumps.

For the construction market, heavy-duty engine-driven construction pumps help contractors dewater excavations, tunnels, foundations, basements, and ditches, saving precious time and money. Gorman-Rupp is one of the world's largest manufacturers of pumps for contractors, and it has built its reputation on its rugged self-priming centrifugal trash pumps.

Gorman-Rupp petroleum pumps fuel the jets that take travelers to their destinations. New vehicles, new transportation systems, and new fuels create a constant demand for new and more efficient pump designs. At Gorman-Rupp, engineers are working today to meet the fuel-handling needs of tomorrow—safely and dependably.

The Patterson Pump division of Gorman-Rupp manufactures an extensive line of centrifugal pumps designed to meet the requirements of automatic sprinkler systems, fire hydrants, and standpipes. These pumps are commonly found in hotels, banks, and factories, and are considered silent sentinels standing ready against the danger and destruction of fire.

The Gorman-Rupp Industries division manufactures an extensive line of original equipment manufacturer (OEM) pumps that are used to meet needs in the appliance, food processing, photo processing, printing, chemical, and medical industries.

For more than 60 years, farmers have put their trust in Gorman-Rupp pumps to irrigate fields, fertilize crops, and dis-

pose of animal waste. Energy-efficient sprinkler irrigation pumps help farmers maximize input power and reduce costly fuel consumption.

Gorman-Rupp considers that the key to its success is its people: "The Pump People," who make sure each pump is manufactured to exact tolerances and continue to design efficient pumps that move the most fluid with the least amount of energy. These people make sure the customer receives the right pump and parts, right on time.

Gorman-Rupp employees take pride in their work and in taking care of their customers. For more information on the Gorman-Rupp Company and the product lines it offers, please visit the company's Web site at www.gormanrupp.com.

OPPOSITE PAGE: GORMAN-RUPP TRASH PUMPS FOR CONTRACTORS ARE USED IN A WIDE ARRAY OF APPLICATIONS. DEWATERING PUMPS, LIKE THIS ONE, ARE IDEAL IN JOBS REQUIRING LONG SUCTION LINES OR IN SITUATIONS WHERE INTERMITTENT FLOWS ARE A PROBLEM. · ABOVE, TOP: GORMAN-RUPP'S NEW MANUFACTURING FACILITY IS LOCATED IN MANSFIELD, OHIO. · ABOVE: STATE-OF-THE-ART, FULLY AUTOMATED MACHINING CENTERS, LIKE THIS ONE AT THE MANSFIELD DIVISION, PROVIDE HIGH-SPEED, HIGH QUALITY MACHINING. · LEFT: LARGE-VOLUME VERTICAL PUMPS MANUFACTURED BY PATTERSON PUMP COMPANY ARE USED FOR FLOOD CONTROL IN LOUISIANA.

GETTING THE WORD OUT

MEDIA & COMMUNICATIONS

COMMUNICATIONS IN THE 20TH CENTURY IS THE STORY OF THE RELENTLESS SPREAD OF INFORMATION AT EVER-FASTER SPEEDS TO AN EVER-WIDER AUDIENCE. BY THE YEAR 2000, PEOPLE ALL AROUND THE COUNTRY—EVEN AROUND THE WORLD—COULD WATCH OR READ THE SAME ITEM SIMULTANEOUSLY IN ONE GREAT SHARED EXPERIENCE.

At the same time, many had also taken advantage of the incredible diversity of media available—from magazines to books, from Internet chat rooms to news Web sites—to tailor news and entertainment to their own particular tastes. Powered by the incredible advances of American industry, communications and the media coexist and often complement each other.

HOT OFF THE PRESSES: NEWSPAPERS AND MAGAZINES

Today, publications are as numerous, varied, and diverse as Americans themselves. There are general-interest news magazines like *Newsweek*, which more than three million Americans read every week. There are niche publications that have circulations of about 1,000 dedicated individuals and cover every topic under the sun, from science to public affairs to hobbies. There are local newspapers that have a national audience, like the *New York Times*, "the paper of record," which has a circulation of 1.2 million. There are national papers that take pains to cover local issues, like *USA Today*, with a circulation of well above two million. There are industry or trade journals, free weeklies at the street corner, a myriad of Web sites providing tailored information to anyone who wants it, and everything in between. Close to 1,000 new magazines are launched each year.

This dizzying array has its roots in the late 19th century. At that time, an affordable alternative to books, which were prohibitively expensive to most people, was sought. Thus the magazine industry was born. Many titles that are familiar today got their start during this period: *McCall's, Good Housekeeping, Popular Science, Vogue.*

Though most publications had a local or regional slant, many carried stories that had a broader interest. Thanks to the telegraph, these articles could be syndicated across the country. In the 1890s in San Francisco, newspaper publisher William Randolph Hearst introduced the "funny papers," or full-color cartoons, and syndicated them to smaller papers. In 1915, Hearst consolidated these regional syndicates to form King Features and United Press International.

Meanwhile, the race was on to create a truly national magazine. In 1883, Cyrus H. K. Curtis of Philadelphia launched the *Ladies Journal*, which would later become the *Ladies Home Journal*. Curtis pioneered techniques for building circulation, promotion, distribution, and even market research. He also sold advertising to raise additional revenue. *Ladies Home*

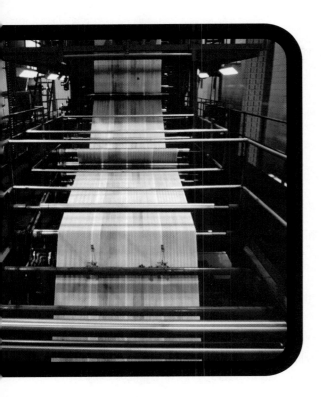

Above: A 1920s newsstand overflows with newspapers and magazines, providing plenty of work for this youngster. • Opposite: A press rolls out the news despite claims the Internet will sound the death knell for print media.

founded in 1922, was the first to inform the American public about the health hazards of smoking.

With the advent of new printing techniques, such as the 1884 invention of the Linotype machine, magazine and media empires were built. For example, in 1909 Condé Nast took a little magazine called *Vogue* and used it as the basis of the Condé Nast Publication empire. Journalist Henry Luce joined with coworker Brit Hadden in 1923 to found *Time*, a general-interest magazine that would report on important issues of the day and place them in context. Today, *Time* has a circulation of 4.5 million, along with sister publications like *Fortune* (founded 1930), *Life*

Journal, today published by the Meredith Corporation, of Des Moines, Iowa, still thrives with 4.5 million readers, a testament to its sound foundation.

In 1897, Curtis took on an even bigger challenge, the *Saturday Evening Post*. Founded as the *Pennsylvania Gazette* by Benjamin Franklin in 1729, this venerable paper had gone downhill in the previous half-century. Curtis transformed it into the definitive middle-class publication. By 1909, the magazine had a circulation of nearly one million; four years later, it passed the two million mark. The *Post* featured general-interest articles, including serials, and made a household name of artist Norman Rockwell, who

produced 332 cover illustrations over 50 years. But the wheel of fortune turned once again. Unable to compete successfully with television in the 1950s and 1960s, the *Post* halted publication in 1969. Several revivals followed, and in the mid-1980s it was bought by the Benjamin Franklin Society.

Many of the new magazines affected national attitudes and even policy during the first half of the 20th century. *McClure's*, founded in 1893, became the voice of the muckrakers. Women's magazines such as *Good Housekeeping, McCall's,* and *Delineator* helped shape the national debate on alcoholic beverages that led to Prohibition in 1919. Later, *Reader's Digest*,

(1936), *Sports Illustrated* (1954), *People* (1974), and *Entertainment Weekly* (1990). In 1989, Time bought Warner Communications and became the world's largest media company. In 2001, America Online purchased Time Warner for $106 billion in a deal that permitted AOL to channel Time Warner content to the Web.

By 1942, magazines abounded. Nevertheless, John H. Johnson spotted an enormous and as yet unexplored marketing opportunity. The Chicago-based Johnson Publishing Company created the *Negro Digest*, modeled on *Reader's Digest*, for the large African American middle class. The energetic Johnson recruited major corporations to advertise to this untapped group. Three years later, Johnson followed up with *Ebony*, a glossy magazine with news and features that was modeled on *Life*, and later *Tan* (1950) and *Jet* (1951). Today, *Ebony* has a circulation of 1.8 million and Johnson remains its publisher and the company's CEO.

All of these national magazines are issued monthly or weekly. What if a newspaper could be written, printed, and distributed nationally every single day, especially in an era when the number of daily papers in a given area was declining? That's the challenge and opportunity Allen Neuharth faced in the early 1980s. Neuharth, chairman and president of the Gannett Company of Arlington, Virginia, which already published 88 daily papers around the country, had a vision: to create a newspaper that would have a broad, national perspective.

Despite the odds, the Gannett Company plowed ahead, and on September 15, 1982, launched the first issue of *USA Today*. As the years passed, *USA Today* established itself as a true general-interest paper, characterized by trademark full-color graphics, charts, and weather maps; articles by

If *USA Today* shook up the newspaper industry during the 1980s, the Internet fundamentally changed it in the 1990s. Today, anyone can get articles from almost any newspaper and major magazine easily over the World Wide Web. Magazines, such as *Wired*, covering the intersection of technology and politics, are integrated with their Web sites. A few publications, such as *Slate* and *Salon*, are completely Web-based. Other Web-based services allow individuals to choose their own news. Meanwhile, desktop publishing software

Association of America, of Vienna, Virginia. The NAA cites research that shows that the majority of on-line readers have remained consistent in their reading of print media. The continued success of such firms as Publishers Printing Company, of Shepardsville, Kentucky, which was founded in 1866 and today prints more than 800 magazine and journal titles, bears this out.

With this in mind, it's instructive to look at how another industry—radio—adapted to a sea change: the introduction of television.

ABOVE: BROADCASTING FROM THEIR CAMPUS STATION, STUDENT DJs ENJOY THE LINK BETWEEN RADIO AND THE RECORDING INDUSTRY. • OPPOSITE, TOP: WILLIAM RANDOLPH HEARST, WHO BEGAN PUBLISHING THE SAN FRANCISCO EXAMINER IN 1887, BUILT A JOURNALISTIC EMPIRE OVER THE NEXT 40 YEARS. • OPPOSITE, RIGHT: THE MARCH 1918 "WIN-THE-WAR" ISSUE OF MCCLURE'S MAGAZINE CONTAINED THE LITERARY/POLITICAL ARTICLES OF AUTHORS SUCH AS IDA TARBELL THAT THE JOURNAL HAD BECOME KNOWN FOR.

celebrity writers; large photographs; and opposing-view editorials printed alongside the editors' piece. The efforts clearly worked. *USA Today* has the largest newspaper circulation in the country, 2.1 million.

makes it easy for anybody to create an attractive newsletter at home.

Is the Internet sounding a death knell for the magazine and newspaper industry? Not according to the Newspaper

DON'T TOUCH THAT DIAL: THE INTRODUCTION OF RADIO

On Christmas Eve 1906, from a makeshift radio station in Massachusetts, came the first radio broadcast, a voice and violin

ORSON WELLES BROADCASTS THE NOVEL THE WAR OF THE WORLDS ON RADIO IN 1938. ATTESTING TO THE GROWING POWER OF THE MEDIUM, MANY LISTENERS THOUGHT HE WAS DELIVERING A NEWSCAST AND PANICKED.

duo. The audience was probably not very large; only a handful of people had radios in their homes, mostly as a hobby. It wasn't until World War I that the technology began to be developed and used in earnest, kicking off a major transformation in mass communications.

The first commercial radio broadcast took place in 1920, when Pittsburgh station KDKA announced the returns of the Harding-Cox presidential election. At the time, there were only about 5,000 radio receivers in the country; by 1924 there were 2.5 million, attesting to the phenomenal popularity of the medium.

Radio became the starting point for two of this country's largest companies. The Galvin Manufacturing Company, which would eventually become Motorola, opened its doors in 1920 and pioneered such radio technology as car radios in the 1930s, walkie-talkies in the 1940s, and transistorized car radios, pocket radios, and the first pagers in the 1950s, to name just a few. In 1919, General Electric formed the Radio Corporation of America (RCA) to market GE and Westinghouse equipment. RCA introduced the Radiola console in 1921, which sold for a pricey $75. Nevertheless, the company sold $11 million worth that year.

After KDKA's coup, there was a rush to capture territory on the airwaves. Even newspaper publishers got into the act. The *Chicago Tribune* debuted station WGN, while the Hearst Corporation started WINS in New York. Soon, Loews Theaters (WHN), Warner Bros. (KFWB), and even department stores like Gimbel Brothers (WIP) and Bamberger and Company (WOR) came up with their own radio stations. Local stores, hotels, even a poultry farm—everyone, it seemed, had a radio station.

In 1923, AT&T hooked up WEAF in New York to Boston, Washington, Philadelphia, and cities in between—16 stations in all. A year later, the network had spread as far west as Minneapolis. In 1926, RCA established the National Broadcasting Company (NBC), which used the AT&T system to reach 10 million listeners across the country.

Instantaneous radio communication brought news and live sports to Americans. President Franklin Roosevelt's "fireside chats" were an important means of public persuasion for his administration, and even today his broadcast speech describing December 7, 1941, as "a date which will live in infamy" can still send chills down one's spine.

But the speed of communication, while important, is still only half the story. Just as important is the culture that grew around radio. In the early days of radio programming, networks did not create shows, they merely broadcast them. Thus, it was up to the businesses that were the show's sponsors to develop content. So Americans tuned in to the *Kraft Music Hall* radio program or listened to comedian Jack Benny's famous tag line "Jell-O Again!" in between his routines.

The shows that resulted were sometimes based on sentiment, other times on whimsy. Many inspired incredible dedication and displayed the growing power and influence of the medium. *Amos 'n' Andy* was so popular during its run in the 1930s that movie theaters, trying to encourage attendance during their early evening shows, would broadcast the 7 P.M. show through their brand-new speaker systems. And in 1938, actor Orson Welles shocked the nation with his reading of H. G. Wells's novel about Martian invasion, *The War of the Worlds.* Many people who tuned in midway through did not realize Welles was reading a story, thought the invasion was real, and panicked.

In those heady days, the radio industry was on top. Newspapers and the burgeoning recording industry felt very threatened. But then came television, and radio was forced to change.

BROADCAST NEWS

In 1912, 15-year-old David Sarnoff was working as a radio operator for the Marconi Wireless Telegraph Company of America in New York when his radio picked up the distress signals of the Titanic. For 72 hours, Sarnoff was the nation's sole source of news about the tragedy. Sarnoff would later go on to head RCA and NBC and revolutionize the broadcasting industry. · Herbert Bayard Swope of the New York World received the first Pulitzer Prize for newspaper reporting in 1917 for his stories about the German Empire. · The first African American radio station was WERD, which began broadcasting in 1949 from Atlanta, Georgia. · When John Walson, an appliance store owner in Mahanoy City, Pennsylvania, had trouble selling televisions because reception was terrible there, he set up an antenna on a utility pole on top of a nearby mountain. Signals received by the antenna were transmitted by wire into his store. Cable television was born on that day in 1948. · Of the 10 most-watched television shows in history, eight were Super Bowls. · It is estimated that 98.6 percent of American homes have a television.

It was with no small sense of irony that in 1981, when Music Television (MTV) debuted, its leaders chose the Buggles' "Video Killed the Radio Star" as the first song to be broadcast. The recording industry, which had felt threatened by radio decades before, now contributed to radio's resurrection after television. The last original radio dramas ended in 1962, but music brought radio back.

Another factor that changed radio—and the music industry as a whole—was recording tape, made from technology that was brought from Germany at the end of World War II. These tapes, which replaced the wax transcription disks that had been used since the early 1930s, could be edited. That simple change enabled actors to work when they wanted to, because they could record a show that could be broadcast at a later time. Bing Crosby was the first to tape a network radio program, which aired on the upstart network ABC in 1946.

With Motorola's invention of the transistorized pocket radio in the 1950s and the rise of "disc jockey" radio personalities, radio was back in play. Today, there are more than 12,000 radio stations and only a little more than 2,000 television stations, although radio advertising revenue is only about half that of the $34.6 billion television brings in.

VIDEO KILLED THE RADIO STAR: THE ADVENT OF TELEVISION

In 1999, 60 years after the first television broadcast, 98.6 percent of U.S. households had a television. How did the great American about-face from radio to TV happen?

Inventors, scientists, and companies had been tinkering with ways to send electronic images by wire for years with varying measures of success, but Philo T. Farnsworth gets much of the credit for producing the first all-electronic television image, in 1927, one year after he joined Crocker Research Labs in San Francisco. Eventually, the company was renamed for him, and Farnsworth went

BELOW: DICK CLARK, WHOSE TV DANCE SHOW *AMERICAN BANDSTAND* HELPED CREATE THE YOUTH CULTURE OF THE LATE 1950S, IS SEATED IN THE AUDIENCE DURING THE FILMING OF AN EPISODE IN LOS ANGELES IN 1964, AFTER THE SHOW MOVED FROM PHILADELPHIA. • OPPOSITE: THE KSTP RADIO AND TELEVISION STATION IN ST. PAUL, MINNESOTA, THE TWIN CITIES' ONLY LOCALLY OWNED STATION, LAUNCHED ONE OF THE NUMEROUS SOCIAL CHANGES TELEVISION WOULD BRING ABOUT WHEN, IN 1950, IT BEGAN BROADCASTING THE NEWS ON A DAILY BASIS.

on to patent technology for scanning, focusing, and synchronizing images and for contrast, controls, and power. In addition to inventing the first cold cathode ray tubes and the first simple electronic microscope, Farnsworth was the first to use radio waves to find direction, creating radar. He also developed a black light to enable sight at night, a technology applied during World War II.

Farnsworth's image-transmitting invention was first used in 1927, when the Bell Telephone system carried live TV images of then-Secretary of Commerce Herbert Hoover from Washington, D.C., to an auditorium in Manhattan. After another decade of refinements, David Sarnoff of RCA presented television to the masses at the 1939 World's Fair in New York. President Franklin Roosevelt became the first president to be seen on TV when the fair's opening ceremonies were later telecast.

In 1941, just as the radio networks CBS and NBC began to run limited television service, World War II intervened. As companies like RCA switched to war production, the growth of TV was suspended. But 40 days after the war ended, RCA was back in business, producing the Model 630TS 10-inch television set. It sold for $375 and 50,000 were made. Three years later, in 1948, RCA purchased the Farnsworth Radio and TV plant and converted the facility to a picture-tube manufacturer.

By 1948, TV was here to stay. That year, just as television played its first major role in covering the presidential election (NBC broadcast the nominating conventions), the beloved *Fred Allen Show*, which had been on radio for 18 years, signed off. By 1950, 108 series that had been on the radio for more than 10 years and 12 that had been on for more than two decades went off the air.

In their place were popular shows like *Texaco Star Theater*, starring former vaudevillian Milton Berle, which debuted in 1948. The first syndicated television show was *Public Prosecutor*, a detective series and game show that went on the air in 1947. Frederick Ziv produced a newsreel series for telecast in 1948, and in 1950, the first episodes of *The Cisco Kid* aired—a syndicated program filmed in color, even though everybody had black-and-white sets—and Sid Caesar's *Your Show of Shows* debuted. Daytime programming began in 1950 with *The Kate Smith Hour*.

Television experienced the same rush that radio did. All of a sudden, independent filmmakers saw an excellent opportunity to produce TV shows. And in 1950, *The Big Show* was introduced. A variety program hosted by Tallulah Bankhead, this was the first program produced by a network and not an ad agency, a great change from the days

of radio. The television production industry was born.

That television helped create and sustain a youth culture is undeniable. In 1956, Elvis Presley's hip-swinging appearance on *The Ed Sullivan Show* not only helped out Ed, whose show had been losing ratings, but also created a bit of a scandal. That same year, popular music and TV mixed again with the launch of *American Bandstand*, hosted by Dick Clark, a live dance show with local Philadelphia teens that showcased the newest and coolest pop singles.

Other social changes were reflected in television. In 1956, Nat King Cole became the first African American artist to have his own network series.

TV also kept Americans more informed than ever. In 1950, KSTP-TV of St. Paul, Minnesota, a subsidiary of Hubbard Broadcasting, became the first television station in the world to offer daily newscasts.

In 1956, Chet Huntley and David Brinkley covered the presidential election and initiated *The Huntley-Brinkley Report*. But it was in the following election that television's power to influence became clear. The 1960 Kennedy-Nixon debates showed a tanned and healthy John Kennedy and a pale, perspiring Richard Nixon. While the majority of those who listened on the radio believed Nixon won the debate, those who saw the debate on television gave the nod to Kennedy.

Just three years later, television reached another unprecedented level of influence in American life by bringing the nation together during the assassination of President Kennedy, his moving state funeral, and the gruesome televised murder of Lee Harvey Oswald. In the ensuing years, television would repeat this role many times, gathering the nation together during events both tragic and triumphal.

CABLE AND SATELLITE: BRINGING TV EVERYWHERE

A key invention that helped the spread of television was the development of cable television, also known as Community Antenna Television (CATV), which was developed in 1948 as a way to improve reception in remote areas. With the debut of Home Box Office in 1972, it soon became an alternative to the "Big Three" networks. Today, cable TV reaches 58.5 percent of American households.

Satellite television provides even more choice than cable. Satellite service began in 1965. By 1976, HBO was able to distribute shows by satellite. It also permitted the establishment of superstations, kicking off the growth of the pay-TV industry and cementing the reputation of one Atlanta entrepreneur.

Georgian Ted Turner began broadcasting his superstation, WTCG, across the nation from the Virgin Islands to Maine and from New York to Hawaii in 1976. After a few years of experimenting with satellite transmission, Turner was ready to risk his fortune for his dream: an all-news cable channel. People thought he was crazy—literally. Only 14 percent of homes at the time had cable TV, and it wasn't clear how many, or if any, would watch news all the time. But Turner pressed on and launched Cable News Network (CNN) on June 1, 1980. As CNN and its various programs such as *Headline News* became more popular, the station began to be known as the "Crisis News Network." Indeed, in June 1989, CNN itself became the news when the Chinese government tried to shut it down during the Tiananmen Square incident. And during the 1991 Operation Desert Storm, even high-level Washington officials watched CNN for the latest reports on what was happening in the Persian Gulf.

CNN also spurred the development of other all-news networks such as NBC's CNBC business and financial news network, launched in 1989, and MSNBC, a joint effort between NBC and Microsoft for a 24-hour news and information cable network and interactive on-line service.

THE NEED TO READ: BOOK PUBLISHING

Throughout a century's advances in news and information media, Americans' appetite for books remains strong. By any measure, the continuing growth of the book market debunks the myth that, in the age of television and the Internet, books would be relegated to the ash heap of history.

The American Association of Publishers reports that in 1999 Americans bought $24 billion worth of books, double the amount of

purchases just 12 years earlier. From trade sales in bookstores and on the Internet to the children's market to textbooks and professional journals, book publishers and retailers continued to play a vital role in informing and educating the public. The currents of economic and technological change have been challenging for industry leaders such as R. R. Donnelley & Sons, Harcourt, HarperCollins Publishers, Houghton Mifflin, Random House, St. Martin's Press, and Simon & Schuster. Yet these companies entered a new century with their role in the information age assured and compelling.

THE NEXT FRONTIER

With key mergers between companies like America Online and Time Warner, it's likely that the World Wide Web and television will become ever more seamlessly integrated. And, despite constant requiems for the newspaper, that medium has survived the introduction of countless technologies and will likely be around through many more.

Communication technology and advances in media have served many purposes. Newspapers fed Americans' appetite for intellectual stimulation and news. Radio brought total strangers into the public's living rooms for the first time, and the public welcomed these visitors. Television let viewers see the violence and destruction of war, the wonder of the moon, and the product of some of the most fertile imaginations ever. At the same time, the news media have let Americans keep better tabs on elected officials and make informed decisions about public policy. Though these media have certainly shaped stories, they have revealed more than concealed. Most important, American communications and media companies have delivered the impossible: shared experiences and boundless choices for everyone.

THE TECHNOLOGY USED IN THIS COMMUNICATIONS SATELLITE HELPED SPAWN CABLE TV, ORIGINALLY DEVELOPED TO IMPROVE RECEPTION. CABLE TODAY REACHES 58.5 PERCENT OF AMERICAN HOUSEHOLDS.

profiles
Media &
Communications

FOR DECADES, BROADCASTERS HAVE SERVED AUDIENCES WITH NEWS, EMERGENCY BULLETINS, EDUCATION, AND ENTERTAINMENT, APPLYING TECHNOLOGICAL INNOVATION AND BECOMING AN INTEGRAL PART OF EACH COMMUNITY'S QUALITY OF LIFE.

BROADCASTING: A LEGACY OF INNOVATION, PUBLIC SERVICE, AND CREATIVITY

"If you serve the public, profit will take care of itself," said Stanley E. Hubbard, founder of Hubbard Broadcasting.

Since the first commercial radio broadcast in 1922, America's broadcasters have served communities with a unique blend of news, information, and entertainment unmatched anywhere in the world. Broadcasters have become heavily involved in so many different activities that they are an integral part of each community's quality of life.

Through the decades, broadcasters have educated audiences with the Nixon-Kennedy debates; they have inspired viewers with Neil Armstrong's walk on the moon; and they have saved countless lives with emergency weather bulletins. Broadcasters have also entertained audiences with classic comedy and absorbing drama. From Jack Benny to Jerry Seinfeld, from *The War of the Worlds* to *The Diary of Anne Frank,* broadcasts remain the primary entertainment medium for millions of Americans every day.

U.S. broadcasting is rooted in localism and community service. The National Association of Broadcasters has documented that the annual value of public service provided by broadcasters is more than $8 billion. That contribution, in the form of airtime donated for public service announcements and money raised for charity and disaster relief, represents more money than the combined amount raised by the top 100 foundations in the United States.

As broadcasters embrace the Internet and move from analog to digital technology, free, over-the-air local radio and television stations are poised for continued innovation. The future is bright, and the U.S. system of broadcasting will undoubtedly remain the envy of the world.

CONUS COMMUNICATIONS COMPANY

SATELLITE NEWS GATHERING—NOW, THE AUDIENCE GOES ANYWHERE

Since the earliest days of TV journalism, one of the great challenges facing broadcasters can be summed up in two words: *miles* and *minutes*. Often, a television station's ability to broadcast a given story in timely fashion boiled down to how far the crew had to travel to cover the story and how long it took the crew to return.

Thus, "local" news was truly that—local—and local TV journalism was to a great extent defined by geography. Television stations were forced to limit their coverage to stories only in their own backyards.

All of that changed in the early 1980s with the development of satellite news gathering (SNG). C-band satellites had been used for several years to transmit programming to television stations, but that technology was not flexible enough for the demands of news coverage.

In 1984, a team of talented engineers in Minneapolis and St. Paul, Minnesota, began experiments in the use of Ku-band technology for the transmission of remote broadcasts. The engineers knew that Ku-band transmissions (unlike C-band) did not need FCC approval for each individual broadcast and that the smaller size Ku-band uplink dishes could be easily transported. In short, the technology was perfect for remote news gathering. The success of their early experiments foretold a seismic shift of dramatic proportions in the business of television news.

Those engineers and their groundbreaking achievement became the foundation upon which CONUS Communications Company was built by Hubbard Broadcasting in 1984, dedicated to SNG and to empowering local television stations with the ability to cover news of interest to their audiences, regardless of location.

It did not take long for the CONUS SNG concept to redefine the television news business. As more and more television stations joined CONUS, the definition of "local news" evolved from "events that occurred locally" to "events that were significant locally, regardless of where they occurred." No longer would viewers have to wait for the networks' evening news—their favorite local

television stations could now deliver national, and eventually international, news by the use of CONUS and SNG.

As a result of the CONUS success, the networks adopted SNG technology for themselves. Eventually, each of the networks set up its own SNG organizations, similar to CONUS, and operates them today in cooperation with affiliated television stations. CONUS, meanwhile, continues its groundbreaking SNG efforts, and remains today the nation's largest independent SNG service.

OPPOSITE PAGE, TOP: PRESIDENT RONALD REAGAN ADDRESSED THE NATIONAL ASSOCIATION OF BROADCASTERS (NAB) CONVENTION IN APRIL OF 1988. · OPPOSITE PAGE, BOTTOM: THE NAB HEADQUARTERS IS LOCATED IN WASHINGTON, D.C. · ABOVE: CONUS COMMUNICATIONS IS BASED IN ST. PAUL, MINNESOTA, WITH OFFICES IN WASHINGTON, D.C., AND LONDON, AND HAS REGIONAL BASES ACROSS THE UNITED STATES. · LEFT: THE INVENTOR OF SATELLITE NEWS GATHERING, CONUS COMMUNICATIONS TODAY PROVIDES PRODUCTION, NEWS, AND PROGRAMMING SERVICES TO LOCAL, NATIONAL, AND INTERNATIONAL BROADCASTERS AND CORPORATE CLIENTS.

WORKING WITH THE NATION'S NEWSPAPERS, THE NEWSPAPER ASSOCIATION OF AMERICA FOCUSES ON VITAL STRATEGIC ISSUES OF READERSHIP, MARKETING, DIVERSITY, PUBLIC POLICY, INDUSTRY DEVELOPMENT, AND NEWSPAPER OPERATIONS.

When people move away from their hometowns, it is quite unusual for them to ask to be sent videotapes of their former local television news program to keep up with what is happening. However, the folks back home often will send them clippings from the local newspaper. Some people even order a subscription to the paper to be mailed to their new address, and others read that newspaper on-line.

People have such an attachment to their newspapers that at the turn of the century, when market researchers Yankelovich Partners asked them what things they would like to see continue into the

21st century, the number one answer, cited by fully 93 percent of respondents, was newspapers. Oreo cookies were a distant second. Newspapers connect with people in a uniquely personal way. People speak of "my newspaper," but not "my television news" or "my Internet site." The daily newspaper is a trusted, reliable, credible communications medium that 85 percent of adults use regularly.

Today's newspapers are not the same black-and-white single products of the last century, when news media consisted of three networks, a handful of national magazines, and a couple of tabloids and broadsheets. People now live in a world and a culture where the newspaper is just one of many news media choices. Nevertheless, newspapers remain a uniquely valued choice, one that people stay with for deep-seated reasons, some logical and some emotional, such as reading that hometown newspaper.

As new technology opens doors of seemingly limitless opportunity, newspapers are expanding their franchise into the on-line and wireless arenas. Nearly all the nation's dailies have an on-line presence, and many are exploring options for wireless delivery of news and information. On-line developments have led to incredible new opportunities for newspapers. Newspapers offer timely, relevant content from a

AMERICA

trusted source that works so well on-line. The Internet, in turn, offers newspapers the chance to put their news in front of readers before tomorrow's paper hits the doorstep, and the unlimited space to explore issues in more depth.

A growing battery of research suggests that more Internet users are visiting newspaper Web sites. Many are younger readers who may pick up a print edition less often. Encouraging as well is the research finding that a strong majority of on-line readers have not altered their use of print media; in fact, a number of people say they read print newspapers more often.

As wireless information delivery continues to be developed, newspapers will have increased opportunities to parlay technological advances into new products and services for readers. But while these on-line and wireless technologies offer new opportunities, they also spotlight one of the challenges for newspapers—namely, the division of audience attention among an increasing number of media outlets.

The Newspaper Association of America (NAA), based in Vienna, Virginia (www.naa.org), whose members constitute nearly 90 percent of U.S. daily newspaper circulation, works with newspapers—large, small, and in-between—to meet challenges and find new opportunities for growth. Whether developing strategies for attracting and keeping advertisers, finding new ways to encourage newspaper sales, exploring news-delivery options, expanding opportunities for diversity, helping to understand new technology, sharing groundbreaking research, or working with the government and Congress, NAA is there. With the support of NAA and other trade associations, the newspaper industry is meeting and conquering these business challenges, and growing.

The industry faces its challenges, though, as competition for people's time and media use continues to fragment the audience. To help newspapers attract more consumer attention, research from an industrywide Readership

Initiative has uncovered the driving forces behind readership— what motivates it, what can be done to capture it, and how newspapers can increase it. The initiative also includes the development of a marketing tool for newspapers to apply in their communities to attract more readers. This is the industry's greatest challenge and opportunity in the early years of the 21st century.

NEWSPAPERS ARE DISTRIBUTED TO 21ST CENTURY READERS IN A NUMBER OF WAYS. OPPOSITE PAGE: SINGLE-COPY SALES TOTAL MORE THAN 19 PERCENT OF ALL NEWSPAPERS SOLD. CUSTOMERS CAN PICK UP NUMEROUS NEWSPAPERS AT CONVENIENCE STORES, COFFEE SHOPS, AND SUPERMARKETS, AS WELL AS ONE WELL-KNOWN WAY—FROM THE NEWS RACK. · ABOVE: RESULTS OF A READERSHIP INSTITUTE STUDY CONDUCTED IN 2000 REVEALED THAT NEARLY 85 MILLION ADULTS TURN TO A NEWSPAPER EVERY DAY FOR A VARIETY OF INFORMATION, BOTH ADVERTISING AND EDITORIAL. · LEFT: ENCOURAGING YOUNG PEOPLE TO BECOME INVOLVED WITH THEIR LOCAL NEWSPAPER CONTINUES TO BE A CHALLENGE. TO REACH OUT TO YOUNG PEOPLE, SOME 950 PAPERS PARTICIPATE IN NEWSPAPER IN EDUCATION PROGRAMS, USING THE NEWSPAPER AS A CURRICULUM TOOL. IN RECENT YEARS, THE INDUSTRY HAS DEVELOPED STRATEGIES TO ATTRACT YOUNG PEOPLE TO THE MYRIAD CAREER OPTIONS AVAILABLE IN THE NEWSPAPER INDUSTRY.

PUBLISHERS PRINTING COMPANY

A SUCCESSFUL FAMILY-OWNED BUSINESS SINCE 1866, PUBLISHERS PRINTING COMPANY PRINTS SPECIALTY MAGAZINES AND JOURNALS ON ITS WEB PRESSES, WITH A KEEN FOCUS ON ADVANCED TECHNOLOGIES AND FINE CUSTOMER SERVICE.

The history of Publishers Printing Company is typical of a lot of companies established in the 19th century that helped transform America into the commercial dynamo that it is today. Founded in 1866 by German immigrant Nicholas Simon, Publishers Printing, which is based in Shepherdsville, Kentucky, started out as a small printing firm, turning out newspapers for local publishers and advertising flyers for local businesses. From those humble beginnings, it eventually grew into one of the finest—and one of the largest—printing resources for professional magazine and journal publishers.

What makes Publishers Printing rare among companies that trace their roots to the 19th century, however, is that it has remained family-owned throughout its history. In fact, since the firm's inception over 135 years ago, five generations of Simons have been at its helm. Unlike the many large family-owned printing firms that have been forced to sell out, close their doors, or watch their once-formidable operations become shadows of their former selves, Publishers Printing has had the good fortune of having a succession of innovative family leaders  who contributed to the firm's growth. And unlike many publicly owned firms, this privately owned family business has been able to maintain just one primary concern throughout its history—serving customers.

"Service to our customers is what separates us from our competition," says Nicholas X. Simon, the company's president who, along with his brother Michael J. Simon, executive vice president, heads the firm today. "Several of our customers today have been with us—and have been happy with us—for more than 30 years. Anyone who takes a walk through our plants will see that we have more people to take care of our customers than our peers have."

The Simons, great-great-grandsons of the founder, give much of the credit for the company's current success to their father, Frank E. Simon, who ran the business from 1946 until his death, in 1990. It was

Frank Simon who, in the 1950s, redirected the company's focus from sheet-fed printing to a web offset operation focused primarily on printing publications. With 1,700 highly trained and dedicated employees, at two spacious, modern Louisville-area plants—a 250,000-square-foot facility in Shepherdsville and a 550,000-square-foot plant in nearby Lebanon Junction, Kentucky—Publishers Printing, through its principal subsidiary, Publishers Press, Inc., caters primarily to short-run publications.

The company today prints more than 800 different magazine and journal titles, 95 percent of which are business-to-business and other special-interest publications. It also prints a number of consumer-type magazines, tabloids, and digests. Each day, some 750,000 copies of magazines, journals, and other publications come rolling off its 23 web presses. Publication press runs can range from as few as 5,000 copies to as many as 500,000.

Publishers Printing adheres to the idea that state-of-the-art technology is a tool that should be exploited to the fullest in printing. Indeed, a list of the technological advancements the company has either pioneered or adapted to the printing business could fill a book. As one example, it was the first printer to produce entire magazines using computer-to-plate technology. The company places such a premium on technology that it even provides training for its customers in the latest technological advancements in printing so that they know how to best prepare their materials for printing by the firm. "We apply tomorrow's technology today," Nicholas Simon says. "It is a philosophy our clients appreciate and benefit from—and it explains why so

many of our customers have maintained long-term relationships with us." The company's mastery of technology tools, along with its consistently fine quality production, have earned it platinum entry, the highest level of achievement, into the GATF/Apple® ColorSync® Registry.

With its dedication to craftsmanship, commitment to superior customer service, and deployment of the latest printing technology, it is not surprising that specialty publishers from coast to coast rely on Publishers Printing to complete their publications accurately, on time, and on budget.

OPPOSITE PAGE: THE CO-PALLETIZED PALLET IS PART OF PUBLISHERS PRINTING COMPANY'S UNIQUE CO-PALLETIZATION/DROP-SHIPPING DISTRIBUTION SYSTEM. THIS SYSTEM DECREASES DELIVERY LEAD TIMES AND REDUCES POSTAL-HANDLING DAMAGE. · ABOVE: THE COMPANY'S NEW DIGITAL-AD DEPARTMENT ACCEPTS ANY TYPE OF COMPUTER FILE FOR ADVERTISEMENTS, REGARDLESS OF FILE FORMAT OR SOFTWARE APPLICATION. · LEFT: MICHAEL J. SIMON (STANDING), EXECUTIVE VICE PRESIDENT, AND NICHOLAS X. SIMON (SEATED), PRESIDENT, ARE GREAT-GREAT-GRANDSONS OF NICHOLAS SIMON, WHO FOUNDED THE FAMILY-OWNED BUSINESS IN 1866. ON THE WALL IS A PORTRAIT OF THEIR FATHER, FRANK E. SIMON, WHO DIRECTED THE COMPANY INTO ITS SUCCESSFUL PRESENT-DAY ERA OF WEB PRESS MAGAZINE-PRINTING OPERATIONS.

CHERBO PUBLISHING GROUP, INC.

CHERBO PUBLISHING GROUP'S QUALITY PUBLICATIONS COMBINE EXCITING PROSE WITH STUNNING PHOTOGRAPHY TO BRING EACH CLIENT'S MESSAGE TO THE WORLD.

Founded on the premise that fine publications should offer the most persuasive, enduring, and cost-effective medium for publication communication, Cherbo Publishing Group, Inc. (CPG) has emerged as the dominant publisher of quality books for commercial, historical, civic, and trade associations.

"Cherbo Publishing Group is a growing, privately held corporation with a talented and experienced staff, modern facilities, and state-of-the-art production and fulfillment technology," says company president, Jack Cherbo. "These, along with our professional sales and marketing organization of proven skill and integrity, our sophisticated network of suppliers and contractors, and our distinguished reputation, all add up to CPG's recipe for success."

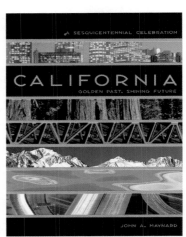

It was Jack Cherbo, a pioneer in the chamber-of-commerce and association publishing industry, and Elaine Hoffman, CPG's executive vice president, who took Cherbo Publishing Group private in 1993. The company was formerly a division of Jostens Inc., a Fortune 500 company and the world's largest maker of school yearbooks and class rings. Jostens pioneered this specialty print business and became the largest international company in the yearbook and class ring industry. Today, Encino, California–based Cherbo Publishing Group has regional offices in Philadelphia, Minneapolis, and Houston, and various marketing facilities throughout the nation.

PUBLICATIONS OF QUALITY

CPG publications—most of which are created in collaboration with a sponsoring agency—promote the economic development of America's cities, counties, and states, both domestically and internationally, and enhance the image and preserve the history of the nation's corporations, associations, organizations, and institutions.

CPG books are editorially reliable, lastingly useful, and uncommonly pleasing to the eye and mind. They offer imaginative conception and design, solid and appealing text and illustrations, quality materials and manufacture, followed by energetic promotion. Each publication is developed, after thorough market research, to meet specific needs of, and provide concrete advantages for, sponsors, corporate participants, and readers. The books' uses are many; those often cited by sponsors include economic development promotion, membership development and retention, personnel recruitment and orientation, as well as client and public relations.

A glance at the topics covered by CPG gives an idea of the scope and variety of its publications. Among these is the current millennium commemorative series, which includes books such as *Texas: An Empire Wide and Glorious* and *Maryland: Anthem to Innovation.* Written by award-winning authors, these beautiful, fully illustrated hardcover volumes celebrate the past, present, and future of U.S. cities, states, and regions, chronicling 20th-century inventions and innovations while extolling the area's quality of life and business environment.

CPG's special interest publications serve to celebrate an anniversary or other special occasion for a corporation, organization, or professional or trade association. Skillfully written and illustrated with period and contemporary photography, these books make ideal commemorative gifts.

CPG also publishes annual metro reports for business and industry, incorporating text, illustrations, and photographs in a softcover format. These books promote economic development by highlighting a city's business and livability advantages for companies or individuals considering a move to the area. Filled with comprehensive information, they include a description of demographics, profiles of local companies and organizations, and other essential information.

International airport histories feature ample illustrations and rich anecdotes that trace the creation and growth of airport facilities and services and the influence of the airports on the surrounding area's economic growth. These books include fascinating historical vignettes and profiles of airport-related businesses and organizations.

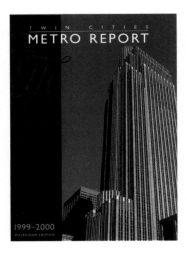

LOOKING TOWARD THE FUTURE

While CPG pays tribute to the cities it writes about, it also contributes to its own community and many others through various organizations, such as the United Way, artistic foundations, and other philanthropic groups. As it looks toward the future, CPG takes on an expanded role, one that will continue to create stunning publications serving corporate and community entities not only in the United States, but also in marketplaces around the world.

CHERBO PUBLISHING GROUP PUBLISHES QUALITY BOOKS FOR BUSINESS, HISTORIC, CIVIC, AND PROFESSIONAL ORGANIZATIONS. CHERBO BOOKS PORTRAY AMERICA'S REGIONS AND ENTERPRISES AND PROMOTE THE ECONOMIC DEVELOPMENT OF CITIES, REGIONS, AND STATES. OPPOSITE: CHERBO'S FINE, HARDCOVER BOOKS INCLUDE THE CURRENT MILLENNIUM COMMEMORATIVE SERIES; THIS VOLUME PORTRAYS THE STATE OF CALIFORNIA. • TOP: SPECIAL INTEREST BOOKS FOR BUSINESSES AND ASSOCIATIONS INCLUDE THIS KEEPSAKE VOLUME ABOUT FAMOUS PUBLIC ARENAS FOR SPORTS AND ENTERTAINMENT EVENTS. LEFT: CHERBO ALSO PUBLISHES SOFTCOVER BOOKS, SUCH AS THIS METRO REPORT ON MINNESOTA'S TWIN CITIES.

POWERING A NATION

OIL, ENERGY, & NATURAL RESOURCES

THE PEOPLE OF THE UNITED STATES, BLESSED WITH ABUNDANT AND DIVERSE NATURAL RESOURCES, HAVE PROSPERED BECAUSE OF THE INGENUITY OF AMERICAN BUSINESS. THE COUNTRY'S OIL, ENERGY, AND NATURAL RESOURCES SECTORS HAVE CREATED JOBS AND WEALTH FOR WORKERS AND A MYRIAD OF PRODUCTS FOR CONSUMERS.

IN SEARCH OF BLACK GOLD

The oil industry could arguably be called the oldest on earth. The hydrocarbon deposits from which oil is extracted are the remains of prehistoric plants and animals. Over the years, man found many uses for oil, mostly medicinal. Marco Polo found that Caspian Sea locals used crude oil to treat camels for mange. The Holy Roman Emperor Charles V kicked off Venezuela's export industry in 1539 by importing crude oil for a gout treatment.

Today, oil products fuel planes, trains, cars, buses, trucks, and motorcycles and heat houses. Chemicals made from oil appear in everything from makeup and toys to sneakers and aspirin, from football helmets to deodorant. Plastics made from petroleum are used in everything from compact discs to computers, TVs, and telephones. The integrated petroleum industry is worth $850 billion, while the oil industry alone employs nearly 1.5 million people.

The first U.S. oil well was drilled in 1859 by Edwin Drake, kicking off oil fever in western Pennsylvania. Drake decided to apply knowledge he had gained from salt mining to oil, and despite the fact that his neighbors thought he was crazy for thinking he could pump oil from the ground, he did just that.

Drake's success attracted the attention of two produce marketers in Cleveland named Maurice Clark and John Rockefeller. In 1863, Clark and Rockefeller opened their own refinery. Within five years, Rockefeller bought out Clark and brought his brothers into the business, which became the nation's largest oil manufacturer. In 1870, the company was renamed the Standard Oil Company of Ohio. By 1885, the Standard Oil Trust was a nationwide network worth $31.5 million and had a lock on about 90 percent of oil bought and sold. Rather than raising prices, however, through efficient operations the company pushed the price per barrel down from 58 cents to 8 cents. In 1894, Rockefeller retired. Standard Oil remained solid until 1911, when the Supreme Court broke it up into 34 entities. (Two of Standard Oil's descendants would reunite in 1999 with the creation of ExxonMobil, today the world's number one integrated oil company.)

Demand for petroleum soared with the development of the internal combustion engine and the arrival of the automobile. In 1907, the Standard Oil Company of California (whose name would be changed to Chevron in 1984) built the first service station in America near its Seattle kerosene refinery. Soon, it was serving more than 200 customers per day. Within the next few

Above: With oil providing 40 percent of U.S. energy needs, these oil rig workers have a critical job. · Opposite: Wind turbines generate power in Tehachapi, California.

years, this field bloomed; in 1916 alone, more than 200 new service stations opened. By the 1920s, crude oil had become a major energy source and also a major industry in "oil patch" states like Texas and Oklahoma.

In the ensuing decades, oil companies spent time and resources further developing the petroleum extraction process. One such company, the New Method Oil Well Cementing Company, was established in Wilson, Oklahoma, in 1919 by Erle P. Halliburton. A year later, Halliburton had patented the Cement Jet Mixer and had worked on 500 oil wells. Investors were impressed by the entrepreneur's aggressive approach, and by 1957, Halliburton Company would have 201 offices in 22 states and 20 foreign countries and by 1999 would become the world's number one provider of oil field services with operations in 120 companies.

In 1973, the oil party abruptly ended when the Arab-based Organization of Petroleum Exporting Countries (OPEC) oil cartel rocked the world with an oil embargo, leading to gasoline rationing in the United States. In 1979, a second blow fell: the Iranian revolution. Gas prices skyrocketed. In response, American oil companies, which were never part of OPEC, sought other sources outside the Middle East. With that additional exploration and the collapse of OPEC's embargo, oil prices dropped again in the 1980s.

By the dawn of the 21st century, the world had produced 650 billion barrels of oil, with another trillion barrels of proven

POWER PLAYS

THE UNITED STATES PRODUCES ONE BILLION TONS OF COAL EACH YEAR; MOST OF IT—APPROXIMATELY 310 MILLION TONS—IS MINED IN WYOMING. · IN 1941, THE CENTRAL VERMONT PUBLIC SERVICE CORPORATION BECAME THE FIRST CENTRAL POWER SYSTEM TO BE RUN BY A WIND TURBINE. · DEDICATED IN 1958 BY PRESIDENT EISENHOWER BY REMOTE CONTROL FROM WASHINGTON, D.C., THE SHIPPINGPORT ATOMIC POWER STATION WAS THE FIRST FULL-SCALE ATOMIC ELECTRICITY-GENERATING STATION IN THE COUNTRY. IT WAS DECOMMISSIONED BY THE DEPARTMENT OF ENERGY IN 1984. · BOULDER DAM, IN BOULDER CITY, NEVADA, OPENED IN 1935 AND IN 1943 BECAME THE FIRST HYDROELECTRIC POWER PLANT TO PRODUCE ONE MILLION KILOWATTS OF POWER. · EACH DAY, MORE THAN ONE MILLION BARRELS OF OIL ARE TRANSPORTED THROUGH THE TRANS ALASKA PIPELINE.

reserves that had not been pumped and 10 trillion more barrels of oil and oil resources present, though difficult to extract, in bitumen and shale oil, among other sources.

With its swashbuckling history of risk-taking, monopoly, embargoes, and environmental questions, oil has always been controversial. Yet one thing is certain: the oil industry will continue to play a major role in meeting the energy needs of the nation and the world.

Fueling the Nation: Natural Gas and Coal

In addition to oil, natural gas and coal are the top energy sources for Americans. Natural gas, a combustible mix of hydro-carbons, provides a full 25 percent of America's energy and forms the basis for plastics, paint, crop fertilizer, and fabrics, among many of its uses. William Hart, the "father of natural gas" in the United States, drilled the first domestic gas well in 1821. By 1998, there were 330,000 wells produc-ing natural gas across the nation. Today, natural gas heats 58 million homes, more than any other energy resource. It is also being used increasingly to power vehicles. There are 700,000 natural gas vehicles in operation around the world; slightly less than 10 percent are in the United States.

energy reserves and providing nearly a quarter of America's energy supply.

Today, coal and other minerals are key components in the everyday lives of Americans and are critical sources for foreign trade, with 1998 exports totaling $3.1 billion. An automobile contains 15 different mineral materials, a computer 30, a color TV set about 35, and a telephone about 40. A carpet alone may contain lime-stone, selenium, lime, soda ash, zeolites, bentonite, titanium, sulfur, and diatomite minerals that come from the mining industry.

two decades of the 20th century, and nearly two-thirds of coal production results from surface rather than underground mining.

Steel: The Backbone of the Industrial Revolution

Steel was the premier material of the Industrial Revolution, thanks in large part to the invention of the Bessemer furnace in 1855 and to the efforts of one man, the Scottish immigrant Andrew Carnegie.

In 1848, 12-year-old Carnegie found work as a bobbin boy in a textile mill in

Above: A geothermal steam plant in Stillwater, Nevada, provides an alternate source of power. Renewable energy such as water, wind, and solar power, generated by companies from coast to coast, contribute 10 percent of America's energy supply. • Opposite: Pump jacks facilitate the extraction of petroleum, one of the world's most valuable resources and an $850 billion industry. Products made from petroleum range from motor and heating oil to chemicals and plastics.

Like oil and natural gas, coal is a fossil fuel, a mineral formed from the remains of trees, ferns, and other plants millions of years ago. It is the most plentiful fossil fuel, forming 95 percent of the nation's fossil

The mining industry has also made substantial strides in extracting the earth's bounty in environmentally sound ways. The coal industry alone reclaimed in excess of two million acres of mined lands over the last

Pittsburgh. He worked his way up there then switched industries, taking a position with the Pennsylvania Railroad. As Carnegie learned more and more about the industry, he began making shrewd investments, such

Molten iron is poured into an open-hearth furnace to make steel. In 1900, thanks to the Bessemer Process and Andrew Carnegie, 28 million tons of steel were produced. The 2000 figure has exploded to 780 million tons.

Photo: © Keith Wood/International Stock

as the $217 he put into the Woodruff Sleeping Car Company, an investment that returned $5,000 the next year. During the last half of the 19th century, Carnegie formed a number of small telegraph and steel companies and combined several of them in 1899 as Carnegie Steel. Sold two years later to financier J. P. Morgan for $480 million, the company was renamed U.S. Steel. The ancestor of today's USX-U.S. Steel Group, U.S. Steel produced more than half of America's steel at the turn of the century. Today, it is still the number one steel maker in the country.

The sale of the steel company made Carnegie the world's richest man; he went on to become one of America's greatest philanthropists. Though the positive impact of the schools and libraries he built cannot be denied, his entrepreneurship provided one more benefit to society: he made steel less expensive and more plentiful. Through his efforts, the price of steel rails dropped from $1,650 per ton in 1875 to $17 per ton in 1898.

In 1900, 28 million tons of steel were produced; 100 years later, that figure had exploded to 780 million. Today, the goods produced by the U.S. iron and steel industries and ferrous foundries total $75 billion in revenue. One of steel's biggest customers is the automobile industry, which purchases a quarter of all steel produced annually.

Because the steel industry uses 2 to 3 percent of the total energy consumed in the United States, it has had a great incentive to become more energy efficient. In the last quarter of the 20th century, the industry reduced energy consumption by 45 percent. In addition, the industry engaged in steel recycling long before collecting cans became popular. Recycling scrap steel saves more energy than producing it from new sources.

The old-fashioned steel industry is quickly moving into the future. Two of America's largest steel makers, AK Steel, of Middletown, Ohio, and Nucor Steel, based in Charlotte, North Carolina, may well be the vanguard for the 21st century. AK Steel, whose beginnings date from 1900 with the founding of American Rolling Mill, is a leading manufacturer of flat-rolled steel. Its research facilities have created cutting-edge products such as carbon and stainless steels coated with antimicrobial compounds. Nucor traces its roots to an automobile company founded by Ransom E. Olds, the founder of Oldsmobile and REO Motor Cars. Today, Nucor is best known for its pioneering work in creating the minimill industry, in which scrap metal is melted in electric arc furnaces much more cheaply than in conventional steel mills. Nucor is also the country's largest steel recycler—10 million tons annually.

THE CHARGE OF THE LIGHT BRIGADE: ELECTRICITY

Flipping a light switch, opening the refrigerator door, booting up a computer—simple, everyday acts that practically everyone performs unconsciously. Yet the world owes a great debt for these conveniences to two of the most prolific inventors in history, one who invented the electric light bulb and one who developed the electricity distribution system that Americans depend on today.

Thomas Edison had already invented a stock ticker, a telegraph, a telephone transmitter, and a phonograph when in 1878 he decided to tackle one of the greatest challenges faced by the inventors of his time: the ability to turn electric power into light. Though arc lamps already existed, they were entirely inappropriate for home use because of the risk of fire. Edison and his research team at Menlo Park, New Jersey, obtained funding from a group of financiers

BELOW: THE POWER CONTROLS BEING INSTALLED ON THIS NATURAL GAS PIPELINE WILL HELP BOOST THE PRESSURE AS THE GAS MOVES THOUSANDS OF MILES FROM THE REGION THAT PRODUCES IT TO THE LOCAL UTILITIES THAT DISTRIBUTE IT. NATURAL GAS HEATS 58 MILLION AMERICAN HOMES, MORE THAN ANY OTHER ENERGY SOURCE. · OPPOSITE: IN OPERATION SINCE 1936, HOOVER DAM IN NEVADA GENERATES MORE THAN FOUR BILLION KILOWATT-HOURS OF HYDROELECTRIC POWER A YEAR, ENOUGH TO SATISFY THE NEEDS OF 1.3 MILLION PEOPLE.

backed by J. P. Morgan and got to work. The company that resulted, the Edison Electric Light Company, would eventually become General Electric, ranked number five among the Fortune 500 companies in 2000.

Although Edison had announced that he would have a light ready within six weeks, he didn't have a patentable product until November 1879. Edison knew of previous experiments with an incandescent lamp, a slender rod heated by a current in a vacuum of glass that prevented the material from burning out or melting. Studying the latest research on vacuums and testing hundreds of materials for the filament, Edison finally devised a bulb that could burn for hundreds of hours. Later, he wrote of his successful effort that the electric light "caused me the greatest amount of study and required the most elaborate experiments" of all his projects.

After the light bulb, Edison turned to the next challenge: how to distribute it. This effort kicked off one of the major technological battles of the late 19th century and had a profound effect on the way electricity was generated and distributed in the 20th century. Edison first demonstrated his new invention in December 1880 by dramatically illuminating Menlo Park and inviting hundreds of spectators. One of the attendees was a noted engineer and inventor who had already begun several successful companies, George Westinghouse.

Westinghouse, who was active in the railroad and natural gas industries and had invented the air brake, was intrigued by Edison's invention but was convinced he had a better way to distribute the electricity. Edison's system, called "direct current" (DC), could only be generated at low voltage and therefore could not travel far. Westinghouse developed an "alternating current" (AC) system that generated high voltages of electricity over longer distances, which were then downgraded to lower voltages that could be used in homes. In 1886, he not only developed a transformer but created a new company, the Westinghouse Electric Company.

Over the ensuing years, the battle between AC and DC was intense, but by the early 1900s, AC had won. Ironically, in 1912, two years before his death, George Westinghouse received the Edison Medal from the American Institute of Electrical Engineers for his services.

Today, just over 100 years after the AC-DC wars, nearly every home in America has electricity. The electric power industry is a $218 billion industry and employs almost 400,000 people, according to the Washington, D.C.–based Edison Electric Institute, an advocacy group for shareholder-owned electric power companies in the United States and associates overseas. Electricity represents nearly 3 percent of gross domestic product and is larger than such other major industries as telecommunications and airlines. Electric

REPLENISHING RESOURCES

PAPER IS THE MOST RECYCLED OF ALL OTHER MATERIALS COMBINED; A FULL 45 PERCENT—OR 47.3 MILLION TONS—OF PAPER USED BY AMERICANS IS RECYCLED. · ACCORDING TO THE SOCIETY OF AMERICAN FORESTERS, EVERY DAY ABOUT FOUR MILLION TREE SEEDLINGS ARE PLANTED THROUGHOUT THE UNITED STATES. · BETHLEHEM STEEL'S FORMER PENNSYLVANIA PLANT IS BEING CONVERTED INTO A 163-ACRE CENTER THAT WILL INCLUDE AN ICE-SKATING RINK, RETAIL STORES, ENTERTAINMENT VENUES, AND THE SMITHSONIAN INSTITUTION'S NATIONAL MUSEUM OF INDUSTRIAL HISTORY. SCHEDULED TO OPEN IN SPRING 2002, IT IS THE LARGEST PRIVATE "BROWNFIELD" REDEVELOPMENT PROJECT IN THE COUNTRY. · THE U.S. DEPARTMENT OF ENERGY IS WORKING WITH THE BUILDING INDUSTRY, ENERGY PROVIDERS, AND OTHERS ON THE MILLION SOLAR ROOFS INITIATIVE TO INSTALL ONE MILLION SUCH ROOFS ACROSS THE NATION BY 2010.

power demand increased eleven-fold between 1950 and 2000, and world demand is expected to double over the next few years.

What powers electric power? More than half of America's electricity supply is generated from coal. Nuclear fuel produces more than 20 percent, and renewable energy, such as water, solar, and wind power, provide nearly 10 percent, as does natural gas. Fuel oil is 3 percent of the energy mix. Like oil and gas, electricity is transported over pipelines. Unlike those two fuels, however, electricity cannot easily be stored. It travels at the speed of light and must be used almost as soon as it is generated.

In an effort to make better and more efficient use of electricity, sophisticated agreements have been signed between power producers in the United States, Canada, and northern Mexico to interconnect transmissions systems to buy and sell power from each other. One of those companies is Enron, of Houston, Texas. Named by *Fortune* magazine as the "most innovative company in America" five years in a row (1996–2000), Enron is credited with almost single-handedly creating a market for the newly deregulated gas and electricity sectors. Enron first got into the game in 1985 when the federal government deregulated the gas industry. In this new environment, Enron's insight was that natural gas was a commodity and could be traded as such. The company has successfully applied this model to electricity, pulp, paper, and most recently, broadband.

SEEING THE FORESTS AND THE TREES: THE PAPER INDUSTRY

No discussion of America's energy and natural resources would be complete without mention of the forest and paper industries.

Ever since the legend of Paul Bunyan and his sidekick, Babe the Blue Ox, these industries have been key components of America's economy.

Forests have been a prime resource for the nation from its earliest days. In the 16th century, there were an estimated 822 million acres of forest, and legend had it that a squirrel could cross the entire continent without setting foot on ground. Forestry in the 19th century was like farming, typically a small, local undertaking. A German immigrant named Frederick Weyerhaeuser would change that.

Weyerhaeuser came to America in 1848 at age 14 with his mother and sister and soon emigrated west. An eager worker, Weyerhaeuser was a day laborer and undertook odd jobs with a railroad construction crew and even a brewery. Eventually, he ended up as a night watchman at a Coal Valley, Illinois, lumberyard and apprenticed for several years until the firm went out of business. Undaunted, Weyerhaeuser bought the company himself and turned it into Weyerhaeuser Timber. Weyerhaeuser's company grew as America grew. From 1859 to 1899, annual domestic

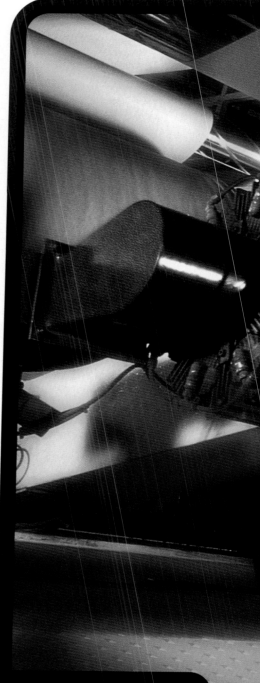

THIS PAPER MANUFACTURING PLANT HAS COME A LONG WAY SINCE BENJAMIN FRANKLIN HELPED BEGIN AMERICA'S FIRST PAPER MILLS. FORESTS ARE STILL A KEY NATURAL RESOURCE.

lumber production rose from eight billion to more than 35 billion board feet.

Weyerhaeuser anticipated many of the industrial organizations of the 20th century, including vertical integration. His company controlled forests, turned logs into lumber, constructed wooden edifices, and eventually worked out agreements with railroads to transport his lumber. Today, Weyerhaeuser, based in Tacoma, Washington, is the second largest forestry

company in the United States, behind International Paper.

The United States is one of the world's top timber-producing countries. The American forest and paper product industries shipped more than $200 billion in goods in 2000. The relationship between the two industries dates back to the 1840s, when papermakers began to use wood pulp (instead of rags) combined with a revolutionary new papermaking technology that

permanently altered an industry that hadn't changed in 2,000 years.

Today, forest and paper companies are well integrated. International Paper, with headquarters in Purchase, New York, is the world's largest producer of forest products, and distributes printing and writing papers, paperboard, and packaging worldwide. Georgia Pacific, based in Atlanta, Georgia, is one of the leading manufacturers, distributors, and wholesalers of building products, producing lumber, siding, doors, and drywall, as well as containers, bathroom tissue, paper towels, adhesives, and other essentials.

The forest and paper industries have also been altered by a growing concern for the environment. In the United States, 33 percent more trees are grown than are harvested, and every year two billion new trees are planted. The same forests in Maine that provided wood for the Continental Navy at the time of the American Revolution are still providing wood today.

As technology improves and new processes are created, America's energy and natural resources industries will continue to work not only to maintain a clean environment but to continue to provide the benefits—from efficient indoor heating to abundant light and electricity—that have contributed to a quality of life unparalleled anywhere else in the world.

profiles
Energy

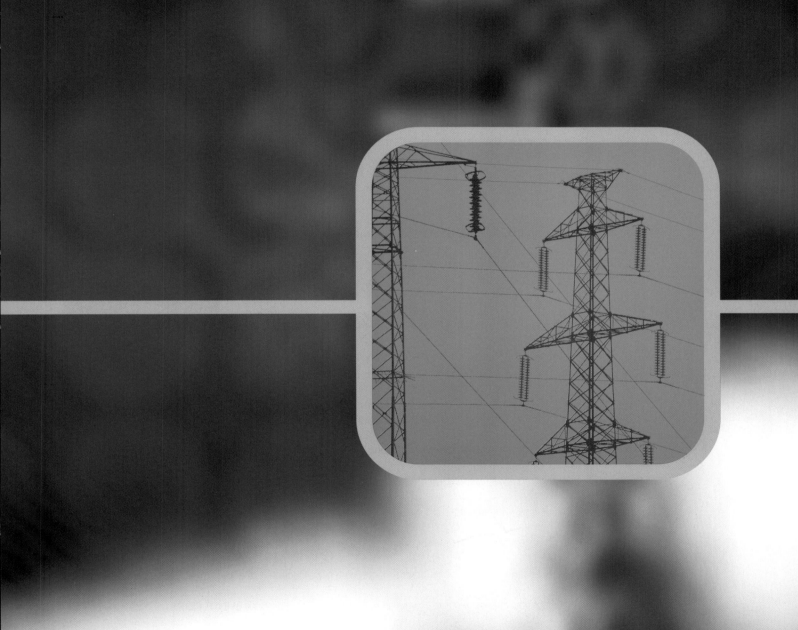

EDISON ELECTRIC INSTITUTE

EDISON ELECTRIC INSTITUTE, THE ASSOCIATION OF SHAREHOLDER-OWNED ELECTRIC POWER COMPANIES, ASSISTS ITS MEMBERS BY ADVOCATING PUBLIC POLICY, EXPANDING MARKET OPPORTUNITIES, AND PROVIDING STRATEGIC BUSINESS DATA.

On October 21, 1879, Thomas Alva Edison successfully burned an incandescent bulb for 40 hours, and soon thereafter came the birth of the electric utility. On January 12, 1933, Edison Electric Institute (EEI) was created to serve the needs of shareholder-owned electric utilities. Today, the lightbulb stands as the symbol of electricity—the universal power source upon which today's society depends and thrives. And EEI stands as the voice of unity for the nation's electric utilities.

ELECTRIC POWER

Although people easily understand the more visible examples of the role of electricity in homes, offices, and industrial plants—for lighting, communications, heating and cooling, and operating appliances and machines of every sort—electric power enables or enhances nearly every object, process, and cultural activity that the world needs and enjoys. From agricultural and medical services to manufacturing and scientific research, transport, and entertainment, a dependable flow of electric current sustains the material fabric and dynamic of modern life. And electricity is inseparably linked with today's single, most influential technology—the Internet.

The generation, transmission, and distribution of electric power in America is a massive, complex $218 billion–plus enterprise that is undergoing unprecedented change brought about by competition. Through this change, electric power companies remain the mainstays of local economic development, help-ing to sustain the growth, strength, and stability of communities nationwide by providing good jobs for nearly 400,000 people, billions of dollars in tax revenues, and diverse local public service programs.

A Changing Industry

The nation's electric power companies, serving residential, commercial, and industrial customers, once included three types of companies: cooperatively owned utilities; self-regulating, government-owned utilities; and the biggest of the three, shareholder-owned power companies.

As the new millennium arrived, America's electric power companies found their industry riding a wave of change, the most important since the electric power industry began. That change centered on restructuring the industry to give consumers a choice of who supplies their power.

As a result of the rapid changes occurring in the industry, electric utilities are undergoing changes as well. Some companies are becoming major players in the electricity generation business by purchasing power plants. Others are taking a different strategic route: divestiture of generation operations in order to concentrate on the transmission and distribution of power. Still others are diversifying their operations with new ventures into such businesses as telecommunications, natural gas, cable television, Internet access, E-commerce, and home security systems. Such activity ensures that companies can compete effectively in evolving markets, efficiently serve customers, and strengthen the nation's economic productivity. These changes also guarantee that customers will continue to enjoy some of the lowest prices for power in the world.

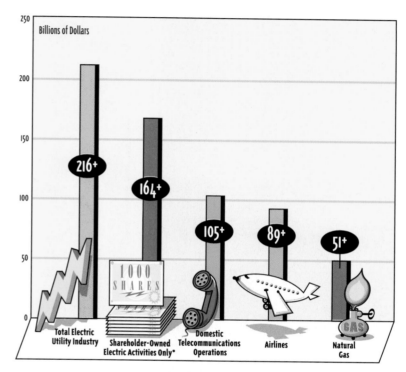

Sources: EEI, FCC, DOT, EIA

* In 1999, total operating revenue for the shareholder-owned electric utility industry totaled $325.6 billion. This figure includes both diversified and non-diversified utility activities. (Source: EEI Financial Review, 1999)

Edison Electric Institute

Edison Electric Institute helps these companies compete effectively and creates a forum for the nation's electric power companies to discuss and share information on the critical issues facing the utility industry.

Sources: EEI, FERC, 2001 Directory of Electric Power Producers and Distributors (© McGraw Hill Energy), and EIA Inventory of Nonutility Electric Power Plants in the United States 1999 (November 2000)

Opposite page: Thomas Alva Edison perfected the incandescent electric light, and soon thereafter, the electric industry was created. • Above: The electric power industry is a large business sector, representing approximately 4 percent of the real gross domestic product of the United States. • Left: In today's electricity markets, there are "traditional" electric utilities, as well as many new electricity suppliers, that are competing in wholesale and retail electricity markets.

EDISON ELECTRIC INSTITUTE

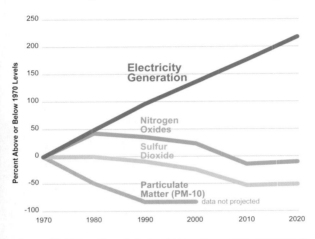

Emissions from U.S. Electricity Generation Since 1970

Percent Above or Below 1970 Levels

Electricity Generation

Nitrogen Oxides

Sulfur Dioxide

Particulate Matter (PM-10)
data not projected

1970   1980   1990   2000   2010   2020

Sources: EIA, 1999 Annual Energy Review, Table 8.3; EIA, 2001 Annual Energy Outlook, Table A8; EPA, National Air Pollutant Emission Trends, 1900-1998, Tables A2, A4, A5

RIGHT: MANY PEOPLE DO NOT REALIZE THAT THE AIR IS CLEANER TODAY THAN IT WAS 30 YEARS AGO. EVEN AS THE GENERATION OF POWER HAS INCREASED DRAMATICALLY OVER THE PAST 30 YEARS, ELECTRIC UTILITIES HAVE MADE SUBSTANTIAL PROGRESS IN REDUCING AIR EMISSIONS. · BELOW RIGHT: A VARIED FUEL MIX PROTECTS AN ELECTRIC COMPANY AND ITS CUSTOMERS FROM CONTINGENCIES SUCH AS FUEL UNAVAILABILITY, PRICE FLUCTUATIONS, AND CHANGES IN REGULATORY PRACTICES. IT ALSO HELPS ENSURE STABILITY AND RELIABILITY IN THE ELECTRICITY SUPPLY, AND STRENGTHENS NATIONAL SECURITY. · OPPOSITE PAGE, TOP: ELECTRICITY MAKES THINGS WORK—IT OPERATES HOMES, OFFICES, AND INDUSTRIES; PROVIDES COMMUNICATIONS, ENTERTAINMENT, AND MEDICAL SERVICES; POWERS COMPUTERS, TECHNOLOGY, AND THE INTERNET; AND RUNS VARIOUS FORMS OF TRANSPORTATION.

Located in Washington, D.C., EEI represents the common interests of some 200 shareholder-owned electric power companies in the United States, along with approximately 45 international affiliates and 100 industry associates worldwide. EEI member companies generate approximately three quarters of the nation's electricity and serve about 70 percent of the population.

EEI OBJECTIVES AND FUNCTIONS

On behalf of its membership, EEI advocates public policy, expands market opportunities, and provides strategic business information. EEI is committed to providing a high degree of value to its members. To that end, EEI creates forums for discussion and information exchange, and continues to be a leader in providing authoritative analysis and critical industry data to its members, Congress, government agencies, the financial community, and other influential audiences. EEI also develops information resources for a wide variety of industry concerns and activities. These unique services include the tracking and reporting of retail competition and restructuring initiatives, the growth of the electric power marketing industry, and utility operating and financial statistics.

An ongoing issue of significant importance to EEI members is keeping the environment clean. The organization provides continual leadership and advocacy to support environmental programs that are based on protecting the public health, that

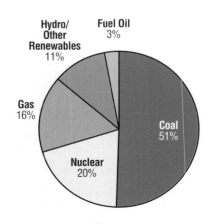

Hydro/ Other Renewables 11%

Fuel Oil 3%

Gas 16%

Coal 51%

Nuclear 20%

Current Generation Mix
(Numbers exceed 100% due to rounding.)
Source: Form EIA-759 and Form EIA-860B

are scientifically sound, and that are achievable in a cost-effective manner. EEI also promotes the industry's strong record on improvement of air quality and dedication to a diversified fuel mix that provides an effective balance for low-cost energy and a healthier environment. During the past 30 years, the voluntary efforts of electric utilities have largely contributed to 30 percent cleaner air—despite a 36 percent increase in electricity generation and a population growth of 30 percent.

On a global level, EEI has expanded its contribution to the industry through its International Affiliate initiative. This special membership of electric utilities outside the United States has raised EEI's profile internationally and has broadened the benefit of cooperation on a number of key issues. These interests of mutual concern include global climate change, the expansion of markets for electric power, international technical standards, and electrotechnologies. Through EEI committee meetings, industry conferences, and special programs, EEI's international outreach effort encourages an ongoing global dialogue addressing critical and emerging electric energy issues. This has become increasingly important as both domestic and foreign companies have increased their investment in foreign countries.

To strengthen EEI's and its members' relationship with key participants in the expanding electric power market, EEI has developed an Associate Program. This effort is designed for the vendors, suppliers, and other organizations committed to advancing the industry. Through a broad range of services, the program provides associates with information resources unavailable elsewhere and the special opportunity to work directly with leaders of the electric power industry.

Electricity and the companies that make it, move it, and market it face a thriving future. Electric power companies are reinventing their industry once again. They will drive the worldwide economy. They will lead improvements in the environment. And supporting them along the way will be Edison Electric Institute.

profiles
Steel Production

AK STEEL CORPORATION

AK STEEL CORPORATION IS A FLAT-ROLLED STEELMAKER WITH A SIGNIFICANT PRESENCE IN THE THREE MAJOR STEEL MARKETS AND A WORLDWIDE REPUTATION FOR OUTSTANDING SAFETY, QUALITY, AND PROFITABLE OPERATIONS.

AK Steel Corporation is a global leader in the steel industry, making steel for products recognized everywhere. The company supplies steel to the major car manufacturers operating in the United States. Its diverse, quality carbon, stainless, and electrical flat-rolled steels are used worldwide by automotive, industrial machinery, and appliance manufacturers; and construction companies. It also makes steel pipe and tubing and snow and ice control equipment. A Fortune 500 company based in Middletown, Ohio, AK Steel generates $4.6 billion in annual sales, employing 11,500 people at its facilities in Indiana, Kentucky, Ohio, and Pennsylvania.

AK Steel was formed in 1994 from a spinoff of the carbon flat-rolled steel business of Armco, Inc. Over the next six years, Armco focused on expanding its core business of specialty stainless and electrical steel processing, becoming one of the nation's largest producers, and AK Steel grew to become one of the world's leading carbon steelmakers. In 1999, AK Steel acquired Armco, creating a uniquely comprehensive, value-added line of steel and steel products.

AK Steel's flat-rolled steel production has a singular presence in the three major steel markets—carbon, stainless, and electrical. As a premier steel producer for automakers, AK Steel supplies carbon and coated steels for automotive body panels as well as stainless steels for automotive exhaust systems. Its stainless steels are found in appliances and in equipment for food processing and chemical, petrochemical, and other industrial applications. AK Steel is one of the nation's only steelmakers producing a full line of energy-efficient electrical steels used in electric motors, power generation and distribution, and lighting systems.

Being competitive in today's global steel market requires commitment to safety, product quality, and productivity, and AK Steel is a record-setting leader in all three categories. Safety is the highest operating priority, and the company has adopted a philosophy of reaching and maintaining a level of zero injuries.

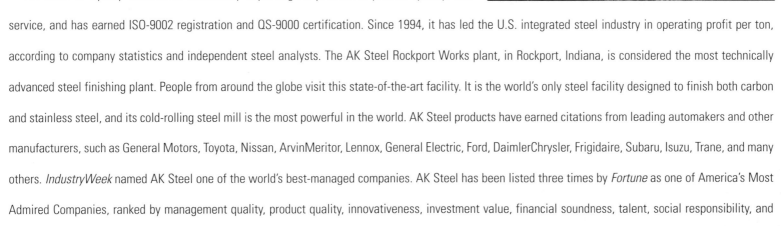

Since 1993, AK Steel has led the American steel industry in every measure of safety performance. The company has been honored with numerous awards, including the Indiana Chamber of Commerce statewide safety award, the Pennsylvania Governor's Award for Safety Excellence, and the National Safety Council Award of Honor. In 2000, Richard M. Wardrop Jr., AK Steel chairman and CEO, was selected by the National Safety Council to receive its first-ever Green Cross for Safety in honor of his longstanding commitment to workplace safety and corporate citizenship.

AK Steel is equally focused on continually improving its processes, product quality, and service, and has earned ISO-9002 registration and QS-9000 certification. Since 1994, it has led the U.S. integrated steel industry in operating profit per ton, according to company statistics and independent steel analysts. The AK Steel Rockport Works plant, in Rockport, Indiana, is considered the most technically advanced steel finishing plant. People from around the globe visit this state-of-the-art facility. It is the world's only steel facility designed to finish both carbon and stainless steel, and its cold-rolling steel mill is the most powerful in the world. AK Steel products have earned citations from leading automakers and other manufacturers, such as General Motors, Toyota, Nissan, ArvinMeritor, Lennox, General Electric, Ford, DaimlerChrysler, Frigidaire, Subaru, Isuzu, Trane, and many others. *IndustryWeek* named AK Steel one of the world's best-managed companies. AK Steel has been listed three times by *Fortune* as one of America's Most Admired Companies, ranked by management quality, product quality, innovativeness, investment value, financial soundness, talent, social responsibility, and use of assets. In crediting its high levels of production, quality, and operating profit, AK Steel cites in good part its rigorous attention to detail in maintaining the complex machinery of its steel plants. The company has received the prestigious *Plant Engineering* North American Maintenance Excellence (NAME) award.

AK Steel operates one of the nation's largest steel research facilities, exploring new manufacturing techniques and working with customers to design new products. It created AgION™ carbon and stainless steels, coated with an antimicrobial compound to prohibit the growth of bacteria and mold. Among the many potential areas for AgION steels are home appliances and equipment for food processing, medical use, laboratories, heating, ventilating, and air-conditioning (HVAC). AK Steel pursues such innovation as part of its ongoing commitment to be well positioned for a bright future.

OPPOSITE PAGE: BASIC OXYGEN FURNACES TURN MOLTEN IRON INTO MOLTEN STEEL AT AK STEEL'S MIDDLETOWN WORKS, HOME TO SOME OF THE MOST PRODUCTIVE STEEL OPERATIONS IN THE WORLD. · ABOVE: AK STEEL'S ROCKPORT WORKS IS THE MOST ADVANCED CARBON AND STAINLESS FINISHING FACILITY IN THE WORLD. THE PLANT'S UNIQUE CARBON AND STAINLESS CONFIGURATION GIVES AK STEEL UNSURPASSED MANUFACTURING FLEXIBILITY. · LEFT: RICHARD M. WARDROP JR., AK STEEL CHAIRMAN AND CEO, WAS HONORED IN 2000 BY THE NATIONAL SAFETY COUNCIL FOR HIS CONTINUING DEDICATION TO WORKPLACE SAFETY AND CORPORATE RESPONSIBILITY. AK STEEL'S INJURY RATE IS ABOUT FIVE TIMES BETTER THAN THE U.S. STEEL INDUSTRY'S AVERAGE.

LEAVE IT TO THE EXPERTS

PROFESSIONAL & BUSINESS-TO-BUSINESS SERVICES

THE 20TH CENTURY WITNESSED TREMENDOUS IMPROVEMENTS IN MANAGEMENT TECHNIQUES AND OPERATIONS OF AMERICAN COMPANIES. FOR CORPORATIONS OF EVER-INCREASING SIZE, MANAGEMENT THEORIES WERE TESTED AND

business strategies perfected. Upgraded financial practices were instituted. New approaches to marketing and advertising, pollution control, and human resources were adopted.

As the century reached its final years, a whole new field of concerns took center stage: keeping up with the changes in information technology and the management of companies' data.

Small businesses experienced these needs and developed many of these proficiencies as well. Linking both large concerns and small enterprises was their need to rely on a vast and expanding array of professional services companies. Though definitions vary, this sprawling sector generally includes services ranging all the way from legal counsel, accounting, data collection, and engineering to advertising, employee recruiting, sanitation, and uniform rentals.

Hoover's, a business network that provides information on business and industry around the world, estimates this sector is a more than $700 billion annual industry. Yet the total grows with companies' needs, especially as many firms increasingly rely on outsourcing to meet basic business functions.

FROM GREAT THEORIES GREAT INDUSTRIES GROW

Before there was consulting, there was "scientific management." Frederick W. Taylor, a talented engineer who had spent time on the factory floor, wanted to find out the best way to do everything. His experience as foreman in a steel mill in the late 1870s convinced him that the two current management styles—pushing factory workers as hard as they could be pushed or letting them get away with as little work as possible—were both wrong. Taylor's insight, revolutionary at the time, was to establish scientifically the reasonable amount of work that should be done over a specific time period.

After observing a top factory worker, Taylor broke down the steps, calculated actual times, then applied the technique of his "time-motion" study to the steel mill. Production jumped. The Taylor System, whose principles were described in Taylor's 1909 publication, *Principles of Scientific Management*, became the model upon which companies were run in the 20th century.

Indeed, *Fortune* magazine called the last 100 years the Century of the Manager. The management theories of two later pioneers, W. Edwards Deming and Peter F. Drucker, are considered just as monumental as those of Taylor and are credited with improving productivity

Opposite: Delighted with the client's response to their strategy, an accounting team calls the home office. · Above: Lawyers consult notes on international trade law.

and influencing the way businesses are run today. Deming, the founder of Total Quality Management, a popular set of creative management principles and practices, is also known for his Fourteen Points, a model for management that helped transform Japan's economy after World War II. His theories still influence how companies are run throughout the world. Drucker, through such books as *The Practice of Management* and *Management: Tasks, Responsibilities, Practices*, became a leading voice in management education.

From the theories and strategies developed by Taylor, Drucker, Deming, and others

arose a great industry whose mission was to help companies grow and increase productivity and profitability through the sound management of people, money, assets, and markets.

Sitting on top of this vital sector are the companies known as the "Big Five" accounting firms. The services of these global powerhouses extend well beyond bean counting and include assurance and advisory, tax, management, outsourcing, merger and acquisition strategy, and information technology counseling.

Recent years have witnessed a flurry of mergers and restructuring; for example, the

spinning off of Andersen Worldwide's management and technology consulting business, which is called Accenture. As of 2000, the Big Five in order of size included:

• PricewaterhouseCoopers, of New York, a $21.5 billion global organization that moved into the number one spot after the 1998 merger of Price Waterhouse and Coopers & Lybrand;

• Andersen Worldwide, a Chicago-based company founded in 1913 by university professor Arthur Andersen;

• New York–based Ernst & Young International, called upon by at least 114 Fortune 500 companies for auditing services;

NYU PROFESSOR PETER DRUCKER, ONE OF THE CENTURY'S LEADING MANAGEMENT EDUCATION VOICES, EXPLAINS THE CHARACTERISTICS OF AMERICAN MANAGEMENT TO TOP POLISH LEADERS VISITING THE STATES IN 1965 FOR A SERIES OF BUSINESS MEETINGS.

$138 billion in annual revenues. As the pace of globalization quickens and the speed of electronic transactions grows, these highly skilled and specialized business experts will no doubt grow in influence and importance.

Alongside the growth of accounting, auditing, and business counseling has come an explosion of demand for legal services. Complex regulations governing hiring and firing as well as environmental and financial controls explain part of this growth. So does the growing litigiousness of American society. The globalization of the economy, with its accent on mergers and international trade law, has also multiplied the demands of large and small firms for lawyers with a diversity of specialties.

There are nearly one million lawyers in the United States working for government, directly for companies, as sole proprietors, or as partners in larger firms. To meet the complex legal needs of America's largest companies, thousands of highly specialized attorneys have organized themselves into

- KPMG International, the product of mergers of Dutch, British, and German companies with a New York firm that traces its roots back to 1897 with the founding of the accounting firm of Marwick, Mitchell & Co.;

- Deloitte & Touche, the U.S. arm of Deloitte Touche Tohmatsu, a New York–based company with 90,000 employees in 130 countries.

Business Week pegs this major slice of the professional services sector at

global firms with offices and affiliates across the country and around the world.

According to *American Lawyer* magazine, the leaders of the $11 billion legal services industry include:

- Skadden, Arps, Slate, Meagher & Flom, a law firm headquartered in New York with 1,322 attorneys and $1.02 billion in annual revenues;

- Baker & McKenzie, of Chicago, with 2,477 affiliated attorneys and $818 million in revenues;

- Jones, Day, Reavis & Pogue, a 1,500-lawyer firm with $595 million in 1999 revenues and roots that date to 1893 Cleveland.

There are also firms that specialize in particular areas. For example, the international firm of Howrey Simon Arnold & White has one of the largest intellectual property, antitrust and competition, and global litigation practices in the world. Fragomen, Del Rey, Bernsen & Loewy, with 19 offices across the nation and abroad, are experts in immigration and nationality law.

The advice provided by those in the legal profession—and in all consulting professions—will become increasingly important and sought after as American companies deal with the complexities of the global economy. Their specialized knowledge and expertise will continue to help America's companies to operate as efficiently, safely, and productively as possible.

THE RISE OF ADVERTISING

During the 20th century, businesses did more than boost the professionalism of their internal practices. Through highly sophisticated marketing, advertising, and public relations efforts, they perfected their sales pitches and helped trigger a wave of consumerism never before witnessed. The growth of advertising and its symbiotic link to both rising incomes and the development of mass media illustrate this dramatic story.

Advertising developed into an art—and a science—in the mid-1800s, when the Industrial Revolution generated an increasingly wealthy and educated population, a communications system that permitted more widespread transmission of information, and, for the first time, a multitude of products for the new middle class to enjoy.

One of the earliest success stories in the advertising industry was N. W. Ayer & Son,

started in 1869 by Francis Weyland Ayer, who named his company for his father both out of respect and out of fear that nobody would take the young Francis seriously. The agency set the standard for the burgeoning industry: "open contract" policies, in which clients paid commission on media rates; a full-service shop with offices in different cities; a new-business department; full-time copywriters and artists; and the nation's first institutional ad campaigns. Today, the company, known for legendary campaigns like "A Diamond is Forever" (deBeers), "I'd Walk a Mile for a Camel" (Camel cigarettes), and "Reach Out and Touch Someone" (AT&T), is a part of

recognized that women, as controllers of the family purse, were the most powerful force in the marketplace and that many of those women read national magazines. He also pioneered the testimonial ad and census-based demographic research and was recognized as "the father of magazine advertising in America." In 1887, his company became the first to write the ads for clients, not just place them. He incorporated his firm, J. Walter Thompson and Co., in 1896. The company, known as JWT, was purchased in 1916 by Stanley Resor.

Above: George Gallup, the famed American opinion pollster, founded the Institute of Public Opinion in 1947. · Opposite: Advertisements like this one for Dr. Pepper, circa 1946, helped trigger an unparalleled wave of consumerism.

IN THE HANDS OF THE PROS

According to *Advertising Age*, the top five of the 100 best advertising campaigns of the 20th century are Volkswagen's 1959 "Think Small" (by Doyle Dane Bernbach); Coca-Cola's 1929 "The Pause That Refreshes" (by D'Arcy Co.); the 1955 Marlboro Man ads (by Leo Burnett Co.); Nike's "Just Do It," of 1988 (by Wieden & Kennedy); and the 1971 McDonald's classic, "You Deserve a Break Today" (by Needham, Harper & Steers). · With its $100,000 bid for the rights to broadcast the 1939 World Series on the radio, the Gillette Safety Razor Company became the first to advertise during a sporting event. · With more than 400,000 members, the American Bar Association is the largest voluntary professional association in the world. · PricewaterhouseCoopers (formerly Price Waterhouse) has tabulated the Academy Awards ballots since 1934.

Chicago-based Bcom3 Group, one of the largest ad corporations in the world. It offers advertising, public relations, and related services to clients like the Coca-Cola Company, Burger King, and the Walt Disney Company.

N. W. Ayer's main competitor was a man named James Walter Thompson. In 1877 in New York, Thompson built a unique advertising agency based on his special insight into the American lifestyle. For example, he

A year after he purchased JWT, Resor entered into a very special merger: he married Helen Landsdowne, a talented copywriter. Landsdowne Resor actively recruited women to be copywriters for JWT and was the first to use sex appeal in ads, beginning with the Woodbury facial soap campaign, which featured the tag line "A skin you love to touch." Under the stewardship of the Resors, by 1927 JWT had become the top ad agency in the country, employing researchers

and psychologists to better understand consumers. In 1947, JWT sponsored the *Kraft Television Theatre*, the first network television program. JWT merged with the WPP Group, today the world's largest advertising firm, in 1987 and counts among its clients Kimberly Clark, Elizabeth Arden, and Qwest.

The interwar period was a time of great growth for the industry. The first radio broadcast, in 1920, opened a revolutionary new outlet for advertising, and by 1938, ad revenue from radio had surpassed that of magazines. It was during this period that Raymond Rubicam and John Orr Young established their agency, Young & Rubicam, in Philadelphia in 1923. Within five years, companies like the Borden Company, Johnson & Johnson, and General Foods became clients. In 1932, Young & Rubicam hired an academic, George Gallup, who had established male-female copy appeal ratings for economy, efficiency, sex, vanity, and quality. In 1935, Gallup started the Gallup Poll, which determined public opinion on issues of the day, and in 1947 left

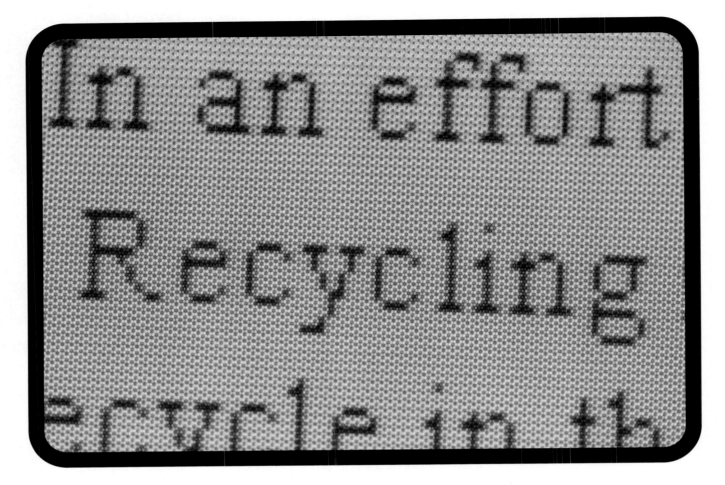

Young & Rubicam to start his own polling company. Today, Gallup's company is one of the leading research and consulting organizations in the world, and Young & Rubicam, like JWT, is now part of the WPP Group.

World War II saw the arrival of television, which made an even bigger splash than radio. In 1941, the first TV spot went on the air, broadcasting to 7,500 TV sets in New York City on NBC's WNBT. The ad featured a Bulova watch ticking for 60 seconds. In 1952, the television industry adopted the A. C. Nielsen ratings, which had been developed for radio in the 1920s and 1930s and which apprised advertisers and their clients of how many prospective customers were watching, and thus how ad dollars could best be spent.

After several decades of mostly uninterrupted growth, the economic stagnation of the 1970s reduced advertising budgets. Meanwhile, increasing globalization led to consolidation in the advertising industry. In

1986, three New York firms, Doyle Dane Bernbach, Needham Harper Worldwide, and BBDO International, merged to create Omnicom Group. With another New York firm, TWBA/Worldwide, joining this team, Omnicom became the largest agency in the world until it was pushed to number two in 2000 by the WPP Group when WPP merged with Young & Rubicam.

By the end of the 20th century, advertising had become a global business with some $450 billion in worldwide revenues. Today, companies like WPP, Omnicom, and New York's Interpublic, the number three firm, offer clients a broad range of public relations and marketing services, principally through their acquisitions of large and small companies in those fields.

As the industry entered the 21st century, the prospect of Internet advertising loomed large in agency strategies. Traditional advertising agencies rushed to set up on-line marketing divisions, like Omnicom's Agency.com.

Yet with on-line advertising lagging well behind initial growth forecasts, the jury is still out as to whether Web-based ads will come to dominate global consumer marketing or simply take their appropriate place as another avenue for companies and their pitchmen.

CLEANING THE ENVIRONMENT

During the last half of the 20th century, increased awareness of and concern for the environment led to the creation of a new industry, one that has experienced tremendous growth. Developing the technologies and practices to clean the environment—not to mention hauling away and recycling the nation's trash—has become a very big business in America. An estimated $150 billion a year is generated by the environmental services and equipment industry.

Ranging from small design and engineering firms to large water-treatment plants, the environmental services industry is diverse and often involves both the public and private sectors. Water supply and treatment facilities, for example, are operated mainly by municipal governments, although many are built by private firms. About 8 percent will likely be privatized in the coming decade.

One of the leaders in the industry is Waste Management, of Houston, the top company in solid-waste management. The firm owns or operates 284 landfills, more than any other company in the industry, and chalks up $12.5 billion in annual revenues.

The Increasing Array of Business-to-Business Services

As the needs of large and small companies grow, and the trend toward outsourcing continues, many businesses in specialized fields are finding that other businesses are their best customers.

There's the office equipment and furniture sector, where the pace is set by New York's IBM, the top supplier of PCs, workstations, servers, and mainframes, and Stamford, Connecticut–based Xerox, the

Framingham, Massachusetts, which has 1,300 stores in the United States, Canada, the United Kingdom, Germany, the Netherlands, and Portugal. Coming in third with $5 billion in sales is OfficeMax, of Shaker Heights, Ohio. The company has approximately 1,000 stores in the United States and Puerto Rico.

Among the top manufacturers of office supplies is the Minnesota Mining and Manufacturing Company, better known as 3M. Famous for its Post-it Notes and Scotch tape, the St. Paul company racked up nearly $17 billion in sales in 2000. Pasadena,

Below: 3M researcher Dr. Spencer Silver developed the adhesive used on Post-it Notes, one of the company's leading products. · Opposite: A computer screen shows a message on recycling, an estimated $150 billion industry.

Manufacturing giants Corning and Allied Signal have divisions that make air pollution–control devices. These are but a few of the companies that have contributed to a major improvement in the environment over the past three decades.

When assessing the environmental improvements in manufacturing and the advances in municipal health through breakthroughs in water treatment and waste management, the contributions of America's design engineers and their companies must not be overlooked. These professionals, working for firms such as San Francisco–based Bechtel Group, complement the work of thousands of innovative smaller firms that design environmental technologies of great diversity and bring them to market.

American business will spend some $1.5 trillion in the first decade of the 21st century to clean the environment, and the environmental services sector will continue its efforts to ensure a quality of life that will enable American companies to operate efficiently and productively.

nation's leader in sales of digital copiers, with more than 30 percent of the market share. Steelcase, with headquarters in Grand Rapids, Michigan, is the world's largest maker of office furniture, recording 2000 year-end sales of $3.8 billion.

The office supply sector is dominated by the Delray Beach, Florida, company Office Depot, which has 950 stores throughout the world and had 2000 sales of $11.6 billion. Right behind Office Depot with nearly $11 billion in sales is Staples, of

California's label-maker Avery Dennison has 200 manufacturing facilities. Among its clients is the U.S. Postal Service for whom the company produces self-adhesive stamps.

Administrative services form another area of commerce and opportunity. Manpower, of Milwaukee, Wisconsin, is the largest temporary-placement agency in the country. The company, founded in 1948 by two lawyers, places more than two million people in jobs per year, earning $12.4 billion in revenues for its recruitment efforts.

Maintaining and processing credit histories is another service area that has seen tremendous growth. This $13.5 billion annual business is dominated by Dun & Bradstreet, Equifax, and Experian Information Solutions. Dun & Bradstreet, of Murray Hill, New Jersey, has a global database of 55 million companies and had more than $1 billion in sales in 2000. The largest credit reporting company in the United States, Atlanta-based Equifax maintains credit records on some 400 million consumers for banks and stores worldwide and also provides consulting on credit risk. Providing similar services is Experian Information Services, of Orange, California. The company has information on 205 million consumers throughout the world.

Other firms provide a plethora of technical services. St. Paul–based Ecolab is a market leader in providing sanitation products and services to hospitals, food service facilities, schools, and other entities. Ecolab posted sales in 2000 of more than $2 billion. Cintas, a uniform rental company with headquarters in Cincinnati, Ohio, is the nation's leading uniform supplier. With 400,000 customers, Cintas had sales in 2000 of $1.9 billion.

As the competition for markets and the need for efficiency accelerate, companies will look even more to the stunning array of firms that are in business to help business.

Trade and Professional Associations

The improvements in management techniques and in the specialization of American business and careers has produced explosive growth in associations. According to the American Society of Association Executives, there are more than 140,000 associations in America, covering virtually every industry, profession, cause, and interest.

Nine out of ten adult Americans belong to at least one association. Millions participate to upgrade their skills, join in advocacy before government, or simply to enjoy the camaraderie of others in their field. The Institutional Labor Advisors Association, for example, is a Washington, D.C.–based organization that consults on all facets of labor-related matters. Also located in the nation's capital is the Reserve Officers Association of the United States, which represents the interests of all active, reserve, former, and retired commissioned officers of the seven branches of the United States uniformed services.

In the wake of such popular demand for the programs and services of associations has come a very big business with a sizable economic impact. Associations employ nearly 300,000 Americans. They rank as a major segment of the health insurance market, purchasing $6 billion in premiums annually. Associations also spend $5.6 billion each year on printing, $2.2 billion on technology, and $56 billion to hold conventions, meetings, and trade shows. That represents a major portion of the $83 billion meetings industry, another service industry whose primary customers are other businesses.

A Bountiful Future

Though part of the strength of America's economy still lies in its strong backs and nimble fingers, in the future it will be what people know and how they apply it that really counts. Professional services of all kinds have together become a vital component of the nation's economy, helping businesses become more productive, professional, and competitive in the knowledge-based global economy of the 21st century. The needs will change and thus so will the players, but the business services industry can look forward to an exciting and challenging future.

A GROUP OF ASSOCIATION EXECUTIVES REPRESENTING HIGH-TECHNOLOGY MANUFACTURING BUSINESSES THROUGHOUT THE NATION HAMMERS OUT THE STRATEGY IT WILL USE WHEN IT GOES BEFORE A GOVERNMENT COMMITTEE TO ADVOCATE FOR CHANGES THAT WOULD BENEFIT THE PROFESSION. ASSOCIATIONS EMPLOY NEARLY 300,000 AMERICANS AND EXIST FOR ALMOST EVERY INDUSTRY, PROFESSION, CAUSE, AND INTEREST.

profiles
Professional Services

HOWREY SIMON ARNOLD & WHITE.

HOWREY SIMON ARNOLD & WHITE IS A DOMESTIC AND INTERNATIONAL POWERHOUSE, WHOSE ANTITRUST AND COMPETITION, GLOBAL LITIGATION, AND INTELLECTUAL PROPERTY PRACTICES ARE AMONG THE LARGEST AND MOST SUCCESSFUL IN THE WORLD.

In this era of increasing globalization, accelerating advances in technology, dramatic consolidations of assets, and ever more complex disputes, today's law firms are expected by clients to respond swiftly and with more experience, resources, and talent than ever before. Excellence is expected and must be delivered. Howrey Simon Arnold & White, LLP, dedicated to being "The Law Firm of Choice" for corporate clients with such needs *and* a home for the very best counselors, litigators, and trial lawyers, meets these challenges.

With practice offices strategically located across the United States—in Washington, D.C.; Houston; Chicago; and both northern and southern California—and in Europe, in London and Brussels—Howrey brings to bear the most talented teams of professionals possible, in any matter and in any venue, from among its more than 500 attorneys and 800 additional professionals and staff members. Its Capital Group includes full-

time professional economists, accountants, financial analysts, environmental scientists, and engineers trained to apply their specific knowledge and skills to clients' needs. Howrey's responsive corporate management model employs a chief financial, operating, and marketing officer, and an innovative board of inside and outside directors.

The sheer volume and scope of the firm's involvement in the nation's commerce and dispute-resolution systems is illustrative. From 1995 through 2000, for example, Howrey attorneys litigated in 49 states, representing clients in more than 1,500 federal and state trial court matters; appeared in more than 430 appeals, including 53 before the U.S. Supreme Court; and appeared in all Federal Courts of Appeals. Another benchmark is the firm's standing among the client communities it serves: The *National Law Journal* has repeatedly ranked Howrey in the top 10 among law firms most used by the top 250 of the Fortune 500 it has surveyed, and as the second most used firm in the United States in both 1999 and 2000. *Global Competition Review*'s survey of international firms named Howrey as the number one antitrust/competition law firm in the world for two consecutive years, 1999 and 2000. And *IP Worldwide*, in 1999 and 2000, ranked Howrey as first among law firms protecting intellectual property rights, in its survey of international companies.

THE PRACTICE

To ensure that each client benefits from its unique array of in-house resources, Howrey deploys uncommon professional skills, imaginatively adapted technology, and a world-class platform of support systems across each of the firm's principal practice groups. Experienced and well-trained lawyers at all levels, in-house economists, accountants, environmental scientists, and a trial site logistics team, for example, support complex litigation. And Howrey's multimedia experts use imaginative presentation technology to vividly communicate complex ideas and evidence to judges and juries.

ANTITRUST AND COMPETITION

Antitrust is the original practice area upon which the firm was founded, in 1956, and built its initial reputation. Today, Howrey's team of more than 180 antitrust attorneys in the United States and in Europe—the largest and most experienced group in the world outside of the U.S. government—includes a large number of former Federal Trade Commission and U.S. Department of Justice officials, several American Bar Association antitrust section chairs, and trial lawyers who have taken more antitrust cases through trial than those of any other firm. In the five years from 1996 through 2000, these veteran specialists have worked on more than 800 mergers and acquisitions, managing them through the U.S. Federal Trade Commission (FTC) and Department of Justice (DOJ) clearance processes, as well as the EU (European Union) Competition office in Brussels. During the same time, litigating and trying more than 500 private antitrust actions, for both plaintiffs and defendants, in virtually every federal district court in the nation, they have accumulated matchless experience in the full spectrum of today's complex antitrust issues.

GLOBAL LITIGATION

Howrey's Global Litigation Group, with more than 125 trial and litigation lawyers, is skilled in handling disputes arising in a number of substantive legal disciplines, including commercial transactions, product liability, insurance recovery, securities, government regulation, white-collar crime, international commercial and government arbitration, and Supreme Court & Appellate litigation. The group's strength lies in its highly trained complement of attorneys and legal assistants, with broad substantive and trial experience, and its capability to bring the strongest possible resources and talent to a dispute, regardless of issue or venue. The group specializes in complex, high-value litigation and arbitration, using the firm's economic and accounting professionals and in-house multimedia and trial site experts to obtain consistently superior results.

TOP: HOWREY SIMON ARNOLD & WHITE ATTORNEYS AND STAFF SHARE A COMMITMENT TO EXCELLENCE. • ABOVE LEFT: HOWREY'S MANAGING PARTNER, ROBERT F. RUYAK, CONTINUES TO DRIVE THE FIRM'S GROWTH.

HOWREY SIMON ARNOLD & WHITE.

INTELLECTUAL PROPERTY

At the heart of Howrey's renowned Intellectual Property practice are nearly 200 intellectual property (IP) litigation, transactional, and trial attorneys, and an array of talented scientists and engineers. Located across the United States and in Europe, they present to clients one of the largest IP practices in the world, with a roster of leaders in the field, including the former U.S. undersecretary of commerce and the director of the U.S. Patent and Trademark Office, and some of the most recognized IP litigators in the nation. Its large complement of lawyer-engineers and lawyer-scientists provides unmatched depth and breadth of knowledge in virtually every discipline. In terms of scope, their expertise covers all aspects of Intellectual Property Strategic Management—from capturing innovations and rights prosecution to licensing, acquisition, disposition, enforcement, and litigation, with specialties in patents, trademarks, copyrights, and trade secrets.

COMMUNITY SERVICE

Howrey believes that it is vital for its lawyers in each community to help those who most need, but can least afford, legal services. Howrey has always been committed to substantial and diverse pro bono work—the provision of the highest quality legal work at no charge to its beneficiaries. The nonlegal staff also participates, through a number of community programs, including mentoring and tutoring.

In 2000 alone, Howrey attorneys and staff members contributed more than 25,000 hours to pro bono matters for more than 100 clients, placing it among the top 25 law firms nationwide. Approximately half the firm's attorneys provided pro bono services, in both routine and impact cases. Among its impact cases, Howrey attorneys represented Baltimore schoolchildren, indigent adoptive children and parents, AIDS clinic patients, and political refugees; battled predatory lending and slumlord property neglect; and pursued workplace

equality. The firm has been recognized for this work with awards from many groups, including the California and Maryland State Bar Associations, the Los Angeles Inner City Law Center, the Washington, D.C., Lawyers' Committee for Civil Rights and Urban Affairs, and the Washington, D.C., Archdiocesan Legal Network of Catholic Charities. In an effort to provide additional services, Howrey has established an innovative intern program with local law schools, which provides the services of law students, supervised by Howrey lawyers, to the indigent.

HOWREY BOOTCAMP™

The steady recruitment of talented young lawyers—essential to maintaining the firm's core strengths and achieving its vision—was dramatically strengthened in 2001 with the launch of a new summer program: Howrey Bootcamp. This five-week program for students who have completed two years of law study, emphasizes

training, hands-on experience, and teamwork. It includes an off-site "camp" that pairs top law students with Howrey's most experienced lawyers in an intensive 14-day training program that teaches practical techniques as participants take charge of a client's problem from initial interview through trial. Using the fact pattern of an actual case, students present motions, discovery disputes, and a trial before senior partners and real judges, who then provide feedback. This "Bootcamp" of trial exercises, seminars, and workshops is combined with three additional weeks of working in one of Howrey's offices, after which successful participants are invited to join the firm. Howrey Bootcamp exemplifies the firm's resolve to attract and retain the most able and dedicated young attorneys upon whom to build its practices, and its sustained commitment to superb training and professional development.

LOOKING FORWARD

For nearly a half-century, Howrey has placed a high value on the human qualities of excellence, commitment, integrity, and teamwork, and has made these characteristics its goals. From the boardroom and workplace to the marketplace and courtroom, Howrey strategically partners with its clients to achieve for them the best possible results in the complex and increasingly challenging business world they face.

JONES, DAY, REAVIS & POGUE

WITH OFFICES ACROSS THE NATION AND WORLDWIDE, JONES, DAY, REAVIS & POGUE PROVIDES LEGAL COUNSEL TO BOTH ESTABLISHED AND EMERGING COMPANIES, FROM LEADING CORPORATIONS TO INTERNET START-UPS.

Jones, Day, Reavis & Pogue traces its roots to 1893, when America was in the midst of an industrial revolution that was rapidly transforming an immigrant nation into a global power. In the late 19th century, Jones Day's founders provided legal counsel to the iron ore, steel, shipping, railroad, and manufacturing companies that, over the next century, became the nation's industrial backbone.

Today, Jones Day ranks among the world's largest and most geographically diverse law firms, with more than 1,500 lawyers, based in 26 offices in centers of business and finance throughout the United States, Europe, and Asia.

FOUNDATION VALUES

As a firm, members are bound together by a set of values that can be traced to Jones Day's earliest days and that continue to govern the institutional behavior of its lawyers and staff. More than anything else, they believe that these fundamental values—integrity, competence, independence, personal accountability, dedication, courage, determination, commitment, understanding, and unity of purpose—convey the essence of Jones Day and the qualities that they bring to each client engagement.

MULTIDISCIPLINARY PRACTICE

Although more than 100 years have passed since the firm's founding, today Jones Day lawyers are in many ways doing exactly what was done in the firm's formative years: providing legal counsel to both established and emerging companies—from more than half of the Fortune 500 to Internet start-ups —as well as to many leading corporations based outside the United States and to individuals.

The aim is to assist clients in finding creative legal solutions to meet their business objectives, whether completing a business transaction, navigating government regulations, resolving litigation, or working through tax issues.

The four major practice groups—Business Practice, Government Regulation, Litigation, and Tax—are supplemented by multidisciplinary teams, as well as by specialized industry practices that provide interdisciplinary services to legally intensive and highly regulated industries. The firm's practice- and industry-based structure brings the talent and experience of the entire firm to bear on matters originating in any office, promotes the exchange of information, and allows for efficient and effective project management within and among the various practices.

At Jones Day the goal is to develop a genuine sensitivity to clients' objectives and a thorough understanding of the economic issues, industry trends, and client concerns implicated by the problems, transactions, and controversies brought to its attention. The firm believes that such an awareness contributes to more creative solutions to clients' problems and, when applied to project planning, provides a measurable value-added dimension to the firm's services. Further, it believes that practice management is key to the efficient delivery of legal services and that such an approach demands a sophisticated level of experience, flexibility, open communication, mutual respect, and support between client and outside counsel.

All Jones Day locations are fully integrated into the firm's practice structure, which facilitates client access to the experience and skills of Jones Day lawyers located throughout the world. All personnel, locations, and practice groups are linked by state-of-the-art communications systems, shared databases, and word-processing systems.

THE FUTURE

"Despite our long and rich history, at Jones Day we have always kept our eyes turned toward the future," says Patrick F. McCartan, managing partner. "We look forward to working together with our clients to meet the challenges of a new century and a new economy."

OPPOSITE PAGE: JONES DAY RANKS AMONG THE WORLD'S LARGEST AND MOST GEOGRAPHICALLY DIVERSE LAW FIRMS, WITH MORE THAN 1,500 LAWYERS, BASED IN CENTERS OF BUSINESS AND FINANCE THROUGHOUT THE UNITED STATES, EUROPE, AND ASIA. · ABOVE: THE FIRM'S FOUR MAJOR PRACTICE GROUPS— BUSINESS PRACTICE, GOVERNMENT REGULATION, LITIGATION, AND TAX—ARE SUPPLEMENTED BY MULTIDISCIPLINARY TEAMS, AS WELL AS BY SPECIALIZED INDUSTRY PRACTICES THAT PROVIDE INTERDISCIPLINARY SERVICES TO LEGALLY INTENSIVE AND HIGHLY REGULATED INDUSTRIES. · LEFT: PATRICK F. McCARTAN IS MANAGING PARTNER OF JONES, DAY, REAVIS & POGUE.

FRAGOMEN, DEL REY, BERNSEN

WITH LAW OFFICES ACROSS THE NATION AND WORLDWIDE, FRAGOMEN, DEL REY, BERNSEN & LOEWY ASSISTS CORPORATIONS AND ORGANIZATIONS WITH ALL MATTERS OF IMMIGRATION LAW AND MULTINATIONAL EMPLOYMENT.

For over a half-century, Fragomen, Del Rey, Bernsen & Loewy, PC, the nation's largest law firm dedicated exclusively to the practice of immigration and nationality law, has been assisting U.S. and multinational employers to expand their businesses and fill critical workforce shortages by hiring foreign national professionals. The result has been a period of extraordinary innovation and job growth, as immigrants have left an indelible mark on American industry in a wide variety of fields, including information technology, telecommunications, pharmaceuticals, and high-tech manufacturing.

With the growing need in the United States for well-trained and educated workers, many corporations must look abroad to recruit and fill professional positions. In addition, global companies are continually sending staff to points around the world on assignment and must deal with foreign work-visa requirements, as nearly every national government worldwide maintains strict controls and quotas on foreign workers. With more than 175 attorneys practicing in 19 offices across the nation and abroad, Fragomen, Del Rey, Bernsen & Loewy (FDB&L) provides representation to multi-national corporations, start-up companies, universities, and other major organizations that employ foreign nationals on a temporary or permanent basis in the United States or abroad.

In addition to institutional clients, the firm represents prominent individuals, including entrepreneurs, professionals, entertainers, and athletes. The firm also has specialized legal practice groups serving the high technology, financial services, and entertainment fields.

FDB&L's services in the area of global visas are unique within the industry. For employees transferred to locations or between assignments outside of the United States, the firm maintains a highly trained

& LOEWY, PC

Foreign Visa Services department to ensure expeditious processing of foreign visa matters. Experienced attorneys, foreign law graduates, former consular officers, and foreign-visa advisers support client needs, and the firm also works collaboratively with a well-established global network of highly qualified and respected foreign immigration attorneys.

Fragomen, Del Rey, Bernsen & Loewy tailors its representation to address the specific needs of each client. The spectrum of legal services, depending on the client goals and expectations, extends from consultation to complete outsourcing of the immigration function. FDB&L works with its clients to devise and implement cohesive immigration guidelines and policies, provide guidance and program support, prepare temporary visa petitions and applications for permanent resident status, and manage immigration status and work authorization matters for the client's entire foreign-national workforce. The firm also coordinates its immigration advice with the client's tax, legal, and financial advisers, since immigration considerations are invariably only a facet of an overall business strategy.

Fragomen, Del Rey, Bernsen & Loewy also advises clients on compliance with the 1986 Immigration Reform and Control Act (IRCA). The firm reviews hiring policies, conducts on-site audits, and trains client staff to properly execute and maintain Employment Eligibility Verification Forms I-9. When necessary, the firm also defends employers against federal charges of hiring undocumented aliens, failing to comply with federal record-keeping requirements, or violating antidiscrimination laws as they relate to foreign national workers.

Government affairs services at FDB&L are seen as essential in helping to promote human resource and international hiring policies critical to its clients' continued growth. The firm's Government Affairs Office, based in Washington, D.C., provides government and public relations assistance in resolving complex immigration issues and promoting regulatory or legislative changes.

Fragomen, Del Rey, Bernsen & Loewy maintains offices throughout the United States and abroad—in Atlanta, Georgia; Buffalo, New York; Chicago, Illinois; Dallas, Texas; Detroit, Michigan; Irvine, Los Angeles, Oakland, Sacramento, San Francisco, and Santa Clara, California; Iselin, New Jersey; Miami, Florida; New York, New York; Phoenix, Arizona; Stamford, Connecticut; Vienna, Virginia; Washington, D.C.; and Brussels, Belgium—ensuring high quality, cost-effective, and timely representation.

FRAGOMEN, DEL REY, BERNSEN & LOEWY IS THE NATION'S LARGEST LAW FIRM PRACTICING EXCLUSIVELY IMMIGRATION AND NATIONALITY LAW WITH 19 OFFICES IN THE UNITED STATES AND ABROAD. SHOWN ABOVE IS THE FIRM'S OFFICE BUILDING IN SANTA CLARA, CALIFORNIA, IN THE HEART OF SILICON VALLEY. PHOTOS, OPPOSITE AND LEFT, © PHOTODISC

INSTITUTIONAL LABOR ADVISORS

INSTITUTIONAL LABOR ADVISORS INTEGRATES ITS EXTENSIVE EXPERIENCE WITH A THOROUGH UNDERSTANDING OF A CLIENT'S BUSINESS TO SUCCESSFULLY ACHIEVE RESOLUTION WHILE ADVANCING THE CLIENT'S BUSINESS GOALS.

Institutional Labor Advisors (ILA) has established a successful track record for helping clients transform labor problems into profits.

The Washington, D.C.–based labor law consulting firm provides clients with a multifaceted approach to resolving significant labor-related issues. ILA's full-service team is equipped to deal with the entire gamut of labor problems. The firm offers expertise in labor matters that include mergers and acquisitions, collective bargaining, strategic planning, governmental relations, administrative and judicial litigation, and resolution of complex employment issues and claims.

ILA works with major corporations across the nation in a variety of industries, ranging from energy and television to manufacturing and construction. Principals William B. Cowen and David S. Smith possess combined experience in labor law that spans more than 50 years. ILA's distinctive approach involves understanding the client's business and integrating a thorough knowledge of labor laws and regulations with the client's business goals.

ILA analyzes a client's goals in relation to current and projected labor commitments and costs, such as health care, work rules, employee benefits, and post-retirement benefits. The firm uses its expertise in activities ranging from structuring mergers and acquisitions to collective bargaining, which helps clients significantly reduce labor liabilities and increase profits.

ILA has worked as the labor advisor to several major companies regarding the merger or acquisition of entities involving hundreds of millions of dollars of employee and post-employment benefit liabilities. The firm conducts due diligence to help identify significant labor issues and costs relating to the transaction itself and to the future operations of the acquired entity. Due diligence procedures include a detailed analysis of labor issues and development of labor-related options for the buyer.

The principals and associates of ILA have collectively bargained scores of labor contracts with a variety of unions over the past three decades. The firm offers complete turnkey bargaining services, including analyzing issues, preparing initial contract offers, drafting final agreements, and creating print-ready agreements. Members of the ILA team have successfully negotiated agreements with unions such as the International Brotherhood of Electrical Workers, the International Brotherhood of Teamsters, Service Employees International Union, United Mine Workers of America, and the United Steelworkers of America, among others.

Additionally, ILA has extensive experience in government relations. The firm represents corporate interests at the state and federal level as it relates to issues such as health and safety, labor, and post-employment liabilities. In addition, ILA members serve as advisors to the U.S. Chamber of Commerce regarding these and other related policy issues.

When necessary, ILA calls upon its supervisory litigation team to resolve major labor issues, including challenges to costly labor arbitration decisions, significant damage actions under the Labor Management Relations Act, and all aspects of litigation under the National Labor Relations Act.

ILA draws on these capabilities with the purpose of enhancing a client's overall business strategy. The group makes a concerted effort to become intimately familiar with a particular company, its industry, its philosophy, and the structure of its operations. ILA consultants look beyond the problem at hand to secure a broader long-term solution.

OPPOSITE PAGE: ILA FOUNDERS DAVID SMITH AND WILLIAM COWEN HAVE BEEN PRACTICING LABOR LAW AND CONSULTING FOR OVER THREE DECADES. • ABOVE: THE ILA GOVERNMENT RELATIONS TEAM REPRESENTS MORE THAN 30 CORPORATIONS. • LEFT: THE GROUP'S BARGAINING TEAM HAS REPRESENTED COMPANIES IN COLLECTIVE BARGAINING WITH MORE THAN 11 DIFFERENT UNIONS.

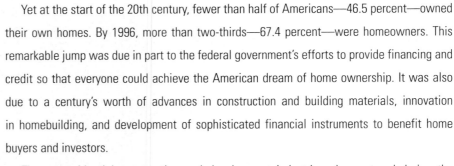

BUILDING A STRONG FOUNDATION

REAL ESTATE, CONSTRUCTION, & DEVELOPMENT

Is there anything that evokes so much sentiment and longing as the home? It is a private sanctuary, a castle.

Yet at the start of the 20th century, fewer than half of Americans—46.5 percent—owned their own homes. By 1996, more than two-thirds—67.4 percent—were homeowners. This remarkable jump was due in part to the federal government's efforts to provide financing and credit so that everyone could achieve the American dream of home ownership. It was also due to a century's worth of advances in construction and building materials, innovation in homebuilding, and development of sophisticated financial instruments to benefit home buyers and investors.

The nonresidential construction and development industries also matured during the 20th century. Worldwide, the construction industry today employs more people than any other, and with changing demographics and increasing wealth, it's likely that this industry will continue to grow and innovate.

STRUCTURAL MATTERS

From wood to stone and brick, from adobe to ice, humans have used wildly varied materials to create shelter for themselves. Even today, the $40 billion building materials industry uses many of the same basic materials in a home or a commercial property that were used hundreds and even thousands of years ago, including nails, wood, and cement.

The latter—the ultrafine powder that binds sand and rocks into concrete—is in fact the world's most widely used building material. Every year, about 1.25 billion tons of cement are produced to create five billion cubic yards of concrete. One reason for cement's popularity is its sheer ubiquity—it is found almost everywhere. The ancient Romans used it to build their baths and the Coliseum. The cement used today, called "portland cement" because its color resembles that of stone from Britain's Isle of Portland, was patented in 1824.

Demand for cement skyrocketed with the development of canal systems in the early part of the 19th century, and many of the industrial age's great inventors worked to refine it further. In 1902, Thomas Edison's Edison Portland Cement Works in New Jersey introduced special long kilns that saved energy and produced a better product. Today, the United States is third in producing this key building material, and 45 U.S. companies operate 118 cement plants. With the authorization of the 1998 Transportation Equity Act for the 21st Century

Photo: Courtesy, Libbey-Owens-Ford Glass Co.

ABOVE: WORKERS CONSTRUCT CONDO FRAMES FROM WOOD, A BUILDING MATERIAL IN USE FOR MILLENNIA. ·
OPPOSITE: INVENTOR MICHAEL J. OWENS MECHANIZED THE GLASS INDUSTRY IN THE LATE 19TH CENTURY.

(TEA-21), which provides $214 billion for new building projects across America, the cement industry will likely stay on an upward path.

Besides cement, there are hundreds of other materials that go into a residence or commercial property, such as pipes, roofing materials, tiles, and glass. CertainTeed, with headquarters in Valley Forge, Pennsylvania, is a leader in the building materials industry, providing everything from ceiling systems to vinyl sidings to decks and railings—practically everything but the proverbial kitchen sink. The company, which began in 1904 as the General Roofing Manufacturing Company in East St. Louis, Illinois, was purchased in 1988 by one of Europe's oldest and largest enterprises, Saint-Gobain, which in the 1600s made glass for the palace at Versailles and today operates a total of 200 plants in the United States, employing 30,000 Americans.

The glass industry would not be where it is today without the foresight and entrepreneurship of a West Virginia glassblower named Michael J. Owens.

To understand Owens's importance to building history, one must recognize that until he came along in the late 19th century, the most important advance in the glass industry had occurred around 300 B.C. with the invention of the blowpipe. For thousands of years, glassmaking was a painstaking process requiring highly skilled workers and lots of time.

At the age of ten, Owens went to work in a glass plant in Wheeling. Based on his experience there, he eventually developed a treadle that allowed a glassblower to open and close a mold with his foot, thereby eliminating the need for a "mold boy" to do it and reducing dependency on child labor.

Owens soon became a leader in the American Flint Glass Workers' Union and led a successful strike against Edward Libbey's New England Glass Company, forcing Libbey to move from Massachusetts to Ohio. Six months later, Owens, who realized that he found glass production more interesting than

union organizing, showed up on Libbey's doorstep in Toledo and asked for a job. Owens became the plant manager and soon began to think about designing a machine that would replace the human glassblower.

Entirely without technical training, but with Libbey's support, Owens designed a prototype and found an engineer to build it. Over the next few years, Owens perfected the machine, which in 1903 could produce 400,000 bottles in 24 hours; by contrast, a master glassblower with a few assistants could manage 216 bottles in a 14-hour day. With this process perfected, Owens turned his attention to mechanizing plate-glass production and opened a plant in West Virginia in 1917 which operated with a minimum of human labor.

In 1932, the Owens-Illinois Glass Company pioneered the development of glass fibers. Envisioned by manager Games Slayter, the material was actually developed by a junior researcher named Dale Kleist, who while welding glass blocks accidentally hit the molten glass with compressed air, creating glass fibers. These new fibers were thin enough to be good insulation but inexpensive enough for widespread use. In 1938, the company teamed with Corning Glass to form a separate company, Owens-Corning Fiberglass Corporation, which produced glass textiles. During the ensuing years, the incredible versatility of Fiberglas became readily apparent—it was used to build hulls for Navy ships during World War II, acoustical tiles, and building insulation. During the 1960s, the uses were expanded to include the creation of underground tanks and pipes, and later, roofing shingles and windows. Today, Toledo, Ohio–based Owens Corning is one of the world's top makers of building materials—a long way from its origins in a West Virginia glassblowing factory.

BUILT TO LAST

As the Egyptian pyramids and Roman roads and aqueducts prove, thoughtful and well-planned construction can last for thousands of years. Today, though the materials and processes have changed, the construction industry is still occupied in building many of the same kinds of structures as their ancient counterparts: roads, bridges, military camps. Some of America's top companies are leaders in this area.

The Bechtel Group, for example, is responsible for more than 19,000 heavy-

Territory to be a railroad grader. He ended up in northern California instead, where he pioneered the use of motorized trucks, tractors, and diesel-powered shovels. In 1919, he expanded his railroad business to include highway building. W. A. Bechtel Company soon became the top heavy-construction company and was responsible for many of the 20th century's most notable public works projects, including the Hoover Dam in the 1930s (completed two years ahead of schedule) and the San Francisco–Oakland Bay Bridge. During World War II, Bechtel mobilized, like many other American companies, and operated shipyards and pipelines.

After the war, Bechtel built upon its storied reputation for orchestrating complex

Trans-Arabian Pipeline, which stretched more than a thousand miles from the Arabian Gulf to the Mediterranean Sea; the prototype nuclear fission reactor; and NASA's Apollo Space Simulation Chamber. Bechtel also was involved in wastewater treatment, pollution abatement, and undersea systems, and built San Francisco's Bay Area Rapid Transit (BART) system in 1972. After the Gulf War in 1991, Bechtel led the engineering effort to extinguish 650 oil well fires that had started during the hostilities.

Also providing a variety of construction services is PBS&J of Miami, Florida. Established in 1960, this firm of 60 offices nationwide offers services in the construction, transportation, environment, project

ABOVE: CONSTRUCTION CRANES RISE IN LAS VEGAS, NEVADA, A REFLECTION OF THE BOOMING ECONOMY AT THE END OF THE 20TH CENTURY. THE $619 BILLION CONSTRUCTION INDUSTRY REPRESENTS 10 PERCENT OF THE NATION'S GDP. • OPPOSITE: BILL LEVITT BUILT THE SUBURBAN DEVELOPMENT OF LEVITTOWN, NEW YORK, SHOWN IN THIS 1950S AERIAL VIEW, WITH FORD-LIKE AUTOMATION AND PRECISION. THE MANNER OF CONSTRUCTION SET A NATIONAL TREND, AND BY 1955, THREE QUARTERS OF NEW HOMES WERE BUILT LEVITTOWN-STYLE.

construction projects in 140 nations on every continent. The Bechtel story starts in 1898 when Peabody, Kansas, farmer and shopkeeper Warren Bechtel loaded up two mules and headed for the Oklahoma

jobs and pioneered a new concept in construction: the turnkey. Bechtel would shepherd the project from start to finish and present the client with a "key" at the end to simply turn it on. Projects included the

management, and other areas. PBS&J has worked on projects with the National Park Service, the Florida Department of Transportation, and the Washington Suburban Sanitary Commission.

Cement masons and concrete finishers prepare the floor of a dam. Cement, the ultrafine powder that binds sand and rock into concrete, is the world's most widely used building material.

single- and multifamily homes but among other services helps people pay for them, maintain them, and insure them. Another giant in the industry, Pulte Corporation, of Bloomfield Hills, Michigan, also started in 1950 and today operates in 41 markets and has constructed more than 250,000 homes.

Since the 1970s, more than 47 million new houses and apartments have been built. One indicator of the future of this sector is the increase in retirement homes and assisted-living residences, an industry that topped $20 billion in 2000, and as the baby boomer generation ages, this trend is likely to continue.

One of the leading companies in building residences for the elderly is Sunrise Assisted Living, founded by Paul Klaasen, a Dutch immigrant, and his wife, Terry, in 1981. Aware that Americans were struggling to take care of older relatives who were in poor health, the Klaasens hatched the idea of creating assisted-living housing for seniors, based upon the *verzorgingstehuizen* in which Paul's grandparents lived in Holland. Residents there essentially took care of themselves, but assistance was available to them as needed.

The Klaasens built their first Sunrise home in Fairfax, Virginia. Soon word spread, and the couple built two more homes. In 1987, Sunrise opened a distinctive Victorian-style mansion which quickly became the Sunrise signature model. Today, there are more than 120 Sunrise mansions in 22 states.

Good Deeds

Land—and the buying, selling, leasing, renting, and management of it—is the source of almost half of the privately owned wealth in the United States. The real estate industry employs about five million

Americans and is tied closely to the country's economic cycle.

In the United States, the $3 trillion commercial real estate market is led by companies like CB Richard Ellis Services, the nation's largest commercial real estate services company. Headquartered in El Segundo, California, the firm has 250 offices in 40 countries and posted sales of $1.3 billion in 2000. New York–based Tishman Realty & Construction's sales for the same period were $1.1 billion. Tishman includes Madison Square Garden and Walt Disney World's EPCOT Center among its clients. Trammell Crow Company, of Dallas, which oversees nearly 300 million square feet of commercial property nationwide and offers other related services both here and abroad, had $760 million in sales.

One of the world's largest residential real estate sales organizations is Century 21, formed from 6,300 independently owned and operated offices across the world. Century 21's 110,000 brokers and agents make up a real estate network for consumers interested in buying or selling homes. One of Century 21's leading competitors, RE/MAX International, based in Greenwood Village, Colorado, has franchises in 34 countries. Among the newest players in the industry is HomeServices.Com, of Edina, Minnesota, which has offices in 12 states and provides mortgage, relocation, and other services.

Managing and funding commercial and residential real estate have in themselves become businesses. One example is the Real Estate Investment Trust (REIT).

Congress created REITs in the 1960s in an attempt to open the real estate market to small investors. A REIT is simply a company that owns and operates real estate, such as apartment buildings, office buildings, shopping centers, or warehouses, and possibly assumes other responsibilities as well. Shareholders invest in REITs in much the same way they would invest in a mutual fund. REITs pay out 95 percent of their taxable income to shareholders every year. Unlike privately owned real estate, REITs are publicly traded on the stock exchange. Today, the REITs have a combined market value of approximately $142 billion.

In the process of buying a house, Americans also generally get a mortgage. The ease of getting a mortgage today is largely due to measures taken in the first part of the century to expand the flow of mortgage money. In 1938, the federal government created Fannie Mae, which became a private, shareholder-owned company 30 years later. Since then, Fannie Mae has provided trillions of dollars for more than 30 million families and is one of America's largest corporations, with $675 billion in assets and $707 billion in net mortgage-backed securities (MBS). These MBSs are an important financial tool that helps primary lenders, such as banks, have funds to make still more loans. In 1999, secondary market investors purchased about 62 percent of all mortgage loans in the United States.

Another secondary market is Freddie Mac, which was chartered by Congress in 1970 and is a stockholder-owned corporation. Like Fannie Mae, Freddie Mac does not provide loans itself, but creates a secondary market for them. Although the two corporations have different approaches, they are similar in structure and regulation.

THE FUTURE OF REAL ESTATE

The bright future of commercial real estate is tempered by long memories of the real estate slump of the late 1980s and early 1990s. The residential real estate market has been growing steadily since the slump, faster than even commercial real estate. In 1997, sales of both new and existing homes reached about $5 billion. And office space continues to be in high demand.

In the coming years, it is likely that the Internet will profoundly impact the profession. On the one hand, information about properties may be easily posted, so real estate agents will feel the need to provide other services and expertise; on the other hand, with so much information around, consumers may want to have a real estate agent act as a filter for them.

The future of the real estate industry—and consequently, the construction and building industries—is intimately tied to the demographics and wealth of Americans. With Americans getting older, and with the younger population increasing, it is clear that the demand for housing will not cease, although it likely will not have such a strong rate of growth.

The trend toward energy efficiency and renewable materials suggests that the industry will move toward more environmentally friendly homes, for example, by using materials like cork instead of plywood for subflooring and by using recycled glass in the creation of fiberglass. One thing is certain: through the efforts of judicious government policies and the boundless imagination and innovation of American industries, more and more Americans are closer to the goal of having their own place to hang their hats.

Photo: © Mason Morfit/FPG International LLC

THE TIN ROOF BEING INSTALLED ON A RED HOOK, WASHINGTON, BUILDING GUARANTEES ITS OWNER LOW MAINTENANCE, ENERGY EFFICIENCY, DURABILITY, AND LONG-TERM SAVINGS.

profiles

Real Estate, Construction, & Development

ANDERSEN CORPORATION

THE WINDOWS AND PATIO DOORS CRAFTED BY ANDERSEN CORPORATION ARE RESPECTED NATIONWIDE AND INTERNATIONALLY BY RESIDENTIAL AND COMMERCIAL BUILDING DEVELOPERS, CONTRACTORS, ARCHITECTS, AND HOMEOWNERS.

Quality is a word frequently used to describe Andersen Corporation and the windows and doors the company makes and markets nationwide and internationally.

Beginning in 1903 as a small lumberyard on the banks of a Wisconsin river town, Andersen Corporation has grown into one of the most highly respected brand names in the window and door industry worldwide. Danish immigrant Hans Andersen and his two sons founded Andersen Lumber Company in Hudson, Wisconsin. Today, the Andersen brand represents a universal benchmark in design and dependability.

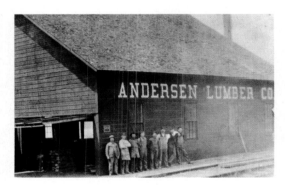

Since 1913, Andersen Corporation headquarters has been located in Bayport, Minnesota. The facility includes the main manufacturing plant, covering 65 acres under one roof. The corporation is privately owned and employs more than 6,000 people. Its commitment to product excellence and customer satisfaction, combined with its dedication to environmental stewardship, employee welfare, and corporate citizenship, has taken the company to the top of its market.

"The values that built the Andersen brand continue to drive this company today," says Donald L. Garofalo, president and chief executive officer. "The founders of Andersen Corporation were passionate about doing the best job possible, and they were committed to understanding customers' needs and providing innovative solutions for the best possible buying experience." With products available in countless sizes, shapes, and styles, Andersen sells millions of vinyl-clad wood windows and patio doors annually throughout North America and in South America, Europe, Asia, and the Middle East.

Energy efficiency is central to Andersen's business philosophy and product design criteria. Andersen is the only window and patio door maker certified by the national environmental labeling organization Green Seal. Andersen also has received recognition for environmental stewardship and exemplary

energy efficiency standards, from the Alliance to Save Energy, the U.S. Environmental Protection Agency and the U.S. Department of Energy. "We set high performance standards, not just for our windows and doors, but also for our manufacturing processes," Garofalo says. "Andersen is committed to manufacturing environmentally sound, energy-efficient products in a responsible manner." Andersen works with its wholly owned subsidiary Aspen Research in developing new technologies. Work focuses on product life-cycle management, development of composite materials to increase performance and efficiency, and elimination or reclamation of manufacturing waste products. This kind of innovation began in 1903 with Hans Andersen's invention of the "10-minute window," the first window produced with pre-made frame pieces in several standard sizes for quick, job-site assembly. In 1932, the company created the first completely assembled, factory-made, wood-frame casement window—the Andersen Master Casement window. In 1964, Andersen introduced the wood-frame gliding door, and in 1966, it created an entirely new category of window products with the introduction of Perma-Shield® vinyl cladding.

Andersen's latest technology is Fibrex™ material—a proprietary composite material made of vinyl and wood-fiber waste from the company's primary manufacturing facility. Andersen uses Fibrex in window and door components and is evaluating its use in a variety of building products.

Renewal by Andersen, Inc., a wholly owned subsidiary of Andersen Corporation, provides homeowners with window and door replacement solutions. Available in selected locations in the United States, Renewal by Andersen consultants coordinate measurement, manufacture, installation, and warranty service for the company's made-to-order window products made of Fibrex material.

Andersen's dedication to giving back to the communities it serves is evident in its long history of philanthropy. The company's corporate citizenship programs give support to Habitat for Humanity International and hundreds of educational, human services, cultural and civic activities, and environmental stewardship initiatives. Andersen

also is an industry leader in product safety, which has resulted in industrywide public safety initiatives and awareness programs.

As Andersen Corporation passes the milestone of 100 years of innovation, partnership, and environmental and community stewardship, its leaders and staff are poised to bring a new century of leadership to the building industry.

PBS&J

PBS&J IS AN ENGINEERING AND PLANNING FIRM THAT PROVIDES COMPREHENSIVE TRANSPORTATION, ENVIRONMENTAL, SITE CIVIL, PROGRAM MANAGEMENT, INFORMATION MANAGEMENT, AND CONSTRUCTION SERVICES NATIONWIDE AND ABROAD.

Since 1960, PBS&J has planned and designed the kinds of facilities that are part of daily life. The firm's founders—Robert P. Schuh, Howard M. "Bud" Post, John D. Buckley, George M. Mooney, and Alex M. Jernigan—were civil engineers who were passionate about their profession. With a common emphasis on quality work, client service, and integrity, these men helped the firm to build a solid professional reputation from which to grow.

A PLAN FOR GROWTH

PBS&J began as a one-office firm in Miami, Florida. By its 10th anniversary, PBS&J had developed a strong south Florida client base and was recognized as one of Florida's strongest consulting engineering firms. As Florida's economy flourished during the 1970s, so did the competition for projects, with more national firms beginning to enter the lucrative Florida market. To remain a major player on its home turf, PBS&J had to increase in size and technical strength.

Fortunately, Florida in the 1980s continued to offer PBS&J fertile ground in which to expand. To a Florida base of 14 offices, PBS&J added five offices in four other states. Expansion moves were never made lightly;

every attempt was made to identify realistic market opportunities and to pursue them by opening offices in just the right locations with just the right managers. In addition to adding new offices, PBS&J continued to expand its resources in established ones.

PBS&J entered the 1990s with a continued drive to expand its geographic base through the strategic acquisition of firms with strong technical expertise and local presence. During this time, the firm worked hard to expand its client base and establish offices from Florida to California and throughout the southeastern United States. The establishment of four separate service lines—transportation, environmental, civil, and construction—provided the management structure necessary to ensure that PBS&J clients would be provided with the highest quality services and products.

Today, with 2,700 PBS&J employees filling 60 offices that span the nation, PBS&J has embarked on a new era of growth—one that emphasizes the multiregional development of its services. Key to this is a strategic initiative that addresses people as well as processes and emerging markets. "We empower our people to be able to respond to their local markets, while still providing them with the advantages of a national firm," explains John B. Zumwalt III, P.E., PBS&J president.

EMPLOYEES: PBS&J's MOST VALUED RESOURCE

Although expanding market recognition is an important initiative of PBS&J, "our firm's success comes down to those one-on-one relationships between our project managers and our clients—our ability to work together

with trust and credibility," says H. Michael Dye, chairman of PBS&J.

PBS&J is committed to providing a work environment that promotes quality work, creativity, and satisfaction. The firm actively seeks ways to assist employees in the development of their professional careers and to foster the next generation of PBS&J leaders. In addition, the firm remains focused on maintaining its core values—values forged from the personal and professional integrity of its founders—to keep PBS&J as a "consultant of choice."

OPPOSITE PAGE, TOP: PBS&J PROVIDES CONSULTING SERVICES TO A WIDE RANGE OF PUBLIC AND PRIVATE CLIENTS, INCLUDING THE FLORIDA DEPARTMENT OF TRANSPORTATION, TURNPIKE DISTRICT. • OPPOSITE PAGE, BOTTOM: ONE OF ONLY A FEW LARGE EMPLOYEE-OWNED CONSULTING FIRMS IN THE UNITED STATES, PBS&J PLANS AND DESIGNS THE KINDS OF FACILITIES THAT ARE PART OF DAILY LIFE, SUCH AS WSSC'S (WASHINGTON SUBURBAN SANITARY COMMISSION'S) NEW SENECA WASTEWATER TREATMENT FACILITIES IN MARYLAND. • ABOVE: WITH OFFICES IN 60 LOCATIONS NATIONWIDE AND 2,500 EMPLOYEES, PBS&J PROVIDES PROJECT TEAMS THAT OFFER A COMBINATION OF LOCAL EXPERIENCE AND NATIONALLY RECOGNIZED EXPERTISE IN TRANSPORTATION, ENVIRONMENTAL, CIVIL ENGINEERING, AND CONSTRUCTION DISCIPLINES. • LEFT: THE PBS&J PORTFOLIO OF PROJECT EXPERIENCE INCLUDES SERVING AS CONSTRUCTION MANAGEMENT CONSULTANT FOR THE NATIONAL PARK SERVICE.

ASSOCIATED GENERAL

THE ASSOCIATED GENERAL CONTRACTORS OF AMERICA ADVANCES THE INTERESTS OF ITS MEMBERS WITH AN INFLUENTIAL INDUSTRY VOICE, AS WELL AS SUPPLYING MANAGEMENT ASSISTANCE, TRAINING MATERIALS, AND OTHER VALUABLE BENEFITS.

With more than six million workers and revenues totaling about 10 percent of the Gross Domestic Product, no industry contributes more to the economic success of the nation than the construction industry. And no organization has done more to further the interests and advancement of that industry in the United States than the Associated General Contractors of America (AGC). AGC and the industry are "Building Your Quality of Life" every day.

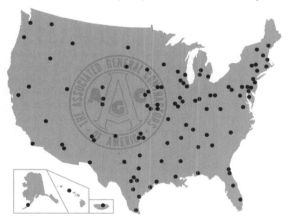

Established in 1918 at the request of President Woodrow Wilson, who recognized the construction industry's importance to the nation's success, AGC is the oldest and largest U.S. construction trade association. Since its founding, it has been dedicated to educating its industry about the latest skills, safety measures, and technology for building quality projects for owners—public and private.

Skill, integrity, and responsibility are the tenets to which AGC subscribes and it is these tenets that

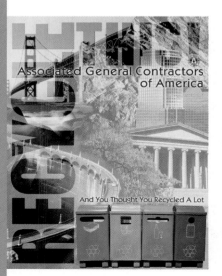

historically have guided the organization in its efforts to improve and advance the industry, create new opportunities for its members, and protect the public interest.

AGC is based in Alexandria, Virginia, and operates through a nationwide network of chapters. Each chapter is its own entity, offering a variety of services designed to satisfy the needs and concerns of its members. AGC represents more than 35,000 companies within the construction industry, including some 8,000 of the leading general contractors in the United States and 13,000 specialty-contracting firms. In addition, more than 14,000 firms and individuals who provide services and/or supplies to the industry also are associated with the organization through its chapters.

AGC members are as diverse as the construction industry itself. They include, among others, nonresidential and public building contractors; heavy and industrial contractors; municipal and utilities; federal highway builders; specialty contractors; and service providers. The organization even has chapters at select universities for students interested in pursuing careers in the construction industry.

Chief among the services AGC provides its members is representation in the halls of government in Washington, D.C., and in state capitals across the nation, providing an influential and effective voice for the construction industry. In fact, for the fourth year in a row, a 2001 survey by *Fortune* magazine ranked AGC as one of the nation's most effective and powerful associations engaged in lobbying activities.

Other member services include networking opportunities for contractors to meet their peers, access to Web-based training materials, management assistance, enhanced communications services, discounts, and a host of traditional benefits. AGC also prides itself on continually providing members with profit-enhancement opportunities, introducing new markets and programs through its publications and its Web site (www.agc.org).

Perhaps the most important service AGC provides is educating young people about the construction industry, encouraging them to consider a career within the industry, thereby ensuring its future. To that end, the organization

makes curriculum programs available for teachers; the programs are designed to give elementary and high school students real-world lessons and activities in the construction field and, at the same time, stress the importance of math, science, social studies, and language arts skills. In addition, AGC provides scholarships to deserving college students pursuing construction industry–related degrees.

Without the construction industry, the United States, undoubtedly, would not be the economic power and vibrant force it is today. And without the Associated General Contractors of America, the construction industry, most likely, would not enjoy its position as one of the most successful and progressive industries in the U.S.A.

OPPOSITE PAGE, TOP: ASSOCIATED GENERAL CONTRACTORS OF AMERICA (AGC) HAS CHAPTERS ACROSS THE COUNTRY, INCLUDING HAWAII AND ALASKA, AND IN PUERTO RICO. · OPPOSITE PAGE, BOTTOM: AGC IS A MAJOR PROMOTER OF CONSTRUCTION MATERIAL RECYCLING, ASSISTING MEMBERS WITH INFORMATION ON NEW AND COST-SAVING TECHNOLOGIES. AGC'S PUBLICATION *RECYCLE THIS!* SHOWCASES COMPANIES, PROJECTS, AND MATERIALS INVOLVED IN SMART RECYCLING ADVANCES THAT ARE PAYING OFF. · ABOVE: AGC'S BUILDUP! PROGRAM CAPTURES THE IMAGINATION OF FIFTH-GRADE STUDENTS LEARNING ABOUT THE CONSTRUCTION INDUSTRY. · LEFT: AGC OUTREACH PROGRAMS INCLUDE SPONSORSHIP OF THE FESTIVAL OF THE BUILDING ARTS, HELD AT THE NATIONAL BUILDING MUSEUM, IN WASHINGTON, D.C.

BUYER'S PARADISE
RETAIL, WHOLESALE, & DIRECT SALES

AMERICAN BUSINESS IN THE 20TH CENTURY PLACED A LIFE OF UNIMAGINABLE MATERIAL ABUNDANCE IN THE HANDS OF AVERAGE CITIZENS—NOT JUST IN THE UNITED STATES BUT AROUND THE WORLD. IT ACHIEVED SUCH A FEAT NOT ONLY BY INVENTING, MANUFACTURING, AND MARKETING A VAST ARRAY OF QUALITY PRODUCTS BUT ALSO BY CONTINUALLY

devising new and creative ways to respond to consumers' growing demands for convenience, choice, and value.

AMERICA GOES SHOPPING

The innovations of two men—Richard Sears and Jeff Bezos—bracket a century of astounding change and growth in American consumerism.

In 1886, Richard Sears began selling watches to supplement his income as a station agent in North Redwood, Minnesota. In 1887, he resettled in the Chicago area and hired watchmaker Alvah C. Roebuck. A year later, the team of Sears and Roebuck formed a company and introduced its first catalogue, which offered only watches and jewelry.

In 1896, Sears Roebuck unveiled its first large general catalogue, which included everything from clothes to jewelry to housewares. The company capitalized on both the growing affluence of the American consumer and the fact that most consumers lived miles from the nation's big cities with no way to get there except by horse or train. Offering convenience and choice unheard of at the time, Sears Roebuck ignited a boom in catalogue shopping.

Flash forward to 1995, the year a young man named Jeff Bezos, not yet 30 years old, opened the virtual doors of his virtual bookstore called Amazon.com on the World Wide Web. The Web was but four years old, accessible to only a small percentage of American households, but Bezos believed that in a few short years an Internet-wired American populace would embrace on-line shopping for its revolutionary convenience and choice. By 1999, Amazon.com had established itself as the largest on-line shopping site. Expanding its product offerings well beyond books, the company now serves 12 million customers from 160 countries and has helped ignite the E-commerce revolution that will reshape buying habits in the new century.

In between the innovations of Sears and Bezos came countless others in response to the ever-growing wealth and ever-changing tastes of the American consumer, innovations devised by some of the most colorful and creative business geniuses in economic history. From James Cash Penney to Wal-Mart's Sam Walton, from Amway's Jay Van Andel and Rich DeVos to the Home Depot's Bernie Marcus, these and many other visionary leaders have shaped the contours of American daily life as much if not more than any politician or general. From the five-and-dime to the shopping mall to the corner convenience store to the mammoth big-box

AS ADVERTISED

14.95
SIZE 10 - 18

ABOVE: A DEPARTMENT STORE SALESPERSON HELPS A CUSTOMER TRY ON A DRESS IN THE AFFLUENT 1950s. • OPPOSITE: BEVERLY HILLS'S RODEO DRIVE REFLECTS AN ABUNDANCE OF HIGH-QUALITY GOODS.

department store, American retailing has created an economic sector responsible for millions of jobs and business opportunities for entrepreneurs around the world.

Any list of the nation's top retailers reveals an interesting mix of older pioneers like Sears and relatively newer giants like Home Depot and Costco.

An innovator in the discount shopping field, Sam Walton opened his first Wal-Mart in Rogers, Arkansas, in 1962. The store sold a wide variety of nationally recognized brands at lower-than-department-store prices. By 1997, the company had reached $100 billion in sales. Today, Wal-Mart is the largest general merchandise retailer in the nation and operates under three divisions, Wal-Mart Stores, SAM's Clubs, and Wal-Mart International.

A more recent arrival on the retail scene, Home Depot was founded in Atlanta in 1978 by Bernie Marcus and Arthur Blank and has

turned millions of Americans into dedicated, do-it-yourself home remodelers. The founders' vision of huge warehouse stores containing tens of thousands of products where shoppers are assisted by well-trained staff (24 hours a day at many locations) has caught on all over America and beyond. Today, Home Depot operates over 1,000 stores in the United States, Canada, Chile, and Argentina.

At Costco, the emphasis is on self-service, and the concept has proven equally popular with cost-conscious shoppers. Founded in Seattle in 1983, the company now operates more than 300 "warehouse clubs" throughout the United States, Canada, Mexico, Korea, Japan, Taiwan, and the United Kingdom, emphasizing low prices on a limited selection of national and private brands.

When it comes to focusing on a special segment of merchandise, Toys R Us leads the pack. Charles Lazarus was just 25 years

old when in 1948 he sought to capitalize on the postwar baby boom by opening a children's furniture store in Washington, D.C. Nine years later he established his first toy supermarket. Today, Toys R Us is an $11 billion business with more than 1,500 toy, children's apparel, and baby-needs stores throughout the country.

Meanwhile, franchising has opened small-business opportunities for hundreds of thousands of American families and at the same time enabled parent companies to vastly expand the reach of their products and their brands. Franchises now account for nearly a trillion dollars in annual sales and more than eight million jobs in 600,000 facilities across the nation.

Consumer demand for convenience and extended shopping hours has given rise to a booming convenience store industry as well. There are now 96,700 convenience stores in the United States, selling in excess of $164 billion worth of gasoline, cigarettes, beer, packaged beverages, snacks, and other food products. Nearly one million workers are employed in these stores, which also provide small-business opportunities for thousands of American families.

HAIL TO THE MIDDLEMAN

Convenience and promises of wide product selection would mean little without a healthy and efficient wholesale trade sector. Mostly hidden from view from the average consumer, wholesalers include establishments primarily engaged in selling merchandise to retailers and to industrial, commercial, institutional, farm, and other businesses. The U.S. Department of Commerce divides this vital sector into those selling durable goods and those selling nondurable goods. By the year 2000, the top products in the latter category included paper, drugs, groceries, and alcohol products; in the former, motor vehicle parts and supplies, furniture, lumber, and electrical supplies.

In general, wholesalers purchase products from a supplier company and deliver them to a retail establishment. By serving as that link, they perform a range of intermediary functions, which vary depending on the line of products handled. These

selection and delivery of all the products their customers want, they quickly comprehend the critical role of the wholesale industry. For the American consumer, the industry delivers choice, competition, and well-stocked store shelves.

According to the National Association of Wholesale-Distributors, the industry racks up $4.4 trillion in annual sales and employs some 6.5 million Americans. While more than 50 percent of America's wholesale and distribution companies are smaller businesses with annual revenues of less than $1 million, a number of big companies are making their mark as well. The Fortune 500 list of top U.S. companies includes 30 firms defined as wholesalers; there are 58 such companies in the Fortune 1000.

The leaders reflect the dominance of the health care, technology, and consumer-foods sectors in the 21st century American economy. Topping Fortune's list is

McKesson HBOC. With $36.7 billion in 2000 revenues, this San Francisco–based company is the nation's largest distributor of pharmaceuticals, health care information systems, surgical products, and other medical supplies. Next, with annual revenues of $30.7 billion, is Ingram Micro of Santa Ana, California, the world's largest wholesaler-distributor of microcomputer products, followed by Cardinal Health, of Dublin, Ohio, selling $29.8 billion in drugs and medical products annually. Based on 2000 revenues, Supervalu of Eden Prairie, Minnesota, is the nation's fourth largest wholesaler. With $20.3 billion in 2000 sales, it is America's largest food wholesaler, supplying 5,700 grocery stores in 48 states as well as operating as a major retailer. And rounding out the top five is food product distributor Sysco Corp. of Houston, the largest North American wholesaler of food products, with $19.3 billion in annual sales.

ABOVE: RICHARD SEARS, WHO FOUNDED SEARS, ROEBUCK & CO., IGNITED A BOOM IN MAIL-ORDER SHOPPING WITH HIS 1896 CATALOGUE. • BELOW: AN ON-LINE SHOPPER MAKES A CREDIT CARD PURCHASE AT A HOME FURNISHINGS WEB SITE, ONE OF MANY WHOSE CONVENIENCE AND CHOICE OF PRODUCTS ARE RESHAPING AMERICAN BUYING HABITS. • OPPOSITE: COST-CONSCIOUS SHOPPERS AT COSTCO WHOLESALE ARE EAGER FOR BARGAINS AT THE GLOBAL DISCOUNTER'S MONTGOMERYVILLE, PENNSYLVANIA, STORE.

functions can include shipping, repackaging, quality control, product research and marketing, inventory control, and even credit to smaller retailers.

There are those who consider wholesaler-distributors as little more than "middlemen" who add to the price of goods. Some believe the industry's role will shrink as technology, E-commerce, and direct-sales arrangements between manufacturers, retailers, and customers grow. Yet, when those who run retail establishments, assembly plants, or hospitals and doctors' offices stop to think what a monumental and time-consuming task it would be to personally arrange for the

A FASHIONABLE OUTFIT CATCHES THE EYE OF A COUPLE OUT WINDOW SHOPPING. WITH MORE CHOICE AND VALUE AVAILABLE THAN EVER BEFORE, CONSUMERS CAN EASILY SPEND THE DAY GATHERING IDEAS.

Direct Selling: A Global Phenomenon

Defined as the face-to-face sale of a consumer product or service away from a fixed retail location, direct selling has not only revolutionized the way people buy things, it has provided low-cost business opportunities for millions of people around the globe.

There were 10.3 million salespeople in the United States as of 1999 with sales of $24.5 billion. In 1993, there were 5.7 million U.S. salespeople who sold $15 billion of products and services. About 55 percent of direct sellers are women, 26 percent are men, and 18 percent operate as two-person teams. Eighty-one percent devote 30 hours or less per week to their businesses, 8 percent spend between 30 and 39 hours, and 11 percent spend 40 hours per week or more.

Direct selling's major product lines include home-family care products (cleaning products, cookware, cutlery, and the like), accounting for 31.9 percent of all U.S. sales dollars. Personal care products (cosmetics, jewelry, skin care) claim 27 percent; services and other miscellaneous products, 18.7 percent; wellness products (weight loss, vitamins, natural medicines), 17.7 percent; and leisure-educational products (books, encyclopedias, toys, games), 4.7 percent.

This form of entrepreneurship is catching on around the world, too. The Direct Selling Association, which is the national representative for the industry before government and conducts market research on its behalf, reports that globally 34.6 million people were engaged in direct selling as of 1999, up from 8.48 million in 1988. Some estimates peg the number of salespeople at closer to 36 million, since the statistics do not include China. Worldwide sales in 1999 totaled $84.5 billion, compared to just $33.3 billion in 1988.

Direct selling has been an integral part of the business landscape since the earliest days of the nation, epitomized by the famous "Yankee peddler." After the Civil War, independent salespeople were recruited to sell the goods of a single manufacturer, and the direct-selling company sales force began to develop.

In 1915, the Fuller Brush Company, of New York, seriously upgraded the profession and introduced the concept of sales organizations by opening branch offices that recruited, trained, and supervised the regional sales groups. The branch manager was either a company employee or an independent salesperson who received a manager's commission on the branch's sales and a standard commission on his personal sales.

By 1920, there were over 200,000 people selling door-to-door. That year, Sears Roebuck and Company began direct sales of the *Encyclopaedia Britannica*. In the 1930s, the direct-selling industry continued to expand. Frank S. Beverage, an executive with Fuller Brush, founded Stanley Home Products in 1931. Today, the company is a division of CPAC, of Leicester, New York, and sells items for personal and home care.

The 1940s saw the development of the "party plan" sales approach. A distributor would ask a woman to host a party in her home during which products were demonstrated and sold. The hostess usually received a percentage of the gross sales to be applied to her own purchases. Thus Tupperware parties and other at-home sales pitches were perfected.

Another major development at this time was the creation of the multilevel marketing distribution channel, known today as network marketing. Under this approach, the independent business person would not only focus on product sales and commission earnings, but on building sales organizations by recruiting other independent businesspeople to become part of his or her "downline." Commissions were earned not only on one's own sales but on the sales of one's recruits.

The 1950s and 1960s saw the direct-selling industry expand dramatically to include companies that still lead the market today. Amway, the largest direct-selling company in the world, with $5 billion in annual sales, was founded in 1959 by Rich DeVos and Jay Van Andel of Ada, Michigan.

GRAND OPENINGS

In 1902, at the age of 26, James Cash Penney opened a dry goods and clothing establishment, the Golden Rule Store, in Kemmerer, Wyoming. The store was later renamed J. C. Penney Company, and today JCPenney's is the nation's fifth largest retailer. · Country Club Plaza, the first suburban shopping center for customers arriving in cars, opened in Kansas City, Missouri, in 1923. · The first enclosed, climate-controlled shopping mall, Southdale, debuted in 1956 in Edina, Minnesota. · Sebastian Spering Kresge founded his first five-and-dimes in Detroit and Memphis in 1897. In 1962, his new concept, the discount department store, opened as Kmart in Garden City, Michigan. Today, the Kmart empire boasts 2,100 stores. · Dayton Hudson has 970 Target stores throughout the nation; the first opened in 1962 in Roseville, Minnesota.

The partners started their company in the basements of their homes. With a proprietary product—L.O.C. (Liquid Organic Cleaner), a concentrated and environmentally safe cleaner, still the first item on the company's product list—and a marketing plan that put business ownership well within the reach of ordinary people, Amway began its meteoric rise. Today, Amway, whose corporate parent is now called Alticor, is comprised of three million independent business owners in 53 markets around the globe.

Another famous name in direct sales got its start back in the 19th century. A New York City bookseller named David McConnell realized that the rose oil perfumes he was giving away were responsible for many of his book sales. He founded the California Perfume Company in 1885 and changed the name to Avon in 1939, in honor of William Shakespeare of Stratford-on-Avon. Today, Avon garners some $5.8 billion in annual revenue. Three million representatives (the proverbial Avon ladies and others) in 139 countries distribute the world's largest selling single brand of cosmetics, fragrances, and toiletries. They also sell an extensive line of fashion jewelry, apparel, and gifts.

Beauty products were also the source of another fortune in direct selling. Mary Kay, based in Addison, Texas, achieved its initial identity and momentum from an extremely charismatic and visionary founder, Mary Kay Ash. In 1963, after a successful career in direct sales, Ash took her life savings of $5,000 and with the help of her 20-year-old son, Richard Rogers, launched Mary Kay Cosmetics. Her personal focus was to provide women with an opportunity for personal and financial success. Mary Kay Inc. has since grown from a small direct-sales company to the largest direct seller of skin care products in the United States, including

BELOW: ALFRED C. FULLER, THE RENOWNED "FULLER BRUSH MAN," IS INDUCTED INTO THE CIRCUS SAINTS AND SINNERS IN NEW YORK IN APRIL 1948. HIS COMPANY BECAME A HOUSEHOLD WORD BETWEEN 1906 AND 1956, WHEN FULLER BRUSH REPRESENTATIVES CALLED ON NINE OUT OF EVERY 10 AMERICAN HOMES. • OPPOSITE: A "RAINBOW" SITS OVER THE KISSIMMEE, FLORIDA, HEADQUARTERS OF THE TUPPERWARE CORPORATION, WHOSE SEALABLE PLASTIC CONTAINERS WERE PROMOTED IN AT-HOME "TUPPERWARE PARTIES" BEGINNING IN THE 1940S.

DOOR THAT KNOCKS ON FULLER BRUSH MAN

the best-selling brand of facial skin care and color cosmetics in the nation (based on most recently published industry sales data). The company now has more than 500,000 independent beauty consultants in 29 markets worldwide.

Another manufacturer of personal care products is Nu Skin Enterprises, of Provo, Utah. Cofounder Blake Roney had just finished college when he pulled together a small group of professionals to develop a line of premium personal care products containing only beneficial ingredients. Beginning with less than $5,000 in capital, Roney, Sandie Tillotson, and several associates founded Nu Skin in June 1984 with 12 personal care products. The company opted to distribute its products through person-to-person marketing so a trained sales force could educate consumers one-to-one about the products' unique benefits. Today, with products licensed in 30 countries, Nu Skin boasts more than 500,000 distributors worldwide and chalks up nearly $1 billion in annual sales.

Health and wellness products form another thriving segment of the direct-sales industry. A pioneer in this sector is

the Shaklee Corporation. Dr. Forrest C. Shaklee Sr. and his two sons, Forrest Jr. and Raleigh, founded the company in 1956 as Shaklee Products in Oakland, California. In 1960, it introduced its first household product, Basic-H, a phosphate-free, concentrated, and biodegradable all-purpose cleaner. Today, the company, headquartered in Pleasanton, California, sells household, personal care, and nutrition products through independent salespeople and has divisions in Canada, Japan, and Mexico.

Alongside these giants of direct selling are innovative upstarts that develop and market unique products and attract legions of dedicated salespeople and customers. Melaleuca, founded in 1985 with just seven employees, is one such company. Guided by president and CEO Frank L. VanderSloot, this Idaho Falls, Idaho, company employs more than 1,300 and has annual revenues exceeding $450 million. Its growth in just over 15 years has earned it a spot on *Inc.* magazine's list of 500 fastest growing companies for five years in a row. The company takes its name from *Melaleuca alternifolia*,

a tree that produces natural antiseptic oil. This substance is used in many of the firm's health care, pharmaceutical, personal care, and home hygiene products. All told, Melaleuca markets over 200 exclusive products geared for everyday personal and household use, with an emphasis on pure, natural ingredients that are favorable to both human health and the physical environment. "We're very proud of these products," says VanderSloot. "But perhaps the most important product companies like ours offer is opportunity—a chance to share in the American dream."

Contributing to America's Good Life

The American marketplace is organized around the principle that a semblance of the good life should be accessible to all. The infinite variety of products in a wide range of prices available to the American consumer reflects this belief. As author and economist Stanley Lebergott has written, "In open societies, human consumption choices share only one characteristic—they are made in the pursuit of happiness."

profiles
Direct Sales

MELALEUCA, INC.

ONE OF THE NATION'S FASTEST GROWING HOME-BASED BUSINESSES, MELALEUCA, INC., OFFERS ADVANCED NUTRITIONAL SUPPLEMENTS; PURE, NATURAL SKIN- AND HAIR-CARE PRODUCTS; AND ENVIRONMENTALLY FRIENDLY CLEANING PRODUCTS.

1770: In New South Wales, Australia, Captain Cook learns that local aborigines treat a number of their ailments with a tea brewed from the leaves of the melaleuca tree, a shrublike tree he names the "tea tree."

2001: In Idaho Falls, Idaho, Melaleuca, Inc.—launched originally to market products based on the melaleuca tree—conducts a $450 million per year business, with an enviable catalog of healthful and therapeutic home hygiene, nutrition, and personal care products.

How melaleuca oil found its way from a miniscule part of Australia into millions of American households—while inspiring a business that in 1991 was described by *Inc.* magazine as America's 37th fastest growing private company and since then has been consistently ranked among the *Inc.* top 2000—is tantamount to an incredible entrepreneurial journey.

In 1985, current Melaleuca president and CEO, Frank L. VanderSloot—at that point content in his post as regional vice president for a Fortune 500 company—received a call from Roger Ball, an old family friend, who had teamed up with an Australian who claimed to have 80 percent of all the melaleuca trees in the world on his ranch. Ball wanted VanderSloot to help the two partners build a company to market Melaleuca Oil, as well as various complementary products.

Reluctant at first, VanderSloot finally agreed, quit his job, moved his family to Idaho, and threw himself into the business with enthusiasm. But he soon discovered seemingly insurmountable problems. After investigating the company's literature, he determined that many of the medical claims the company had been

making about Melaleuca Oil were outside the bounds set by the U.S. Food and Drug Administration. He also discovered that many of the products lacked credible research and that the company's marketing plan was based on a multilevel marketing scheme that was probably illegal in all 50 states. Finally, VanderSloot discovered that the company's Australian partner did not control anything near 80 percent of the world's melaleuca trees. In fact, he owned barely 5 percent of them. Sales plummeted.

Not surprisingly, the decision was made to close down Oil of Melaleuca, Inc., which had taken off with such great promise.

What happened next is the stuff of marketing history. Out of failure, VanderSloot learned the secret to Melaleuca's current success.

"I learned," says VanderSloot, "that a lot of ordinary, hardworking people want to get ahead, but that they have no real way to do it. Though America is supposed to be the land of opportunity, with corporate mergers and buyouts, it is nearly impossible for the little guy to get in."

"Little wonder that throughout the ages there has been a popular cry to redistribute wealth," he continues. "The problem is that socialism and communism just haven't worked, and of course, they never will. I realized that what we need is not the redistribution of money, but the distribution of *opportunity*."

VanderSloot knew that Melaleuca Oil really did have great therapeutic potential. And with his newfound knowledge that significant numbers of people longed for the opportunity to secure an independent income, he developed new formulas, as well as an innovative new marketing plan.

He rearranged his deal with the original owners, became a partner in the business, invested his life savings, and set out to

establish a brand new organization. He met with chemists, pharmacists, doctors, attorneys, and other experts of various stripes, then he launched Melaleuca, Inc., in September 1985. With a loyal office staff of seven, he developed a mission statement that pledged to "enhance the lives of those we touch by helping people reach their goals" and vowed to "never charge more for our products than what they are worth."

VanderSloot's efforts paid off when, in 1991, he accepted the prestigious Blue Chip Enterprise Award from the U.S. Chamber of Commerce. This award recognizes companies that overcome great adversity on their way to success. In 1998, VanderSloot was named "Idaho Business Leader of the Year" by Idaho State University, and in 2001, he was named "Entrepreneur of the Year" for the northwest United States.

Today, in the *Melaleuca Country Catalog*, there are more than 200 top-of-the-line nutritional supplements; fast-acting natural cures for aches and pains; economically and ecologically sensible laundry and cleaning products; and luxurious, beneficial shampoos, bath gels, skin care preparations, and cosmetics for both men and women. Indeed, VanderSloot and his scientists guarantee that the products distributed by Melaleuca are of a higher quality—and are a better value—than any to be found in a grocery store.

"Today, we are in the position where top scientists approach us with their inventions," notes VanderSloot. "They sometimes spend years developing awesome products with no way to take them to market. Melaleuca becomes that avenue to the marketplace. PROVEX*CV*, a revolutionary heart-protection supplement containing specific varieties of grape skin and grape seed, was developed at the University of Wisconsin; our best-selling vitamin and mineral Vitality Pak, processed with a fructose compound that allows the body to fully assimilate minerals, was developed by scientist David Mitchell; and our Access Fat-Conversion Activity Bars were developed from the research of Dr. Larry Wang into adenosine, a nucleoside involved in the body's capacity to metabolize fat."

RIGHT: ALL OF MELALEUCA'S PRODUCTS ARE BASED ON IN-DEPTH SCIENTIFIC AND CONSUMER TESTING. MADE WITH RESEARCH-BASED FORMULAS OF NATURAL INGREDIENTS, EACH OF MELALEUCA'S PRODUCTS IS DESIGNED WITH THE CUSTOMER'S TOTAL WELLNESS IN MIND. · OPPOSITE PAGE, TOP: FOR ITS ABILITY TO SUCCEED IN THE FACE OF TREMENDOUS ECONOMIC CHALLENGES, MELALEUCA WAS RECOGNIZED WITH THE U.S. CHAMBER OF COMMERCE 1991 BLUE CHIP ENTERPRISE AWARD. · OPPOSITE PAGE, BOTTOM: MELALEUCA'S COMMITMENT TO ITS CUSTOMERS LED THE COMPANY TO DEVELOP A STATE-OF-THE-ART CALL CENTER WHERE PRODUCT SPECIALISTS FIELD NEARLY 400,000 ORDERS PER MONTH.

And how does Melaleuca market its products? For a $29 investment, marketing executives can buy comprehensive information on every product and a 12-month subscription to the company's monthly magazine. Then, using the catalog, along with knowledge of the real science behind every product, they can market the line to their friends, neighbors, and relatives. Their customers order from the catalog each month, and Melaleuca pays commissions to whoever gave the customer the catalog. Moreover, since Melaleuca ships every order directly to the customer, executives don't have to contend with stocking products or managing inventory.

In April 2001, the Melaleuca head office sent out 162,000 commission checks, ranging from $2.03 to more than $185,000. In 2000, two independent marketing executives made more than $1 million, while more than a few executives took home hundreds of thousands of dollars.

"Our business is actually tailored to supplement people's existing incomes," VanderSloot says. "Many marketing executives sell Melaleuca products part-time." For those starting out, the average income is $1,500 per month. And while this alone can make a significant impact on the average family budget, the potential for growth is substantially greater.

Also, with its loyal customer base, the company has been able to negotiate good rates on a number of services on behalf of its customers. For example, Melaleuca's Preferred Customers—those who have a minimum standing order for $35 worth of products each month—can now enjoy substantially reduced rates for Internet access, airline tickets, and long-distance telephone service.

Currently, Melaleuca signs somewhere between 17,000 and 20,000 new households every month. It is already in one out of every 200 households in the United States and Canada, and it recently opened branches in Hong Kong, Taiwan, Japan, and Australia.

Finally, on the key to leadership, VanderSloot offers, "I have learned that people want to have a dream. They want to have hope. It is an awesome responsibility that we have as leaders, that people are following us. It is important that we live worthy of their trust in us. We must provide them substance, with superior products, and financial reward in proportion to their contribution. We really are redistributing opportunity.

"And the result is not only fun, it's incredible!"

profiles
Retail & Wholesale

THE NATIONAL ASSOCIATION OF CHAIN DRUG STORES IS A VOICE FOR 33,000 COMMUNITY CHAIN PHARMACIES, REPRESENTING THE CONCERNS OF HEALTH CARE CONSUMERS AND RETAILERS IN AN INCREASINGLY REGULATED WORLD.

Chain pharmacies are America's corner drug stores—with more than a century of service meeting community health care needs and providing the patient care and convenience Americans have come to expect.

Since the days of tin ceilings and soda fountains, when the pharmacy was Main Street's main meeting place, the spirit of enterprise has helped build a national network of chain drug stores that now serve thousands of communities and millions of customers every day. Never before has pharmacy played so

important a role in the nation's health care. Chain pharmacies fill more than 60 percent of the over 3 billion prescriptions dispensed annually in the United States. As drug therapy becomes a more common and critical element of medical care, pharmacists have become the trusted partners with physicians in guiding patient care and offering advice and counseling. Chain pharmacies also play a key role in the economic life of their communities, employing more than 435,000 Americans and ringing up more than $160 billion in annual sales.

The first chain drug stores appeared in 1850, the brainchild of enterprising owners who recognized the enormous potential of stores that had become the social and shopping hubs of their communities. The owners were retail entrepreneurs who took advantage of shared ideas and volume buying, leveraging their good names to build more and more stores.

The National Association of Chain Drug Stores (NACDS) is the voice for the nation's 33,000 community chain pharmacies, representing the concerns of health care consumers and retailers in an increasingly regulated world. Founded in 1933 in the wake of the Great Depression of 1929, NACDS

OF CHAIN DRUG STORES

was the creation of six chain drug store executives who met at New York City's Vanderbilt Hotel to create an organization that would give them "a unified voice" in government.

The founders' challenges at the time: A spate of antichain legislation, a drive to ban drug store soda fountains, and, as *Chain Store Age* magazine described it, "the activities of various pressure groups to put across selfish legislation that makes it necessary for legitimate business to be constantly on guard and adequately organized."

Today, NACDS remains that unified voice, working hard to ensure that Americans have free choice and easy access to medications, promoting the important role pharmacists play in patient care . . . and still battling the occasional piece of "selfish" legislation.

Now representing the largest component of pharmacy in the nation, NACDS is pleased to count among its members more than 95 percent of all chain drug companies and supermarkets and mass merchants with pharmacies. Among its many policy initiatives, NACDS is:

- working to ensure that the nation's neediest senior citizens can obtain the prescription drug coverage they need;

- working with insurers, health maintenance organizations (HMOs), and government health plans to promote fair compensation for pharmacy services;

- monitoring tax and regulatory issues, as it works to ensure a healthy business environment for its members.

On the educational front, NACDS is working to support and expand pharmacy education and training to help provide a qualified, dedicated workforce to meet the growing demand for pharmacists.

NACDS and its member pharmacies also are enthusiastically involved in their communities, sponsoring good works on the local level and supporting

charities that promote the health and welfare of Americans nationwide. NACDS is a partner in America's Promise, The Alliance for Youth, and maintains an industrywide commitment to help young families lead healthy lives and contribute to their communities.

The nation's chain pharmacies play a crucial role in both America's health care system and in community life. NACDS is proud to strengthen and support that role.

AMERICA
THE PLACE TO BE

TOURISM & HOSPITALITY

The ancient Romans could arguably be called the first tourists. Their empire stretched across one million square miles, from Spain to Syria. They traveled over roads paved in stone to historic sites in Greece and Asia Minor, stopping for the night at inns along the way.

Today's tourists zoom across America's superhighways and stay overnight in hotels or motels with all the amenities. And, because of the way foreign visitors' dollars are counted, travel and tourism has become the United States' largest export industry. Not bad for an industry that barely existed a century ago.

'There Is No Profit in the Tourist Business'

Rome wasn't built in a day, and neither was America's tourism industry. In fact, the United States was nearly 100 years old before anyone thought to promote tourism for tourism's sake. Pioneers and explorers had been heading west for generations, but theirs were journeys for business purposes, rarely if ever for pleasure.

That all changed in 1888 when Ward Foster, a travel expert, opened the Ask Mr. Foster travel agency. Less than 25 years later, the company had plush offices in upscale department stores, hotels, and resorts. The elite agency was eventually bought by Carlson Companies, of Minneapolis.

Not everyone had Foster's foresight. Around the same time, the Wells Fargo company briefly entered the action but after four months left the industry. J. C. Fargo stated, "There is no profit in the tourist business, and even if there were, this company wouldn't undertake it." Fargo turned out to be wrong, and in 1915, a subsidiary, American Express, opened a travel department. Today, American Express, headquartered in New York City, is the world's number one travel agency, with more than 1,700 offices worldwide.

Getting There Is Half the Fun

The travel industry grew slowly in those early days. People journeyed primarily by ship and rail. It wasn't until the invention of the automobile that travel and tourism as an industry really took off. By 1912, 37 states had highway departments, and the unofficial federal highway system began to take shape. Freed from the constraints of distance, Americans eagerly traveled the countryside to see what there was to see.

Travelers, of course, need a place to stay. But there were few choices in the early days. In 1900, there were only 10,000 hotels around the country, located primarily in downtown areas.

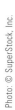

ABOVE: WITH MT. RUSHMORE IN THE REAR-VIEW MIRROR, A 1950S FAMILY WITH TRAILER IN TOW HEADS OUT ON THE OPEN ROAD. • OPPOSITE: RENOWNED BOURBON STREET IN NEW ORLEANS LIGHTS UP THE NIGHT.

provided well-stocked writing desks, small sewing kits, and free morning newspapers. It was said that Statler "built and operated hotels the way his contemporary, Henry Ford, built automobiles."

Like Ford, Statler soon found himself challenged by eager competitors. One pretender to the throne was Conrad Hilton, whose first experience with hotels was his own family's bed-and-breakfast. In 1907, the first Hilton Hotel was created from six unused rooms in his parents' house in San Antonio, New Mexico. After working in his father's general store all day, Hilton would meet trains at the local station and solicit guests. After a number of business and political ventures throughout the next decade, Hilton landed in Cisco, Texas, in 1919. Although he went there to buy an interest in a bank, Hilton instead bought the Mobley Hotel on a hunch. That purchase was the first step on his way to building an empire that in 1999 would total 1,800 owned, partially owned, managed, or franchised hotels. Despite financial troubles during the depression, Hilton managed to get out of debt, and in 1949 purchased the most famous hotel in America, the Waldorf-Astoria. Five years later, he purchased the Statler chain itself.

The competition certainly benefited hotel customers. One by one, hotels added amenities. The Hotel Statler in Boston was the first to add radios in individual rooms. In 1927, the Statler in Detroit was the first to put a central "air condition" system in every public room, a practice that would spread to nearly every hotel in the country by the 1940s. In 1946, the Westin debuted the first guest credit card. The New York City Roosevelt Hotel was the first to put television sets in guests' rooms, followed soon after in 1951 by Hilton, the first chain to do so. In-room

They were either luxurious, like the brand-new Waldorf-Astoria in New York City, which like other first-class hotels featured steam heat, baths on each floor, effete, continental-style service; red plush; and gilt trim. Or, they were uncomfortable and chilly, and a traveler going solo often had to share a room with a complete stranger.

Entrepreneurs like E. M. Statler saw an opportunity: create comfortable, affordable rooms with unpretentious service. His first Statler Hotel, built in 1900, was a temporary hotel for the Pan American Exposition in Buffalo, New York. The exposition proved to be a fiasco, topped off by the assassination of President McKinley on the steps of the Music Hall. Nevertheless, Statler broke even and went on to found the Statler chain of hotels, which revolutionized the hotel business by creating a model of standardization, efficiency, and customer service. Statler was the first to put bathrooms in every room. His system of back-to-back bathrooms and shared plumbing is still in use today. Even though rooms with private baths cost the hotel guest more, Statler believed that this amenity gave him a competitive edge. He also coffee, minibars, direct-dial telephones, in-room cable, and in 1999, in-room personal computers—over the next few decades, hotel guests became accustomed to having many of the comforts of home at a hotel.

GAS, FOOD, LODGING

General Motors' famous 1950s advertising campaign "See the USA in Your Chevrolet!" aptly expressed the spirit of postwar America: enthusiastic, optimistic, and ready to roll. By the 1940s, modern superhighways began to appear, culminating in the Federal-Aid Highway Act of 1956 that provided for the Interstate Highway System.

The fuel that powered the engines of the new, prosperous travelers was gasoline. Gas stations were found almost everywhere. One Georgia businessman named William Stuckey, who had survived the Great Depression by selling pecans door to door, decided to include gas stations next to the pecan shops he had built along the highways. His idea grew into a national network of convenient highway pit stops where weary travelers could fill their tanks with gas and their stomachs with pecans, fruit, sandwiches, and coffee.

Roadside motels became abundant as well, but how could travelers know that the one they chose would be clean, safe, and comfortable?

motels were often less savory. It was sometimes difficult for travelers to figure out before taking a room whether the establishment was charming, clean, and comfortable or a nightmare.

Wilson was not pleased with this situation. Moreover, as the father of five, he was appalled at the price that hotels charged for

to the motels, forcing the family to drive a while before finding a place to eat breakfast in the morning.

While some people would have grumbled and walked away, Wilson recognized that he couldn't be the only irritated parent in America. He figured there were a lot of them, people who would be happy to find a

ABOVE: A VACATION AT THE BEACH, SUCH AS THIS FAMILY IS EXPERIENCING, WAS MORE EASILY ACCOMPLISHED AFTER THE HOLIDAY INN OPENED IN 1952, DELIVERING MUCH-NEEDED FAMILY AMENITIES SUCH AS FREE MEALS FOR CHILDREN. DEMAND FOR THIS TYPE OF MID-RANGE FAMILY HOTEL SOON SKYROCKETED. • OPPOSITE: LEE LAWRIE'S *ATLAS* SCULPTURE ON THE PLAZA AT ROCKEFELLER CENTER HAS COME TO SYMBOLIZE THE CENTER ITSELF, A MASTERPIECE OF 1930S ART DECO URBAN DESIGN SAID TO ENCAPSULATE THE VERY ESSENCE OF NEW YORK.

A Memphis homebuilder named Kemmons Wilson asked himself the same question as his family drove to Washington, D.C., in 1951. Though there were reliable hotels located in city centers, roadside

children: two dollars each, even though his kids had brought their own bedrolls so they could sleep on the floor in their parents' room. An additional difficulty was the lack of appropriate family restaurants convenient

reliable, standardized roadside motel room with a clean restaurant nearby. With that clear vision, Wilson entered the motel business. "And," he told his wife, "if I never do anything else worth remembering

Fresh air and superb scenery make family hikes like this, along the lake at the foot of northern California's Mount Shasta, among the nation's most popular outdoor vacation activities.

in my life, children are going to stay free at my motels."

Upon returning home, Wilson set to work and began building his first motel in Memphis. He named it Holiday Inn, after a Bing Crosby movie Wilson's draftsman had recently seen. It was completed in 90 days and opened in 1952, a year to the day after that inspirational car trip. The Holiday Inn featured 120 air-conditioned rooms, each with free television (other motels rented TVs for a dollar), plus a restaurant, a gift shop, and a swimming pool on site. Telephones, ice, and free parking were standard amenities.

Demand for a mid-market hotel like Holiday Inn exploded. By the end of the 1950s, about 65 percent of travelers fit into that category, and Wilson had opened up 100 Holiday Inns around the country. A decade later, in the early 1970s, one Holiday Inn was opening somewhere in the world every two days. Holiday Inns had become the first billion-dollar food-service and lodging company in history.

Wilson, of course, didn't do all this alone. Despite the initial success of the Holiday Inn chain, he had difficulty in interesting fellow homebuilders to join his company. So once again, Wilson turned frustration into opportunity and became a pioneer in the franchise business, offering investors the chance to purchase the rights to the Holiday Inn name and build and operate the hotels themselves.

Today, the Holiday Inn chain is owned by the British company Bass. With 1,500 hotels worldwide, the name is the largest single hotel brand and the most widely recognized in the world. And, true to Wilson's vision, in the United States and Canada, kids still stay—and eat—free at the Holiday Inn.

Kemmons Wilson wasn't the only person to notice the dearth of family amenities. Howard Dearing Johnson, the son of a tobacco merchant, would found his own motel-restaurant empire by filling this need. Johnson grew up in Wollaston, Massachusetts, where he ran his father's cigar stores. He eventually branched out on his own, buying a small patent medicine store in the middle of town. He had a staff of 75 boys to deliver newspapers and a soda fountain that served three flavors of ice cream: vanilla, chocolate, and strawberry.

Three flavors weren't enough for Johnson, a true ice cream lover. In 1925, he borrowed $2,000 to open a corner drug store in Wollaston. He quickly realized that ice cream could be his biggest seller if he could offer customers a unique flavor. Johnson developed a special vanilla and chocolate based on his mother's recipes, and as sales exploded, he opened a stand at a nearby beach and expanded his offering to 28 flavors of superior ice cream. By 1928, he was selling almost $250,000 a year worth of the frozen treat.

Over the years, Johnson added more stands and expanded the menu. He opened the first Howard Johnson's restaurant, in Quincy. It was a great success, but one restaurant wasn't enough for Johnson. In 1935, he found another individual interested in running a restaurant, trained him, and opened a second Howard Johnson's, in Cape Cod. In doing so, Johnson, like Holiday Inn's Wilson, became a pioneer in the franchising industry. The restaurant's distinctive design, with its blue walls and bright orange roof, became a hallmark of the chain. Over the next seven years, despite the depression, Johnson opened 25 more restaurants along local highways. In the coming years, he also developed a "central commissary" concept in which food was processed in centrally located, company-operated plants then shipped to restaurants. This kept quality consistent.

Next, Johnson went into the motel industry. In 1954, with 400 restaurants around the country, the first Howard Johnson Motor Lodge franchise was opened, in Savannah, Georgia. By 1975, there were over 1,000 restaurants and 500 motor lodges throughout the United States and Canada.

Yet the company was hit hard by the oil crises and rising gas prices of the 1970s.

FIRST-CLASS FIRSTS

According to the American Society of Travel Agents, the top 10 U.S. destinations are Orlando, Las Vegas, San Francisco, New York, Los Angeles, Seattle, Honolulu, San Diego, Miami, and Denver. · The word MOTEL, a combination of MOTOR and HOTEL, was coined by Arthur Heineman in 1925 when he opened the Milestone Motor Hotel, in San Luis Obispo, California. A two-room bungalow with kitchen went for $1.25 a night. · Woodstock, Vermont, opened the first ski lift, a tow rope, in the nation in 1934. · The world's largest amusement park is the 364-acre Cedar Point in Sandusky, Ohio. The 131-year-old park is home to Millennium Force, which at 310 feet has the biggest drop of any roller coaster in the country. · Atlanta's Hartsfield International is the nation's busiest airport, serving more than 80 million passengers annually.

Competition from fast-food giants like McDonald's further complicated the picture. The firm went through several changes in ownership but refocused its mission on global growth and on capitalizing on its unique and fondly considered brand name. Today, Howard Johnson International, based in Parsippany, New Jersey, boasts 500 hotels in 14 countries. And 28 flavors of ice cream are still sold in Howard Johnson's Ice Cream Shops across the nation.

The middle of the 20th century was a time of tremendous growth for the hotel-motel industry. In 1949, it began expanding beyond U.S. borders with the opening of the Caribe Hilton in San Juan, Puerto Rico. In 1954, the largest merger took place when Hilton purchased the Statler hotel chain for $111 million, at the time the largest real estate transaction in history. And in 1957, J. W. Marriott opened his first hotel.

Like Howard Johnson, Marriott did not start out in the hotel business; he was a food entrepreneur. A native Utahan, Marriott decided to move to Washington, D.C., and went into business for himself on May 20, 1927. He brought with him a franchise of Sacramento, California–based A&W Root Beer and opened a nine-seat root beer stand right in the middle of the city. Marriott lured his first customers with the radio broadcast of Charles Lindbergh's famous flight. A few months later, recognizing that ice-cold root beer would only sell well in the summer, Marriott added some spice to his menu: Mexican food, like chili and tamales, and barbecued beef. He opened his first drive-in store in Washington, D.C., in July 1927 and named it Hot Shoppe.

The Hot Shoppes chain grew, and soon Marriott opened a Hot Shoppe near the Hoover Airfield (now the site of the Pentagon) in Arlington, Virginia. Passengers and crew alike would take food "to go" before their flights. This gave Marriott an idea. In October

BELOW: THE SUCCESS OF THE FIRST HOWARD JOHNSON'S RESTAURANT IN QUINCY, MASSACHUSETTS, IN THE 1930S LED ITS FOUNDER TO FRANCHISE MORE THAN 400 AROUND THE COUNTRY WITHIN TWO DECADES. TODAY, THE COMPANY HAS 500 HOTELS IN 14 COUNTRIES—AND ICE CREAM SHOPS ACROSS THE NATION. • OPPOSITE: MONTICELLO, THOMAS JEFFERSON'S VIRGINIA HOME AND THE ONLY HOUSE IN AMERICA DESIGNATED AS A WORLD HERITAGE SITE, IS AMONG NUMEROUS HISTORICAL ATTRACTIONS RUN BY PRIVATE, NONPROFIT ORGANIZATIONS.

1937, he pioneered in-flight catering and soon branched out to government cafeterias and hospitals. Twenty years later, Marriott opened his first hotel, also in Arlington. In 1968, the newly renamed Marriott Corporation began a fast-food restaurant division with its Roy Rogers restaurants.

By 1996, the enormous corporation had begun to split up its operations into different divisions covering everything from food and facilities management to senior-living services. Today, the $400 million, Bethesda, Maryland–based Marriott International, which also includes the Ritz Carlton and Ramada properties, is the largest lodging company in the world.

On the Road Again

Americans' travel habits changed dramatically in the second half of the century as they left their cars at home and traveled by plane. Yet they still needed transportation when they reached their destination. Filling this void was Hertz, the first car rental company to offer an airport location, which opened at Chicago's Midway Airport in 1932.

John Hertz did not invent the business that bears his name. Hertz, a former boxing promoter and president of Yellow Cab and Yellow Truck and Coach Manufacturing Company, bought the company from Walter Jacobs, who opened his first car rental operation in Chicago at the age of 18. Jacobs repaired and repainted a dozen Model T Fords and put them to work. Within five years, his business had grossed $1 million.

After Hertz purchased the company in 1923, he named it Hertz Drive-Ur-Self System and hired Jacobs as the top operating and administrative executive. In 1953, Jacobs became Hertz's first president. After a number of mergers, buyouts,

and divestitures, Hertz became the world's largest car rental company, and now has 6,000 locations in 140 countries and a fleet of 500,000 vehicles. The car rental business that started with a dozen Tin Lizzies is today a $14 billion industry.

To See What There Is to See

As a new century begins, not only have Americans' modes of travel changed; so have their travel patterns, pointing the way toward a new path for the industry. Families are trading in the traditional two-week vacation for shorter trips, but parents who go on business trips are more likely than ever to bring their children. In 1998, family vacations accounted for 72 percent of all vacation trips.

Those vacations are most likely to involve camping, hiking, and biking, the most popular outdoor vacation activities in America. In 1999, America's National Parks logged more than 436,000,000 visits. Private companies also provide recreational and historical attractions for the public benefit. For example, 300,000 people every year visit the privately owned Natural Bridge in the Shenandoah Valley in southwestern Virginia, a 23-story rock formation that Thomas Jefferson, who originally owned the property, called "the most sublime of Nature's works." In Maine, companies like International Paper and Champion own parts of the North Maine Woods, which occupies more than two million acres of private lands and is open to camping and

hiking. This park looks like true wilderness but is actively managed for timber. And, since the 1930s, the electric power industry has provided recreational facilities for hunting, fishing, and camping on the buffer acres surrounding the land.

Americans are also big shoppers; it's one of the top activities for travelers. Outlet malls have become increasingly important; 37 percent of all travelers said they visited a discount mall in 1997. In the state of Virginia—where one can see Thomas Jefferson's home, Monticello; George Washington's home, Mount Vernon; Colonial Williamsburg; Arlington National Cemetery; Civil War battlefields; and the nation's first settlement of Jamestown— the number one tourist destination is Potomac Mills outlet mall, which draws 17 million people per year. Cultural and historic tourism isn't dead, however; more than

50 million adults visit museums and cultural sites every year.

Perhaps the ultimate in shopping-oriented vacations is a visit to the Minneapolis-based Mall of America. Built on the site of the old Met Stadium, the

mall opened in 1992. The Mall of America employs more than 12,000 people and has more than 500 stores and a seven-acre amusement park. With tourist traffic between 35 and 42 million visits every year, the mall and related activities

TRAVEL LORE

The restoration of Colonial Williamsburg, Virginia, was the brainchild of William Goodwin, a pastor and professor at William and Mary College. It was Goodwin who in 1926 convinced John D. Rockefeller Jr. to spend the millions needed to rebuild the town. Today, Williamsburg draws about 4.5 million visitors annually. · The United States welcomed more than 24 million foreign tourists in 1999. The majority came from Japan (4.8 million), The United Kingdom (4.3 million), and Germany (2 million). · In 2000, nearly 430 million people visited the national parks. · Perhaps a reflection of the popularity of the 1997 film *Titanic*, more than five million people booked passage on a cruise that year. A $500 million replica of the ill-fated ship is scheduled to set sail in 2002.

contribute $1.2 billion to the economy of Minnesota.

Minnesota is not alone in attracting visitors. Travel and tourism is the first, second, or third largest employer in 29 states and generates 7.6 million jobs for Americans. Almost two million work in hotels alone, and according to the National Restaurant Association, travelers and visitors account for half the sales at table-service restaurants with checks totaling over $25, for a grand total of $20 billion in annual sales.

For the Amusement of All

One of the most popular types of vacation involves a visit to a theme park. Attendance at theme parks rose steadily during the 1990s, ending the century with year 2000 revenues of $10 billion. In 2000, more than 175 million people visited the top 50 theme parks in the country. The Magic Kingdom at Walt Disney World in Orlando, Florida, led the way with 15.4 million guests, followed by Disneyland (13.9 million), Epcot (10.6 million), Disney-MGM Studios (8.9 million), and Animal Kingdom at Walt Disney World (8.3 million).

Probably the best-known theme park in the world—and the one that started it all—is Disneyland. In the 1950s, Walt Disney began plans for a site to be called Mickey Mouse Park, which would feature

Above: Riders on Perilous Plunge at Knott's Berry Farm in Buena Park, California, plummet 115 feet down a water chute at a 75-degree angle. Thrill rides like this help Knott's retain its people-pleasing reputation. • Opposite: Paradise Pier recreates California's seaside amusement parks of old at Disney's new California Adventure, the company's second Anaheim park. California Adventure joins the Magic Kingdom in Orlando and Disneyland in Anaheim as top U.S. vacation attractions.

lifelike statues of Mickey and Donald Duck and where guests could take pictures and ride around in a small train. Realizing that his vision was larger than the 11 acres in Burbank, California, where he had

originally planned to build the park, across from his movie studio, Disney purchased 200 acres of orange groves in Anaheim to the south. In 1955, the gates to Disneyland opened, welcoming children to "The

Happiest Place on Earth." The Walt Disney Company would later open the previously mentioned parks in Florida, as well as parks in Paris and Tokyo. Today, Tokyo Disneyland has the largest attendance of

any theme park in the world (16.5 million visitors in 2000).

Holding second place in the industry is Six Flags, which operates 40 theme and water parks across the country, from Six Flags Great Adventure in Jackson, New Jersey (3.5 million guests in 2000) to Six Flags Magic Mountain in Valencia, California (3.3 million visitors in 2000). The company had more than $1 billion in sales in 2000.

The public's fascination with movies, movie stars, and Hollywood led to the establishment of another group of very popular theme parks. Universal has been letting the public peek behind the curtain since 1915 when to celebrate its gala opening in Hollywood it allowed visitors to observe the set of movies in production for only 25 cents. The Universal Studios Tour opened in 1964, kicking off more than three

decades of growth and expansion, including a drive-through King Kong ride that initiated a new era in theme park design in 1985. In 1990, Universal opened in Florida. By 1999, the Islands of Adventure, Portofino Resort, and Universal CityWalks in both Orlando and Hollywood (California) had opened to the public. The Universal theme parks welcomed more than 19 million visitors in 2000.

theme parks make the company a major conservator, with their collection of 65,000 mammals, birds, reptiles, and fish.

Taking a Gamble

While a trip to a theme park is almost always a sure bet for a good time, many Americans like to try their hand at games of chance at one of the nation's many gaming centers. In 1997, gross revenues from all U.S. gaming sources exceeded $50 billion—in other words, more than $1 for every $10 spent on leisure goods and services. Most of this went to casinos, including nearly 100 located on riverboats or dockside and 260 on Indian reservations. This is an enormous advance for an industry that by 1910 had been banned in every state and which was regarded as unsavory until a federal crackdown in the 1960s introduced strict standards for the industry.

With the advent of new laws legalizing gaming, especially state lotteries, casinos came of age. The first popular destinations were Las Vegas and other Nevada sites. In 1976, gaming was legalized in Atlantic City, New Jersey, revitalizing that resort town.

For years, such towns drew an adults-only crowd who came for the

shows and the Cirque du Soleil. Video arcades, rides, and restaurants that cater to children are also big draws. And the look of Las Vegas has changed; there are casino replicas of the ancient pyramids of Egypt, and the cities of Venice, New York, and Paris. Another casino, the Bellagio, resembles an Italian villa complete with a magnificent fountain, botanical gardens, and an art gallery showcasing van Goghs and other masterpieces.

The Journey Ahead

At the dawn of the 21st century, the travel industry is poised to change once again as consumers drift away from using commission- and fee-based travel agents. Consumers are taking matters into their own hands and increasingly using the Internet for travel services and information. Airlines, hotels, and cruise lines have been on the Web since 1994. In 1997, 29 million travelers used the Internet. That figure boomed to 85 million in 1999. Yet many industry analysts believe that travel agencies will maintain a secure place in the Internet era as consumers rely on the Web mainly to compare prices and book basic trips, while looking to agents for expert counsel. On-line travel accounts for

THE NEW YORK NEW YORK HOTEL & CASINO IN LAS VEGAS, NEVADA, IS PART OF THE CITY'S NEW LOOK. GAMING CENTERS LIKE LAS VEGAS HAVE REVAMPED THEIR STYLE AND THEIR OFFERINGS IN AN ATTEMPT TO CAPTURE THE ATTENTION OF A LUCRATIVE GROUP: FAMILIES.

Anheuser-Busch, based in St. Louis, Missouri, is another company that has successfully branched out into the theme park business. During the 1970s, the company bought or created Busch Gardens, Sesame Place, and SeaWorld, among others. In 2000, 21 million people visited Anheuser-Busch attractions. In addition to offering fun-filled family outings, Anheuser-Busch

gambling and the floor shows. But savvy entrepreneurs realized they were missing out on a lucrative group: families. Today, many casinos are partnering with movie studios and other entertainment entities to form entertainment locations that are appropriate for adults and children alike. In Las Vegas, for example, there are shows the entire family can enjoy, like magic

only about 1 percent of the $101 billion of travel products sold by travel agents.

Like the ancient Romans, Americans are a peripatetic people. The urge to travel and see what there is to see will always lure the adventurer in everyone. And American business will help make it possible to travel safely, sleep soundly, and eat well every step of the way.

ON THE MOVE

TRANSPORTATION, LOGISTICS, & INFRASTRUCTURE

Just weeks before the turn of the last century, a naysayer writing in the Literary Digest summed up his assessment of the future of U.S. surface transportation this way: 'The ordinary horseless carriage is at present a luxury for the wealthy, and although its price will probably fall in the future, it will never of course come into as common use as the bicycle.'

A New Industry Revs Up

It is not hard to see why the transportation skeptics reigned in 1900 America. While the nation had come a long way since the days of Thomas Jefferson, when it took him four days to make the journey from Philadelphia to Baltimore, horses (animal and iron), steamships, and bicycles still moved the country. It had been just four years since automobile pioneer Charles Edgar Duryea sold his first car, assembled part by part and piece by piece in his shop in Springfield, Massachusetts. As of 1900, there were just 8,000 cars registered throughout the entire country and only 10 miles of paved roads. This handful of motor vehicles shared the roads with some 18 million horses and 10 million bicycles.

Yet expanding incomes, the desire for personal mobility, the needs of a growing economy, and the vision of business pioneers like Henry Ford soon made the horseless carriage the only carriage Americans wanted to have. By 1923, one in four American families owned an automobile, thanks in large part to Ford's assembly-line innovations that drove the price of cars down to a level average citizens could afford. Today, in a nation of 273 million people, there are more than 210 million registered motor vehicles and Americans log 2.5 trillion miles a year. More than $140 billion in autos and parts are produced annually by an industry that directly employs 210,000 Americans and indirectly employs millions more.

More than just a modern convenience, the car became a defining feature of 20th-century American culture—at least as significant as television and the computer. One can chart the fads and fashions of the nation through the rise and fall of automobile makes and models. Many Americans can mark the chapters of their lives through the cars they owned. The development of the automobile unleashed a tremendous dynamic force throughout the economy and culture, spawning dozens of related industries, from highway construction to drive-through restaurants, and raising to prominence some of the century's most colorful and controversial figures, from Henry Ford to Lee Iacocca, from Ralph Nader to Richard Petty.

In 1890, historian Frederick Jackson Turner declared the "closing" of the American frontier. But as far as Americans were concerned, there was a great big continent in between the shores of the Atlantic and Pacific yet to be explored, and there was no better way to see it, move throughout it, and develop it economically than with the motor

ABOVE: KEY FIGURES IN THE BUILDING OF SAN FRANCISCO'S GOLDEN GATE BRIDGE GIVE IT THEIR APPROVAL. ·
OPPOSITE: THE LICENSE PLATE OF A 1955 CHEVY REFLECTS THE JOY AMERICANS FELT OUT ON THE ROAD.

vehicle. The decentralization of American cities, the movement to the suburbs, and the rise of the great sunbelt commercial centers like Dallas's Metroplex, Southern California's Inland Empire and Orange County, the Atlanta area's Cobb County, as well as the San Francisco Bay Area's Silicon Valley can all trace their roots to the availability of reliable cars, cheap gas, and good roads.

In the last quarter of the 20th century, critics liked to remind Americans of the costs of their car culture: the impact on the environment, the decline of city centers and the loss of community, the dependence on foreign oil, urban and suburban gridlock, and the deaths of more than 40,000 people each year in traffic accidents. But Americans have made it clear that, rather than abandon individual mobility, they want these problems solved through the same technological ingenuity that brought them modern cars and highway systems.

Industry has responded with cleaner, more efficient engines, safer and more reliable vehicles, and computer-designed traffic management systems. It has also developed a surer sense of the changing, sometimes fickle attitudes of the consumer. U.S. carmakers acknowledge being asleep at the wheel in the late 1970s while the Japanese and others made inroads into the domestic car market, scooping up as much as 25 percent by 1980. ("We built some lousy cars" is how the plain-speaking Lee Iacocca put it.) But in the 1990s, American manufacturers were the first to spot an exploding demand for sport utility vehicles and light trucks, which by the end of the century together accounted for more than half of new vehicle sales.

As with many industries, globalization has become the watchword in the auto industry. In response to growing trade frictions with the United States during the 1980s, the Japanese auto industry, led by Toyota, established production facilities here that by the end of the decade could produce some 1.6 million vehicles a year for the domestic market. Yet U.S. automakers have been busy "going global," too, building lucrative markets like Mexico and forming joint ventures in developing countries throughout the world. In 1998, globalization reached a new plateau when Chrysler, one of America's venerable "big three," merged with Germany's Daimler-Benz, becoming the DaimlerChrysler company.

Delivering the Goods by Rail and Truck

Despite what is likely to be an everlasting love affair with the automobile, 20th-century Americans eagerly embraced other transportation choices. The early years of the century brought with them the opening of subway and bus systems in metropolises like New York that whisked hundreds of thousands of riders through the city daily. By 1946, the average American was taking 178 trips a year on mass transit, a number that then steadily declined until a resurgence began in the 1970s.

For much of the 20th century, intercity passenger rail service struggled to find its niche in a transportation world increasingly dominated by cars and planes. From the end of the Civil War until the onset of World War I, no other mode of transportation came close to rivaling the rails. At its peak in 1916, some 254,000 miles of track crisscrossed America.

But severe challenges arose. The federal government seized the railroads for the duration of World War I and returned them in a decrepit condition. And the growing popularity of cars, buses, trucks, and airplanes took its toll—as did the depression, another world war, and numerous regulations. In 1971, the federal government created Amtrak to take over the remaining, and mostly money-losing, rail passenger service, to preserve a treasured legacy of rail travel and to protect communities that remain heavily dependent on rail, such as those along the Washington–New York–Boston corridor. Amtrak trains today cover more than 22,000 route miles and carry 21 million passengers annually.

ABOVE: THE IMPROVED ABILITY OF MODERN FREIGHT TRAINS LIKE THIS ONE TO MOVE RAW MATERIALS AND FINISHED GOODS ALL OVER THE WORLD, WITH INCREASING SPEED AND SOPHISTICATION, ACCOUNTS FOR THE RESURGENCE OF THE RAILS IN THE 20TH CENTURY. • OPPOSITE: MODEL T FORDS MAKE THEIR WAY BY BOAT TO AN EASTERN PORT, WHERE THEY WILL BE DELIVERED TO A DEALER. THANKS TO ASSEMBLY-LINE INNOVATIONS THAT DROVE THE PRICE DOWN, BY 1923 MORE THAN ONE IN FOUR AMERICAN FAMILIES OWNED AN AUTOMOBILE.

Yet it is the rail's improved ability to move the raw materials and the finished goods of a great industrial power that accounts for its resurgence in the 1990s and will define its essentiality in the new century.

For railroads, along with trucks, ships, planes, and pipelines, are moving hundreds of billions of goods all over the world—and they are doing so with increasing speed, efficiency, and technological sophistication.

The importance of an economy's logistics system (the manner in which it moves products through the entire chain of production, sale, and use by the end consumer) cannot be overstated in a global economy.

These travelers are among the more than 200,000 that pass through the Chicago O'Hare International Airport every day, making it the chief economic engine of the Midwest.

Free-trade agreements, for example, will not have their desired impact if each trading party cannot seamlessly and efficiently move goods from plant to port to retailer to consumer. Likewise, e-commerce companies, for all their promise of consumer choice and convenience, are still at the mercy of the nation's physical transportation system and its shippers to get the product to the consumer once he or she clicks on the mouse.

Changes in the manufacturing process, whereby components are brought together from all over the world for assembly in a centralized location on a just-in-time basis, have also spurred the demand for and development of shipping that is reliable, cost-effective, global, and traceable at a moment's notice.

Trucking is easily the largest and most far-reaching of all modes, comprising 81 percent of total freight transportation revenues, employing 9.5 million Americans, and accounting for 5 percent of the nation's gross domestic product. The development of modern cabs for the nation's estimated five million truck drivers, clean and efficient diesel engines, and tough industry standards on safety have improved trucking's productivity. One of the most respected names in the business is Volvo Trucks North America. The company, headquartered in Greensboro, North Carolina, manufactures heavy-duty commercial trucks including long-haul models and work rigs, as well as diesel engines and rear-suspension systems.

One of the leaders in less-than-truckload shipping is the Overnite Transportation Company, of Richmond, Virginia. Founded in 1935, the company provides comprehensive transport services to 45,000 cities and towns within the United States and overseas.

Rail cargo is essential to some of America's most important industries, carrying 70 percent of the motor vehicles shipped from manufacturing sites, 64 percent of the nation's coal, and 40 percent of its grain and farm products, according to the Association of American Railroads, a Washington, D.C.–based advocacy group representing the major rail freight companies and Amtrak. Growing faster than either trucking or rail, air cargo now hauls more than 18 billion ton-miles of goods through the skies each year.

But the future of freight transportation will be defined by intermodalism, the combining of one or more means of transportation to move a product from producer to customer or from one company facility to another. Customers care little or not at all about the means of conveyance; it is service, speed, and surety that have become the hottest commodities in shipping.

Understanding the shipping needs of the new American economy is what led Frederick Smith to found Federal Express in 1971 and it is what explains the continued success of competitor United Parcel Service. Between them, the two companies operate more than 1,100 aircraft and 200,000 vehicles, offer service in 200 countries, and make well over four billion deliveries a year. Teaming up with Internet vendors, these package-delivery and logistics companies will be a key component in America's transformation to an e-commerce economy.

LAYING THE FOUNDATION FOR GREATNESS: AMERICA'S INFRASTRUCTURE

The 20th-century development of America's infrastructure—the roads, highways, bridges, dams, ports, pipelines, intermodal shipping links, and municipal facilities covering a vast continent—is a substantial factor in the nation's strength as an economic and military superpower. No element of this basic foundation has had such a broad impact on the promotion of shared economic progress throughout the nation as its system of roads and highways.

BELOW: THE NEW NAVAL AIRCRAFT CARRIER U.S.S. PRESIDENT TRUMAN IS SHOWN DOCKED IN LOS ANGELES HARBOR IN 2000. NAMED IN HONOR OF THE 33RD U.S. PRESIDENT, IT WILL SUPPORT AMERICAN INTERESTS ABROAD. • OPPOSITE, TOP: FEDEX PACKAGES ABOUT TO BE LOADED ON A PLANE WILL BE DELIVERED WITH THE SPEED AND CERTAINTY AMERICANS HAVE COME TO EXPECT. • OPPOSITE, BOTTOM: THE WABASHA STREET BRIDGE IN ST. PAUL, MINNESOTA, WAS RECENTLY REBUILT AT A COST OF $35 MILLION TO SUPPORT COMMERCE WELL INTO THE 21ST CENTURY.

the U.S. Department of Commerce, the nation's transportation infrastructure is a tangible asset worth more than $1.5 trillion, an asset that acts as the life-supporting circulatory system of the world's greatest economy.

And with two-way global trade now exceeding $2 trillion a year and accounting for some 20 percent of gross domestic product, America's more than 100 public ports represent a vital link to an increasingly interdependent world economy. Commercial port activities create jobs for 1.4 million Americans and establish the communities in which they are located as

America's first road linked New York and Boston in 1673. Little more than a dirt trail, it was called the Boston Post Road. Men were posted at intervals along the way, each one responsible for relaying mail and messages along his section to the next post until he reached his big-city destination. The federal government's first large-scale highway construction project was started in 1810 and was to stretch from Baltimore all the way to the Mississippi River. But in 1830, construction was stopped at Vandalia, Illinois. After all, the reasoning went, who would need these big interstate roads when canals and railroads would work better?

During the 20th century, few argued that a massive program of building paved roads and highways linking every corner of the land would be needed to spur the development of a vast continent and ensure the mobility of a restless people. From the Shackleford Good Roads program during the Woodrow Wilson administration to the National Highway System

begun during the Dwight D. Eisenhower administration, America experienced a road-building boom.

Today, there are 3.9 million miles of public roads in the United States, including 45,744 miles of interstate highways. The transportation construction industry, which not only built these roads but also the nation's 5,415 airports, 3,750 waterports, and 2,382 mass-transit stations, is a $153 billion-a-year business accounting for 1.6 million American jobs. According to

hubs of international commerce and intermodal transportation.

Throughout U.S. history, few values have been more cherished than America's mobility, the idea that there is always a new frontier in business or in life down the road or around the world. Thanks to outstanding 20th-century developments in transportation, logistics, and infrastructure, America greets the new century with a modern, efficient foundation for prosperity that is second to none.

profiles
Transportation, Logistics, & Infrastructure

Photo inset. © Digital Stock

320

OVERNITE TRANSPORTATION

One of the nation's largest less-than-truckload carriers, Overnite Transportation Company provides high quality regional, national, and international shipping through its network of more than 170 service centers.

From its humble beginning 66 years ago, ferrying goods from local Virginia farms, Overnite Transportation Company grew to become one of the largest movers of furniture and textiles in the 1940s. Later, when America went to war, Overnite went, too. During World War II, Overnite trucks carried the blankets and uniforms worn by American troops in the European theater to ports for transport across the Atlantic. After the war, when Americans returned to the United States with an insatiable appetite for the finer things in life, Overnite expanded across the nation to transport building materials needed for the postwar housing boom and the goods needed to fill those homes.

Today, Richmond, Virginia–based Overnite is the seventh largest less-than-truckload (LTL) carrier in the nation, with a modern fleet of more than 4,000 tractors and 18,000 trailers serving 45,000 cities and towns in the 48 contiguous states, Alaska, Hawaii, Guam, Canada, Mexico, Puerto Rico, and the U.S. Virgin Islands.

Spirited entrepreneurs Harwood and Calvin Cochrane started the company in the early 1930s. Despite scant resources during the Great Depression years, the brothers persevered. In 1935, Harwood Cochrane took over the traffic lanes himself, beginning a steady business expansion that continues to this day.

In 1957, after years of growth, Overnite became a publicly traded company on the New York Stock Exchange. In 1986, Overnite was acquired by the Union Pacific Corporation, one of America's largest companies, whose financial strength and state-of-the-art transportation technology allowed Overnite to reach its full potential. Today, through its nationwide network of service centers, Overnite employs 13,000 people and enjoys annual sales in excess of $1 billion.

COMPANY

SERVICES AND ENHANCEMENTS

Overnite's standard service, Advantage Overnite, is adjusted to suit each geographic region. In addition, Advantage Guaranteed and Advantage Expedited are available to meet specific customer needs. Advantage Overnite provides full-state coverage in 32 states east of the Rocky Mountains, with 97 percent–plus service reliability.

Advantage Guaranteed, available to direct points in the continental United States and Canada, provides customers with an extra blanket of security, ensuring that shipments will be available for delivery at specified destinations or the delivery is free. Advantage Expedited combines ground and air transport to rush time-critical shipments worldwide. Continuing to expand its services, in 2000, Overnite unveiled Guaranteed Pickup Service, becoming the first carrier in the nation to provide nationwide pickup with an on-time guarantee for direct LTL shipments.

SPECIAL EXPERTISE

Overnite offers a number of special services. SSD, the company's truckload division, provides superior full-load trucking with satellite-linked, 24-hour tracking and driver communication. Overnite's Assembly and Distribution programs link shipments from or to multiple locations, helping customers improve transit times while reducing warehousing costs. Government Services is Overnite's award-winning provider of LTL transport across land and ocean for the U.S. government. The company's Trade Show Division is experienced in delivering complex displays and equipment to convention halls and arenas across the nation.

Long a leader in its field, Overnite has moved into the 21st century, making optimal use of fully integrated technology with a host of on-line services. Its MyOvernite.com service gives customers secure, easy access to all their relevant shipping information, including electronic transmission of document images, bills of lading, status reports, and delivery receipts, as well as real-time news and shipping schedules. For additional information, visit the company's Web site at www.Overnite.com.

OPPOSITE PAGE: PROVIDING LOCAL, REGIONAL, AND NATIONWIDE COVERAGE, MORE THAN 4,800 OVERNITE VEHICLES TAKE TO AMERICA'S ROADS EACH DAY. • ABOVE: OVERNITE TRANSPORTATION COMPANY HAS BEEN RECOGNIZED AS ONE OF THE NATION'S LEADING TRUCKING GIANTS SINCE 1935. • LEFT: "OUR PEOPLE MAKE THE DIFFERENCE" IS NOT MERELY A SLOGAN AT OVERNITE TRANSPORTATION, BUT THE COMPANY'S CREED FOR MORE THAN 66 YEARS.

VOLVO TRUCKS NORTH AMERICA

WITH CORE VALUES OF QUALITY, SAFETY, AND RELIABILITY, VOLVO TRUCKS NORTH AMERICA BUILDS TRUCKS SUPERIOR IN PERFORMANCE, DESIGN, ENVIRONMENTAL CARE, AND DRIVER COMFORT, AND OPERATES PREMIER TRAVEL PLAZAS.

When it comes to making trucks—big, over-the-road trucks—it's tough to match Volvo for quality, safety, and reliability. Sweden-based automotive giant AB Volvo, which has been recognized for generations world-wide for superior vehicles, has been making great trucks since 1928. Today, the Volvo Truck Corporation is one of the world's leading heavy truck and engine manufacturers. Its Greensboro, North Carolina–based affiliate, Volvo Trucks North America, established in the United States in 1981, carries on the Volvo tradition in the western hemisphere.

Volvo Trucks North America manufactures heavy-duty commercial trucks with day cabs or sleeper cabs. Volvo Trucks models range from long-haul trucks—such as the premium Volvo 770, which features, among other things, an integrated sleeping compartment, kitchen, office, and entertainment center—to work rigs specifically designed for use in logging, construction, aircraft fueling, and refuse processing.

Besides trucks, Volvo Trucks North America markets first-rate, technologically advanced heavy-duty diesel engines and rear-suspension systems. The trucks and their engines are assembled at the company's state-of-the-art plants in the New River Valley area of Virginia; sales and leasing of Volvo Trucks products are handled through a network of more than 200 dealers across North America.

To oversee the smooth delivery of its trucks and the operation of its service centers, Volvo Trucks maintains field offices in Chicago, Illinois, and Salt Lake City, Utah; as well as in Ontario, Canada, and in Mexico City, Mexico. Volvo Trucks export operations are handled in Fort Lauderdale, Florida. And, to support its service operations—available through over 200 service locations in the United States and Canada—the company maintains up-to-date parts-distribution centers in Westerville, Ohio; Memphis, Tennessee; Union City, California; and Mississauga, Ontario, Canada.

Volvo Trucks considers that the real backbone of its operations, however, is its dedicated workforce of some 2,800 individuals nationwide, who are highly trained and motivated to work with energy and passion to create premier transport-related products.

In addition to its truck business, Volvo Trucks has a majority ownership interest in the U.S. truck stop chain Petro Stopping Centers. These leading travel plazas provide truck operators and travelers in 29 states not only with diesel and gasoline fueling facilities, oil-change and light repair services, restaurants, and convenience stores, but also with showers, laundry facilities, entertainment centers, Internet kiosks, and business services.

With its ownership stake in Petro and its range of ancillary services designed to help customers manage their businesses and acquire and finance new or pre-owned truck vehicles, Volvo Trucks is able to provide customers with a total ownership experience and a complete solution to the challenges faced in operating the transportation side of a business. Volvo Trucks stands ready to help its customers be successful by providing them with service and support at every turn.

The fundamentals that set Volvo Trucks apart are its core values of quality, safety, and reliability. Any company worth its salt stands for something, and at Volvo Trucks, the company stands for quality—in the performance, design, and finish of the products it manufactures, in the processes it uses, and in the people it employs. Quality also distinguishes Volvo Trucks in the service and support it provides for its customers, with whom it builds strong, lasting relationships based on trust.

Safety, meanwhile, has long been a passionate pursuit at Volvo Trucks. Volvo Trucks is a leader in the heavy-truck industry in safety research and development, ensuring that the products it manufactures are among the safest and most environmentally sound in the world and that its levels of excellence will increase with each new generation of trucks and truck engines the company introduces.

As for reliability, Volvo Trucks customers depend on the company to consistently be innovative in its thinking, fair-minded in its business practices, and capable of delivering products and services that meet or exceed their expectations. Dependability is a fundamental trait that Volvo Trucks also requires of its employees, vendors, and business partners. It is a trait the company firmly believes its customers deserve.

Opposite page: Volvo Trucks VN model highway tractors feature advanced design, uncompromising quality, and superior safety and driver comfort. · Above: This Volvo VN 770 is shown at a Petro Stopping Center, one of the 29-state chain of leading travel centers, in which Volvo has a majority ownership interest. From financing to services on the road, Volvo is committed to offering its customers a total transportation solution. · Left: The new Volvo VHD vocational truck combines toughness and serviceability with driver comfort and safety.

ASSOCIATION OF AMERICAN

The Association of American Railroads supports North America's major freight railroads and Amtrak with research and support programs, electronic information exchange, and public policy advocacy.

The industry that once defined the destiny of modern America has, since deregulation in 1980, transformed itself into a newly powerful driving force for U.S. economic growth in the 21st century. From 1980 to the start of the new millennium, the railroads invested more than $247 billion in advanced technology and equipment and achieved outstanding improvements in both shipping rates and operational efficiency, with enhanced safety records and expanded customer services. Today, U.S. freight railroads move millions of cargo tons for customers every day and directly contribute $13 billion to the economy annually, plus billions of dollars in purchases. Not surprisingly, the rail companies involved in such complex and dynamic enterprises have long benefited from cooperating on matters of critical interest to all of them. The Association of American Railroads (AAR) was organized in 1934 to represent the industry and to facilitate joint action for its members and the public.

Headquartered in Washington, D.C., AAR conducts research and develops programs and initiatives; provides information, coordination, and support services related to railroad operations, traffic, and finances; facilitates information exchange among railroads and their customers and suppliers; and advocates for its members on legislative matters.

Forging Ahead, Then and Now

In 1830, the Baltimore and Ohio Railroad—with its first 13 miles of track—launched America's swift journey from fledgling society into modern nationhood. For the next century, no single industry was more influential than the railroads in enabling the new nation to forge its resources and energies into a coherent whole. On the vast web of steel rails that came to link burgeoning cities, towns, and agricultural regions, the iron horse and the steel rail made a national economy possible. By 1917, 1,500 U.S. railroads operated a quarter-million miles of track and employed nearly

RAILROADS

two million people. By the 1970s, however, federal regulation of the railroads that had begun in 1887 had

effectively prevented the industry from capitalizing on the emerging technology and economic forces of

the late 20th century. To cope with this crisis, Congress crafted the Staggers Rail Act of 1980, which

enabled railroads to establish their own routes, tailor their rates to the market, and compete effectively.

The law's positive effects were dramatic. Labor productivity jumped 285 percent between 1980 and

1999, and shipping rates dropped an effective 57 percent, saving customers tens of billions of dollars.

And because of an explosive growth of rail intermodal service, cargo equal to that of nine million trucks

per year is now carried by rail intermodal trains.

ASSOCIATION OF AMERICAN RAILROADS MEMBERS

- Burlington Northern Santa Fe Railway
- CSX Corporation
- Canadian National Railway
- Canadian Pacific Railway
- Kansas City Southern
- Norfolk Southern
- Union Pacific Railroad
- RailAmerica
- Amtrak
- Ferrocarril Mexicano
- FerroSur
- Transportación Ferroviara Mexicano

LEADING-EDGE TECHNOLOGIES FOR THE NATION'S TRAINS

Sophisticated technology accelerates the newly vitalized railroads and improves their performance. The

most dramatic symbol may be today's $2 million, 6000-horsepower locomotives, which generate twice the

pulling power of previous models built just 10 years earlier. Railroads have purchased more than

8,000 new and rebuilt locomotives since 1990. The newest units reduce maintenance and increase fuel

efficiency. More than 440,000 new freight cars, built with lighter-weight, stronger materials, were added

to the freight car fleet. Railroads are the most fuel-efficient ground transportation mode.

Less visible, but more impressive still, are the astonishing advances made possible by computerized

operations. A 140-car train can be operated with just a two-person crew. Vast, automated switching yards are managed by small teams of technicians who can

process thousands of freight cars per day, making up dozens of trains and sending them on their way. Efficiency and

safety go hand-in-hand. Since 1980, accident rates dropped by two-thirds, and employee injury rates fell 70 percent.

The Internet has been harnessed to make doing business with the railroads easier and more efficient, including

tracking shipments, ordering cars, handling bills of lading, and estimating time-of-arrival information via the industry's

common Web site (www.steelroads.com).

America's railroads have again proven their strengths and resilience. With the informed, guiding assistance of the AAR,

the nation's railroads continue their dynamic contribution to America's economy—as they have for nearly two centuries.

OPPOSITE PAGE: COMPUTERIZED CONTROL CENTERS LIKE THIS ONE ARE USED BY TODAY'S HIGH-TECH RAILROAD INDUSTRY TO CONTROL OPERATIONS OVER THOUSANDS OF MILES OF RAIL LINE FROM A SINGLE LOCATION. · ABOVE: A FLEET OF MORE THAN 20,000 MODERN LOCOMOTIVES—WITH MORE THAN 65 MILLION TOTAL HORSEPOWER— DELIVERS THE FREIGHT FOR AMERICA'S FREIGHT RAILROADS.

AMERICAN ROAD & TRANSPORTATION

THE AMERICAN ROAD & TRANSPORTATION BUILDERS ASSOCIATION ADVOCATES STRONG FEDERAL INVESTMENT IN THE NATION'S TRANSPORTATION INFRASTRUCTURE AND PROMOTES EFFICIENCY FOR THE TRANSPORTATION CONSTRUCTION INDUSTRY.

Behind the headlines of today's high-tech and high-flying industries—from satellite communications and E-commerce to CT scanning and microsurgery—runs a dependable, unifying reality. No matter how sophisticated or elaborate its products or services, every enterprise in America depends upon the nation's infrastructure of highways, airports, and public transportation. And although people largely take its prodigious benefits for granted, this transportation system not only ensures America's economic prosperity, but also contributes vitally each day to the success of every facet of national and local community life.

The bare facts of the system reveal its importance: nearly four million miles of public roads; 5,415 airports; 6,185 miles of urban transit; 200,000 miles of freight and passenger railway; and 3,750 waterport terminals. One government estimate values the nation's roads, bridges, airports, and mass transit facilities in excess of $1.5 trillion.

But the system's operating dynamics are more compelling still, for not only is the network continually expanding to meet growing transport needs, it must also be constantly maintained and renewed. U.S. transportation construction is a $200 billion-per-year industry—a greater proportion of the gross domestic product than farming, petroleum, or motion pictures. And more than 2.2 million private and public sector jobs are generated by transportation construction economic activity.

A CENTURY OF SERVICE TO THE U.S. TRANSPORTATION CONSTRUCTION INDUSTRY

Not surprisingly, so vast a system embraces diverse disciplines, resources, and skills in countless communities and a great many companies, large and small, whose common interests are vitally affected by federal, state, and local legislatures and judiciaries. For the last century, these common interests of the

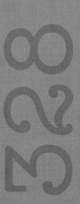

BUILDERS ASSOCIATION

transportation construction industry have been actively advocated for and coordinated by an uncommonly energetic trade group, the American Road and Transportation Builders Association (ARTBA).

Headquartered in Washington, D.C., ARTBA is a full-service association with more than 5,000 members, whose eight membership divisions reveal its industry's diversity: contractors, planning and design, transportation officials, traffic safety, materials and services, public-private ventures in transportation, research and education, and equipment manufacturers. ARTBA holds annual meetings and conferences, maintains standing committees, policy advisory councils, and professional development sections that work on issues to promote the effectiveness and efficiency of the transportation construction industry.

COORDINATING TRANSPORTATION RESOURCES ACROSS AMERICA

Perhaps most importantly, however, ARTBA advocates strong federal investment in the nation's transportation infrastructure to meet public needs. Since its inception in 1902, the association has maintained a strong lobbying role. Among the major historic steps in the industry's development that were influenced by ARTBA action are the Federal-Aid Road Act of 1916—the first sizable appropriation of federal funds for road improvements, which established the federal government's role in transportation development; the Federal-Aid Highway Act of 1956, which saw the creation of the Highway Trust Fund; the creation of a cabinet-level U.S. Department of Transportation; the 1998 Transportation Equity Act for the 21st Century; and the 2000 Aviation Investment and Reform Act for the 21st Century. As with other major trade associations, ARTBA is an important participant in the continuing debate to balance national, regional, and local resources to achieve the healthiest and most productive balance of resource allocation and priorities, not only in Washington, but in communities all across America.

ARTBA's unique federation structure and its 100-year track record have no parallel in the U.S. construction industry. A diverse and talented volunteer leadership, active chapters, grass-roots members, and a highly qualified interdisciplinary staff all work together to make ARTBA today's driving force in transportation construction.

AMERICAN ROAD & TRANSPORTATION BUILDERS ASSOCIATION
1902 ★ 100th ★ 2002
ANNIVERSARY

CONTINENTAL AIRLINES

CONTINENTAL AIRLINES RANKS AMONG THE WORLD'S MOST SUCCESSFUL AIR TRANSPORT ENTERPRISES, OPERATING 2,500 DEPARTURES DAILY TO 136 DOMESTIC AND 92 INTERNATIONAL DESTINATIONS.

Built on one of airline history's longest records of pioneering innovation, which began in 1937, Continental Airlines today ranks among the world's most successful air transport enterprises. In 2001, Continental operated some 2,500 departures daily to 136 domestic and 92 international destinations. Operating major hubs in Newark, Houston, and Cleveland, Continental serves more international cities than any other U.S. carrier, with flights throughout the Americas, Europe, and Asia.

Successfully weathering the industry's turbulence following U.S. airline deregulation in 1978, Continental has enjoyed an enviable ascent since 1995. Under the leadership of Gordon Bethune, company chairman and CEO, the carrier's operational efficiency, industry reputation, and profits have soared. In 2000, Continental delivered its sixth consecutive year of profitability.

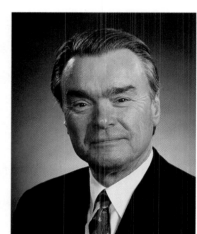

FLY TO WIN

During a period when its industry struggled to overcome adverse public opinion about service and reliability, Continental proved itself a commendable exception. Airline customers repeatedly voted Continental the top carrier for customer satisfaction, earning it the *Frequent Flyer* magazine/

J.D. Power and Associates award for long flights in 1999 and both long flights and short flights in 2000. Continental was number one or two in the J.D. Power study for the past five years, and has won more awards for customer satisfaction than any other airline. Continental was also named the "2001 Airline of the Year" by *Air Transport World* magazine, the industry's leading monthly publication. As recipient of the same honor in 1996, Continental

is the first airline to receive the coveted "Airline of the Year" distinction twice in five years.

FUND THE FUTURE

Through robust finances and fleet modernization, Continental has reduced its average jet-fleet age

to make it one of the industry's youngest. In 2000, for example, the airline accepted delivery of 28 new Boeing jets and retired 19 older planes; aircraft orders and

leases ensure fleet commonality and tailored growth.

Continental continued to expand its hubs in New York/Newark, Houston, and Cleveland from 1995 to 2000, significantly increasing destinations served from all

three cities. Planned improvements involving these centers include a new international terminal at Houston's Bush Intercontinental Airport and completion of the New

York Global Gateway project, featuring high-speed train service from New York City's Pennsylvania Station and World Trade Center to Newark International Airport.

MAKE RELIABILITY A REALITY

Continental continued to distance itself from other airlines by ranking number one in on-time performance for the year 2000, according to the U.S. Department of

Transportation. While setting the industry standard for transporting people to their destinations safely, on time, and with superior service, Continental continues

its leadership efforts in persuading the U.S. Congress to properly fund vital modernization and efficient operation of the nation's air traffic control system.

WORKING TOGETHER

Central to Continental's success is a long-standing determination to ensure that its people are genuinely valued and

actually enjoy coming to work. Continental's employees are active decision makers, enjoy a work environment of dignity and respect, and are rewarded with performance-based incentives. Since 1995, Continental has paid more than $545 million—over one-half-billion dollars—to its employees in profit sharing funds, and has distributed more than $118 million in bonuses. These and many other actions help account for the inclusion of Continental by Fortune magazine on its annual list of the "100 Best Companies to Work For" in 1999, 2000, and 2001.

OPPOSITE PAGE, TOP: GORDON BETHUNE IS CHAIRMAN AND CEO OF CONTINENTAL AIRLINES. · OPPOSITE PAGE, BOTTOM: CONTINENTAL EMPLOYEES TAKE PRIDE IN THE AIRLINE'S THIRD CONSECUTIVE RANKING ON FORTUNE MAGAZINE'S "100 BEST COMPANIES TO WORK FOR" LIST. · ABOVE: COMFORTABLE SEATS, SPACIOUS AISLES, AND EXCEPTIONAL FOOD SERVICE ARE JUST SOME OF THE REASONS FOR CONTINENTAL'S POPULARITY WITH CUSTOMERS. · LEFT: CONTINENTAL PRIDES ITSELF ON PROVIDING CONSISTENTLY EXCELLENT CUSTOMER SERVICE.

A Vision for the Future

'The emergence of a truly entrepreneurial economy in the United States during the last 10 or 15 years is the most significant event to have occurred in recent economic and social history.'
—Peter Drucker, 1999

Today's entrepreneurs, like their predecessors throughout history, don't rest with the mere invention of a breakthrough product or critical technology, nor are they satisfied to see their inventions merely become new toys of the rich and privileged. They transform their products and technologies into dependable, affordable, and ubiquitous tools that are placed within reach of average people and improve the lives of all. And in doing so, they change society as a whole.

The transforming power of the Internet, for example, impacted the U.S. economy and the lives of Americans with a speed and force never before seen. The Internet quickly became a global phenomenon as well. Talk of a "New Economy" quickly spread, an economy in which the old rulebook and old industries would be discarded in favor of a new empire built on technology, information, multimedia, and electronic commerce—all developed and offered to consumers by vast, global companies.

Indeed, along with the spread of capitalism around the globe, business analysts rank the revolution in information technology as the most profound economic and social trend of the times. They see an economy driven chiefly by technology in the way it used to be driven by the housing and auto industries.

There is little question that information technology—much of it invented and popularized by American companies—is rapidly changing the way businesses, employees, consumers, and families around the world work, think, shop, and conduct financial transactions. The Internet has both shrunk and linked the world, rendering vast differences and old geographic borders irrelevant or, at least, less significant.

Information technology and the vast array of Internet exchanges conducted on and with that technology have made Americans and American companies more productive and prosperous. But as the nation enjoys the fruits of these empowering tools, the jury is still out as to just how much the Internet age will alter the economic and social life of the country. Is the Internet really a life-altering development, or just another communications tool? Some trendspotters have already moved on, declaring that the U.S. economy and society are already in transition again, this time moving from an information age to a biotechnology age.

The 'Old Economy:' Built to Last

Meanwhile, the "Old Economy" enters the new millennium in fine shape, thank you.

At least 100 of the companies that appeared on the 2000 list of the Forbes 500 were also on the list in 1955. And while a "low-tech" retailer like Wal-Mart has climbed rapidly on the list to number two (and is the largest private employer in the United States), a company that literally wrote the book for the computer and Internet age, Microsoft, stands at number 84.

One other basic reality about U.S. economic strength is illustrated by the list: In 2000, as in other years, the top 500 companies in America employed just 10 percent of the workforce. The small-business sector has always been and remains in this period of globalization and high technology the backbone of the American enterprise system.

In a 1999 speech, Federal Reserve Board Chairman Alan Greenspan considered the question of whether America has a New Economy or has simply improved the great free enterprise system it already had with new tools and new techniques. His conclusion:

"Although there doubtless have been profound changes in the way we organize our capital facilities, engage in just-in-time inventory regimes, and intertwine our newly sophisticated, risk-sensitive financial system into this process, there is one important

caveat to the notion that we live in a New Economy, and that is human psychology.

"The same enthusiasms and fears that gripped our forebears are, in every way, visible in the generations now actively participating in the American economy. . . .

"Hence, as the first cut at the question, 'Is there a New Economy?' the answer in a more profound sense is no. As in the past, our advanced economy is primarily driven by how human psychology molds the value system that drives a competitive market economy. And that process is inextricably linked to human nature, which appears essentially immutable and thus anchors the future to the past."

AN IMMEASURABLE CAPACITY FOR GREATNESS

As the men and women of American business begin the new century and a new millennium, they see an exciting future anchored to a glorious past. The new technologies they created have immeasurably expanded the free enterprise system's capacity for great achievements. But it is the bedrock values of that system that will drive the business community and America to those achievements: the values of hard work, individual initiative, free and fair competition, and commitment to community.

It is the limitless capacity of American free enterprise to empower the dreams and aspirations of everyday people everywhere

that accounts for America's strength prosperity, and humanity. Yes, American businesses and entrepreneurs build grea products, companies, and financial empires But, more important than all that, American business builds dreams.

As Winston Churchill advised, it is time to see free enterprise and the businesses that make free enterprise work for wha they truly are—the strong horse pulling the whole cart. American business has delivered higher levels of prosperity to more lev els of society than any other community in human history. A bright future awaits i Americans never forget that when busines does well, its capacity for helping people and giving life to their dreams is unlimited

Bibliography

nt. "Computers in Classrooms: Lessons Learned." *The Washington Post*,
ry 25, 2000, A17.

n. "Billions Served: An Interview with Norman Borlaug," *Reason*, April 2000.
//www.reason.com>.

rid. *From Mutual Aid to the Welfare State: Fraternal Societies and Social Services
–1967*. Chapel Hill: University of North Carolina Press, 2000.

ry. "Inventors of the Modern Computer: Graphical User Interface—The Apple
About the Human Internet, May 10, 2001. <http://www.inventors.about.com/
e/inventors/library/weekly/aa043099.htm.

alter J. *The Smithsonian Book of Flight*. New York: Wings Books, 1996.

nnings. *Audience Ratings: Radio, Television, Cable*. Hillsdale, N.J.: Lawrence
m Associates, Publishers, 1988.

heodore, Louis Hicks and Ben J. Wattenberg. *The First Measured Century: An
ated Guide to Trends in America, 1900–2000*. Washington, D.C.: American
rise Institute, 2000.

ordon. *The Encyclopedia of American Facts and Dates*. 10th ed. New York: Harper
Publishers, 1997.

. "This Week in Business History." *The Arizona Republic*, February 7, 2000, D2.

Allan T. "Learning From Las Vegas." *The Wall Street Journal*, February 7,
A36.

Hal. *Syndicated Television: The First Forty Years, 1947–1987*. Jefferson, N.C.:
land & Co., 1989.

eople Who Most Influenced Business This Century." *Los Angeles Times*, October
99, U1–12.

Sandra. "Green Around the Edges." *The Washington Post*, April 22, 2000, G1.

oug. *So Who the Heck Was Oscar Meyer?: The Real People Behind Those Brand
s*. Fort Lee, N.J.: Barricade Books, 1996.

ugh. *A Century of Pop: From Vaudeville to Rock, Big Bands to Techno, A Hundred
of Music That Changed the World*. Chicago: A Capella Books, 1998.

n, David. *The Fifties*. New York: Ballantine Books, 1993.

Robert, and Aaron Singer. *The Economic Transformation of America Since 1865*.
o, Fla.: Harcourt Brace & Company, 1994.

Robert E. *Henry R. Luce: A Political Portrait of the Man Who Created the
can Century*. New York: Charles Scribner's Sons, 1989.

t D. "A New Era of Bright Hopes and Terrible Fears." *Business Week*, October 4,
<http://www.businessweek.com>.

"Human Genome to Go Public." *CNN.com*, February 9, 2001.

    <http://www.cnn.com/2001/HEALTH/02/09/genome.results>.

"Indicators of the Century." *Time*, December 31, 1999, 36.

Kane, Joseph Nathan, Steven Anzovin, and Janet Podell. *Famous First Facts: A Record of
First Happenings, Discoveries, and Inventions in American History*. 5th ed. New York:
H. W. Wilson Company, 1997.

Landro, Laura. "The Bellagio: Where Luxury Is a Crap Shoot." *The Wall Street Journal*,
March 3, 2000, W1.

Lebergott, Stanley. *Pursuing Happiness: American Consumers in the Twentieth Century*.
Princeton, N.J.: Princeton University Press, 1993.

Leeds, Jeff. "In Spite of Losses, Campaign Media Consultants Still Win Big." *Los Angeles
Times*, April 18, 2000, A1.

Lenzner, Robert, and Carrie Shook. "The Unstoppable REIT Juggernaut." *Forbes*, December
29, 1997. <http://www.forbes.com>.

Magill, Frank N., ed. *Chronology of Twentieth-Century History: Business and Commerce*.
Vol. 1 and 2. London: Fitzroy Dearborn Publishers, 1996.

Maltin, Leonard. *The Disney Films*. New York: Crown Publishers, 1984.

_____. *The Great American Broadcast: A Celebration of Radio's Golden Age*. New
York: Penguin Putnam, 1997.

Michaels, James W., and Dirk Smillie. "Webucation," *Forbes*, May 15, 2000,
<http://www.forbes.com>.

Moukheiber, Zina. "Tiny Abiomed Looks for a Pulse Long After the Jarvik-7." *Forbes*, April
17, 2000. <http://www.forbes.com>.

News Front. *The 50 Great Pioneers of American Industry: Classics Edition*. Maplewood, N.J.:
C. S. Hammond and Company, 1967.

Norris, Floyd, and Bockelmann, Christine. *New York Times Century of American Business*.
New York: McGraw-Hill, 2000.

Page, Jake. "Making the Chips That Run the World." *Smithsonian Magazine*, January 2000,
36–46.

Pritchard, Peter. *The Making of McPaper: The Inside Story of USA Today*. New York:
Andrews and McMeel, 1987.

Public Broadcasting System. "American Masters: Neil Simon."
<http://www.pbs.org/wnet/americanmasters/database/simon_n.html> (2001).

Rasmussen, Cecilia. "First Transcontinental Flight Was a Rough One." *Los Angeles Times*,
March 26, 2000, B12.

The Reader's Digest Association. *Our Glorious Century*. Pleasantville, N.Y.: The Reader's
Digest Association, 1994.

Robinson, James W. *The Excel Phenomenon*. Rocklin, Calif.: Prima Publishing, 1997.

Rogers, Adam, and David A. Kaplan. "Get Ready for Nanotechnology." *Newsweek Extra*, winter 1997–98.

Scism, Jack. "Old Values Remain as Bank Grows." *News & Record* (Greensboro, N.C.), June 17, 1996, B4.

"Service Sector Jobs and the Current Economy." Melinda Penkava, host. National Public Radio, *Talk of the Nation*. November 16, 1999.

Shaw, John. "The Influence of Space Power Upon History (1944–1998)." *Aerospace Power Chronicles*, March 16, 1999. <http://www.airpower.maxwell.af.mil/airchronicles/cc/shaw.html>.

Sobel, Robert, and David Sicilia. *The Entrepreneurs: An American Adventure*. Boston: Houghton Mifflin Company, 1986.

Stewart, Thomas A. et al., "The Businessman of the Century." *Fortune*, November 22, 1999, 109–28.

Stone, Amey. "Business and Education: Learning to Work Together." *Business Week*, Online Special Report, July 22, 1999. <http://www.businessweek.com>.

Streitfeld, David. "Gateses Add $5 Billion to Foundation." *The Washington Post*, January 25, 2000, E1.

Symonds, William C. "Industry Outlook 2000—Services (Education)." *Business Week*, January 10, 2000. <http://www.businessweek.com>.

Symonds, William C. et al., "For-Profit Schools." *Business Week*, February 7, 2000, 64–76.

Waldrop, Mitchell. "The Trillion Dollar Vision of Dee Hock." *Fast Company*, October 1996. <http://www.fastcompany.com>.

Webb, Michael, ed. *Hollywood: Legend and Reality*. New York: Little, Brown and Co., 1986.

"Welcome to the Inventors Club!!!" *Girltech.com*, 1999. <http://www.girltech.com/Invention/IN_invention_intro.html>.

Whittemore, Hank. *CNN: The Inside Story*. Boston: Little, Brown and Co., 1994.

Zellner, Wendy. "Going to Bat For Vouchers." *Business Week*, February 7, 2000, 76–78.

In addition to the sources listed above, Web site postings by the following entities provided information used in this publication:

Advertising Age; Alvin Ailey American Dance Theater; American Association of Health Plans; American Association of Port Authorities; American Association of Publishers; American Association of Railroads; American Council on Education; American Council on Life Insurance; American Farm Bureau; American Hotel and Motel Association; American Institute of Architects; American Lawyer; American Plastics Council; American Road & Transportation Builders Association; American Society of Association Executives; American Telephone and Telegraph (AT&T); American Textile Manufacturers Institute; American Trucking Associations; America Online; AmeriCares; Amgen; Amtrak; Amway; Andersen Consulting; Anheuser-Busch; AOL Time Warner; Archer Daniels Midland Company; Associated Press; Avon; Bank of America; Bass Hotels/Holiday Inn; Bechtel; Bethlehem Steel; Birdseye; Boeing; Bristol-Myers Squibb; Bureau of Labor Statistics; Burlington Industries; Cable News Network (CNN); Capital Research Center; Cargill; Carnegie Mellon University; Carrier; Caterpillar; Centex; Century 21 Real Estate; CertainTeed; Chemical Manufacturers' Association; Chrysler; CIGNA; Citibank; The College of William and Mary; CUNA Mutual Group; Curtiss-Wright; Deloitte & Touche; Direct Selling Association; The Dismal Scientist; Dow; E. I. du Pont de Nemours and Company; Eli Lilly and Company; Encyclopedia.com; Enron; Ernst & Young; Exxon/Mobil; Fannie Mae; Federal Express; Flow International; Footwear Industries of America; The Foundation Center; Fox Entertainment; Freddie Mac; Frigidaire; General Motors; General Nutrition Centers; Giddings & Lewis; Gillette; The Great Atlantic and Pacific Tea Company; Harvard University; Health Insurance Association of America; Hertz; Hewlett-Packard; Hilton; The Home Depot; Hoovers Online; Howard Johnson; Infoplease.com; Ingersoll-Rand; Insurance Information Institute; Intel; International Business Machines (IBM); International Franchise Association; Investment Company Institute; JCPenney; Johns Hopkins University; Johnson & Johnson; Jones International University; J. Walter Thompson; Keds; Knott's Berry Farm; KPMG; Kraft Foods; Kroger; Levi Strauss; Lockheed Martin; Lucent Technologies; Mall of America; Marriott; Mary Kay; Massachusetts Institute of Technology (MIT); Maxfield and Montrose Media; McDonald's; MCI WorldCom; Medtronic; Microsoft; Milliken; Motorola; National Aeronautics and Space Administration (NASA); National Air Transportation Association; National Association of Broadcasters; National Association of Convenience Stores; National Association of Home Builders; National Association of Manufacturers; National Association of Real Estate Investment Trusts; National Association of Wholesaler-Distributors; National Broadcasting Company (NBC); National Foundation for Teaching Entrepreneurship; National Highway Transportation Safety Administration; National Inventors Hall of Fame; National Restaurant Association; National Retail Federation; National Theatre of the Deaf; Netscape; New York Stock Exchange (NYSE); NIKE; Nonprofit News; Notre Dame University; Nuclear Regulatory Commission; Owens Corning; Pennsylvania Cable Television Association; PepsiCo; Pharmaceutical Research and Manufacturers of America; Pharmacia Corporation; Portland Cement Association; PricewaterhouseCoopers; Princeton University; Prudential; Public Broadcasting Service; Pulte; Raytheon; RCA; RealEstate.com; Reliance Insurance; Revlon; Rotary International; Sprint; Stanford University; Starbucks; Sun Microsystems; Target; Travel Industry Association; Tricom Chemical; United Airlines; United Parcel Service (UPS); University of North Carolina; University of Pennsylvania; U.S. Census Bureau; U.S. Department of Agriculture; U.S. Department of Defense; U.S. Department of Education; VF Corporation; VISA; Wal Mart; The Walt Disney Company; Washington Scholarship Fund; Wegmans; Welfare to Work Partnership; Wine Institute; World Food Prize Foundation; World Wide e-Processing; X Prize Foundation; Yale University; Young & Rubicam

Index

341

343